During times of universal deceit,
telling the truth becomes a revolutionary act.

George Orwell

Have nothing to do with the fruitless deeds
of darkness, but rather expose them.

Ephesians 5:11 (NIV)

Contents

Chapter 1

A Heavenly Encounter

In a dream, for instance, a vision at night,
when men and women are deep in sleep,
fast asleep in their beds –
God opens their ears
and impresses them with warnings...'

Job 33:15a, The Message

There are dreams that you forget and there are dreams that you remember. This book stems from a dream that I'll never forget – a dream that transformed my way of seeing the world and which, in turn, changed my life.

Before I had the dream in question I was constantly preoccupied with the Lord and hungry for the deeper things of God. Day after day I was seeking after more of God's presence and yet had not experienced the breakthrough in my life.

One night I climbed into bed, sighed and confided in my wife, 'I need to seek and know the Lord more.'

What I didn't know was that this cry of my heart was about to be answered within a matter of hours.

At some point during the watches of that momentous night in October 2009 I had an extraordinary experience.

9

I will try to describe it, even though human words seem inadequate.

I was lying horizontally on my bed when suddenly I felt myself being lifted up and rising slowly through the ceiling and then the roof of my house. As I was being transported higher and higher into the night sky, I looked down and could see the houses below. I was not afraid. Rather, I felt an unusual tranquility. I just knew that I was being lifted by God.

I continued to ascend until I rose up above the clouds. There I rested, hovering in the deep blue and starry night sky. Still in a horizontal position, I knew that I was now directly above my house, which was hidden from my view.

As I waited there for what seemed to be no longer than a few seconds a large pair of hands appeared out of a bright white cloud formation. These hands were pressed together as if in prayer and were moving slowly towards me.

As they reached me the right side of my torso opened spontaneously and formed a rectangular cavity.

The hands gently placed something inside.

As these hands moved away, the cavity in my side began to close in the same manner as it had opened.

I then began to descend just as I had ascended. As soon as I touched my bed, I woke up. I lay there wondering what on earth had just happened to me for a few moments before I fell asleep again.

As soon as I reentered my dream state, I found myself standing in a bright white room. There was a corridor to the left of me. I looked and I saw God standing there. He spoke to me saying, 'someone has come a great distance to see you.'

At that moment the shadow of a man appeared around the corner of a corridor to the left side of the room. His footsteps were silent as he approached me. I knew immediately from his appearance and radiance that he was an angel.

He walked directly towards me, magnificent, regal and dignified. As he did so I caught myself wondering why an angel would travel such a distance to meet me.

I stood motionless and in silence, nervous but at peace.

The angel stood around six feet tall and wore a bright white garment. His face was very dark and shiny. He had the appearance of a Nigerian man in his mid 50's. His eyes were like white lights and his demeanor was calm, serious and authoritative.

The angel stood directly before me, so close that we were almost touching chest to chest. He lifted his head and eyes upwards and communicated with the Lord. Even though he was silent I was able to understand. He said, 'what would you like me to say?'

I was surprised that the angel had journeyed such a vast distance at the bidding of the Lord, and yet did not know what message to bring. I was full of expectation as I waited for the words he would impart to me. With the faintest nod of his head, the angel indicated that he had heard God's answer. But I was unable to hear or perceive what the Lord had said. All I understood was that God's words were private, between him and the angel alone.

Then the angel placed his left hand upon my back and placed his right hand directly on my heart.

He spoke only one word: 'LOVE'.
And then the vision abruptly ended.

I awoke at around 6am the next morning to hear the clear voice of the Holy Spirit. He asked me directly in my right ear, 'Will you not tarry with me one hour?' I did not respond, however, and fell back to sleep. I awoke again about ten minutes later. A second time the Holy Spirit spoke, but this time with great urgency and gravity, 'Will you not tarry with me one hour?' I jumped out of bed, repenting for not obeying the first time, and hurried downstairs. I entered the lounge where I had the sweetest time of communion with God that I had not enjoyed for many months.

Later in the morning I explained to my wife what had happened in the night. I told her that the Lord had put something into my side. She asked me what it was. I replied that I didn't know.

'Why didn't you ask him?' she asked.

'I didn't think to,' I replied.

'You need to ask!' she retorted.

So for the next five days I went before God and sought an understanding of the dream.

The answer emerged as I began to recognize the urgency of the context in which I had received the dream.

At that time, the European Union was ratifying the Lisbon Treaty – a Treaty which would come into force in January 2010 with the appointment of the first permanent President of the EU.

I had previously not paid too much attention to what seemed like an insignificant political development. In addition, I was not particularly knowledgeable about the activities of the European Union or politics in general for that matter. However, during that week of seeking the Lord, I began to experience an increasing sense of danger regarding the EU. In fact, I couldn't get this rising sense of peril out of my mind. As I continued to pursue

God's interpretation of the revelation he had given to me, he began to impress upon me the terrible and woeful consequence of Britain's further integration into this European Union.

I turned to prayer, interceding with passion and researching the ins and outs of the EU with diligence.

It was during this praying that God opened my eyes for the first time not only to the political events that were unfolding but also their significance from the perspective of Biblical prophecy.

At the same time the Lord also brought to my remembrance a powerful vision I had received back in 1991 and connected it with what he was now showing me in 2009. This earlier vision is described in my book, *Beyond Earthly Realms* and was given at the time of the drafting of a new EU treaty, known as the Maastricht Treaty. That treaty created the European Union and the single European currency which is used today. That vision lasted over ten hours and was followed by other visions concerning Europe, the second coming of Christ, and many other topics.

It was now Sunday, day five of seeking God after my dream experience.

While I was preparing for church, I became strongly compelled to get down on my knees before the Lord right where I stood. I fell to the floor and urgently prayed from deep within my spirit: 'Lord, give me a heart and a spirit like Daniel and do not let me bow down to any ungodly world system or power. To you alone, Lord, I bow down. I repent of unknowingly and unwittingly bowing down to any world system.'

Instantly a joy and a peace flooded my soul. It was as if that prayer had lifted a veil off my heart and mind and I was now enjoying an unprecedented freedom.

I always arrive early at church to set up the computer for the worship service and to run through the songs with the worship team. As Simon the worship leader began to sing I was quite unexpectedly taken in my mind to the place where I had hovered above the clouds five nights earlier. There I was able to watch again as the Lord's hands approached me. This time, however, I saw that he put six enveloped letters into my side. My heart began to race as I felt instantly convicted that I must urgently write warning letters to Her Majesty the Queen, the then Prime Minister Gordon Brown, and David Cameron leader of the Conservative party who is now the Prime Minister. The letters would warn them of impending calamity should Britain continue to be a part of the European Union.

My heart now felt like it was burning and I became consumed with the urgency and immediacy of the task before me. The Lord wanted these letters written and posted without delay. I knew I could not procrastinate for a moment. I performed my duties at church that Sunday and went home. I wondered what I should write but the Lord said, 'Put pen to paper and you will know what to write.' Over the next three days I wrote three letters.

During that time I could hardly eat or sleep. It was as though the Lord was pushing me in every waking moment to write to these high level leaders.

Finally the letters were written. I ran to the post box and dropped them in. An intense relief flooded my soul and I knew that my mission had been accomplished.

What effect the letters had I do not know. But what I do know is that God wanted them written for a purpose and that my role was simply to be obedient and trust that they would accomplish whatever they had been set out to do.

I still had three more letters to write and so I waited on the Lord. It was January 2012, the time of the amendment of the Lisbon Treaty to tackle the problem of the failing Euro currency. My heart was stirred again in the same manner as with the first three letters back in 2009. I felt compelled to write an urgent warning letter, this time not for the leaders of the nation, but for all people around the world. The fourth warning letter is what you are about to read in this book. I believe this is an end time prophetic wake up call.

Trumpet Blast Warning is accordingly a comprehensive expression of what the Lord is continuing to work in me as a result of the dream I had back in 2009. It is a warning message. It is not intended as an in depth study of the topics covered because each would fill entire volumes. Furthermore it has not been written to answer eschatological questions – theological questions concerning the order and nature of events during the final years of planet earth.

In *Trumpet Blast Warning* I explain that current events and biblical prophecy are converging in such a way as to indicate that we are heading towards the most climactic period in the history of the world.

Throughout the Bible the prophets, apostles and Jesus Christ himself warned that the world would not always continue as it has but would one day come to an end. The Apostle Peter warned, 'the day of the Lord will come like a thief. The heavens will disappear with a roar; the elements will be destroyed by fire, and the earth and everything in it will be laid bare' (2 Peter 3:10). This fast approaching climax to all history – referred to as the end of days, Armageddon, or the Apocalypse – has been sign posted throughout the Bible. As Christians, we have been warned to be prepared. Unbelievers are to be warned too and encouraged to find faith in Christ Jesus before it is too late.

What then of the angel's message to me, containing the one word 'LOVE'?

In the weeks and months after my dream, I felt more and more drawn to the figure of the prophet Daniel in the Old Testament Scriptures. Daniel was a man given dreams, and indeed the interpretation of dreams, during a time of national crisis. The Jewish people of his day were in exile in Babylon (modern Iraq) and were in great distress. Daniel, a man called to stand for God in a pagan and political arena, began to have dreams about the future course of the world – dreams which he was called at points to share with the leading governmental figures of his day.

With such a challenging calling it was imperative that Daniel received a revelation of God's love. When times are turbulent, God's servants are not to live from fear but from love. They are not to be unsure of their position before God but certain of the fact that the Father himself loves them dearly (John 16.27). This was true of Daniel too. God revealed his love for the prophet not just his plans.

So in Daniel chapter 10 – a chapter that impacted me at a very deep level back in 2009 – we read,

'Suddenly, a hand touched me, which made me tremble on my knees and on the palms of my hands. And he said to me, "O Daniel, man greatly beloved, understand the words that I speak to you, and stand upright, for I have now been sent to you."' (vv.10-11, NKJV).

Daniel received two things here. He received a touch from God. He also received a word from God that he was 'a man greatly beloved.'

Daniel needed to know the LOVE of God before he heard and transmitted the plans of God.

Put another way, Daniel had to learn that intimacy is the true foundation for prophecy.

When Daniel received the subsequent vision from the angel in chapter 10 he fell into great sorrow because of the tough times that were coming. Whereupon the angel gave him a fresh word about the love of God and an additional word about knowing

God's shalom, his peace. 'He said, "O man greatly beloved, fear not! Peace be to you; be strong, yes, be strong!"' (Daniel 10.19, NKJV).

In the months after my dream in October 2009 I knew two things. I first of all knew that God was warning me about calamitous times ahead. I secondly knew that I wasn't to live out of fear but out of love. I was to live with the blessed assurance that the Lord loves me dearly not with a sense of insecurity about my position before him.

And I believe that this word is for you too. Please read this book with the knowledge that God loves you and wants you to know his peace within the storm.

And please read it knowing that he loves this world and that his passionate longing is for everyone to know him as their Lord before it is too late.

For it is in that place of knowing him personally that we all find safety and rest when the wind is strong and the waves are high.

So my prayer is that the Holy Spirit will bring you a touch and a word from God so that you might live from a centre of love not a centre of fear.

And my prayer is that all of us will be ready for the things that are to come.

In these days the words of Jesus to 'watch' and to 'be prepared' are echoing throughout the heavens.

Here on earth the Lord is declaring with a loud voice that we must get ready now (Matthew 24:42:44).

Do you hear His voice?

He who has an ear let him hear! (Revelation 3:22)

Chapter 2

Mass Media, Mass Deception

*By skilful and sustained use of propaganda, one can make a
people see 'heaven as hell, or a most wretched life as paradise'*
Adolf Hitler [1]

With the advent of the digital age and the development of new
technologies it is true to say that we have become affected in an
unprecedented way by the propaganda disseminated through
mass media.

We are conditioned by what we watch, listen to and read.

We understand world affairs through the eyes of people with a
definitive and covert agenda.

Defining our Terms

What do we mean when we talk about the mass media and
about propaganda?

Mass Media refers to any medium used to reach vast numbers
of people, whether electronically – through television, internet,
radio, touch pads and cell phones – or through printed media
– such as newspapers, magazines etc.

Propaganda is the transmission of information which is
often deceptive in nature and advances a political ideology or

viewpoint with the express aim of influencing peoples' attitudes and making them believe in something that is untrue.

The point I want to make here is this: simply taking what is said in the mass media and believing it is folly. The people behind these media have an agenda. They want you to see the world in a way that advances their cause. They want you to conform to their agenda.

Thomas Jefferson, third president of the United States memorably stated in a letter in 1807: 'nothing can now be believed which is seen in a newspaper. Truth itself becomes suspicious by being put into that polluted vehicle... Perhaps an editor might begin a reformation in some such way as this. Divide his paper into four chapters, heading the first, Truths; second, Probabilities; the third, Possibilities; the fourth, Lies. The first chapter would be very short.'

If that was true as far back as 1807 when the technologies supporting the mass media were markedly less advanced – how much more true it is today.

The Power of the Mass Media

Governments and corporations around the world have for a long time understood the enormous influence and power they yield over the masses through propaganda transmitted through the mass media.

The propagandist Edward Bernays is regarded as the father of Public Relations. Born in Vienna in 1891 he was the nephew of Sigmund Freud. In 1892 the Bernays family moved to New York. Later Bernays would be hired by Woodrow Wilson and other US presidents, the US army and many large corporations to spearhead and engage in propaganda campaigns. He published many scholarly works on propaganda which are still used today in universities worldwide.

Due to the negative connotations associated with the term propaganda after its use by the Germans in World War 1, Bernays coined a new term and rebranded it Public Relations.

Bernays wrote: 'if we understand the mechanism and motives of the group mind, is it not possible to control and regiment the masses according to our will without their knowing about it?... The conscious and intelligent manipulation of the organized habits and opinion of the masses is an important element in democratic society. Those who manipulate this unseen mechanism of society constitute an invisible government which is the true ruling power of our government. We are governed, our minds molded, our tastes formed, our ideas suggested, largely by men we have never heard of.'[2]

And again,

'In almost every act of our daily lives, whether in the sphere of politics or business, in our social conduct or our ethical thinking, we are dominated by the relatively small number of persons... who understand the mental processes and social patterns of the masses. It is they who pull the wires which control the public mind.' [3]

According to Bernays the true ruling power belongs to an invisible government, not what we see showcased via the mainstream media. This unseen group is made up of those who control the masses through complex propaganda techniques and deceive the people into believing that their ideas are their own, when in reality they have been strategically implanted.

Joseph Goebbels, Hitler's Minister of Propaganda, stated that Bernays' work was the blueprint used by the Nazis to seize control of Germany.[4] Adolf Hitler understood perfectly well the power of propaganda and the importance of gaining mind control over the masses. He devoted two chapters to the subject in his book *Mein Kampf.*

'The receptivity of the great masses is very limited, their intelligence small, but their power of forgetting is enormous. In consequence of these facts, all effective propaganda must be limited to a very few points and must harp on these in slogans until the last member of the public understands.' [5]

And again,

'The most brilliant propagandist technique will yield no success unless one fundamental principle is borne in mind constantly and with unflagging attention. It must confine itself to a few points and repeat them over and over.' [6]

It was by means of carefully orchestrated propaganda techniques that Hitler would influence the people of Germany, Europe and the world.

The People's Receiver

When Adolf Hitler rose to power in 1933 he appointed Joseph Goebbels as his 'Minister of Public Enlightenment and Propaganda'. In this role Goebbels was given total control over the press, radio, cinema and theatres. At Goebbels' request the 'People's Receiver' was developed, an affordable radio receiver designed to pick up only the stations of the Reich, ensuring that Nazi propaganda could be listened to as opposed to foreign broadcasts. Listening to foreign stations actually became a criminal offence. Later the penalty would be death.

Of propaganda Goebbels said this: 'never lose sight of the fundamental principle of all propaganda, the constant repetition of the most effective arguments,' and, 'propaganda means repetition and still more repetition!' 'I keep dinning it into my people over and over: repeat it until even the densest has got it.' [7]

When Germany was overrun by the Allies in 1945, Hitler was on the brink of launching a cable television system much like

22

what George Orwell was later to describe in his novel 1984. He was intending to use this to broadcast Nazi propaganda around Germany. The plans were first discovered by Soviet soldiers in the ruins of Berlin in 1945. A document written by engineer Walter Bruch – who invented the PAL color television system – entitled, 'Plan to supply people's transmitter to German homes', was presented to Hitler. The document claimed that the laying of a broadband cable between Berlin and Nuremberg had begun. The documents also revealed that Hitler had been planning a complex series of public television screens, including in laundries so that housewives could tune in. Joseph Goebbels, the brainchild behind the plan, said: 'we'll be able to show whatever we want. We'll create a reality, which the people of Germany need and can copy.' [8]

Albert Speer, Hitler's Minister for Armaments and War Production, believed that it was by utilizing all technical means to broadcast and disseminate Nazi propaganda that Hitler's dictatorship of Germany was established and sustained. He said at the Nuremberg trials: 'Hitler's dictatorship differed in one fundamental point from all its predecessors in history. His was the first dictatorship in the present period of technical development, a dictatorship which made complete use of all technical means for the domination of its own country. Through technical means like the radio and the loud-speaker, eighty million people were deprived of independent thought. It was thereby possible to subject them to the will of one man.' [9]

Today Hitler's scheme has not only been fully realized but has gone far beyond what he could ever have possibly imagined. Our world is now awash not only with televisions in homes and public places but with the technological ability to broadcast via the internet on all kinds of devices including the cell phone. Goebbels' chilling statement has reached its prophetic fulfillment. Through television a reality has been created which fosters dependency and exposes the masses to endless hours of daily manipulation and lies.

Primetime Propaganda

In the late 1940s the Central Intelligence Agency (CIA) began a secret project known as Project Mockingbird. The operation was to recruit and put on the CIA payroll American news agencies and journalists in order to buy influence behind the scenes at the major media outlets and to become distributors of government propaganda.

William Colby, former CIA Director said: 'the CIA owns everyone of any significance in the major media.' [10]

Former CIA intelligence officer William B. Bader, on briefing members of the Senate Intelligence Committee, said: 'there is quite an incredible spread of relationships. You don't need to manipulate Time magazine, for example, because there are [Central Intelligence] Agency people at the management level.' [11]

Nothing has changed. Today minute by minute this strategy is being used at our expense. Through television programs – whether news, shows or movies – we are being conditioned and programmed into believing lies, lies that are to do with politics, economics, the climate, health, terrorism, war and so on.

A book entitled *Primetime Propaganda* by Ben Shapiro documented how popular American television programs such as Happy Days, Sesame Street and Friends were laced with political messages. While The Sunday Telegraph reported that the British government spent nearly £2 million funding television programs that were indistinguishable from regular shows, commissioned by ministers to show their policies and activities in a sympathetic light.

In 2012 the British Broadcasting Corporation (BBC) was accused of being the European Union's propaganda arm after it admitted to receiving £3 million in grants from the European Union since 2007. Furthermore, the corporation revealed that its commercial arm, BBC Worldwide, borrowed more than £141 million from the European Investment Bank since 2003. This led Tory MP Priti Patel to ask, 'how can a public service broadcaster demonstrate genuine impartiality on European issues if it is in receipt of EU funds?'

MP for Lincoln, Karl McCartney, commented that 'there has long been concern by many at what can only be described as Left-wing reporting, particularly, though not solely, in matters relating to Britain's relationship with Europe....Even Mark Thompson, the BBC's director general, has accepted the corporation had previously been guilty of a "massive" Left-wing bias. Mr Thompson has also admitted that the BBC's coverage of Europe had been "weak and rather nervous"...in the light of these EU loans, and the BBC's often one-sided coverage of EU matters, it is now incumbent on the BBC to explain very clearly to the British people how it intends to ensure the organization's impartiality, in respect of its Left-leaning reporting, in the future. Until such time, I think people will quite rightly continue to question what influence the EU exerts, financially or otherwise, over "our" BBC.' [12]

Finally propaganda techniques can now be fully exerted with the most deceptive and far reaching effects ever known, positioned as it is today in the perfect environment of the digital age. Its influence and efficacy is now beyond all limitations.

These overt and more obvious forms of mind control through television propaganda have been used for decades. However in this digital age a whole new covert opportunity has presented itself to governments and corporations which surpasses all past efforts to control the masses.

Television and Hypnosis

A character in the movie *Network* makes this impassioned plea about the realities concerning television technology: 'you're beginning to think that the tube is reality and that your own lives are unreal...In God's name, you people are the real thing; we're the illusion.' [13]

That should be a wake-up call not only to the characters in the movie and those watching the film. It should be a wake-up call for all of us.

Television presents a world of illusion.

It is not a window onto reality.

It is a window onto what people want us to see.

For a long time governments and media corporations have understood the ability to control the mind through various techniques. In fact many mind control ideas were taken from Nazi Germany. After World War Two, the American government under President Truman authorized what was called 'Operation Paperclip', the transporting of Nazi scientists from Germany to America to continue research in various programs ranging from new rocket design to mind control.

MK-Ultra was borne out of one such Nazi program. Project MK-Ultra was a covert CIA human experimentation program, using many methods to control the mental state and modify the behavior of a person.

One method used was hypnosis. A declassified CIA document dated 7th January 1953 reads, 'these subjects have clearly demonstrated that they can pass from a fully awake state to a deep H [hypnotized] controlled state...by telephone, by receiving written matter, or by the use of code, signal, or words...It has also been shown by experimentation...that they can act as unwilling couriers for information purposes.' [14]

A person under a hypnotic trance becomes extremely vulnerable to suggestion from outside sources. The American Psychological Association says this: 'when using hypnosis, one person (the subject) is guided by another (the hypnotist) to respond to suggestions for changes in subjective experience, alterations in perception, sensation, emotion, thought or behavior.'

Mind control or hypnotic trance can be induced by various means. In the case of MK-Ultra it was through the use of mind-altering drugs. More traditional methods would be by optical fixation, where the patient fixes a steady stare at an object.

When a person is under hypnotic suggestion different waves of the brain become active. A person moves from Beta waves to Alpha and Theta waves. Once in the Alpha wave state a person becomes receptive to suggestion. Electricity is used to communicate with the billions of neurons that make up the human brain. The electrical activity of the brain is known as brainwaves. These brainwaves emit electrochemical impulses of different frequencies. These brainwaves can be broadly divided into four categories and are emitted at different stages of brain activity:

Beta – normal waking consciousness with frequencies ranging from 13-60 Hertz

Alpha – physical and mental relaxation with frequencies of 7-13 Hertz

Theta – drowsiness and reduced consciousness of 4-7 Hertz

Delta – deep sleep or seizure of 0.1-4 Hertz.

In 1969 scientist Herbert Krugman monitored brainwaves to discover the effects of television watching on the brain and found that in less than a minute a person's brainwaves switched from Beta waves – active and logical thought – to Alpha waves – a meditative and trance-like state that is open to suggestion, as in hypnosis.

Television is accordingly a very effective medium for deceiving the masses through the transmission of propaganda. Even the very act of watching TV induces a docile and subservient response in the viewer and opens the mind to suggestion.

A Powerful Delusion

Furthermore it has been found that signals can be embedded into a television broadcast to elicit an emotional response in the viewer, thereby transforming the common television set into a sophisticated weapon to control the emotions of the viewer.

Here is just one example of many that reveal this to be present fact not future science fiction:

In *Nervous system manipulation by electromagnetic fields from monitors*, inventor Hendricus G Loos says that 'physiological effects have been observed in a human subject in response to stimulation of the skin with weak electromagnetic fields that are pulsed with certain frequencies near 1/2 Hz or 2.4 Hz, such as to excite a sensory resonance. Many computer monitors and TV tubes, when displaying pulsed images, emit pulsed electromagnetic fields of sufficient amplitudes to cause such excitation. It is therefore possible to manipulate the nervous system of a subject by pulsing images displayed on a nearby computer monitor or TV set. For the latter, the image pulsing may be imbedded in the program material, or it may be overlaid by modulating a video stream, either as an RF signal or as a video signal. The image displayed on a computer monitor may be pulsed effectively by a simple computer program. For certain monitors, pulsed electromagnetic fields capable of exciting sensory resonances in nearby subjects may be generated even as the displayed images are pulsed with subliminal intensity.'
(15)

Whether this technology will be used to control the masses in the future remains to be seen. But what is certain is that we are now being programmed to believe in a certain kind of way via television. We are being deceived into believing a different kind of reality to one that actually exists. Propaganda is so insidious that we do not even know it is happening.

This is the weapon formed against us. The Bible prophesies that in the last days the inhabitants of the earth will be deceived. Revelation 13:14 says, 'he [Satan] deceived the inhabitants of the earth.' 2 Thessalonians 2 explains that in the end of days people will be deceived because they refused to love the truth and so will live under a powerful delusion. That prophecy is being fulfilled now. Through the manipulative use of television a powerful delusion is deceiving the inhabitants of the earth.

Television has become a drug in the western world and while its people have become anaesthetized through watching endless hours of often mindless programming, and being conditioned through it, governments have been busy behind closed doors implementing new policies, signing treaties, taking away our democratic freedom and stripping us of our God-given civil rights.

When democracy is but a distant memory television will be utilized to its fullest and most horrifying effect. A weapon of mass mind-control the like of which the world has never known will be enlisted, giving rise to a tyrannical world government.

Chapter 3

The March Towards World Government

We shall have world government whether or not you like it, by conquest or consent
James Warburg, February 17, 1950 [1]

Today America would be outraged if UN troops entered Los Angeles to restore order. Tomorrow they will be grateful. When presented with this scenario, individual rights will be willingly relinquished for the guarantee of their well-being granted to them by the World Government
Henry Kissinger, Secretary of State to President Nixon [2]

Ever since the dawn of history people have harbored an ambition to rule the world, from Babylon to the Roman Empire, from Napoleon to Adolf Hitler's Nazi Germany. But while these dictatorships and others have arisen through military conquest, a new dictatorship has been rising in our time which does not employ the historical and overt method of war. Unnoticed and shrouded in secrecy, veiled by the strategic use of propaganda in the mass media, a world government is covertly being orchestrated every day. Incrementally, over a period of decades, this world government has been taking shape and now in our time, the final phases are being implemented.

The establishment of the League of Nations in 1919, after the

31

end of the First World War, was the embryonic beginning of world government. Its stated priority was to maintain world peace. Consisting of 58 member countries, the League of Nations would endure until its failure to prevent war when Hitler withdrew from the league and World War Two quickly ensued. However, this would only serve to strengthen the plan for world government and after Hitler's defeat in 1945 the United Nations was founded, replacing the League of Nations.

John D Rockefeller Jr (1874-1960) was a committed globalist who funded and supported the League of Nations. He was so committed to globalism that in 1946 he bought and donated the land on which the United Nations headquarters now stands on the banks of the Manhattan River in New York.

The Rockefeller family has long been a part of the secretive group known as the Bilderberg Group, founded by Joseph Retinger – a politician and 33rd degree Mason.

In 1954, under the guidance of the Dutch royal crown and the Rockefeller family, the most powerful people in the world met for the first Bilderberg meeting in the Netherlands at the Hotel de Bilderberg. Its purpose was to debate current world issues in an off-the-record manner, hidden from the eyes of the media.

Since 1954 the Bilderberg Group has met annually and has represented the elite and the wealthy of the western nations – presidents, prime ministers, state secretaries, politicians, royalty, bankers, financiers, the World Bank, International Monetary Fund, European Union, United Nations and NATO representatives, media moguls, military leaders, businessmen and others. Bilderberg participants are sworn to secrecy and any collaborating news outlets such as The Washington Post, The New York Times and Los Angeles Times [3] are forbidden to report anything. With many media chiefs actually belonging to the group, and agreeing to the press embargo, it is little wonder that they have achieved the obscurity they have.

Having said that, it should astonish all of us that so many influential and high ranking individuals can meet in one place over a weekend, once every year, and that so little or no media coverage is given to the gathering at all.

When you consider the list of invites this becomes even more startling. Attendees have included Prince Charles and Prince Philip of the British Royal Family, US Presidents, Prime Ministers Margaret Thatcher, Tony Blair, Gordon Brown, German Chancellor Angela Merkel, Rupert Murdoch of News Corporation (Fox News), David Rockefeller of Chase Manhattan Bank, Donald Rumsfeld – US Secretary of Defense, President of the European Commission – Jose Manuel Barroso, Mario Monti (now Italian Prime Minister), Timothy Geithner – President of the Federal Reserve Bank of New York and Bill Gates – Chairman of Microsoft, to name but a few.

Jim Tucker in his book, *The Bilderberg Diary* writes: 'if 120 film stars, or 120 professional football players, gathered secretly each year, in a sealed-off resort patrolled by armed guards, you would bust your butts to learn what transpired. Why, then, is there no curiosity when 120 of the world's most distinguished leaders in finance and politics gather in that way?' [4]

Precisely! Why has the very existence of the Bilderberg meetings remained shrouded in secrecy? Why does no one know about the topics of discussions in those meetings, or the conclusions reached? The answer to this can be found in a revealing comment made by David Rockefeller when he stated in June of 1991, 'we are grateful to the Washington Post, the New York Times, Time Magazine and other great publications whose directors have attended our meetings and respected their promises of discretion for almost forty years... It would have been impossible for us to develop our plan for the world if we had been subjected to the lights of publicity during those years. But the world is more sophisticated and prepared to march towards a world government. The supranational sovereignty of an intellectual elite and world bankers is surely preferable to the national auto determination practiced in past centuries.'

The Real Agenda

The purpose of the Bilderberg Group as stated on their official website is 'three days of informal and off-the-record discussion about topics of current concern especially in the fields of foreign affairs and the international economy.' However, for many years Daniel Estulin, investigative journalist and author of the book *The Bilderberg Group* has investigated Bilderberg and obtained vital information from those meetings which reveals that the Bilderberg Group's aims are less than virtuous.

Estulin documents that the Bilderberg group wants to create 'one international identity' by destroying the national sovereignty of nations through subversion. They want to control people through the following:

- creating a 'zero-growth society' (prosperity means progress and progress makes it difficult to enslave humanity)
- 'artificially manufactured crises' for the purpose of confusing and demoralizing humanity (making people unable to decide their own futures)
- the 'global control of all education' (eliminating the true past allows for the globalist dream to be realized)
- further empowerment of the United Nations
- the establishment of an American Union much like the European Union through the Western Trading Bloc and its expansion
- the development of NATO into the UN's world army
- the transformation of the International Court of Justice into the sole global legal system
- the formation of a Socialist welfare state where obedient slaves will be rewarded, and those not bowing to the system exterminated [5]

David Rockefeller brazenly admits in his own Memoirs that he is working towards a world government: 'for more than a century, ideological extremists at either end of the political spectrum have seized upon well-publicized incidents to attack the Rockefeller family for the inordinate influence they claim we wield over American political and economic institutions. Some even believe we are part of a secret cabal working against the best interests of the United States, characterizing my family and me as "internationalists" and conspiring with others around the world to build a more integrated global political and economic structure – one world, if you will. If that's the charge, I stand guilty, and I am proud of it.' [6]

The very name Bilderberg also gives us a clue to the true activities of the group. It is often purported that the Bilderberg Group gained its name after the hotel of its initial meeting. According to Estulin however, the name has a more sinister history. Prince Bernhard of the Dutch royal family was an officer in the German Reiter SS Corp in the early 1930s and was on the board of a German chemical group, Farben Bilder. Estulin writes that Bernhard was inspired through his Nazi history in corporate management to call the group the Bilderberg Group after Farben Bilder, in memory of the Farben Bilder executives who organised Heinrich Himmler's 'Circle of Friends' who were elite wealth builders during Hitler's Nazi Germany. [7] We should remember that Hitler's dream was one of world domination and that the Nazi Bilder Group was given the role of resourcing the creation of this totalitarian dystopia.

The European Union

The Rockefeller family and the Bilderberg Group have been influencing and coordinating efforts to form a world government from the time of the League of Nations to the time of the United Nations. It should therefore not surprise us to learn that the creation of the European Union is also the work of these same globalists and a part of the overall strategy to see the plan for a world government fully realized.

Leaked papers from a 1955 Bilderberg Group conference summary confirm that the Bilderbergers were at the heart of establishing a European Union and also the single euro currency. Under the heading 'European Unity', the paper reads, 'it might be better to proceed through the development of a common market by treaty rather than by the creation of new high authorities...' and, 'it was generally recognized that it is our common responsibility to arrive in the shortest possible time at the highest degree of integration, beginning with a common European market.' Just two years later in 1957 the European Economic Community was created with the Treaty of Rome. Concerning the euro currency the paper says, 'a European speaker expressed concern about the need to achieve a common currency, and indicated that in his view this necessarily implied the creation of a central political authority.' [8]

The EU Observer carried a story in March 2009 also confirming the Bilderberg link with the creation of the euro currency. Etienne Davignon, former president of the European Commission and current chairman of the Bilderberg Group, openly admitted that Bilderberg had helped to create the euro:

'A meeting in June in Europe of the Bilderberg Group – an informal club of leading politicians, businessmen and thinkers chaired by Mr Davignon – could also "improve understanding" on future action, in the same way it helped create the euro in the 1990s, he said. When we were having debates on the euro, people [at Bilderberg events] could explain why it was worth taking risks and the others, for whom the formal policy was not to believe in it, were not obliged not to listen and had to stand up and come up with real arguments.' [9]

Furthermore, the Telegraph, in the year 2000, reported that declassified American government documents from the 1950s revealed that the Rockefeller foundation and Joseph Retinger, the Bilderberg founder, had their hand in building what is now the European Union. The documents show that America was working aggressively behind the scenes to push Britain into a European state and gave instructions for a campaign to promote a fully fledged European Parliament. It was signed by General William J Donavan, head of wartime Office of Strategic Services – what would later become the Central Intelligence Agency.

Files released by the US national archives reveal that Washington's 'American Committee for a United Europe' was its main instrument for structuring the European program. According to the article, the US role in the creation of a European Union was a covert operation, including funding from the Rockefeller and Ford foundations. A memo dated June 11th 1965 advised Robert Marjolin the vice-president of the European Economic Community to pursue monetary union by stealth.[10]

Contrary to what we are made to believe the creation of the European Union has not been a product of democratic decision-making by the people of Europe but has rather been the result of underhanded orchestration by a secretive elite with an agenda that goes far beyond the geographical boundaries of Europe.

The American Union

Another union unknown to most is the embryonic North American Union. This proposes the merger of Canada, North America and Mexico with a plan to have a single currency, much like the euro, called the amero. [11] The EU would therefore be the blueprint for the creation of the NAU. Again, incrementally and by stealth, the NAU has been developing but at a much faster rate than the EU.

The year 1987 would mark the beginnings of the NAU with the signing of the North American Free Trade Agreement (NAFTA) in Washington by President Reagan and Canadian Prime Minister Brian Mulroney.

Later in 2001 Mexico's President, Vicente Fox, after calling for the creation of a North American common market in 2000, would agree the 'Partnership for Prosperity' in Washington with President Bush.

In 2005 the Security and Prosperity Partnership was signed by President Bush, Paul Martin of Canada and Vincente Fox of Mexico. [12]

In his book, The Late Great USA, Jerome E. Corsi shows how this agreement was a full-frontal assault on American sovereignty. Saying that, 'Bush's goal to create a North American Union with no borders, a shared currency, and utterly no voice for average Americans in their own futures is the real reason he won't enforce immigration laws.' Corsi claims:

'A North American Union would not just be the end of America as we know it but the beginning of an EU-like nightmare – a bureaucratic coup d'etat foisted upon millions of Americans without their knowledge or consent.'

American and European Union

David Rockefeller of the Bilderberg Group founded the Trilateral Commission in 1973 for the purpose of fostering closer relationship with the United States, Europe and Japan. G. Edward Griffin, in his book *The Creature From Jekyll Island*, writes of the Trilaterial Commission, 'the TLC was created by David Rockefeller to coordinate the building of The New World Order... an end run around national sovereignty, eroding it piece by piece.' The objective is to draw the United States, Mexico, Canada, Japan, and Western Europe into political and economic union. Under slogans such as free trade and environmental protection, each nation is to surrender its sovereignty 'piece by piece' until a full-blown regional government emerges from the process. The globalist agenda has been by stealth to incrementally set up political unions for the purpose of forming a world government.'

As the political unions of the EU and NAU are in place they will merge together as will other political unions like the Asia Union. This is taking place with the EU and the US. On the 30th April 2007, Chancellor Merkel of Germany, European Commission President Jose Manuel Borosso and the then US President George Bush met together for a press conference on the White House lawn to announce the results of a recent US-EU Summit. Bush said, 'I thank the chancellor and José very much for the trans-Atlantic economic integration plan that the three of us signed today. It is a statement of the importance of trade. It is a commitment to eliminating barriers to trade. It is a recognition that the closer the United States and the EU become, the better off our people will be. So this is a substantial agreement and I appreciate it.' [13]

It was clear that no small agreement had been signed at the Summit. The White House described what was essentially an end to US independence:

'[The US-EU Summit] adopted a

- framework on transatlantic economic integration which lays a long-term foundation for building a stronger and more integrated transatlantic economy, in particular by fostering cooperation to reduce regulatory burdens and accelerating work on key 'lighthouse projects' in the areas of intellectual property rights, secure trade, investment, financial markets, and innovation
- declaration on political and security issues, including the seemingly mutually exclusive goals of combatting terrorism and working towards visa-free travel for all EU and U.S. citizens by creating conditions by which the Visa Waiver Program may be expanded
- joint statement on energy security and climate change that commits the United States to working collectively with the EU to ensure secure, affordable, and clean supplies of energy and tackling climate change [14]

Signing Away our Sovereignties

For world government to succeed the national sovereignty of a nation must first be compromised and then abolished. This is one of the globalist's number one weapons in their quest for world supremacy.

The destruction of a nation's sovereignty renders that nation powerless of independent authority. To achieve this, the globalists use a crisis as a pretext to create a treaty between countries. Once the treaty is ratified, any existing age-old laws of the land and constitutions of the countries involved become undermined and with each amendment of the treaty more and more sovereignty is simply whittled away. Eventually nations become mere provinces within unions controlled by unelected bureaucrats whose primary and underlying hidden purpose has always been to remove the sovereign power from that nation and subjugate it.

This is conquest − but curiously enough no military action has been required to gain control, yet country after country is invaded and the march towards world government becomes an ever closer nightmare.

This is how the European Union was formed − after the crisis of the Second World War amid an atmosphere of fear that war could happen again in Europe.

In 1951 Belgium, France, Germany, Italy, Luxembourg and the Netherlands formed the European Coal and Steel Community. In 1957 those six countries signed the Treaty of Rome, establishing the European Economic Community (EEC), and a European Court of Justice was also formed. In 1965 the Merger Treaty was signed merging the European Coal and Steel Community, the European Atomic Energy Community and the European Economic Community into one single structure − the European Economic Community.

Skipping forward to the Single European Act signed in 1986 was the first major and important mile stone in a revision of the Treaty of Rome. The revision would set an objective to establish a Single Market by December 1992.

Another giant leap forward for the globalist agenda was the Treaty of Maastricht signed in 1992 establishing the European Union. This would see the morphing of the EEC into what is now known as the European Union – a fully functioning regional government with its own flag, anthem, and passports bearing the name European Union, usurping national passports.

Maastricht also paved the way to the single euro currency adopted in 2002. Since Maastricht, other treaties have been signed but none as far reaching and powerful as the Treaty of Lisbon signed in December 2007 and entering into force in December 2009.

The Lisbon Treaty

The Lisbon Treaty was a reworking of the failed EU constitution rejected by the French and the Dutch in a 2005 referendum. European Commission President Jose Manuel Barroso said of the EU constitution, 'we cannot say that the treaty is dead.' He was right and in 2007 the re-born EU constitution, in the form of the Lisbon Treaty, was forced upon and signed by all member states.

In one fell swoop a treaty came into being which allowed the EU wide and sweeping powers over the current twenty seven member nations of Europe. Vast amounts of power have now been shifted to a foreign parliament. All member nations, including Britain, are governed by unelected bureaucrats in Brussels.

Deceived by the mainstream media and the then British Prime Minister Edward Heath, with most newspapers encouraging a 'yes' vote for a Common Market in the 1975 referendum, the

British people had no idea that by voting 'yes' they were voting for the destruction of British Sovereignty. Neither did they know the campaign was supported by the CIA. CIA operative Cord Meyer Jr became the head of a CIA station in London for the duration of the Referendum whose job was "to do what it takes" to secure a "Yes" vote in favour of Britain staying in the EEC.[15] Heath said of the Common Market in 1973, 'there are some in this country who fear that in going into Europe we shall in some way sacrifice independence and sovereignty. These fears, I need hardly say, are completely unjustified.' [16]

Today however the EU has become a far cry from the early days of the Common Market and now over 75% of British law is made in Brussels, demonstrating that unelected bureaucrats have effectively more power than British MPs.

Over 25,000 EU laws affect Britain. Laws are passed in the EU parliament at around 300 an hour! Because British politicians have given the EU precedence over British law, Parliament has no choice but to enact EU laws. These laws are made by the European Commission – a group of unelected bureaucratic traitors who have taken an oath not to act in the interests of their own country.

In an economic crisis where austerity is the talk of the day, Britain is paying around 50 million pounds a day for the privilege of being a member of the EU, with an EU annual budget of 8 billion.

EU President Herman van Rompuy is reported to receive a salary earning more than US President Barack Obama.[17] While the head of the European Union's High Representative for Foreign Affairs, Baroness Ashton earns a salary larger than Hilary Clinton.[18]

In 2004 the European Commission dismissed Marta Andreasen, EU chief accountant, after she spoke out against the European Union's 'Enron-style' book-keeping. Andreasen said, 'I encountered evidence of structural fraud embedded in the European Commission systems. High officials knew this was the case, and still is the case. I am the one who has behaved as a real European – and I have paid for it with my job.' [19]

Global Governance

The Lisbon Treaty has literally transformed the EU into a 'United States of Europe.' Notably the new treaty allowed for a first permanent President of the European Council. With such a new and powerful position becoming available it would be expected that the people of Europe would have a say in the so called democratic decision making of the EU and elect such a person to power. Not so. The President of Europe was not elected at all. Herman van Rompuy was appointed behind closed doors in a secret meeting chaired by Bilderberg's Viscount Etienne Davignon. The author of an article for The Guardian wrote before Rompuy's appointment,

'Van Rompuy met Kissinger at a closed session of international policymakers and industrialists chaired by Viscount Etienne Davignon, a discreetly powerful figure in Brussels who was vice-president of the European commission in the 1980s. The viscount currently chairs the Bilderberg Group, the shadowy global freemasonry of politicians and bankers who meet to discuss world affairs in the strictest privacy... Van Rompuy, it seems, attended the Bilderberg session to audition for the European job...' [20]

Rompuy was previously the president of Belgium, an artificial state created by globalists in 1830 as a political experiment, a blueprint for the EU. To understand Belgium is to understand the EU. Belgium lacks patriotism; in fact, if you visit you will see a distinct lack of national flags. EU flags are seen flying from their government buildings.

Belgium is also of course home to the Brussels European Parliament. It is a country sadly without identity, consisting of

6 million Dutch people living in the north, and 4 million French living in the south. Lode Claes, Flemish philosopher, wrote in his book The Absent Majority, that 'without identity and a sense of nationhood, there can be no democracy or morality'.

The Lisbon Treaty is the fulfillment of all past EU treaties that reduce Britain and all other member countries into states within a union. This union takes precedence over national constitutions and parliaments, causing them to be controlled by a system of unelected bureaucrats with the character and shape of a dictatorship more akin to the old Soviet Union. This union has resulted in the abolition of individual national sovereignty and democracy in favor of a move towards an eventual dictatorial world government.

With the birth of the new 'United States of Europe' it was significantly and remarkably announced by the new EU president, Herman van Rompuy that 2009 also became the first year of global governance:

'We're living through exceptionally difficult times – the financial crisis and its dramatic impact on employment and budgets, the climate crisis which threatens our very survival, a period of anxiety, uncertainty and lack of confidence. Yet these problems can be overcome through a joint effort between our countries....2009 is the first year of global governance with the establishment of the G20 in the middle of the financial crises. The climate conference in Copenhagen is another step towards the global management of our planet – our mission, our presidency is one of hope, supported by acts and deeds.' [21]

The G20

Nineteen countries and the European Union compose the G20 – a group of twenty finance ministers and central bank governors from twenty major economies. The G20 is yet another step closer towards a world government with the consolidating and merging of economic powers. The United Nations Climate

Conference also referred to by Rompuy was held in December of 2009 in Copenhagen. The former science advisor to British Prime Minister Margaret Thatcher, Lord Christopher Monckton, says the climate conference was actually a guise to lay the foundation for a world government:

'At Copenhagen this December, weeks away, a treaty will be signed – Your president will sign it. Most of the Third World countries will sign it, because they think they're going to get money out of it. Most of the left-wing regimes from the European Union will rubber stamp it. Virtually nobody won't sign it. I read that treaty and what it says is this: that a world government is going to be created. The word government actually appears as the first of three purposes of the new entity – The second purpose is the transfer of wealth from the countries of the West to Third World countries, in satisfaction of what is called, coyly, climate debt – because we've been burning CO_2 and they haven't. We've been screwing up the climate and they haven't. And the third purpose of this new entity, this government is enforcement.' [22]

2009 saw the birth of a 'United States of Europe', the establishment of the G20 and an attempt, although it failed, by the United Nations to set up an agreement that would effectively create a world government. All these events happening together at one time are far from coincidental; they represent a massive push by the globalists to see their vision finally accomplished. Nations are being destroyed and supplanted by a global plan to unify every country under one international law. The end result will be world government.

But how is it possible that politicians can openly commit acts of treason by signing treaties that literally destroy national sovereignties and enforce international laws and regulations upon the people without little or no protest at all? In fact, in most cases the people are in agreement with their actions. We have already looked at how, through a strategy of perpetual propaganda disseminated through the mainstream media, the masses have either been blinded to the realities around them or they have been conditioned and deceived to believe that the pursuit of entertainment is far more important – leaving them either totally preoccupied or too caught up in the pleasures of life to care.

There is however another mind-control strategy used by the globalists which enables a fast and effective reaction from the people, allowing for such treaties and agreements to be passed – and that is the strategy of FEAR.

Through fear people will agree to practically anything as was clearly stated by a leading member of Hitler's Nazi Germany, Hermann Goering:

'Naturally the common people don't want war; neither in Russia, nor in England, nor in America, nor in Germany. That is understood. But after all, it is the leaders of the country who determine the policy and it is always a simple matter to drag the people along, whether it is a democracy or a fascist dictatorship or a parliament or a Communist dictatorship. The people can always be brought to the bidding of the leaders. That is easy. All you have to do is to tell them they are being attacked...It works the same in any country.' [23]

In the next chapter we will look at the way crises induce fear which then create the fertile conditions for leaders to implement changes which societies would not tolerate in the normal course of events.

In other words, we will look at the way the globalists are using mind control strategies to restrict liberties and advance their agenda.

Chapter 4

Creating a Climate of Fear

You never let a serious crisis go to waste.
And what I mean by that, it's an opportunity to do
things you think you could not do before

Rahm Emanuel, former Chief of Staff to Barack Obama [1]

We are on the verge of a global transformation.
All we need is the right major crisis and the nations will
accept the New World Order

David Rockefeller [2]

At the end of the last chapter we looked at the way in which governments create a climate of fear in order to create an atmosphere of compliance towards changes that would not normally be accepted within a society.

How then is this fear generated?

What are the mechanisms by which a government instills the kind of panic in which people are prepared to cede the ground on which they enjoy their civil liberties?

The answer is through a crisis. The intentional orchestration of frightening crises is one of the most successful means for inducing a change of mind within large numbers of people.

Crises, in short, are the means by which minds are controlled.

47

Crises are being created by those with a globalist agenda.

Crises are the launch pad for world government agendas.

Problem/Reaction/Solution

We need to understand here that a crisis is a powerful weapon in the hands of the globalist and it is currently through crises that world government moves ever closer into actualization.

To do that, the globalists are using a strategy known as the Hegelian Dialectic.

The Hegelian Dialectic creates a series of circumstances which guide our thoughts and actions towards a predetermined solution.

The Hegelian Dialectic derives its name from Georg Wilhelm Friedrich Hegel, a German philosopher (1770-1831). Hegel revolutionized European philosophy and was a forerunner to Marxism. Karl Marx used Hegel's dialectic theory to support his economic theory of communism and it was on this philosophical foundation that the ideology of the Soviet Union was built.

In simplistic terms the Hegelian Dialectic brings about change in three simple steps – Thesis, Antithesis and Synthesis.

Step 1 **The Thesis:** manufacture or exploit a **problem** (war, terrorist atrocity, earthquake, flood etc)

Step 2 **The Antithesis:** evoke the required **reaction** (fear, panic, anxiety)

Step 3 **The Synthesis:** offer a **solution** (in the case of terrorism, the enacting of unconstitutional laws which give more power to the police and military over civilian lives, more surveillance, justification for invasion and so on).

Under any other scenario the solution would have been flatly opposed by the people. But now, as a result of the crisis, the people cry out for the very solution they would have opposed which in turn is the solution that the globalists wanted and planned all along. The people now feel free from fear but are actually enslaved more than ever before to the government.

The Hegelian Dialectic is effective because it creates the illusion that the people are in control of their own destinies and that democracy is alive and well. It keeps the people in the dark as to what is truly going on. It also creates a certain dependency upon the government and the people look to it as though it is their only hope – when the exact opposite is true.

This is therefore the most effective deception.

For the globalist, the Hegelian cycle looks like this:

Let's look at a few examples of this kind of cynical exploitation of peoples' minds through the use of fear-evoking crises.

The Euro Crisis

The euro crisis has been used to implement further integration of the twenty seven countries of the EU, particularly the seventeen countries of the Eurozone.

What is the problem? The media has informed us that the end of the euro and the collapse of the EU are imminent.

What reaction has this instilled? The media have instilled fear that the European Union dream is in grave danger and that it must be rescued at all costs, because the effects of the disintegration of the EU would be catastrophic not only for Europe but for the rest of the world.

What has the solution been? We have been persuaded to buy into a deeper integration of the EU nations with a new fiscal pact. Rather than demonstrate against the latest encroachments by the EU, the people accept a greater loss of national sovereignty, relieved that a total meltdown of the Continent has been averted.

Climate Change

What is the problem? We are told that our actions are having devastating and potentially world-ending affect on the planet's climate. This problem is heralded aggressively through the mainstream media and propagandized through big budget Hollywood movies like *2012*. In addition, we hear scaremongering and ridiculous claims from high ranking officials which all help to instill fear in the people and create the illusion that there is a serious problem that needs solving.

For example, Herman van Rompuy, EU President, said during his first press conference in 2009, 'we are living through exceptionally difficult times…the climate crisis which threatens our very survival, a period of anxiety.' [3]

Prince Charles wildly declared at the Copenhagen climate conference in the same year, 'the grim reality is that our planet has reached a point of crisis and we have only seven years before we lose the levers of control.' [4]

What kind of reaction has this engendered? In the face of an imminent climatic apocalypse – allegedly within seven years – the public has been motivated to support climate policies through anxiety rather than through considered debate.

What has the solution been? We have agreed to a draft treaty to reduce carbon emissions which consents to a global centralization of political, economic and environmental power via the United Nations!

Terror in London

On the morning of 7th July 2005 a series of coordinated bombs exploded in London, targeting civilians during the rush hour and leaving 56 dead and 700 more injured.

Terrorism was cited as the problem here and the reaction was widespread panic.

What were we persuaded to accept as a result? New laws were passed in the name of security which involved a considerable loss of civil liberties, including free speech. There was an increase in the surveillance of UK citizens and subsequently a leap forward in the advancement of the police state agenda.

Michael Meacher, former Minister of State for the Environment under Tony Blair said of the 7/7 attacks:

'7/7 we call it…it's a very convenient way of ensuring there is fear, ensuring there is control, and ensuring that those who are in the know – and of course we cannot tell you because it is all secret – are in a position of extreme power.' [5]

All this of course reveals that elements within the UK government, and indeed other governments too, are developing solutions to crises, whether real or manufactured, which are helping to advance the globalist agenda.

Chapter 5

Government Sponsored Terrorism

It's a very convenient way of ensuring there is fear, ensuring there is control

Michael Meacher, Former Minister of State for the Environment under Tony Blair [1]

Once the people are terrorized, you can force a police state on them
Mae Brussell, Journalist [2]

In order to bring a nation to support the burdens of maintaining great military establishments, it is necessary to create an emotional state akin to war psychology. There must be the portrayal of external menace

John Foster Dulles, Secretary of state under President Eisenhower [3]

A false flag operation, otherwise known as an act of government sponsored terrorism, is a clandestine operation orchestrated by criminal elements of a government or political entity designed to further its own political agenda with the intent to deceive its own people into believing the operation was carried out by an opposing entity. The name 'false flag' is derived from the subversive tactic of flying the colors or flags of a country rather than its own.

53

Let us take a brief look at some examples of false flag operations.

The Reichstag Parliament Fire

The Reichstag parliament fire took place on the night of February 27 1933, just one month after Hitler's Nazi party came to power.

It was orchestrated by Hitler's president of the Reichstag, Hermann Goring, and by Joseph Goebbels, minister of propaganda, who blamed the attack on a German Communist Party plot against the government. The only evidence the Nazis produced was a mentally handicapped young man by the name of Marinus van der Lubbe who was conveniently discovered behind the Reichstag and later found guilty and executed. As a result of the attack, civil liberties were suspended. Mass arrests of Communist party members and all parliamentary delegates ensued. This action resulted in their parliamentary seats becoming empty. Hitler was thus able to bring the Nazi party to a majority and consolidate his dictatorial power.

In 2008, 75 years later, van der Lubbe finally received his pardon. An article in The Guardian reads, 'an unemployed Dutch bricklayer who was made a scapegoat for one of the defining moments of 20th-century German history has been pardoned for his crime 75 years later. Marinus van der Lubbe, 24, was beheaded after being convicted of setting fire to the Reichstag, an event Hitler used as a pretext to suspend civil liberties and establish a dictatorship.' [4]

The false flag operations of Hitler did not stop with the Reichstag. In order not to appear as the aggressor but rather as the defender, another event was staged to justify the Nazi invasion of Poland on the night of August 31, 1939. Known as 'Operation Himmler', this involved – among other events – an action in which German convicts were forced to dress as Poles, taken to the Polish-German border, drugged and then shot to make it look as though they had been killed while attacking German troops.

From what we know of the atrocities committed by the Nazi regime it is no surprise that Hitler's government engaged in false flag operations. It is however a much harder and disturbing leap to entertain the possibility that our own governments in Britain, Europe and America could ever be complicit and active in such heinous crimes against its own people. Tragically, however, history provides us with many such examples.

Operation Gladio

Operation Gladio was created by the CIA and NATO as a strategy to stop communist influence in Italy and Western Europe after World War II. In reality Gladio was a terrorist network involved in false flag operations designed to deceive civilians into believing that Communist and leftist groups were responsible for atrocities. Trains, buses and even schools were targeted. In 1978 it would be Gladio which would assassinate the former Prime Minister Aldo Moro because, against the wishes of Washington, he was planning to include Communists in the government. The assassination was then blamed on the Red Brigades. The deadliest attack occurred in 1980 at a railway station in Bologna in which eighty five people were killed and a further two hundred injured.

A document uncovered by a Turkish journalist revealed the connection between NATO, the United States and Gladio. The 140 page manual, 'Field Manual 30-31,' provides detailed advice on the subjects of sabotage, bombing, killing, torture, fake elections and how to carry out acts of violence in times of peace and blame it on the Communist enemy.

The manual reads, 'there may be times when Host Country Governments show passivity or indecision in the face of Communist subversion and according to the interpretation of the US secret services do not react with sufficient effectiveness...

US army intelligence must have the means of launching special operations which will convince Host Country Governments and public opinion of the reality of the insurgent danger. To reach this aim US army intelligence should seek to penetrate the insurgency by means of agents on special assignment, with the task of forming special action groups among the most radical elements of the insurgency... These special operations must remain strictly secret. Only those persons acting against the revolutionary uprising shall know of the involvement of the US Army in the internal affairs of an allied country. The fact, that the involvement of forces of the US military goes deeper shall not become known under any circumstances.' [5]

In 1990 the European Parliament passed a resolution condemning Gladio, calling for a, 'full investigation into the nature, structure, aims and all other aspects of these clandestine organizations.'

The resolution singled out the United States for special criticism, protesting against the efforts of US officials to encourage the establishment in Europe of such a network. [6]

Operation Ajax

Operation Ajax involved the 1953 overthrow of the democratically elected Prime Minister of Iran, Mohammed Mosaddegh. It was orchestrated by the United Kingdom's MI6 intelligence agencies and United States CIA for the purpose of retaining control of Iran's oil.

Street thugs, clergy, politicians and Iranian army officers were all bribed to take part in a propaganda campaign to oust Mosaddegh and his government. According to declassified CIA documents the most feared mobsters were hired by the CIA to stage riots. Buses and truck loads of CIA paid men were also brought in from Tehran in order to take over the city. Approximately 300 people died in the conflict and Mosaddegh was deposed and arrested. [7]

Based on this kind of data, it is hard not to ask questions of other events in the Middle East, such as the 2010 Arab uprisings. Could it be that these were orchestrated by western intelligence to gain the upper hand in the Middle East?

Operation Northwoods

Operation Northwoods was a false flag US government proposal in 1962 to commit acts of terrorism against its own citizens in US cities as a pretext for military intervention with Cuba. The previously classified document was unearthed in 1997 by the John F Kennedy Assassination Records Review Board. Operation Northwoods had the written approval of all members of the Joint Chief of Staff. However, upon presentation of the plan to President John F Kennedy, it was rejected.

The document entitled 'Justification for US Military Intervention in Cuba' stated:

'The desired result from the execution of this plan would be to place the United States in the apparent position of suffering defensible grievances from a rash and irresponsible government of Cuba and to develop an international image of a Cuban threat to peace in the Western Hemisphere.'

Operation Northwoods called for innocent people to be shot on American streets and for a wave of terrorism to strike Washington DC, Miami and other states. It called for fleeing Cuban refugee boats to be sunk at sea, for innocent people to be framed for bombings they did not commit, and for a plane to be hijacked and destroyed in an effort to implicate the Cuban government and provoke a response.

The most incredible part of the plan involved the idea of flying a passenger plane full of college students. The plane would take off with the students and drop down off the radar and be secretly flown back to the United States while another pilotless and remotely controlled plane would take its place. While flying over Cuba the plane would transmit a 'may day' message saying it was under attack by Cuban MIG aircraft, the plane would then be remotely destroyed.

The previously top secret document included some of the following plans;

- Start riots near the base main gate
- Blow up ammunition inside the base and start fires
- Sabotage a ship in the harbor
- Sink a ship near the harbor entrance and conduct funerals for mock-victims
- Blow up a US ship in Guantanamo Bay and blame Cuba
- Blow up an unmanned drone vessel in Cuban waters. A US air/sea rescue operation would ensue to evacuate remaining members of a non-existent crew. Newspapers would carry casualty lists to cause a 'helpful wave of national indignation'
- Develop a Communist Cuban terror campaign in the Miami area, in other Florida cities and even in Washington blaming refugees seeking a haven in the US
- Sink a boatload of Cubans en route to Florida whether real or simulated
- Explode plastic bombs in carefully chosen spots, arrest Cuban agents and release prepared documents substantiating Cuban involvement
- Paint an F-86 plane to convince air passengers they saw a Cuban MIG. The pilot of the passenger plane would announce it was a Cuban MIG further convincing the passengers
- Hijackings against civil air and surface craft to appear to continue as harassing measures condoned by the government of Cuba
- An elaborate plan to create the illusion that a chartered civil airliner full of college students en route from the US

to Jamaica, Guatemala, Panama or Venezuela had been shot down by a Cuban aircraft while flying over Cuba. An exact duplicate of the plane would be created using a registered aircraft belonging to the CIA. The duplicate plane would be substituted and the passengers would board it under false names. The original registered aircraft would be converted to an unmanned drone. The duplicate plane carrying the college students would then be landed in a field and the passengers evacuated. The drone plane would continue to fly its planned route and while flying across Cuba it would transmit a MAY DAY message stating that it was under fire from a Cuban MIG aircraft. The plane would be destroyed via a radio signal. The incident would then be authentically reported to the US by radio stations in the Western Hemisphere instead of the US having to try and sell the lie

- Create an incident to make it look as though Communist Cuban MIGs had shot down a US military aircraft over international waters in an unprovoked attack. A pre-briefed pilot with a false identity while flying near the Cuban island would broadcast once only that he had been hit by Cuban MIGs and was going down. At this exact moment a submarine or similar would scatter plane debris and a parachute approximately 15-20 miles off the Cuban coast. The pilot however would continue to fly low altitude and land at a secure base at which time the plane would be stored and given a new tail number. The pilot would then assume his real identity. It would then appear that the pilot and plane were indeed missing. Other pilots flying in the area upon seeing the plane debris in the water would be convinced that the event had really happened and they would have a 'true' story to tell. Later a ship could be dispatched and aircraft parts retrieved giving yet more weight and evidence to the validity of the incident. [8][9]

We have just looked at documented evidence of past false flag operations including those either implemented or drawn up by our own governments – the train station bombings in Italy, the assassination of a political leader through Gladio in the 1980s, the orchestrated uprising in Iran, the ousting of Iranian Prime Minister Mohammed Mosaddegh, and finally the proposed elaborate and ingenious plan to hijack planes through Operation Northwoods.

If historically false flag operations have been used to further a political end, could it be that they are still being used to this day?

It would surely be naïve to believe otherwise.

Many people find this idea too disturbing. How could western governments be responsible for such barbaric and evil acts against its own people? Is not this kind of behavior only reserved for so-called 'rogue states'? Or is this just what we have been led to believe?

Chapter 6

Disturbing Questions

An error does not become truth by reason
of multiplied propagation, nor does truth
become error because nobody sees it

Mahatma Gandhi [1]

If we choose, we can live in a world of comforting illusion

Noam Chomsky [2]

By now we should realize that we have been conditioned to believe in a false reality created through the philosophy of 'problem, reaction, solution' and disseminated through the controlled mainstream media. We are saturated daily by the news constantly telling us how things are in the world. We have been bombarded with deception and illusion through a number of propaganda techniques. This is the continual information war, to win the hearts and the minds of the people.

Remember that Hitler's minister of propaganda Joseph Goebbels stated, 'propaganda means repetition and still more repetition!' 'I keep dinning it into my people over and over: repeat it until even the densest has got it." [3]

This is what is happening today. The mainstream media propagates the same ideas over and over again until they become accepted as incontestable truth.

This unceasing repetition has conditioned us to believe in many falsehoods, such as the view that our western governments are intrinsically good and that other governments of the world are defective or even evil. Other nations are either labeled as 'rogue states', part of the 'axis of evil', or we are told that they are harboring weapons of mass destruction. I am not saying that these other governments are necessarily acting in goodwill either. But it is important to realize that often our leaders and the mainstream media are guilty of vilifying other nations in order to stir up support for actions that would otherwise be rejected. We must never forget how George Bush and Tony Blair confidently declared that Saddam had WMDs in Iraq. 'I have absolutely no doubt at all that we will find evidence of weapons of mass destruction programs,' stated Blair. [4] But these weapons have never been found! This was not a mistake. This was a lie. The WMD claim was the flawed premise upon which the invasion of Iraq in 2003 took place.

Consider more recently the saber rattling between the West and Iran.

Iran has invaded no one in 200 years. Yet we constantly hear in the news that Iran is closer than ever to building a nuclear bomb which it will be ready to use. If it is true that Iran is building a bomb, what is to say that the real purpose for this is not self-preservation? Kenneth N. Waltz American political scientist writes, 'despite a widespread belief to the contrary, Iranian policy is made not by 'mad mullahs' but by perfectly sane ayatollahs who want to survive just like any other leaders.' [5]

The truth is that the mainstream media goes to great lengths to denigrate anyone who dares to question established versions of events and expose inaccuracies and contradictions.

This was vividly demonstrated in a segment broadcast on CNN in which author Jonathan Kay calls those who question established realities 'paranoid individuals', 'firebrands' or 'kranks'. He defines so-called 'kranks' as people who are usually in their 40s and 50s. These people are college professors, computer scientists, technical minds, mild-mannered individuals and very intelligent people. He includes theologian professor David Ray Griffin as an example. [6]

Despite the media spin, we have already seen in this book how the West has been actively involved in false-flag operations. The big question is, what about now? Is this still happening today?

This is a very disturbing topic and one that many are not prepared to address. But to refrain from asking questions because the answer might be too disturbing is tantamount to burying our heads in the sand. We can, as Noam Chomsky said, 'choose to live in a world of comforting illusion', or we can take upon ourselves the mantle of Moses, Daniel, Esther or John the Baptist. Under God's direction and anointing they did not bow down to the world's systems but rose up in the power of God and stood against the tyrannical government and leaders of their day, becoming harbingers of truth in a time of oppression and deception.

September 11th 2001

Two terrorist attacks in our recent history not only shocked but also changed the world in which we live. The 9/11 and the 7/7 London bombings were both allegedly perpetrated by Islamic extremists. However, closer examination of both these events has confirmed that the US and UK governments were involved in a massive cover-up operation, concealing evidence and blatantly lying to the public about what really happened. The controlled mainstream media only served to support the government's story of events, not only through the news but also through documentaries created to answer those who have dared to question the official narrative.

The question is why would we be lied to unless there was something to hide?

Let us take a concise look at the many discrepancies in both the stories of the September 11, 2001 attacks and the July 7, 2005 London bombings.

We begin with September 11th and a statement by Paul Craig Roberts, assistant secretary of the US Treasury under Ronald Reagan: 'it is a non-controversial fact that the official explanation of the collapse of the WTC buildings is false.' [7]

September 11, 2001 – or 9/11 as it's often referred to – is the day on which four coordinated attacks were carried out on the United States, attacks in which almost 3,000 people lost their lives.

The official story of events according to the FBI, the 9/11 Commission Report and the mainstream media, is that nineteen al-Qaeda Islamic militant terrorists hijacked four passenger planes and flew them into the World Trade Center Twin Towers in New York City, the Pentagon in Arlington, Virginia and into a field in Shanksville, Pennsylvania (this fourth plane was supposed to target Washington DC).

The Twin Towers hit by two of the hijacked passenger jets collapsed within only two hours of the attack and according to the official account did so as a result of the intense fires caused by the impact of the airplanes.

There is however a considerable amount of compelling evidence to suggest that the official story is untrue.

Firstly, let us take a brief look at the official 9/11 Commission Report.

The 9/11 Commission Report, prepared by the US government's own National Commission on Terrorist Attacks on the United States, was issued on July 22 2004. This report has, however, been questioned by a number of high ranking officials.

Former FBI Director Louis J Freeh, writing in the Wall Street Journal's opinion page, said of the report that it ignored – or 'summarily rejected' – 'the most critical piece of intelligence that could have prevented the horrific attacks.' Freeh also said that it is 'a good time for the country to make some assessments of the 9/11 Commission itself.'

Freeh, who resigned his position only months before the attacks, claimed that the US government knew of the identity of the bomber's ringleader Mohammed Atta one year prior to the attacks. Freeh states that 'military officers assigned to Able Danger [a military intelligence operation] were prevented from sharing this critical information with FBI agents.' This intelligence, Freeh writes, is 'undoubtedly the most relevant fact of the entire post-9/11 inquiry. Yet the 9/11 Commission inexplicably concluded that it was not historically significant.'

The final 9/11 Commission report concluded that 'American intelligence agencies were unaware of Mr Atta until the day of the attacks.' However, Freeh disclosed that ten days before the release of the report, commission staff met with a Navy officer who said that Mr Atta had been identified as an al-Qaeda member and told the Commission that 'Able Danger' had identified Mohammed Atta to be a member of an al-Qaeda cell located in Brooklyn.

Congressman Weldon who has worked to shed light on these claims said 'there's a cover up here, it's clear and unequivocal.'
(8)

Even some staff members and commissioners of the report have concluded that the Pentagon's initial story was possibly an effort to fool the commission and the general public. Thomas H. Kean, former New Jersey Republican governor who led the commission said, 'we to this day don't know why NORAD [North American Aerospace Command] told us what they told us, it was just so far from the truth…It's one of those loose ends that never got tied.'

In fact the 9/11 Commissioners knew that military officials had lied to them. False information was provided by NORAD and the FAA for over two years after the attacks in testimony and in media appearances. Authorities suggested that US air defenses had reacted quickly, that jets had been scrambled in response to the hijackings, and that fighters were prepared to shoot down the hijacked plane if it threatened Washington. However, audio tapes and other evidence from NORAD clearly revealed that the military never had any of the hijacked planes in their sights.

John Farmer, former New Jersey attorney general who led the staff enquiry, said, 'I was shocked at how different the truth was from the way it was described...The tapes told a radically different story from what had been told to us and the public for two years...This is not spin. This is not true.' [9]

Many errors have been published in the 9/11 Commission Report, including errors surrounding Waleed al Shehri, one of the alleged hijackers. According to the Commission Report he was on board American Airlines Flight 11 which crashed into the North Tower of the World Trade Center.

The 9/11 Commission Report states:

'Three members of his hijacking team...Sugami, Wail al Shehri, and Waleed al Shehri were selected in Boston...All five men cleared the checkpoint and made their way to the gate for American 11...The Shehri brothers had adjacent seats in row 2 (Wail in 2A Waleed in 2B), in the first class cabin. They boarded American 11 between 7:31 and 7:40 [10]. Reports from two flight attendants in the coach cabin, Betty Ong and Madeline Amy Sweeney, tell us most of what we know about how the hijacking happened. As it began, some of the hijackers – most likely Wail al Shehri and Waleed al Shehri, who were seated in row 2 in first class – stabbed the two unarmed flight attendants.' [11]

However, contrary to the report, on 23rd September 2001 the BBC reported that hijack 'suspects' were alive and well. The story stated that 'Saudi Arabian pilot Waleed Al Shehri was one of five men that the FBI said had deliberately crashed American Airlines flight 11 into the World Trade Center on 11 September. His photograph was released, and has since appeared in newspapers and on television around the world. Now he is protesting his innocence from Casablanca, Morocco. He told journalists there that he had nothing to do with the attacks on New York and Washington, and had been in Morocco when they happened. He has contacted both the Saudi and American authorities, according to Saudi press reports.' [12]

Within weeks of the attacks many of the hijackers accused by the FBI were found to be alive, appearing in various news stories around the world. Yet these men inexplicably still appeared in the final 9/11 Commission Report published in 2004 as having been part of the hijacking team aboard the planes!

Abdulaziz Alomari

According to the FBI Abdulaziz Alomari accompanied Mohamed Atta and helped him hijack and pilot Flight 11 into the North Tower. Alomari protested his innocence to a London based newspaper 'Asharq Al-Awsat'. 'The name [listed by the FBI] is my name and the birth date is the same as mine, but I am not the one who bombed the World Trade Center in New York.' [13] The Saudi Embassy in Washington defended Alomari saying that his passport was stolen in 1996. The story of Alomari still being alive was also reported by the BBC.

Saeed Al-Ghamdi

Saeed Al-Ghamdi apparently hijacked flight 93 which crashed into a field in Pennsylvania. Al-Ghamdi said, 'I was completely shocked. For the past 10 months I have been based in Tunis with 22 other pilots learning to fly an Airbus 320. The FBI provided no evidence of my presumed involvement in the attacks...You cannot imagine what it is like to be described as a terrorist – and a dead man – when you are innocent and alive.' [14]

Salem Al-Hamzi

The FBI claimed that Al-Hamzi was onboard Flight 77 that crashed into the Pentagon. However according to a story in the Guardian, Salem Al-Hamzi was alive and living in Saudi Arabia and worked at a government owned petroleum and chemical plant and had never visited the United States. [15]

Ahmed Al-Nami

Identified by the FBI, Al-Nami apparently was onboard Flight 93. Al-Nami from Riyadh is an administrative supervisor with Saudi Arabian Airlines and was in Riyadh on September 11. Al-Nami, who never lost his passport, said it was 'very worrying' that his identity had been used and published by the FBI without any checks. Al-Nami said, 'I'm still alive, as you can see. I was shocked to see my name mentioned by the American Justice Department. I had never even heard of Pennsylvania where the plane I was supposed to have hijacked crashed.'[16]

The BBC would later change their stance on an original story they published in 2001, 'Hijack 'suspects' alive and well', and even admitted to editing the archived story, 'to make it as clear as possible that there was confusion over the identity. In an effort to make this clearer, we have made one small change to the original story. Under the FBI picture of Waleed al Shehri we have added the words, 'A man called Waleed Al Shehri' to make it as clear as possible that there was confusion over the identity. The rest of the story remains as it was in the archive as a record of the situation at the time.' [17]

The article also published a statement from the FBI at the request of the BBC: 'the FBI is confident that it has positively identified the nineteen hijackers responsible for the 9/11 terrorist attacks. Also, the 9/11 investigation was thoroughly reviewed by the National Commission on Terrorist Attacks on the United States and the House and Senate Joint Inquiry.

Neither of these reviews ever raised the issue of doubt about the identity of the nineteen hijackers.' [17]

Omissions and Distortions

David Ray Griffin, Christian theologian and author of *The 9/11 Commission Report: Omissions and Distortions,* lists over 100 omissions and claims made by the Commission and says that the entire report is constructed in support of one big lie: that the official story about 9/11 is true.

Here are just some of the omissions noted by Griffin:

1. The omission of evidence about Mohamed Atta – such as his reported fondness for alcohol, pork, and lap dances – which is in tension with the Commission's claim that he had become fanatically religious
2. The obscure evidence that Hani Hanjour was too poor a pilot to have flown an airliner into the Pentagon
3. The omission of the fact that the publicly released flight manifests contain no Arab names
4. The omission of the fact that fire has never, before or after 9/11, caused steel-frame buildings to collapse
5. The omission of the fact that the fires in the Twin Towers were not very big, very hot, or very long-lasting compared with fires in several steel-frame buildings that did not collapse
6. The omission of the fact that, given the hypothesis that the collapses were caused by fire, the South Tower, which was struck later than the North Tower and also had smaller fires, should not have collapsed first
7. The omission of the fact that WTC 7 (which was not hit by an airplane and which had only small, localized fires) also collapsed – an occurrence that FEMA admitted it could not explain
8. The omission of the fact that the collapse of the Twin

Towers (like that of Building 7) exemplified at least ten features suggestive of controlled demolition

9. The omission of the fact that President Bush's brother Marvin and his cousin Wirt Walker III were both principals in the company in charge of security for the WTC

The Towers

Between 2002 and 2006 NIST, the National Institute of Standards and Technology, studied the destruction of the World Trade Center and reached the conclusion that the collapse of the towers was caused by the combined effects of the impact of the airplanes and the fires.

The towers, however, were specifically designed to withstand the impact of a passenger plane – one the size of a Boeing 767.

Frank DeMartini, World Trade Center project manager, who died a hero on September 11th after rescuing 70 people from the North Tower, said of the towers, 'the building was designed to have a fully loaded 707 crash into it. That was the largest plane at the time. I believe that the building probably could sustain multiple impacts of jetliners, because this structure is like the mosquito netting on your screen door – this intense grid – and the jet plane is just a pencil puncturing that screen netting. It really does nothing to the screen netting.' [18]

Furthermore John Skilling, who was the head structural engineer for the World Trade Center, said in a 1993 interview that if a jetliner impacted one of the towers, 'there would be a horrendous fire...A lot of people would be killed' but 'the structure would still be there.' Leslie Robertson, a member of Skilling's firm, also supported the Frank DeMartini statement and said that the buildings were designed to withstand the impact of a Boeing 707. Hyman Brown, construction manager of the Twin Towers goes further and attests that 'it [the WTC] was over-designed to withstand almost anything including hurricanes, high winds, bombings and an airplane hitting it.'

The official story is that intense fires caused the steel to melt and the buildings to collapse but neither before nor after 9/11 has a steel-framed building ever collapsed because of fire.

In 1991 the 38-storey high One Miridan Plaza in Philadelphia caught fire and burned for more than nineteen hours. FEMA reported that although the beams and girders sagged, the columns continued to bear their load without obvious damage. (19)

In 2005, the Windsor building in Madrid Spain, a 32-storey tower building framed in steel-reinforced concrete, burned for almost a day and completely engulfed the upper ten stories of the building – but it did not collapse. (20)

In 2009, a fire at the 44-storey Mandarin Oriental Hotel in Beijing raged for more than five hours. The blaze which was filmed on CCTV shows the building enveloped in flames, and yet it did not collapse. (21)

In 2010, fire broke out in a 28-storey skyscraper in Shanghai, China. The building became completely engulfed in flames and burned for four hours until firefighters brought the blaze under control. Once again the building did not collapse. (22)

The fires in the above examples burned for much longer and with much greater intensity than the ones in the World Trade Center towers but they did not collapse. However, the South Tower – we are told – collapsed after just 56 minutes of fire and the North Tower collapse occurred after burning for just 102 minutes. (23)

It is also important to note the white color of the flames, captured by video footage during the Windsor building fire. This evidence showed that there was a lot of oxygen burning. When comparing the flames that came from the World Trade Centers they were significantly smaller, dark red in color and black smoke was seen pluming from the buildings.

Physicist Professor Steven Jones explains that the black smoke coming from the towers is indicative of an oxygen starved fire. A fire starved of oxygen cannot produce intense heat. This therefore makes it scientifically impossible to conclude that steel could melt under such conditions.

Steel begins to melt when it reaches almost 2800° Fahrenheit. An open fire fueled by hydrocarbons, such as kerosene (jet fuel), can reach temperatures of maximum 1700° Fahrenheit, which is way below the melting point of steel at 1100 degrees.

Brian Clark, a survivor, confirms that the fires were not intense by virtue of the fact that he was able to make his way down the South Tower from a position above the plane's impact. Clark said in an interview, 'when I looked down there I didn't see flames, I just sensed that it was the right thing to go in there and try and test it, we would go as far as we could until we were stopped by flames, and when we came to the 78th floor...and there were flames licking up the other side of the wall...it wasn't a roaring inferno I sensed that the flames were maybe starved for oxygen right there...in the interior, we kept going and we got on to the 74th floor and we got down that far – normal conditions – the lights were on, fresh air coming up from below.' [24]

Video footage that was taken as the attack unfolded and shown around the world also revealed the temperature within the buildings could not have been intensely hot. In the exact point where the plane had impacted the North Tower not long before, a woman could be seen standing and apparently not suffering from the effects of heat. Surely if the temperatures were high enough to melt steel the woman would have had no chance of surviving there.

NIST commissioned numerous tests to verify how the towers came to collapse. Kevin Ryan, former manager at Underwriters Labs – one of the companies who conducted the tests for NIST – challenged the final NIST report and went public. Within a week he lost his job.

Ryan explains that the primary theory tested was the so-called pancake theory – the theory that the floors collapsed on top of each other, with the columns being left unsupported. However, the floor models tested in furnaces at much hotter temperatures for much longer periods of time did not collapse in the tests. A few months later the government updated their report stating not only that the floors did not collapse but that they had also done tests on the few samples saved from the fire zones and those tests proved that the temperatures were very low. Ryan reiterated, 'the temperatures were not hot enough to even soften steel.'

NIST came out with a summary statement saying that the floors did actually collapse and the steel did soften. NIST solved this problem by using a computer simulation and replaced the 'pancake theory' with the 'inward bowing theory'. According to the institute the heat weakened the floors which started to curve inwards as did the walls. Ryan states that the computer simulation was manipulated. 'They doubled one thing, they cut something else in half...for example...they double the time that the computer model exposes columns to fire, 90 minutes instead of what we know as 45 or 50 minutes...' [25]

The Collapse

If we are to believe the official story of the collapse of the twin towers then something unexplainable happened on that day. The towers fell at close to free-fall speed. This means that there was almost no air resistance to slow down the speed of the fall.

For example, if a weight was dropped from a height of 400 meters – the approximate height of the towers – it would take around nine seconds to hit the ground. According to the 9/11 Commission Report the collapse of the South Tower took just ten seconds – almost free-fall speed. For this to have happened every floor in the tower would have to give way before hitting the next floor, otherwise resistance would have occurred as one floor came into contact with the next floor and so on and the tower would not have fallen in just ten seconds.

Dave Heller is a building engineer with degrees in physics and architecture. He writes:

'There is a method that has been able to consistently get skyscrapers to fall as fast as the...buildings of the World Trade Center fell on 9/11. In this method, each floor of a building is destroyed at just the moment the floor above is about to strike it. Thus, the floors fall simultaneously – and in virtual freefall. This method, when precisely used, has indeed given near-freefall speed to demolitions of buildings all over the world in the past few decades...This method is called controlled demolition...Controlled demolition would also explain the seismic evidence recorded nearby of two small earthquakes – each just before one of the Twin Towers collapsed. And finally, controlled demolition would explain why...steel skyscrapers... collapsed in essentially the same way.' [26]

The late William Christison, former senior analyst for the Central Intelligence Agency for twenty nine years, concurs that the buildings came down in this way. 'All of the characteristics of these demolitions show that they almost had to have been controlled explosions.' [27]

Further evidence of controlled demolition being used to bring down the towers can be seen by the fact that they not only fell at near free fall speed but that they also perfectly reflected a demolition implosion – falling in on themselves – and collapsing into their own foot print – a classic hallmark of a planned building demolition.

Demolition implosion is a technique used when it is necessary to minimize the damage of other buildings in close proximity. Implosionworld.com writes on their website:

'The only time a building is truly 'imploded' is when exposures (other structures or areas of concern) completely surround it. When this situation exists, the blaster has no choice; he must make the building collapse in on itself. This is by far the trickiest type of explosive demolition project, and there are only a handful of blasting companies in the world that possess enough experience...to perform these true building implosions.' [28]

Eyewitness Accounts

Eyewitnesses at the scene, many of them firefighters, consistently described explosions and loud bangs indicative of a controlled demolition. The following are from a document published by the New York Times after having won a Freedom of Information lawsuit against the City of New York in 2005.

'It actually gave at a lower floor, not the floor where the plane hit, because we originally had thought there was like an internal detonation explosives because it went in succession, boom, boom, boom, boom, and then the tower came down.'

Ed Cachia, Firefighter, FDNY

'It was weird how it started to come down. It looked like it was a timed explosion...'

Dominick Derubbio, Battalion Chief, FDNY

'The lowest floor of fire in the South Tower actually looked like someone had planted explosives around it because the whole bottom I could see – I could see two sides of it and the other side – it just looked like that floor blew out. I looked up and you could actually see everything blew out on the one floor. I thought, geez, this looks like an explosion up there, it blew out.'

Brian Dixon, Battalion Chief, FDNY

'I got up, I got into the parking garages, was knocked down by the percussion. I thought there had been an explosion or a bomb that they had blown up there.'

Michael Donovan, Captain, FDNY

'I should say that people in the street and myself included thought that the roar was so loud that the explosive – bombs were going off inside the building.'

James Drury, Assistant Commissioner, FDNY

'Some people thought it was an explosion. I don't think I remember that. I remember seeing it, it looked like sparkling around one specific layer of the building...My initial reaction was that this was exactly the way it looks when they show you those implosions on TV.'

Thomas Fitzpatrick, Deputy Commissioner for
Administration, FDNY

'It could have been as a result of the building collapsing, things exploding, but I saw a flash flash flash and then it looked like the building came down...[It was at] the lower level of the building. You know like when they demolish a building, how when they blow up a building, when it falls down? That's what I thought I saw.'

Stephen Gregory, Assistant Commissioner, FDNY

'As we are looking up at the building, what I saw was, it looked like the building was blowing out on all four sides. We actually heard the pops. Didn't realize it was the falling – you know, you heard the pops of the building. You thought it was just blowing out.'

Joseph Meola, Firefighter, FDNY

'At first I thought it was – do you ever see professional demolition where they set the charges on certain floors and then you hear "Pop, pop, pop, pop, pop"? That's exactly what – because I thought it was that.'

Daniel Rivera, Paramedic, EMS

'It almost actually that day sounded like bombs going off, like boom, boom, boom, like seven or eight, and then just a huge wind gust just came...'

Thomas Turilli, Firefighter FDNY

76

'And then I just remember there was just an explosion. It seemed like on television they blow up these buildings. It seemed like it was going all the way around like a belt, all these explosions.'

Rich Banaciski, Firefighter, FDNY

The Mysterious Collapse of Building Seven

Many people do not realize that on 9/11 a third building collapsed.

Building 7 was a 47-storey building that stood at the World Trade Center site. It was mainly occupied by significant government organizations, the IRS (Internal Revenue Service), the US Secret Service, the CIA, the Securities and Exchange Commission, the Mayor's Office of Emergency Management, and finally insurance and financial institutions.

It was not hit by a plane but mysteriously collapsed in the same fashion as the South and North Towers just seven hours later at virtual freefall speed within just six seconds.

The official story is that falling debris from the collapse of the North Tower damaged it and started fires in the building. Curiously the 9/11 Commission Report does not mention the collapse of Building 7 at all, another remarkable omission by the report – especially considering the fact that it was the third steel framed building in history to collapse due to fire, and all on the same one day! In fact, an investigation into the reasons for the collapse was not carried out until 2008, and then only after much public pressure.

The collapse of building 7 only adds more weight to the evidence that controlled demolitions brought down the towers. Here we have a building that was not hit by a plane and, contrary to reports, was not a towering inferno. If it was, why was this not captured on camera by the many photographers and TV crews reporting on the day?

Interestingly enough another building, building 5 – within the World Trade Center complex – sustained considerable structural damage due to the Twin Tower collapses. Building 5, visibly an inferno, was captured on video – yet Building 5 remained standing.

The 2008 report carried out by NIST – the National Institute for Standards and Technology claims a 'New Phenomenon' and an 'extraordinary event' occurred for the first time ever in the collapse of Building 7. NIST's Building & Fire Research Laboratory Director, Shyam Sunder, said, 'what we found was an uncontrolled building fire similar to those we have seen in other tall buildings caused an extraordinary event. The collapse of World Trade Center 7 was primarily due to fires. This is the first time that we are aware of that a building over fifteen stories tall has collapsed primarily due to fire.'

One question this raises is if it was certainly a 'new phenomenon', and indeed an 'extraordinary event', with Building 7, how on earth did anyone have forewarning concerning its collapse? Forewarning is confirmed not only by many eyewitness emergency workers but also from news outlets which apparently received information about the collapse and unwittingly reported on it too early.

Both the BBC and CNN incredibly reported that Building 7 had collapsed or was collapsing prior to the event actually happening. Over one hour before it fell, CNN's Aaron Brown – while looking at a perfectly stable Building 7 – reported that the building 'has collapsed or is collapsing', while the BBC reported over twenty minutes before the collapse, 'the 47 storey Salomon Brothers building [Building 7] close to the World Trade Center has also collapsed.' Behind the BBC reporter, Jane Standley, Building 7 can be clearly seen still standing on the skyline.

Firefighters were also captured on video saying, 'keep your eye on that building, it'll be coming down soon.' Firefighter Tiernach Cassidy describes it thus: 'then, like I said, building seven was in imminent collapse. They blew the horns. They said everyone clear the area until we got that last civilian out. We tried to give another quick search while we could, but then they wouldn't let us stay anymore. So we cleared the area. ... So yeah, then we just stayed on Vesey [Street] until building seven came down.'

Deputy Fire Chief Nick Visconti said, 'now World Trade Center 7 was burning and I was thinking to myself, how come they're not trying to put this fire out? [Chief, Frank Fellini] said, '7 World Trade Center, imminent collapse, we've got to get those people out of there.' I explained to them that we were worried about 7, that it was going to come down and we didn't want to get anybody trapped in the collapse. One comment was, oh, that building is never coming down, that didn't get hit by a plane, why isn't somebody in there putting the fire out?'

If the collapse of this steel structure was a new phenomenon and an extraordinary event then surely it would have been totally unexpected. This does not make any sense.

To shed some light on how there could have been prior knowledge of the collapse, we must go to Larry Silverstein, New York City real estate investor and developer, and owner of the World Trade Center complex, who made an extraordinary statement in a 2002 PBS documentary, *America Rebuilds*. Silverstein said, 'I remember getting a call from the, er, fire department commander, telling me that they were not sure they were gonna be able to contain the fire, and I said, "We've had such terrible loss of life, maybe the smartest thing to do is pull it." And they made that decision to pull and we watched the building collapse.' The word 'pull' is a term used in the field of demolition.

This is an astonishing statement to make for two reasons – one, it is in complete contradiction to the NIST report which concluded that the building had collapsed due to fire; two, to rig a building for demolition that is apparently an inferno, and also to carry this out in only a few hours, would surely be a logistical impossibility. The only conclusion to draw from Silverstein's statement is that Building 7 had to have been prepared in advance of the attacks.

The late Danny Jowenko was the owner of Jowenko Explosieve Demolitie, a controlled demolitions company in the Netherlands. Jowenko, a controlled demolitions expert, upon being shown 2006 footage of the destruction of Building 7 said, 'this is professional work, without any doubt.' He was then told that the building was brought down on 9/11. Jowenko responded in disbelief, 'are you sure it was the 11th? That can't be.' After continued analysis of the video, Jowenko said, 'I think this is obviously a building that has been imploded...If this is the consequence of the WTC towers coming down...that would greatly astonish me. I can't imagine it. No.' Later in 2007 Jowenko reaffirmed his conclusion when asked if Building 7 had been brought down by explosives: 'Absolutely,' he said, 'I've looked at the drawings, at the construction, and it couldn't have been done by fire.'

Finally there is yet more evidence that supports the story of controlled demolition. Found amongst the smoldering debris of all three buildings weeks after the collapse was the presence of molten metal. Many eye witness accounts testified to seeing pools of molten metal literally streaming at the World Trade Center site even weeks after the event.

So what is the relevance of this molten metal? Government reports admitted that the temperatures within the buildings were not anywhere near high enough to cause steel to melt. So what is the explanation?

Professor Steven E. Jones from the Department of Physics and Astronomy, Brigham Young University, offers some answers. Jones maintains that the molten metal that was repeatedly observed and reported in the rubble of the World Trade Center buildings is consistent with the use of high-temperature cutter-charges such as thermite – routinely used to melt, cut and demolish steel. [29]

Resident Jeanette McKinley, who lived directly across from the South Tower, saved dust that blew into her apartment after the collapse of the towers and presented it to Professor Jones for examination. Jones found that the dust was like a snapshot of the residue produced by the tower during its collapse. In analyzing the dust Jones found that it contained metal droplets indicating the use of a substance called thermite. Also found in the sample was barium. Jones states that barium nitrate and sulphare are a part of the military patent on what is known as Thermate. Thermate is Thermite with sulphare and barium nitrate added to make it cut more rapidly through steel. Jones says that barium is a very toxic metal and ordinarily you would not expect to find it in the large concentrations found at the World Trade Center sites. Jones said, 'the fact that we see it...in the dust, is a very strong indication to me that the military form of thermite has been used.' [30]

Summary of our Findings

To sum up, we have looked at the staggering errors of the 9/11 Commission Report, including the mistaken identities of the hijackers, how the NIST report concluded that the towers were brought down by fire, despite the fact that steel towers subjected to much longer fires have never collapsed before, how the black smoke is indicative of an oxygen starved fire and how a survivor testified to the fire being starved of oxygen.

We have looked at how steel only melts at temperatures at around 2800° Fahrenheit, a temperature 1100 degrees higher than what could have been in the towers, how NIST manipulated their computer simulation of the towers collapse, how the towers fell at near freefall speed, an effect only produced by controlled demolition, and how eye witness accounts referred to explosions and what they said looked like a controlled demolition.

We have looked at the mysterious collapse of Building 7, how it was reported before it happened, the conflict between the official NIST report that the building came down as a result of fire and Silverstein's seeming admission on the contrary that it was 'pulled', and the demolitions expert Danny Jowenko's reaction to video footage, 'this is professional work, without a doubt.'

Finally, molten metal found at the sight and the analysis of dust produced during the collapse was evidence of the use of thermate, a military form of thermite which cuts rapidly through steel.

The Pentagon

According to the official story, five al-Qaeda terrorists hijacked American Airlines Flight 77 on September 11th 2001. It was allegedly piloted by one of the terrorists, Hani Hanjour. It was deliberately slammed into the west side of the Pentagon, the headquarters of the United States Department of Defense in Arlington County, Virginia at 9.37am.

Pilots for '9/11 Truth' state that Hanjour would have had to have been an accomplished airline pilot in order to pull off such a maneuver. However, according to evidence this was not the case. Hanjour attended the Pan Am International Flight Academy in Phoenix, Arizona. Instructors at the flight school found that Hanjour's piloting skills were so shoddy and his grasp of English so inadequate that they questioned if his pilot's license was authentic. A former employee at the school said that he was considered by staff to be a very bad pilot. 'I'm still to this day amazed that he could have flown into the Pentagon. He could not fly at all.' [31]

Later in August of 2001 Hanjour attended three test runs at Freeway Airport in Bowie, Maryland, this time taking to the skies in a single engine Cessna 172. However, instructors Sheri Baxter and Ben Conner found that Hanjour had trouble controlling and landing the plane. [32]

How is it possible that Hanjour was not only able to pilot a Boeing 757 but also to perform the maneuver that struck the Pentagon? Considering he had trouble controlling and landing a four-seat single-engine Cessna 172, this is most doubtful.

There is one final important story to mention that further indicates the public has been fed many lies concerning the Pentagon incident.

Two phone calls were allegedly made by CNN commentator Barbara Olson, a passenger on Flight 77, to her husband Ted Olson who was the then US Solicitor General. According to Ted Olson these calls were made using an onboard phone. However Ted Olson changed his mind on this a few times saying that Mrs Olson called him from her cell phone. The problem with this story is that cell phone technology in 2001 would have only allowed a call if the plane was flying at a slow speed and at a low altitude. According to the 9/11 Commission report Barbara's first call was made between 9:16 and 9:26. At this time however, according to the flight data recorder information, the plane would have been flying at an altitude of over 25,000 feet and a speed of 324 mph – too high and too fast to have made a call. Ted Olson's story then changed to his wife using the onboard phone rather than a cell phone which sidestepped the technological issue. However the onboard phone claim is also at odds with the facts. According to an American Airlines spokesperson, Boeing 757s did not have onboard phones for passengers or crew use. Did Ted Olson lie or were the calls a fabrication? [33]

July 7, 2005 attack on London

On July 7th 2005 a series of coordinated bombs exploded targeting rush hour commuters using London's public transport. According to the official narrative four home-grown Islamic terrorists detonated four bombs, three on the London Underground tube trains and the fourth on a double-decker bus in Tavistock Square. With 56 dead and 700 more injured this was one of the deadliest attacks in the nation's peacetime history.

Considering the enormity of the crime one would expect that a thorough and extensive public inquiry would have been carried out. Indeed it was Tony Blair, then Prime Minister who stated before the Commons in December 2005, 'I do accept that people, of course, want to know exactly what happened and we will make sure that they do...We will bring together all the evidence that we have and we will publish it so that people, the victims and others, can see exactly what happened...But I really believe that at the present time, if we ended up having a full scale public inquiry when actually we do essentially know what happened on July 7, we would end up diverting a massive amount of police and security service time and I don't think it would be sensible.' (34)

Instead of this, then, a narrative concerning the London bombings would be compiled and written by a senior civil servant. When questioned about the report not being independent of the government, the then Home Secretary, Charles Clarke insisted that this did not mean that the government was attempting to cover anything up. 'Certainly, there is no question of a cover-up of any kind,' he said. (35)

In 2011 the survivors and relatives of those who died in the bombings eventually abandoned their long battle to force the government to hold a public inquiry citing that the proceedings would not only be unsuccessful but would also cause further distress to those affected by the attacks. (36)

In any case even if a full public inquiry had ever been granted by the British government it would not only have been unsuccessful but would have been a complete and utter farce from beginning to end for one simple fact.

Just one month prior to the bombings on June 7th 2005 the Inquiries Act coincidentally became law. The act was designed to provide a framework for future inquiries, set up by Ministers into events that have caused or have potential to cause public concern. [37]

At the time many voices criticized the new Inquiry Act law. Amnesty International contended that 'any inquiry would be controlled by the executive which is empowered to block public scrutiny of state actions.' Canadian Judge Peter Cory, who was commissioned by the British and Irish governments to investigate state collusion in six high profile murders in the Cory Collusion Inquiry, said, 'it seems to me that the proposed new Act would make a meaningful inquiry impossible. The Commissions would be working in an impossible situation. For example, the Minister, the actions of whose ministry was to be reviewed by the public inquiry, would have the authority to thwart the efforts of the inquiry at every step. It really creates an intolerable Alice in Wonderland situation.' Furthermore Chris Smith, member of the US House of Representatives, damningly declared, 'the bill pending before the British Parliament should be named the 'Public Inquiries Cover-up Bill." [38]

Under the new act:

- the inquiry and its terms of reference would be decided by the executive; no independent parliamentary scrutiny of these decisions would be allowed
- the chair of the inquiry would be appointed by the executive and the executive would have the discretion to dismiss any member of the inquiry
- the decision on whether the inquiry, or any individual hearings, would be held in public or private would be taken by the executive
- the decision to issue restrictive notices to block disclosure of evidence would be taken by the executive. [39]

Lord Saville of Newdigate, the chair of the Bloody Sunday Tribunal of Inquiry, said, 'As a Judge, I must tell you that

I would not be prepared to be appointed as a member of an inquiry that was subject to a provision of this kind.' [40]

The question is, why was an act passed into law just one month prior to an unprecedented attack on London – a law that passed full control of every aspect of any inquiry to the executive – a law that allows the State to block any investigation of State actions, to shut down avenues of inquiry at any time, to quash the publication of any evidence and so on?

With the possibility of no sensible public inquiry we are left with the British government's own version of events as detailed in the Home Office 7/7 report released on May 11th 2006. But as with the US Government's 9/11 Commission Report, so too the UK's Home Office 7/7 report was riddled with many unbelievable omissions and errors about a day that abruptly and violently ended the lives of so many, bolstered the continued war on terror, changed the course of domestic security policy and advanced the Orwellian big brother agenda in a nation that was already the most surveillance-saturated country in the world. [41]

On comparing the evidence available with the narrative of the official government report it is clear that, contrary to Blair's promise, the document fails to give a full account of what actually happened, or to provide all of the evidence that Blair promised.

Here are just a few examples of many that prove the official story is seriously lacking as a professional and credible account of what happened on that day:

The official account stated that the four bombers caught the 7.40am Thameslink Luton to King's Cross train; '07.40: The London King's Cross train leaves Luton station.' [42]

However it was reported by witnesses and Thameslink employees that the 07.40 train was cancelled on that morning. [43]

86

According to the report, 'Gold Command' police who were already in place due to the G8 summit taking place in Scotland were quickly deployed to the scenes. [44]

Gold Command police is a hierarchical framework for the command and control of major incidents and disasters. There is surprisingly no mention at all in the report for another more credible reason that these Gold Command officers would have been in the vicinity on that day. A terrorist rehearsal operation was being carried out at the exact time that the attacks took place.

Visor Consultants, a private company was running a terrorist rehearsal operation in London, not only at the exact same time but also at the exact same locations as the real attacks were being carried out.

Peter Power, the Managing Director of Visor Consultants appeared on BBC Radio 5 shortly after the attacks saying, 'at half-past nine this morning we were actually running an exercise for...a company of over a thousand people in London based on simultaneous bombs going off precisely at the railway stations where it happened this morning, so I still have the hairs on the back of my neck standing upright!'

Interviewer Peter Allen replied, 'to get this quite straight, you were running an exercise to see how you would cope with this and it happened while you were running the exercise?'

Powers answered, 'precisely, and it was, er, about half-past nine this morning, we planned this for a company and for obvious reasons I don't want to reveal their name but they're listening and they'll know it. And we had a room full of crisis managers for the first time they'd met and so within five minutes we made a pretty rapid decision, 'this is the real one' and so we went through the correct drills of activating crisis management procedures to jump from 'slow time' to 'quick time' thinking and so on.' [45]

Staged terror and military drills were not unique to 7/7 alone, but also occurred during the attacks of September 11th 2001.

There is no mention in the report of any prior warnings of the attacks, despite the fact that the Israeli National News reported that then Israeli Finance Minister, Benjamin Netanyahu was in London on that day, due to attend a conference at the Great Eastern Hotel, and was warned not to attend moments before the explosions. This suggests some foreknowledge of the attacks. [46]

Also in London on the day of the attacks was Rudi Giuliani, mayor of New York City at the time of the 9/11 attacks. Immediately after the London explosions the official story was that a power surge had occurred. It had not yet been announced that bombs had exploded or that it had been a terrorist attack. However, Guiliani commented, 'I was right near Liverpool [Street] Station when the first bomb went off and was notified of it and it was just to me very eerie to be right there again when one of these attacks takes place.' Did Giuliani assume it was an attack rather than a power surge, or was he too like Netanyahu given prior warning? [47]

Andy Hayman, Assistant Police Commissioner said, 'the bombers are all certain to have been caught on many cameras during their journey....we will end up with very good pictures that will identify them.' [48]

The report states that, 'the 4 were identified together by CCTV at various points before the bombings.' [49]

But despite the claim of both the report and Hayman only one very poor image of the four men apparently together was shown to the public, with additional CCTV images released later on 1st August 2008. However these images failed to provide conclusive proof of the men's guilt. The Mail Online wrote in an article entitled 'Conspiracy fever: As rumors swell that the government stage 7/7, victims' relatives call for a proper inquiry'. It claimed that 'a still CCTV photo of the four bombers arriving at the station in Luton is the only one of the four men together on July 7. Controversially, no CCTV images, either still or moving, of them in London have ever been released. The Luton image is also contentious: the quality is poor and the faces of three of the bombers are unidentifiable.' [50]

It is important to understand that during the time of the attacks the average person in London was scrutinized by 300 cameras a day with 6,000 cameras in the London Underground alone! In fact London has been described as 'the surveillance capital of the world.' [51] There should be an abundance of CCTV images and footage of the four alleged bombers together! But remarkably there is not. In fact the single piece of evidence that shows the four alleged terrorists together only shows the face of one of the men. The other three are not even identifiable!

Also noteworthy is the fact that the four CCTV cameras on the number 30 bus that exploded in Tavistock Square were apparently not functioning that morning. But no explanation in the official story is given as to why.

Scotland Yard sources said, 'it's a big blow and a disappointment. If the cameras had been running we would have had pin-sharp close-up pictures of the person who carried out this atrocity. We don't know if the driver forgot to switch them on or if there was a technical problem but there are no images.' [52]

But an independent July 7th researcher received the following communication from Stagecoach stating that the cameras could not be operated by the vehicle driver ruling out the idea that the driver forgot to turn them on. 'The set up of the cameras also means they cannot be accessed or switched off by the vehicle driver.'

So why were the number 30 bus cameras not working on that day? Of course if they had been, as Scotland Yard stated, we would have had a pin-sharp close-up of the bomber – conclusive evidence – but unfortunately we have nothing.

As Hayman confidently stated, all the bombers should have been caught on the many CCTV cameras during their journey. London is known as the 'surveillance capital of the world', invading the privacy of thousands of innocent people every day, but when it really came down to it and the CCTV was needed to do its job, they captured absolutely nothing of any conclusive significance to incriminate any of the men! This one point alone should raise serious questions.

Many other inconsistencies surrounding the official Home Office report abound:

- Identification documents for Mohammad Sidique Khan were mysteriously found at three of the four bomb sites. Two days after the bombings Khan's documents were found at Edgware Road and Aldgate and five days after that other property of Khan's was found at Tavistock Square. Khan was allegedly responsible for the Edgware Road incident which happened almost one hour before the bus blew up. The question is how did Khan's documents find themselves also at Aldgate and Tavistock Square, especially considering he would have been dead by the time the bus bomb exploded? Could it be that Khan's documents were planted to incriminate him? [53]
- Omitting to mention that Haroon Rashid Aswat, alleged to have ties with al Qaeda and wanted by the US who British police sources, originally told the media he was linked to the 7/7 bombings. But according to terrorist expert John Loftus, Aswat was being hidden by the British Secret Service, MI6 and was working for the British government. [54]
- The mention of the video confession of Khan. 'There is a video statement by Khan, shown on al Jazeera television… indicating his intention to martyr himself through a

terrorist attack.' [55] In the so-called confession Khan actually makes no reference to blowing himself up or his intention to attack London. In a court of law this would amount to no evidence at all since he makes no direct mention of the crime he is accused of.

- The official report stated that the bombs were 'homemade, and that the ingredients used were all readily commercially available and not particularly expensive.' [56] Christophe Chaboud head of the French Anti-Terrorism Co-ordination Unit, sent to London to assist in the criminal investigation, told Le Monde newspaper that the explosives used were of military origin. Chaboud described this as, 'very worrying...we're more used to [terrorist] cells making home-made explosives with chemicals.' Chaboud then surmised how the terrorists could have got their hands on military grade explosives by saying, 'they had someone on the inside who enabled them to get them out of the military establishment.' [57]

- The official report records that there was no evidence of remote detonation to explode the bombs. However, Vincent Cannistraro, former head of CIA's counter-terrorism centre, said that 'mechanical timing devices' had been recovered. [58] While the World Tribune reported, 'Al Qaida employed light but advanced bombs detonated by timers in last week's bloody strike on London's mass transit system. British officials said authorities have determined that the four bombs that blew up in subways and a bus in London on July 7 were composed of less than 4.5 kilograms of explosives each. They said the bombs were small enough to fit in a knapsack and were detonated by timers rather than suicide attackers.' [59]

So were the men suicide attackers or were their bombs detonated from a remote location?

The question of whether suicide bombers were responsible was raised by the Mirror newspaper in an article exclusive, 'Was it Suicide?' The story asked if the bombers had been tricked into killing themselves so that their secrets would remain hidden.

The article reads, 'police and MI5 are probing if the four men were told by their al-Qaeda controller they had time to escape after setting off timers. Instead, the devices exploded immediately. A security source said: 'if the bombers lived and were caught they'd probably have cracked. Would their masters have allowed that to happen? We think not.' 'Another intelligence source added, 'whoever is behind this didn't want to waste their best operatives on a suicide mission. Instead they used easily recruited low-grade men who may have believed they'd walk away.' [60]

The story offers an interesting hypothesis and the evidence is compelling. It cites that the terrorists bought return rail tickets, pay and display car park tickets, that none of men shouted the cry of 'Allah Akhbar!' – the hallmark of an Islamic suicide bomber – and that two of the alleged bombers had strong personal reasons for staying alive. Why would the men purchase return rail tickets if they did not intend to return? And why would they bother to buy a pay and display car park ticket for a car that they had ostensibly abandoned?

The suggestion in the article that the men did not know that they would be blowing themselves up is an interesting theory especially when coupled with the terrorist drill that was reported to have been taking place at the exact same time and at the exact same locations. Is it possible that as a part of the drill, suicide bomber actors were also used, only to find that when the time came for them to play their role real bombs were detonated? This would provide the perfect cover for those responsible and create the illusion that these men were indeed suicide bombers.

A History of Patsies

Throughout history unwitting people have been used as so called terrorists by governments in false flag operations to further a political agenda. These people are known as patsies. A patsy is a person who has been set up by conspirators to take the blame for a criminal act that they did not commit.

Consider the following incidents where patsies have been used:

Marinus van der Lubbe was found at the back of the German Reichstag building after it was set ablaze in February 1933. He was blamed for the fire and punished by execution. Later it would be found that the Reichstag fire was in fact a false flag operation carried out by the Nazis in order to bring Hitler to power. [61]

Pietro Valpreda, called by the mainstream media 'the monster of Piazza Fontana', was convicted for the 1969 Piazza Fontana bombing in Italy but was found innocent sixteen years later. The real culprits of the bombing belonged to Operation Gladio's strategy of tension created by NATO and the CIA. [62]

The Guildford Four – Paul Michael Hill, Gerard Conlon, Patrick Armstrong and Carole Richardson were all charged with the IRA pub bombing attacks in the 1970s. It would later be found that confessions made by the four came as a result of police coercion through intimidation, torture and threats against family members. The four were released on 19th October 1989 after having their convictions quashed. [63]

The Maguire Seven – Anne Maguire, Patrick Maguire, Patrick Maguire (son of Anne and Patrick), Vincent Maguire, Sean Smyth, Patrick O'Neill and Patrick Conlon – were all charged with possessing nitroglycerine and for turning their household into a factory for making bombs. They were tried and convicted on 4th March 1976. The convictions of the seven were overturned in 1991 after it was found that the handling of scientific evidence used to originally convict them was unsound and corrupt. On February 9th 2005, six months before the July 7th bombings, Tony Blair issued an apology to the families of both the Guildford Four and the Maguire Seven. [64]

The Birmingham Six – Hugh Callaghan, Patrick Joseph Hill, Gerard Hunter, Richard McIlkenny, William Power and John Walker – were accused and sentenced to life imprisonment in 1975 for the Provisional IRA Birmingham pub bombings. However, they too were declared innocent after their convictions were declared unsafe and unsatisfactory in March 1991. According to Hill, the men while in police custody were, 'tortured and framed', beaten, subjected to mock executions, threatened with being thrown off a high rise building and burnt with cigarettes. The six men were awarded from £840,000 to £1.2 million in compensation. [65]

Problem/Reaction/Solution

We may never know what really happened in London on July 7th 2005. But what we can be sure of is that we have not been told the truth. We have been fed a string of lies from beginning to end by the British government. However, what we do know is that through 7/7 a political agenda was advanced through the cycle of Problem – Reaction – Solution. Both 9/11 and 7/7 were used to advance significantly the political agenda for world government. In the wake of both these incidents the globalists were able to push forward their big brother plan to enslave and control the masses through the expansion of surveillance, the implementation of draconian laws, the proliferation of the police state and the military invasion and intervention into Islamic countries through the so called 'war on terror' – all characteristic and essential elements that form the basis of a globalist vision obsessed with world domination.

Consider the USA's military interventions in foreign nations. We have been led to believe that the plan for military intervention in Afghanistan and Iraq came as a response to the attacks of 9/11. But this is simply not the case – 9/11 was a crisis used for the purpose of changing the hearts and minds of the American people, and the world. It was used as the justification for a US led invasion into these countries in what was actually a game plan for economic and military supremacy.

A document called 'The National Security Presidential Directive' had already been conceived and drawn up prior to 9/11. The document dealt with military operations in Afghanistan and even included a plan to persuade the Afghan government to turn over al-Qaida leader Osama bin Laden. At which point of course he had not been implicated as the mastermind of 9/11. [66]

A report written by members of the Council on Foreign Relations, an influential foreign-policy think tank, of which David Rockefeller is the Honorary Chairman, called *Rebuilding America's Defenses* was published by The New American Century in September 2000.

The document revealed Bush's intention to take military control of the Gulf region whether or not Saddam Hussein was in power. It stated, 'while the unresolved conflict with Iraq provides the immediate justification, the need for a substantial American force presence in the Gulf transcends the issue of the regime of Saddam Hussein.'

So, it was irrelevant whether or not Saddam was complicit in 9/11 as was repeatedly insinuated by the Bush administration, or harboring weapons of mass destruction. Bush was going in anyway and Saddam created the perfect excuse.

The publication also provides insight into the planned destiny of America and its role in the coming world government and its belief that it should usher in a 'Pax Americana', Latin for American Peace. This is a revealing allusion to the term 'Pax Romana,' originally created and used by the Roman Empire. The document speaks of the establishment of a US military presence in every part of the world. It goes on to say that one way to rapidly achieve the goal of this 'Pax Americana' would be if an outside enemy would attack the US. Just one year later

9/11 occurred and the globalists got their wish.

Michael Meacher MP, former Environment Minister in Blair's government, said of the document, 'this is frankly a demand for full spectrum dominance by the United States. I think the most chilling aspect of the project for New American Century document is this kind of transformation of our foreign policy. This kind of strengthening of America's defenses is a revolutionary change and is not going to happen at all quickly, without a new catalyst of massive proportions, for example a new Pearl Harbor.' [67]

In conclusion, Meacher summarized the war on terror and its aim to advance world government when he said, 'the "global war on terrorism" has the hallmarks of a political myth propagated to pave the way for a wholly different agenda – the US goal of world hegemony, built around securing by force, command over the oil supplies required to drive the whole project.' [67]

The voice of James Warburg echoes down through the decades, 'we shall have world government whether or not you like it, by conquest or consent.' [68] We are reminded that it is inevitable – nothing can stop the globalist wheels from centuries of turning to arrive at this pivotal point. World government is a certain and approaching reality and should come as no shock.

But then we should remember – long ago it was prophesied that a future tyrannical world government would rise during the final stages of world history.

Chapter 7

The Final Empire

A fourth kingdom on earth, which shall be different from all other kingdoms, And shall devour the whole earth, trample it and break it in pieces
Daniel 7:23 (NKJV)

And authority was given him over every tribe, tongue, and nation
Revelation 13:7b (NKJV)

If we are to understand the momentous events taking place in today's world, then we will need to look at the Bible. The Bible offers a fascinating and detailed insight into the future and serves as an invaluable warning message to the last generation.

The Bible includes many predictions. One prophetic book is particularly relevant because it tells of the formation of a tyrannical world government presided over by a charismatic and evil dictator. It portrays a final empire to reign on the world stage that will usher in the climax of history. I am referring to the Book of Daniel in the Old Testament.

Prophecies of the Future

Daniel was born in approximately 623 BC. When he was a young man he was taken into captivity by King Nebuchadnezzar from

Israel to Babylon around 586 BC. While in exile Daniel chose not to defile himself with the pagan religion that surrounded him and so God gave him the ability to understand visions and dreams of all kinds.

As a result of his insight and wisdom, Daniel was promoted to the royal court of King Nebuchadnezzar and became the ruler over the entire province of Babylon. During this time the king received a troubling dream. Daniel was found to be the only person in the kingdom that was not only able to interpret the dream but also to tell the king of the related dream that he had received.

Nebuchadnezzar's dream, as described by Daniel, was of a great image of a man, resplendent and awesome in appearance. The man had a head of gold, chest and arms of silver, stomach and thighs of bronze, legs of iron, and feet a mixture of clay and iron.

In the dream a stone was cut, but not with human hands, and struck the image on its feet of clay and iron and smashed them into pieces.

Then the iron, clay, bronze, silver and gold were crushed together like chaff and were blown away in the wind until no trace of the image was left.

The stone that struck the image then became a great mountain and filled the entire earth.

Daniel went on to interpret the dream, explaining that the king was the golden head of the image. The chest and arms of silver represented a second kingdom that would arise after him. The stomach and thighs symbolized a third kingdom of bronze that would emerge and rule the entire earth. Finally a fourth kingdom would appear. The legs of iron, as well as its feet and toes partly of iron and clay, would crush the previous kingdoms. This Empire will be strong to crush (as with iron) but also fragile and divided (as with clay). The stone represented the Kingdom of God which would crush these earthly kingdoms and last forever (Daniel 2:31-45).

The head of gold represented Nebuchadnezzar's Babylonian empire (605–539 BC), the gold being symbolic of the great wealth and power of Babylon. After Nebuchadnezzar died the empire began to break apart.

The chest of silver represented the Medo-Persian empire established by Cyrus (539 BC). According to history this empire was stronger but not as wealthy or resplendent as its Babylonian predecessor. The silver was symbolic of being stronger than gold but of less value.

The stomach and thighs of brass represented the Greek empire led by Alexander the Great (330 BC). The Greek empire had less wealth than both the Babylonian and Medo-Persian empires, brass being less in value than gold and silver, but also much tougher – brass being symbolic of the military might of Alexander's empire.

The legs of iron represented stage one of the Roman Empire in the time of Christ, iron being symbolic of the power to conquer through military force. The Romans subdued the known world like no others before them. The feet of iron and clay represented, as most scholars of prophecy agree, stage two of the Roman Empire. We can also refer to this as the revived Roman Empire – an Empire like the first one and which will arise in the last days of world history. The feet of clay mixed with the iron reveal that this second manifestation of the Roman Empire is powerful but divided and therefore fragile.[1]

Years later Daniel himself would receive a vision parallel to the earlier dream of King Nebuchadnezzar. This time however, he did not see a statue or an image of a man symbolizing the four empires but rather four ferocious beasts.

'After this I saw in the night visions, and behold, a fourth beast, dreadful and terrible, exceedingly strong. It had huge iron teeth; it was devouring, breaking in pieces, and trampling the residue with its feet. It was different from all the beasts that were before it, and it had ten horns. I was considering the horns, and there was another horn, a little one, coming up among them, before whom three of the first horns were plucked out by the roots. And there, in this horn, were eyes like the eyes of a man, and a mouth speaking pompous words.' (Daniel 7: 7-8, NKJV)

It is this fourth beast of Daniel's vision, as well as the fourth part of the statue, that we need to understand because it is prophetic of the second appearance of the 'Roman Empire' which will rise at the end of time. Interesting to note here that of all the beasts it is about the fourth that Daniel asked for more understanding.

'Then I wished to know the truth about the fourth beast, which was different from all the others, exceedingly dreadful, with its teeth of iron and its nails of bronze, which devoured, broke in pieces, and trampled the residue with its feet; and the ten horns that were on its head, and the other horn which came up, before which three fell, namely, that horn which had eyes and a mouth which spoke pompous words, whose appearance was greater than his fellows. I was watching; and the same horn was making war against the saints, and prevailing against them' (Daniel 7:19-21 NKJV).

Here we are introduced to both a dream and a vision about a final world power that will rise onto the global political stage at the end of history. We know of its timing as both the dream and the vision conclude with the following statements,

'And in the days of these kings the God of heaven will set up a kingdom which shall never be destroyed; and the kingdom shall not be left to other people; it shall break in pieces and consume all these kingdoms, and it shall stand forever.' (Daniel 2:44, NKJV)

'...Then the kingdom and dominion, And the greatness of the kingdoms under the whole heaven, Shall be given to the people, the saints of the Most High. His kingdom is an everlasting kingdom, And all dominions shall serve and obey Him.' (Daniel 7:27)

The additional information that Daniel received which was not included in the dream of Nebuchadnezzar is the detail of the ten horns which symbolizes ten kings or kingdoms (Daniel 7:24, king and kingdom being interchangeable in the original). It also depicts an eleventh more powerful horn with eyes like a man that rises up and speaks against God, making war against the saints and prevailing against them.

This is the introduction to what the bible calls the Antichrist, the man of sin, or the man of lawlessness who will rule the final empire – a tyrannical world government. We will look at this subject in Chapter 8 – The Rise of the Antichrist.

Approximately 675 years later the Apostle John was imprisoned for his faith on the Greek island of Patmos. He received a powerful vision, a kind of sequel if you will to Daniel's earlier vision in which more details are revealed:

'Then I stood on the sand of the sea. And I saw a beast rising up out of the sea, having seven heads and ten horns, and on his horns ten crowns, and on his heads a blasphemous name... And all the world marveled and followed the beast. So they worshiped the dragon who gave authority to the beast; and they worshiped the beast, saying, "Who is like the beast? Who is able to make war with him?"...Then he opened his mouth in blasphemy against God, to blaspheme His name, His tabernacle, and those who dwell in heaven. It was granted to him to make war with the saints and to overcome them. And authority was given him over every tribe, tongue, and nation. All who dwell on the earth will worship him, whose names have not been written in the Book of Life of the Lamb slain from the foundation of the world.' (Revelation 13:1-8, NKJV)

We can be sure from John's description that the beast referred to here is the same beast of Daniel's vision. However John is given some interesting additional information. The beast not only has ten horns but also seven heads. John also describes how the beast will be given power and authority to rule over the whole earth and that everyone will worship him.

Later John describes even more details concerning the beast:

'So he carried me away in the Spirit into the wilderness. And I saw a woman sitting on a scarlet beast which was full of names of blasphemy, having seven heads and ten horns...And on her forehead a name was written:

MYSTERY, BABYLON THE GREAT, THE MOTHER OF HARLOTS AND OF THE ABOMINATIONS OF THE EARTH.' (Revelation 17:1-4, 5, NKJV)

'Here is the mind which has wisdom: The seven heads are seven mountains on which the woman sits.' (Revelation 17:9, NKJV)

'And the woman whom you saw is that great city which reigns over the kings of the earth.' (Revelation 17:18, NKJV)

Here we learn that a prostitute, who is symbolic of 'that great city which reigns over the earth,' sits astride the beast and that the seven heads are actually symbolic of seven mountains.

The details of both Daniel's and John's visions are vital in helping us to interpret and confirm that what is going on today is indeed the fulfillment of biblical prophecy and a fulfillment of those dreams and visions describing a second stage Roman Empire, or world government, rising today.

How can we be sure of this?

The Apostle John helps us to understand by describing the following things that he saw:

- A great city that reigns over the kings of the earth
- The beast had seven heads which were seven mountains and ten horns that were kings or kingdoms
- A woman sitting on a scarlet beast with blasphemous names written on her forehead
- It would be called 'Mystery, Babylon the Great, the Mother of Harlots, and of the Abominations of the Earth'

In John's day the great city that reigned over the kings of the earth was Rome. The ancient city of Rome was built on seven hills. They were the Aventine, Caelian, Capitoline, Esquiline, Palatine, Quirinal and Viminal hills. In ancient Rome prostitutes were required to wear a label with names written on their foreheads. According to most bible scholars Babylon meant Rome to the early Christians, Babylon being a metaphor for every kind of abomination.

In 1957, it would be in Rome that a treaty would be signed establishing what would become the European Union. The beast or kingdom of Daniel and John's visions had ten horns – ten kings or kingdoms. The European Union has interestingly divided the world up into ten regions – could these be the eventual ten kingdoms? The regions are clearly displayed on the official website of the EU: 1. North America, 2. Central America and the Caribbean, 3. South America, 4. Western Europe, 5. Eastern Europe and Central Asia, 6. the Mediterranean and Middle-East, 7. Africa, 8. North-East and South Asia, 9. South-East Asia, 10. Australia and the Pacific.

1968 would see the birth of a group known as the Club of Rome, founded in Rome. The group would be champions for the cause of world government. Today they describe themselves as 'a group of world citizens, sharing a common concern for the future of humanity.' Conspicuous Honorary members of the Club of Rome are Queen Beatrix of the Netherlands and Prince Philippe of Belgium, two prominent participants of the secretive Bilderberg Group who hold to the same world government ideals.

A Club of Rome report entitled, *Mankind at the Turning Point*, by authors Mihaljo Mesarovic and Eduard Pestel, provides further evidence that this club is working towards world government: 'a 'world consciousness' must be developed through which every individual realizes his role as a member of the world community…It must become part of the consciousness of every individual that the basic unit of human cooperation and hence survival is moving from the national to the global level.' [2]

Another report by the same authors reveals that The Club of Rome has also divided the world up into ten regions. [3] Furthermore a United Nations document entitled, *Millennium Development Goals Report 2009*, under the heading 'Regional Groupings' on page 55 also displays the world divided up into ten regions.

It is no coincidence that modern day Rome is once again central to the idea of world government. This is a fulfillment of biblical prophecy.

The Revived Roman Empire

The original Roman Empire enjoyed two centuries of unprecedented stability and prosperity known as the Pax Romana, Latin for Roman Peace. By the year 324 Christianity had become the official religion of Rome, by decree of Emperor Constantine who was the first Roman emperor to 'convert' to Christianity. Constantine is well known for his merging of Babylonian beliefs with the Christian faith. This new form of Christianity bore little resemblance to the early church as recorded in the New Testament. Constantine held the office of pontifex maximus, the chief priest of the Roman religion. Later this same title was to be conferred on the Pope of the Roman Catholic Church. The origins of the title are intriguing.

The city of Pergamum, located in the Roman province of Asia (modern Turkey), was a haven for idolatry and the worship of pagan gods. The Babylonian cult of the Magians could be found there. The title of the high priest of the Magians was 'Chief Bridge Builder', meaning someone who spans the divide between mortals and Satan and his demons. In Latin the same title was known as 'Pontifex Maximus' – the name now given to the Pope! [4] Of further interest is the fact that Pergamum also became the home of the mother-child cult of Babylon that would later be moved to Rome. This leads us to ask important questions regarding the office and nature of the Pope and the true origins of the devotion towards the Madonna and Child, a central icon of Roman Catholicism.

Beginning in the late 4th century the empire began to fall apart with the western part of the empire ending in 476. The eastern part continued and is known today as the Byzantine Empire. However, the Roman Empire never completely died. Just as Daniel saw in his vision the fourth beast was different from the others. There were both legs and feet; in other words, the Empire would appear in a second stage. This beast would lie dormant for a time and then slowly rise again in the last days.

The sleeping beast of the Roman Empire would be awakened some 324 years later when the Holy Roman Empire – 962–1806 – proclaimed itself to be the successor of the Western part of the Roman Empire.

The territory of the Holy Roman Empire was centered on the Kingdom of Germany, but included other territories.

In 962 Otto I was crowned Holy Roman Emperor by the Pope and from then on the concerns of the Kingdom of Germany were strongly connected with those of Rome and the Pope, even though Charlemagne, Charles the Great, was looked upon as its true founder.

Charlemagne was crowned on Christmas Day in 800 by Pope Leo III as the first Emperor of the Romans since the fall of the Roman Empire. Charlemagne's empire united most of Western

Europe for the first time since its break up. Known as the Father of Europe, Charlemagne promoted the formation of a common European identity. In 1512 the name of the Holy Roman Empire was officially changed to the Holy Roman Empire of the German Nation. We will see that this is a significant name change because Germany – both past and present – is the central power influencing the rebirth of the revived Roman Empire today.

From Roman Empire to European Superstate

Charlemagne receives homage to this day through what is called the Charlemagne Prize, a prestigious European prize awarded by the German city of Aachen to those who contribute to the ideals of Charlemagne – the restoration of the Roman Empire – or in today's words – a European Superstate. Most of the kings of Germany who reigned over the Holy Roman Empire were crowned in Aachen.

Notable figures have been recipients of the prize since its inception in 1949, including Winston Churchill, Edward Heath, Henry Kissinger, Francois Mitterrand, Helmut Kohl, Queen Beatrix of the Netherlands, Tony Blair, Bill Clinton, Pope John Paul II and Angela Merkel.

The Charlemagne Prize was the brainchild of Kurt Pfeiffer. Pfeiffer was previously a member of the Nazi Party and of five other Nazi organisations.

It should come as no surprise that a Nazi would be inspired to found the Charlemagne Prize to award those who have been instrumental in supporting and creating the European Superstate as this was of course the original Nazi plan for Europe.

Nazi Roots

It would not only be the Charlemagne Prize that would have Nazi beginnings. Today's European Union has an uncanny

106

resemblance to Hitler's original plan for a European Superstate. Given the fact that prominent Nazi leaders were instrumental in the construction of the EU, this too is no surprise.

Walter Funk, Hitler's economics minister, began drawing up the plans for a post-war 'Europäische Wirtschafts Gemeinschaft', translated 'European Economic Community' in Berlin in 1941.

Key points to the plan were a common European Currency, harmonization of European Rates of Exchange, a European Agricultural Economic Order, a Common Labour Policy and The European Regional Principle.[5]

Funk was a prominent Nazi official also serving as State Secretary at the Ministry of Public Enlightenment and Propaganda. He signed the decree which advanced the policy for economic extermination of Jewish enterprises. He was convicted at the Nuremberg trials. On his release in 1957 Funk helped to promote the new European Economic Community in schools and universities. The European Economic Community, the name decided upon under Hitler's Nazi Germany, was adopted and used after the signing of the Treaty of Rome in 1957, which created the foundation of what is now called the European Union. Funks' blueprint for the EEC is practically identical to the structure used by the EU today!

Walter Hallstein was a member of leading Nazi organizations. Hallstein qualified as a Nazi leadership officer and became an army officer in 1942 and was also involved in the preservation of Nazi doctrine in universities and the promotion of Nazism in German law. [6]

Hallstein shockingly became the first President of the Commission of the European Economic Community serving from 1958–1967. Hallstein was awarded the Charlemagne Prize in 1961.

Paul Henri Spaak was involved in the development of the

Belgian National Socialist Party. Spaak showed his loyalty to the Nazi regime when he said in 1938, 'some people wish to lead us into a policy of solidarity with the democracies against the Fascist states. I refuse to stick to such a policy.' He concluded, 'if Great Britain and France want to help Czechoslovakia by invading Germany through Belgium, they will be treated as invaders.' [7]

Spaak was appointed the first President of the Common Assembly of the European Coal and Steel Community from 1952-1954 which later became the EEC. Notably Spaak was also appointed as the first ever President of the United Nations General Assembly from 1946–1957 and was also Secretary General to NATO from 1957–1961. Spaak was also a recipient of the Charlemagne Prize awarded in 1957.

The appointment of individuals with political ideologies such as these must lead us to question the character, ethics and intentions of these political organizations.

Hitler's Anthem

The chosen anthem of the European Union happens to be the work of a former Nazi Party member, Herbert von Karajan. The anthem is from Beethoven's Ninth Symphony – the famous 'Ode to Joy.' In 1985 it was adopted as the official anthem of the European Community. Herbert von Karajan conceived the arrangement of the new anthem which was protected by copyright and belonged to the Nazi Party from 1935 to 1945. [8]

The symphony was also played to mark the end of Hitler's 53rd birthday celebrations.

Goebbels birthday speech and his comments regarding the symphony are noteworthy.

'As the powerful Ode to Joy sounds and a sense of the greatness and scope of these times reaches even to the most remote

German hut, as its sounds reach to distant countries where German forces stand watch, each of us, man or woman, child or soldier, farmer or worker or civil servant will know both the seriousness of the hour and the joy of being a witness and a participant in this great historical epoch of our people. We call the eternal power that rules over us the Almighty or God or Fate or the Good Father, he who as the Ninth Symphony says, lives beyond the stars. We ask the Almighty to preserve the Führer, to give him strength and blessing, to favor his work, to increase our faith, to make our hearts steadfast and our souls strong, to give our people victory after its battles and sacrifices, to bring the times to fulfillment.' [9]

Adolf Hitler, Holy Roman Emperor

Hitler's rise to power in 1933 and his obsession with relics from the Holy Roman Empire further illustrates the fanatical quest to see the Roman Empire rise again. Discovered in a heavily fortified bunker under Nuremberg Castle were Hitler's stolen treasures from the Holy Roman Empire. Among the hallowed relics was the Spear of Destiny said to be the spear that pierced Christ's side at his crucifixion. Legend has it that whoever possessed the spear would conquer the world. Past rulers of the Holy Roman Empire, Constantine, Charlemagne and Barbarossa, certainly believed this to be the case – all making sure they had the mystical spear in their possession. [10]

An eerie quote from Hitler when he first encountered the spear at a museum in Vienna provides evidence of his belief that he not only considered himself to be the new Emperor of the Holy Roman Empire but also of the world.

'I stood there quietly gazing upon it for several minutes quite oblivious to the scene around me. It seemed to carry some hidden inner meaning which evaded me, a meaning which I felt I inwardly knew yet could not bring to consciousness...I felt as though I myself had held it before in some earlier century of history. That I myself had once claimed it as my talisman of power and held the destiny of the world in my hands...' [11]

This belief was also echoed by Joseph Goebbels, Hitler's Minister of Propaganda:

'The Führer gave expression to his unshakable conviction that the Reich will be the master of all Europe. We shall yet have to engage in many fights, but these will undoubtedly lead to most wonderful victories. From there on the way to world domination is practically certain. Whoever dominates Europe will thereby assume the leadership of the world.' [12]

Other notable clues to the revival of the Roman Empire through Nazi Germany were the famous Nazi salute, the Nazi Standard and the emblem used by Hitler's Third Reich, all having counterparts in the Roman Empire.

Also today's coat of arms of Germany is almost an exact copy of the emblem of the Holy Roman Empire emblem. Does Germany therefore consider itself to be the continuation of the Holy Roman Empire?

All four emblems bear some likeness to each other as illustrated here.

The Seat of Satan

Hitler's obsession with religious antiquity would take on a more obviously sinister tone. In the book of Revelation we read the following: 'And to the angel of the church in Pergamos write..."I know your works, and where you dwell, where Satan's throne is. And you hold fast to My name, and did not deny My faith even in the days in which Antipas was My faithful martyr, who was killed among you, where Satan dwells." (Revelation 2:12-13 NKJV)

Pergamum was a thriving and influential city within the Roman Empire. It is intriguing that John would make such a strong statement concerning Pergamum being the place where Satan has his throne! But John had every good reason to say this and we will learn that this expression was far from figurative.

Pergamum was the center of emperor worship; in fact, it boasted three temples dedicated to the worship of the Roman Emperor[13], one of which was called the Temple of Pergamon, with an altar dedicated to emperor worship. Refusal to acknowledge the divinity of the emperor resulted in ritual murder upon the altar. [14]

From 1878–1886 a German engineer called Carl Humann excavated 'Satan's Throne', known as the Pergamon Altar. With the agreement of the Turkish government all the fragments were painstakingly transported stone by stone to Germany and became the property of the Berlin museum. It was eventually showcased in Berlin's Pergamon Museum in 1930 alongside the Ishtar Gate.

Three years later Hitler came to power.

As if lured by the satanic influence that it embodied, a grand reproduction was commissioned for his Nazi rallies in Nuremberg, and it was from the place of 'Satan's Throne' that Hitler delivered the 'Final Solution' – what we now know to be

111

the systematic extermination of the Jews in the Holocaust.

The Gates of Hell

Also housed at the Pergamon Museum in Berlin is the Ishtar Gate. The Ishtar Gate was one of the gates to the city of Babylon, dedicated to Ishtar the Babylonian goddess of love and war and through which ran what was called the Processional Way, adorned with symbols of monsters and snake dragons. According to myth, Ishtar descended into hell. Arriving at its gates she cried for them to be opened lest she break them down and allow the dead to escape and devour the living.

'If thou openest not the gate to let me enter,
I will break the door, I will wrench the lock,
I will smash the door-posts, I will force the doors.
I will bring up the dead to eat the living.
And the dead will outnumber the living.' [15]

It is noteworthy that the European city of Berlin became the center for these two archaeological structures.

Just three years after they went on display to the public Hitler would announce from 'Satan's Throne', the final solution. In response, the 'Gates of Hell' were flung wide open and the cries of Ishtar, the goddess of war, were uttered like the fulfillment of a prophecy, 'and the dead will outnumber the living.' Approximately 9.5 million Jews lived in Europe before the Nazi takeover in 1933. But by 1945, most European Jews – two out of three – had been murdered. [16]

Hitler of course did not get to see the fulfillment of his vision to rule over the European Superstate and the world. However, the evidence shows that although Hitler died, the self-same spirit that drove him continued to live on and worked behind the scenes to accomplish what he set out to achieve.

So far we have looked at the prophetic visions of both Daniel and John which point to a 'revived Roman Empire' during the final stages of Earth's history. We have seen that the revived empire began with the rise of the Holy Roman Empire, which later became the Holy Roman Empire of the German Nation; that Hitler considered himself to be the Holy Roman Emperor; that the European Union was a fulfillment of the Nazi plan for Europe and that Hitler's vision was not only to rule Europe but the entire world.

Now we will examine some further evidences within the adopted symbolism of the European Union that are both remarkable and disturbing.

Unveiling the European Union

During the discussions over the draft text for the European Constitution, as well as the later reworked constitution for the Lisbon Treaty, a decision was made to exclude any reference to God or Europe's Judeo-Christian roots. Despite this judgment however, striking religious and biblical themes are undeniably woven into the very fabric of the European Union.

The twelve starred flag of the European Union was designed by Arsène Heitz who worked at the Council of Europe. Heitz a devout Roman Catholic, acknowledged in a 2008 interview that the design was derived from the Apostle John's apocalyptic writings in the book of Revelation 12:1: 'now a great sign appeared in heaven: a woman clothed with the sun...and on her head a garland of twelve stars.'

Heitz belonged to the Order of the Miraculous Medal which identifies itself with the symbol of the twelve stars encircling the Virgin Mary.[17] According to evangelist and prophecy writer David Hathaway, Heitz hopes that one day Mary will be incorporated into the design of the EU flag.[18]

In Catholic doctrine Mary the mother of Christ is referred to as the Queen of Heaven. This belief is based on Revelation 12:1.

But this is an erroneous interpretation. Bible scholars agree that when examined against the backdrop of all scripture the 'woman' actually represents the church/Israel and the twelve stars represent the twelve apostles. Nevertheless, because of this verse Mary is known as the Queen of Heaven in the Catholic Church.

On December 8th 1955, the day that the Catholic Church celebrated the Feast of the Immaculate Conception of the Virgin Mary, the new European flag was adopted and unveiled at the Château de la Muette, Paris.

In addition the following year in 1956 the Council of Europe donated a stained glass window to Strasbourg Cathedral. It portrayed the Virgin Mary, Queen of Heaven with child, and a twelve star halo above her – the exact representation of the EU flag!

It is accordingly incontrovertible. The EU flag embodies a powerful religious theme inspired by Roman Catholicism but whose roots lie in the ancient Babylon religion as we will later see.

Another symbol adopted by the European Union is the woman riding the beast, as detailed in the vision of the Apostle John in Revelation 17. This dovetails with the theme of the EU flag's allusion to the Queen of Heaven.

'So he carried me away in the Spirit into the wilderness. And I saw a woman sitting on a scarlet beast which was full of names of blasphemy, having seven heads and ten horns...And on her forehead a name was written:

MYSTERY, BABYLON THE GREAT, THE MOTHER OF HARLOTS AND OF THE ABOMINATIONS OF THE EARTH." (Revelation 17:1-4, 5, NKJV)

The woman that John refers to is identified in Greek mythology as Europa from where Europe gets its name. According to Greek mythology Zeus disguised as a white bull desired Europa while she was gathering wildflowers in a seaside meadow. Taken by the bull's beauty Europa climbed onto its back at which point Zeus dived into the sea. Arriving in Crete, Zeus raped her. Europa bore three sons. After her death she received divine honor as the 'Queen of Heaven'. [19]

In Jeremiah 7:17-19 and 44:15-19, the prophet Jeremiah wrote about the 'Queen of Heaven'. She is identified in the Bible as the Babylonian goddess Ishtar and not as Mary the mother of Christ!

All over Europe the image of Ishtar the 'Queen of Heaven' riding the beast can be found, most notably at the Council of Europe building in Brussels and the EU parliament area of buildings in Strasbourg – the two faces of the European Union. It can also be seen at the Brussels airport, on a UK stamp commemorating the 2nd European Parliamentary elections, a 1948 German funf deutsche mark currency note, a May 2000 copy of Germany's Der Spiegel Magazine, 'Guten Morgen Europa,' and again in 2004, 'Das Neue Europa.' It is also on the Greek Euro coin – a prophetic symbol in itself. Greece is being raped by the EU – locked in the economic prison created by the EU to subjugate it.

In January 2013 the European Central Bank announced the second series of Euro banknotes. All new banknotes will include a portrait of Europa the 'Queen of Heaven' within the watermark and hologram. The first 'Europa' banknote was rolled out in May 2013. [20]

Babylon and Rome in Europe

We have seen how Satan's Throne and the Ishtar Gate – both symbols of Babylon and Rome – were shipped to Berlin. There is however another site bordering Germany that blatantly transmits the same messages.

Strasbourg, France, is the official seat of the European Parliament, opening in 1999 at a cost of $400 million. The tower section of the parliament building was designed to look unfinished – a symbolic statement to the continual development and expansion of the EU. [21]

The architects were inspired by Roman amphitheatres [22] and its unfinished facade does look reminiscent to Rome's Colosseum. The building is also obviously and unashamedly modeled on the famous 1563 painting by Pieter Brueghel – The Tower of Babel! The allusion to Brueghel's painting was reinforced on an official European Commission poster featuring the Tower of Babel with a builder's crane in the background, with brick shaped Europeans involved in its construction. The poster's slogan read, 'Europe: Many Tongues, One Voice'. Hovering ominously above the tower were the twelve stars of the EU flag – Not as they usually appear however, but bizarrely inverted to form pentagram stars, the occult symbol for Satan!

Brueghel deliberately created his tower painting to represent both the tower of Babel and the Roman Colosseum – symbols of rebellion against God and persecution towards those who would not take part in the practices and beliefs of Rome. The Bible records that Nimrod built the tower whose name in the Hebrew language literally means 'we will rebel'. On entering the modern day EU structure of the parliament building, open to the sky above, it is certainly reminiscent of Rome's ancient colosseum and it is not hard to imagine the jeering spectators looking down upon the gladiators or indeed the Christians as they were thrown to the wild animals.

When looking at both the parliament building and the painting together the suggestion is clear – Babel's Tower and the Colosseum are truly visible.

Rabbi Daniel Lapin, author of *Tower of Power, Decoding the Secrets of Babel*, said he was told that the architects were asked to make it resemble the Tower of Babel. Lapin provides fascinating insight into the story of Babel that can be found in Genesis chapter 11. He says that the story serves as God's warning concerning tyrannical government and how it enslaves its citizens for its own purposes. The story ends with God mercifully causing division among the people by confusing their languages, bringing an end to the construction of that city and thereby freeing the people from its undemocratic power.[23]

The poster has many meanings. Firstly the Tower of Babel is an outright statement regarding the EU and its vision to build a government akin to Babel's, in direct rebellion against God.

The depiction of brick-shaped people is interesting. According to Lapin, bricks in the Bible refer to man, or of being manmade and identical. Stones refer to God, or of being God-made – unique and individual. No one stone is the same. The tower, we are explicitly told in the Genesis account, would be built using bricks not stone. Lapin explains that the bricks point to people being uniformly shaped to build the government. That is people control or enslavement.

The crane in the background shows that the EU intends to continue building where the Babylonians left off. The Babylonians could not complete the city as they became scattered due to the language barrier that was created by God. The slogan, 'Europe: Many Tongues, One Voice' is a rebellious proclamation that the EU plans to go against God's dispersion of the people through dividing their languages and that it intends to reverse its affects and enable the builders to continue.

Finally the inverted stars which form the occult pentagram reveal without doubt that evil powers are controlling the institutions of the European Union.

Regardless of the decision of the European Union to try and eradicate any Judeo-Christian roots in Europe it seems that whichever way one turns it is an unmistakable fact the institutions themselves are not only using strong biblical symbolism but that the symbolism itself is apocalyptic in nature and serves to send us a powering warning message that we are indeed living in the closing chapters of earth's history.

Germany and the European Union today

In 1945 Germany was divided and became two states – East Germany and West Germany. It was reunited in 1990 with the collapse of the Berlin Wall. Germany was one of the founding members of the European Community in 1957.

Since Germany's unification in 1990 it has become the dominant power within the European Union and Chancellor Angela Merkel its de facto leader. In 1990 Nicholas Ridley, Secretary of State for Trade and Industry under Margaret Thatcher's Government, voiced his concerns that the European Union was actually 'a German racket designed to take over the whole of Europe'. He was forced to resign for his comments but now 22 years later it seems his words are coming true. [24]

This too was the fear of Margaret Thatcher who was forced to resign her premiership in 1990, politically disempowered for her stance against the advancing European superstate. Thatcher was opposed to German unification and was alarmed that they would become an 'unstoppable force' in an unbalanced Europe.[25] Then French President Francois Mitterant told Mrs Thatcher that a united Germany might 'make even more ground than Hitler had', and that Europe would have to bear the consequences.[26]

Today Germany is the foremost political and economic power in the European Union. It is the largest contributor, providing 20% of the EU budget. Germany has the fourth largest economy in the world, is the third largest exporter and importer of goods, and boasts a high standard of living.

In 2005 Angela Merkel was elected Chancellor of Germany.

Born in 1954 Merkel is Germany's first female Chancellor. She is listed 4th place in Forbes 'The World's Most Powerful People.'

In 2007 Merkel became the President of the European Council and also chaired the G8.

Merkel was central in the construction of the EU Lisbon Treaty. She was also instrumental in the forming of the Transatlantic Economic Council in 2007, an agreement that bound both the European and the US economies together.

As predicted Germany has certainly grown in power and influence since the collapse of the Berlin Wall in 1990. It is able to wield its weight not only in Europe but also in the world. This is why Merkel's Germany is seen as pivotal in dealing with the European financial crisis.

In 2007 the European Central Bank proposed a fiscal union of the EU member countries. The Fiscal Stability Treaty was signed on 2 March 2012 by all member states except the Czech Republic and the UK. On 1 January 2013 it entered into force. The treaty requires national budgets to meet certain targets. Failure of any member country to do so will result in fines. Complete economic integration of the eurozone is where this crisis is taking Europe – a European Superstate. In 2010 Germany put pressure on other member states to adopt a balanced budget law with strict budgetary discipline [27] and in 2011 Merkel vowed to create a 'fiscal union' across the eurozone with wide-ranging powers to avert a so called catastrophe, insisting that treaty changes and tighter regulation of erring eurozone members was the only way out. She also dismissed the claim that Germany was trying to dominate Europe as 'absurd'.[28]

Max Keiser of 'Financial War Reports' thinks otherwise and explains that he believes Germany will ultimately emerge as the superpower from this crisis:

'When you have, let's say the bankers in Germany, to give an example of the Eurozone, they have cut off the supply of credit to the rest of the continent with the purpose of strangling those countries' economies, and then we are seeing that right now, when these countries give up their sovereignties effectively, or their fiscal sovereignty over to Germany, as they are doing now and they get through this course of action of basically doing a buyout...then Germany can turn the credit back on again, then the economy begins to flow, you have inflation again and you have employment again, but by then Germany will be in control. Germany will run Europe. This is something they've tried a few times before. Many people call this the Fourth Reich....it's something that obviously would benefit Germany. The actions by the countries to stop this from happening are not being taken by these countries unfortunately, because the politicians who run these countries, Spain, Italy, Germany, Greece are extremely corrupt, they're extremely corrupt and you can buy them quite easily, and they've all been bought off. So this is great for Germany in the long run, I think that Germany will emerge as really the sole superpower because China's economy looks like its breaking apart, the US is horrible, and the UK is very weak, so Germany could ultimately achieve its long term goal.' [29]

Certainly Germany is becoming more and more central to the backbone of the European Union. In a strategic move Germany's capital Berlin was chosen as the location to deliver the first ever State of Europe speech on 9th November 2010, delivered by Herman van Rompuy, President of the European Council from none other than the steps of the notorious Seat of Satan – the Pergamon Altar – which appears to be beguiling politicians once again. Rompuy was introduced by Germany's Chancellor, Angela Merkel, who curiously moved residence to live directly opposite the museum that houses the Seat of Satan after she came to power in 2005.[30]

Rompuy's opening words are intriguing;

'Ladies and Gentlemen, it is an honor to be addressing you at this place and time. Above all because I am the first politician you have invited to give the annual "Europe Address". And then because it is my privilege to do so in the Pergamon Museum, and on 9 November*. This place and that date are linked to so much history! There is a sense of powerful and ancient forces driving us in two directions. The Gods of Olympus before and behind us, 2300 years old, take us to Greek civilization and Pergamon with its temples, fountains, libraries and theatres...' [31]

What a statement to make at the first ever State of Europe speech and while standing on the very steps of the Seat of Satan in Berlin, Germany.

'There is a sense of powerful and ancient forces driving us... the gods of Olympus before and behind us..." What exactly is Rompuy saying here?

Is he suggesting that powerful spiritual forces are in fact driving the EU?

---

*9 November 1918 is commemorated as armistice day, during the night of the 8/9 November 1938, Berlin's synagogues were set on fire and the Berlin wall came down 9 November 1989.

Chapter 8

The Rise of the Antichrist

At the time of supreme peril I must die a martyr's death for the people. But after my death will come something really great, an overwhelming revelation to the world of my mission. My spirit will rise from the grave, and the world will see I was right

Adolf Hitler [1]

It is certain that Adolf Hitler understood that he and his political party were being driven by powerful and ancient forces. This is confirmed not only by Hitler's occultic fascination with artifacts, such as the spear of destiny and the Seat of Satan, but also by his connections with satanic societies.

Often missing from the annals of history is the fact that Hitler and other Nazi party members were heavily involved with the occult in their fanatical quest to dominate Europe and the world. The evils committed by Hitler were not at all the work of a madman, as history often records, but the work of a man consumed by the very powers of hell itself.

Hitler became associated with a satanic society known as the Thule Society, also called the German Brotherhood of Death Society, which used the swastika symbol on their emblem. This was later adopted by his Nazi Party. Even today the Thule Society logo has similarities with the Nazi swastika and lightning bolt symbols, although the society goes to great lengths to disassociate itself with its Nazi history. At the time

123

the swastika was also used by the Freemasons until its image was forever tainted by the evils of Nazism. It was subsequently dropped from public usage. [2]

The society also used the skull and bones symbol which were visible on the peaked caps worn by the Nazi SS. Rudolf von Sebottendorf founded the Thule Society in 1918. Sebottendorf was a Freemason and an occultist; it is therefore little surprise that he would carry the swastika of the Freemasons over to his newly formed society, which was really a kind of off-shoot or extension of Freemasonry. The belief in the supremacy of a master race – the Aryan race – was promulgated by the society and those wanting to join had to sign a "blood declaration of faith" concerning their ancestry, declaring that no Jewish blood or coloured blood flowed through their veins. [3]

Dietrich Eckart, one of seven founders of the Nazi Party, and himself associated with the Thule Society, claimed that he had received a satanic revelation, and that it was his destiny to prepare the vessel of the Antichrist, the man who would inspire the world and lead the Aryan race to world conquest. Upon meeting Hitler, Eckart said, 'here is the one for whom I was the prophet and forerunner.' [4]

Furthermore, Alfred Rosenberg a member of the Nazi Party who was first introduced to Hitler by Eckart allegedly believed himself to be the prophet of the Antichrist and that Hitler was possessed with the 'Beast of Revelation'. [5]

The Thule Society pays tribute to Satanists such as Aleister Crowley and Helena Blavatsky.

Crowley, born in 1875 was also known as the 'The Great Beast 666', and is recognised as the greatest Satanist of the 20th century. Crowley was also a high degree Freemason. Crowley said of himself, 'I was not content to believe in a personal devil and serve him, in the ordinary sense of the word. I wanted to get hold of him personally and become his chief of staff.' [6]

The Satanist Helena Blavatsky was one of the founding members of the Theosophical Society which also influenced Hitler – an organisation formed in 1875 for the advancement of occultism which too had ties with Freemasonry, as in fact it still does to this day. This group likewise incorporated the swastika into its society seal. It was Blavatsky who, like the Thule Society, promoted the idea of the Aryan race, or the master race – about which Hitler became obsessed, and which resulted in the extermination of the Jews. Blavatsky believed that the Aryan race was descended from the people of the mythical Atlantis and that the Semitic races were an offshoot of them. She wrote concerning the Semite, 'the Semites, especially the Arabs, are later Aryans – degenerate in spirituality and perfected in materiality. To these belong all the Jews and the Arabs.' [7]

Blavatsky's writings concerning Satan reveal plainly that the society was Satanic to its very core: 'it is Satan who is the god of our planet and the only god,' 'and this without any allusive metaphor to its wickedness and depravity. For he is one with the Logos, 'the first son, eldest of the gods...' [8]

Blavatsky said that the purpose of the society was to prepare humanity for the arrival of a world teacher that would direct the evolution of humankind. One can only conclude that the teacher Blavatsky was awaiting would be nothing less than Satanic in origin. This same belief is reflected in the teachings of Alice Bailey who denounced her personal Christian faith and became a teacher of the occult. [9]

In 1915 Bailey became associated with the writings of Blavatsky and her Theosophical Society. Bailey quickly rose to influence within the society. Bailey claimed that she had been visited by Kuthumi, one of the 'Masters of the Ancient Wisdom' and from this experience she published 24 occultic works.

In 1919 Bailey's husband Foster, a 32nd degree Freemason, became the National Secretary of the Theosophical Society. Soon after the Baileys founded the Lucis Trust in 1922 under the name Lucifer Publishing Company, which later became known as the Lucis Publishing Company. Lucifer was the name given to Satan before his decision to rebel against God and he was cast out of heaven. Isaiah 14:11-13 read, 'how you are fallen from heaven, O Lucifer, son of the morning! How you are cut down to the ground, you who weakened the nations!' (NKJV) It is noteworthy that Lucifer was cast down to earth and weakened the nations. The name Lucifer means light-bearer.

The Lucis Trust acts as the publishing arm for Bailey's books, for the Arcane School – an occultic training school, World Goodwill and other groups. World Goodwill has been given United Nations recognition and the Lucis Trust consultative status within the United Nations Economic and Social Council. In fact at one point the Lucis Trust offices were actually located within the United Nations Plaza. The Lucis Trust distributes occultic books worldwide and boasts thousands of members, including influential internationalists and Bilderbergers such as Henry Kissinger and David Rockefeller.[10]

The Hidden Nature of the United Nations

When looking at the United Nations many people consider it to be a benevolent organization striving to protect human rights and foster world peace – a powerful force for good in an otherwise fractured world. However, this is simply a propaganda mask shrouding its true identity and corrupt intentions, one of which we will now see is distinctly religious, occultic in nature, and setting the stage for the arrival of the Antichrist.

In 2009, UN Secretary General, Ban Ki-moon said, 'our times demand a new definition of leadership – global leadership. They demand a new constellation of international cooperation – governments, civil society and the private sector, working together for a collective global good.'

To this aim the United Nations has what it refers to as 'Civil

126

Society Organizations' – 'UN system partners and valuable links to civil society'. These societies it says 'play a key role at major United Nations Conferences and are indispensable partners for UN efforts at the country level. NGOs are consulted on UN policy and program matters. The UN organizes and hosts, on a regular basis, briefings, meetings and conferences for NGO representatives who are accredited to UN offices, programs and agencies.'

The Lucis Trust is listed as one such society playing a key role.

As stated by the UN, the areas of Lucis Trust expertise and fields of activity are Culture, Human Rights, Humanitarian Affairs, Sustainable Development and Values. [11]

The relationship between World Goodwill of the Lucis Trust and the United Nations is also clearly stated in World Goodwill's Purposes and Objectives: 'the work of World Goodwill is based on the principles of brotherhood, human unity, sharing and cooperation; and on the fundamental rights and freedoms embodied in the United Nations Universal Declaration of Human Rights.' It further states, 'World Goodwill is an accredited non-governmental organization with the Department of Public Information of the United Nations. It maintains informal relations with certain of the Specialized Agencies and with a wide range of national and international non-governmental organizations. World Goodwill is an activity of the Lucis Trust, which is on the Roster of the United Nations Economic and Social Council.' [12] Finally an objective of World Goodwill is 'to support the work of the United Nations and its Specialized Agencies as the best hope for a united and peaceful world.' [12]

One of the three main purposes of World Goodwill is 'to cooperate in the work of preparation for the reappearance of the Christ.' [12] One has to ask a vital question here: the reappearance of which Christ? Certainly they cannot mean the Christ of the Bible. How could an occultic organization whose name is derived from Lucifer himself be waiting for the Christ of the Bible? They surely would not recognize Him if He came. Remember Blavatsky, from whom Alice Bailey drew her inspiration, believed Satan to be the god of this planet and the only god.

Jesus himself warned us about false Christs and that their appearing are a sign of the closing of the age:

'Now as He sat on the Mount of Olives, the disciples came to Him privately, saying, "Tell us, when will these things be? And what will be the sign of your coming, and of the end of the age?" And Jesus answered and said to them: "Take heed that no one deceives you. For many will come in my name, saying, 'I am the Christ,' and will deceive many.' (Matthew 24: 3-5, NKJV)

'Then if anyone says to you, 'Look, here is the Christ!' or 'There!' do not believe it. For false Christs and false prophets will rise and show great signs and wonders to deceive, if possible, even the elect. See, I have told you beforehand. "Therefore if they say to you, 'Look, He is in the desert!' do not go out; or 'Look, He is in the inner rooms!' do not believe it.' (Matthew 24:23-26, NKJV)

The purposes and objectives of World Goodwill in the section 'The Reappearance of the Christ' reveal further the beliefs of this United Nations organization and confirms its role in end time Bible prophecy.

They believe that we are living in a time of preparation for a new civilization and culture in a new world order and are waiting for the arrival of a new spiritual dispensation, that a World Teacher, the Christ, will appear, invoked by the masses in all parts of the world. This 'christ' they believe, is expected by Christians and all other faiths who refer to him under different names such as the Imam Mahdi of Islam, the Messiah of Judaism, Krishna of Hinduism and Lord Maitreya and

128

Bodhisattva of Buddhism. Conclusively we can see that this awaited 'Christ' is not the Christ of the Christian Bible. How can he be? Firstly, each so called 'Christ' teaches a different doctrine and embodies conflicting character traits with one another. Does the coming 'Christ' suffer from a multiple personality disorder? The Bible says that the true God is not the author of confusion (1 Corinthians 14:33 NKJV).

Secondly, how can Christ who is God's Son, according to the Bible, be the Imam Mahdi of Islam, when Islam says that God has no son? Certainly a true Muslim would not agree with the teachings of the Lucis Trust – that the Mahdi and the Christ of the Bible are one. And how can Krishna and Christ be the same person when they have different mothers who lived in different places and at different times? Christ was born in Bethlehem, Judea, to the son of Mary who lived in Nazareth, Galilee in the late 1st century AD. Krishna was born in Mathura, Utter Pradesh, to the son of Devaki who lived approximately 3000 years prior to Christ's birth. The Christ that is to come is the Christ that was first born in the flesh to Mary in Bethlehem. He is not the Christ of any other faith or the incarnation of Maitreya as taught by Blavatsky's Theosophy, or Alice Bailey's so called 'Cosmic Christ.' In fact, Theosophy even denies that the historical person of Jesus of Nazareth ever existed. Blavatsky made it clear and simple that their 'Christ' is not the Christ of the Bible when she wrote, 'the coming of Christ means the presence of CHRISTOS in a regenerated world, and not at all the actual coming in body of 'Christ' Jesus....Christ – the true esoteric SAVIOUR – is no man, but the DIVINE PRINCIPLE in every human being.' [13]

The Bible says that he who does not believe that Jesus came in the flesh – that is, was born in Bethlehem to Mary of Nazareth – is a liar and the Antichrist (2 John 1:7). The writers of the gospels stressed further the vital doctrine that Christ was made flesh – that He became a man. After Jesus had died upon the cross and rose on the third day, we are told that He shared a breakfast of bread and fish with the disciples (John 21:1-14).

Even after His supernatural resurrection Jesus was not a spirit, He was still a man of flesh. Then Thomas, who doubted that is was Jesus, put his hand into the physical wound of Christ and believed, exclaiming, 'my Lord and my God' (John 20: 24-29). Finally, Jesus said that in the same manner (bodily flesh) that He would leave, He would return – the biblical Jesus will return in bodily flesh! This is how we can recognize who Jesus is when He comes.

The Bible has a stark warning for us concerning the teachings of the Lucis Trust. 1 John 2:22 states, 'who is a liar but he who denies that Jesus is the Christ? He is Antichrist who denies the Father and the Son' (NKJV). And 1 John 4:3 says, 'every spirit that doesn't confess Jesus is not from God. This is the spirit of the Antichrist, which you have heard is coming and is now already in the world' (CEB).

We can see that the Lucis Trust is not waiting for the return of the Jesus of the Bible. Actually Alice Bailey was very clear on this point when she wrote, 'the Christ who will return will not be like the Christ Who (apparently) departed...If men look for the Christ who left His disciples centuries ago they will fail to recognize the Christ who is in process of returning...It matters not to Him of what faith a man may call himself.'

On the contrary – it matters a great deal to Christ if a man is placing his hope in any other person or faith than in Christ alone. Jesus himself said, 'I am the way, the truth, and the life. No one comes to the Father except through me' (John 14:6 NKJV). And again, 'I am the Gate for the sheep. All those others are up to no good – sheep stealers, every one of them' (John 10:7-8, the Message).

In fact, Bailey's Lucis Trust teachings bear no resemblance at all to the beliefs of Christianity or to the teachings of the Bible – and any Christian references used by them are an attempt to cover up the true nature of their occultic teachings under the guise of pseudo-Christianity and to deceive those who do not have understanding. Jesus described these kinds of teachers as being ferocious wolves disguised as sheep: 'beware of false prophets, who come to you in sheep's clothing, but inwardly they are ravenous wolves' (Matthew 7:15, NKJV).

Lucis Trust denies both the true Father and the true Son – its members do not confess the Jesus of the Bible. We are therefore left with one disturbing reality. If the United Nations are not waiting for the true Christ, then who are they waiting for?

Paul-Henri Spaak, first president of the United Nations General Assembly apparently did not care when he made this damning statement, 'we do not want another committee, we have too many already. What we want is a man of sufficient stature to hold the allegiance of all the people and to lift us up out of the economic morass into which we are sinking. Send us such a man, and whether he be God or devil, we will receive him.' [14]

Further evidences of the religious aspirations of the United Nations go beyond the Lucis Trust and can be found inside the United Nations building itself. Since 1957, located on the west side of the public lobby, is a meditation room dedicated to world peace for peoples of all faiths and religions. Dag Hammarskjöld, then Secretary General of the United Nations, personally planned and supervised every detail of the creation of the meditation room. The room is all but empty except for an abstract mural and a 6 ½ ton rectangular block of polished iron in the centre, illuminated by a single spotlight. The abstract mural was created 'to evoke a feeling of the essential oneness of God' and the iron block an 'altar to the God of all...' in accordance with the teachings of Theosophy 'dedicated to the God whom man worships under many names and in many forms.' [15]

Dr Robert Muller, United Nations Under Secretary General for 40 years, when speaking at the 20th Anniversary of the Meditation Room in 1977, further illustrated the UN's religious agenda and beliefs when he said, 'meditation, prayer, dream, hope, vision, monitoring, guidance, foreseeing and planning all go hand in hand in so many different ways at the United Nations. For me the tall building of the U.N. is an edifice of human hope and dream jutting into the universe and receiving from that universe increasingly clearer messages. Perhaps we have reached a time of cosmic evolution…Little by little, a planetary prayer book is thus being composed by an increasingly united humanity seeking its oneness, its happiness, its consciousness and its full participation in the continuous process of creation and miracle of life. Once again, but this time on a universal scale, mankind is seeking no less than its reunion with the "divine," its transcendence into ever higher forms of life. Hindus call our Earth "Brahma," or God, for they rightly see no difference between our Earth and the universe. This ancient, simple truth is slowly dawning upon humanity. Its full flowering will be the real, great story of the United Nations.' [16]

Muller holds no punches here, and is quite clear about his aspirations concerning the United Nations. The UN building jutting into the universe is to communicate with the divine – one cannot help but remember again the story of Babel here – so it appears that the fascination with Babel is not only reserved to the European Union alone. According to Muller the final full flowering of the United Nations will be mankind reuniting with the "divine". This is a disturbing thought when considering that Theosophy's "divine" means Lucifer or Satan himself!

But Muller goes even further, even presuming to speak for God concerning the UN when he said, 'and God saw that all nations of the earth, black and white, rich and poor, from North or South, from East and West, and of all creeds were sending their emissaries to a tall glass house on the shores of the River of the Rising Sun, on the Island of Manhattan, to stand together, to think together, and to care together for the world and all its people. And God said: "That is good". And it was the first day of the New Age of the Earth'. [17]

Another group that meets regularly in the Meditation Room – and which is listed under the United Nations Civil Society

Organizations – is the Aquarian Age Community. Their beliefs correspond to those of the Lucis Trust.

Psychologist Susan MacNeil's article (which was written for the group) entitled, 'the Spiritual Work of the United Nations and the Liberation of Humanity,' reveals that the group's reach has influenced and introduced Ambassadors and UN staff to UN Meditation. She goes on to say that General Secretaries Kofi Annan and Ban Ki-Moon believe the UN Meditation Room to be both important and significant. She divulges that the Meditation Room is situated right below the General Assembly. This she believes represents 'significant alignment'.

MacNeil refers to meditation with 'alignment' – focusing together until an 'at-one-ment of soul and mind occurs' – believing that no other body can best accomplish this than the United Nations. Once this 'alignment' has been 'effectively concluded,' writes MacNeil – quoting from *The Rays of the Initiations* by Alice Bailey – 'you have, therefore, as a guarantee of the return of Christ into public recognition..." Finally MacNeil writes, 'it is a sacred call to strengthen the path of return for the Lord of Love. The Spiritual Work of the United Nations and the Liberation of Humanity meditation is, to my mind, a response to the invocative cry of humanity...' [18]

Facilitating this 'liberation of humanity' meditation and the so called 'cry of humanity', the United Nations have adopted into their Rules of Procedure Rule 62 – a 'Minute of Silent Prayer or Meditation.' The official UN website writes the following, 'immediately after the opening of the first plenary meeting and immediately preceding the closing of the final plenary meeting of each session of the General Assembly, the President shall invite the representatives to observe one minute of silence dedicated to prayer or meditation.'

The United Nations take very seriously the act of meditation. Sri Chinmoy, the UN's official meditation leader from the 1970's until his death in 2007, wrote the following words and music for this UN 'hymn' called "UN Meditation" which was sung at the 20th Anniversary of the Meditation Room.

UN Meditation a soulful cry
To reach the vastness of oneness sky
United Nations Meditation Group
A simple Truth-serving all-loving troup
United Nations Meditation Room
To stop for good the birth of
Cosmos doom UN Meditation
A soulful cry [19]

Furthermore, a meditation prayer entitled "The Great Invocation" has been adopted and used by United Nations associated groups. Written by Alice Bailey, who apparently received it while in a trance through a member of the so called "Spiritual Hierarchy" – Djwal Khul – the invocation is a call for 'Christ' to return to earth.

The prayer reads as follows:

The Great Invocation

From the point of Light within the Mind of God
Let light stream forth into the minds of men.
Let Light descend on Earth.

From the point of Love within the Heart of God
Let love stream forth into the hearts of men.
May Christ return to Earth.

From the centre where the Will of God is known
Let purpose guide the little wills of men –
The purpose which the Masters know and serve.

From the centre which we call the race of men
Let the Plan of Love and Light work out
And may it seal the door where evil dwells.

Let Light and Love and Power
restore the Plan on Earth.

The so called 'restoration of the Plan on earth' referred to in the prayer is important.

Firstly we need to gain some understanding about what the plan is. In her book 'The Externalization of the Hierarchy', which opens with the Great Invocation meditation, Alice Bailey makes it clear that part of the 'Plan' relates directly to the Jews.

Bailey writes, 'the Jews are instruments in the working out of the Plan for the production of certain syntheses and to bring humanity to certain realizations and decisions.'

Bailey believed that the Jews represent the energy and the life of a previous solar system and that they are the descendents of a people that failed to 'make the grade'. According to Bailey's teachings the Jewish race was the highest product of that past solar system and this is why the Jew has insisted upon being separated from all other races, because they brought with them from the previous system the belief that his race was the 'chosen people.' Bailey writes that now the Jew 'must learn the lesson of absorption and cease his wandering'.

Bailey believed that not only should the so called insistent beliefs of the Jew have been relinquished long ago, but that their belief has also governed the law of marriage, which also should have ceased thousands of years ago. This helps us to discern why and how the sanctity of traditional Judeo-Christian marriage is under vehement attack in the western world – it is nothing less than part of an occultic agenda instigated by the Luciferic teachings of Alice Bailey and others.

It is Judaism, teaches Bailey, that has caused the stirring up of hate and global tensions. One of the ways to bring about world peace is for the Jewish people to undergo what she calls 'racial fusion' and a letting go of 'his own separative tendencies and of his deep sense of persecution'. Once the Jew understands that the law of karma is working out against him because of 'his racial acts and deeds of conquest, terrorism and cruelty,' then the solution will follow.

However, as yet, Bailey writes, the Jew neither shares understanding, love or right action in helping to arrive at the solution. Bailey writes, 'this problem is also capable of solution if properly recognized for what it is, and if coupled with an effort by the Jews themselves to solve it, and to be cooperative in the world efforts to adjust their problem. This they have not yet done because the average Jew is lonely and unsettled, able to do little to put himself right before the world.'

Hitler believed the same but was less choosy with his words: 'only when this Jewish bacillus infecting the life of peoples has been removed can one hope to establish a co-operation amongst the nations which shall be built up on a lasting understanding.' [20] Of course Hitler's answer for the solution to the problem differed; as we know from the outcome of Goring's infamous memo which referred to the, 'Final Solution of the Jewish Problem.'

Bailey writes that the major racial problem for many centuries has been the Jewish race, and it is this she believes that brought Germany to a critical point. Bailey describes the Nazi view – which she was apparently opposed to – concerning Judeo-Christian beliefs: 'Christian teaching and Christian ethics must necessarily be eliminated... Christianity must also be overthrown because it is based on Jewish sources; the rule of Christ must come to an end...'

Bailey then describes her view concerning Judeo-Christian beliefs. Bailey blames the Apostle Paul and later theologians of the church for incorrectly interpreting Scripture so as to 'bridge the gap between the spiritual future of the world and the Jewish dispensation which should have been passing out.'

She goes on to say that the teachings of the Son of God have been largely ignored and that the 'failure of Christianity can be traced to its Jewish background...' In her view 'loving action' and 'loving service', should have been taught instead of 'the blood sacrifice' and the emphasis on the 'existence of a wrathful God, needing to be placated by death, and which embodied the threats of Old Testament Jehovah in the Christian teaching of hell fire.' [21]

Exactly where the difference lies between Bailey's beliefs concerning Nazi ideology and her own teachings is confusing, to say the least. According to Bailey, the Nazis wanted to overthrow Christianity because it was based on Judaism. They believed the rule of Christ must come to an end. Bailey teaches that the so called failure of Christianity can be attributed to the fact that it is based on Judaism, and that the atoning blood sacrifice of Jesus Christ was a mistake.

Let us make no mistake here. Bailey, like Nazism, makes it clear – Judaism should be eliminated, or in Bailey's more diplomatic phraseology, 'absorbed' or 'racially fused' and that Christianity is by default a failure because it is based on Judaism. By declaring Christianity a failure, is not Bailey also attempting to overthrow Christianity? And by suggesting that the blood sacrifice of Christ was a theological error, is she not also proclaiming that the rule of Christ should come to an end?

Considering the ideas of Theosophy's founder Blavatsky, the anti-Semitic sentiments taught by Bailey should come as no surprise at all. We mentioned earlier how Blavatsky promoted the belief of the Aryan race which influenced Hitler and led to the holocaust. Bailey, taking her beliefs from Blavatsky, had strong feelings concerning the Jewish race too. Although Bailey did not condone the atrocities committed against the Jewish race throughout history, we can see that her rationale concerning the Jews is indeed disturbing and certainly does not help to stem the tide of Jewish persecution that exists to this day.

In 1953 Bailey wrote of the Jews, 'their aggressive history as narrated in the Old Testament is on a par with present-day German accomplishment...Today the law is working, and the Jews are paying the price, factually and symbolically, for all they have done in the past...They have never yet faced candidly and honestly (as a race) the problem of why the many nations, from the time of the Egyptians, have neither liked nor wanted them. It has always been the same down the centuries. Yet there must be some reason, inherent in the people themselves, when the reaction is so general and universal. Their approach to their direful problem has been one of supplication, or of distressed complaint, or of unhappy despair. Their demand has been for the Gentile nations to put the matter right, and many Gentiles have attempted to do so. Until, however, the Jews themselves face up to the situation and admit that there may be for them the working out of the retributive aspect of the Law of Cause and Effect, and until they endeavor to ascertain what it is in them, as a race, which has initiated their ancient and dire fate, this basic world issue will remain as it has been since the very night of time.' [22]

The encouragement of this kind of shocking teaching must lead to a stark indictment of the United Nations. What exactly are they thinking, listing under their Civil Society Organizations the Lucis Trust, whose apparent expert field of activity is culture, human rights, humanitarian affairs and values? What about the culture and the human rights of the Jewish people – who the founder of the Lucis Trust believes should be eradicated? What about the rights of Christians and the values taught in Christianity, which Bailey says are nothing more than a 'failure' because they are based on Judaism? These ideas do not sound expert at all they sound racist, anti-Semitic, anti-Christian and in truth resonate more with Adolf Hitler's Nazi ideology. Bailey gets away with this malevolent teaching because she has carefully packaged it with the terminology like the 'Plan of the Great Invocation' in order to hide her true, demonic agenda.

Hitler and the Antichrist of the Bible

When taking into account everything we have discovered so far – the Nazi roots of the European Union, the anti-Semitic and anti-Christian teachings propagated through the United Nations Civil Society Organization, the Lucis Trust, and the UN's own occultic aspirations – it is not too difficult to imagine how the Bible prophecies concerning the rise of the Antichrist could easily be fulfilled in our day.

I believe that the chilling words spoken by Hitler – that after his death there would be an overwhelming revelation to the world of his mission, that his spirit would rise from the grave and the world would see that he was right – are in the process of being fulfilled in our time. I do not mean that Hitler's own spirit is making an appearance, as Hitler himself was deceived into believing, but that the demonic spirit of the Antichrist which took possession of his body is re-emerging in our time.

Could it be that we have become so dumbed down and conditioned through various propaganda techniques, as well as distracted by the engineered pursuit of materialism, that we cannot see what is rising up before us? We turn on the news and blindly believe everything we are told and if anyone does dare to question it they are immediately ridiculed. Is it possible that we have become blind and that what is actually happening before our very eyes through these political institutions today is nothing less than the rise of Hitler's original mission but repackaged in a more subtle way?

We should remember that during the rise of Nazism, the people and also the church were not able to recognize that the Satanic forces of hell itself were being unleashed before them in the person of Adolf Hitler. Incidentally it was partly the people's blindness and avid support of him that inadvertently aided the Satanic scheme to find its fruition. This should be a lesson for all of us to have a discerning heart concerning our own political leaders today.

We saw earlier that according to the beliefs of both Rosenberg and Eckart, Hitler was possessed by the spirit of the Antichrist. They were therefore convinced that he was appointed to fulfill the works of darkness as prophesied in the Bible. Judging by Hitler's actions it is not too difficult for us to arrive at a similar conclusion, and it is from this place of understanding that a vitally important picture begins to take shape, serving as a window for us into the future of our world.

By looking at Hitler and Nazi Germany we can see a microcosm of the world to come as prophesied in the Bible. Hitler's Germany was just the beginning, in which he did not fail in his mission, but rather provided the impetus to significantly advance the occultic agenda to institute a one world government presided over by an evil dictator. Just five days after Hitler's alleged suicide on 25th April 1945, the United Nations drafted the UN Charter and officially came into existence six months later on 24th October 1945. Six years later in 1951 what would become the European Union was formed. Both of these have been significantly influenced by Hitler's Nazi ideology because Nazism is the manifestation of the spirit of the Antichrist.

In understanding our world now and the time approaching its end, it is vital for us to recognize that a repackaged form of Nazism is reappearing, shrouded and hidden in darkness with names and symbols designed to conceal its hellish identity. The coming world government will therefore by nature manifest the same racist ideas such as anti-Semitism. Indeed, this idea already exists within the United Nations. This will eventually lead to crimes of incalculable evil – the instituting of similar laws and the implementation of the same brutal actions and practices perpetrated by Nazi Germany, except this time on a global scale. We can see this happening now. This is why the government controlled mainstream media only focuses on the plight of the Palestinians, while at the same time portraying Israel in a negative light. I am not saying here that Israel is without its faults, but that the reporting is always tipped to highlight the Palestinian problem. This dupes the masses and rallies their support against the Jew – exactly as Hitler did in Nazi Germany. This is nothing less than a part of the age-old occultic agenda to eliminate the Jewish people from the face of the earth – a strategy which the mainstream media is responsible for propagating.

Now let us look at what the Bible has to say specifically concerning the character and the mission of the Antichrist, after which we will examine further evidence revealing how Hitler and his Nazi regime embodied the very spirit of the Antichrist, proving that Hitler initiated the fulfillment of the prophesied Antichrist to come.

The Antichrist of the Bible

The word Antichrist in the bible literally means 'against', 'opposite' or 'in place' of the Messiah.

The name Antichrist appears in the Christian Bible four times;

'Little children, it is the last hour; and as you have heard that the Antichrist is coming, even now many Antichrists have come, by which we know that it is the last hour.' (1 John 2:18)

'Who is a liar but he who denies that Jesus is the Christ? He is Antichrist who denies the Father and the Son.' (1 John 2:22)

'Every spirit that does not confess that Jesus Christ has come in the flesh is not of God. And this is the spirit of the Antichrist, which you have heard was coming, and is now already in the world.' (1 John 4:3)

'For many deceivers have gone out into the world who do not confess Jesus Christ as coming in the flesh. This is a deceiver and an Antichrist.' (2 John 1:7)

From these passages we can see that the Bible teaches that

the Antichrist is coming and at the same time that many Antichrists have already come and it is this that tells us that the end is approaching. We can see that the Biblical image of the Antichrist does not exclusively refer to one single person, but can apply to anyone who denies that Jesus is the Christ, or denies the Father and the Son, or who does not confess that Jesus Christ came in the flesh – all these beliefs are Antichrist in character. The Bible does however single out one specific person who it refers to as the Antichrist. He will be the dictator of a totalitarian world government. It is this figure on whom we are focusing in this chapter.

It is important to note that Christian theology has not obtained the doctrine of the coming Antichrist from these four verses alone. There are many other prophesied references to the Antichrist recorded throughout the Bible that describe him under different titles. Let us take a look at just a few of them here.

The little horn: He will have eyes like a man and speak arrogantly. He will persecute or wear out the saints and will have a plan to change sacred festivals and laws (Daniel 7:8; 25).

A king with fierce expression: He will be able to understand sinister schemes, be a master of deception, gain great strength but not by his power alone and he will persecute and kill the Jews (Daniel 8:23-24).

The deceiver: Through him deception will prosper (Daniel 8:25).

The peace maker: Through him the nations will feel secure. Once he has deceived the nations into believing in the false peace he has established he will rise up and destroy many and take his stand against the Messiah, Jesus Christ (Daniel 8:25).

The people of the prince: He will destroy the city and the sanctuary (Daniel 9:26).

The one who makes desolate: He will make a peace treaty and then break it (Daniel 9:27).

A vile person: He will speak peace and seize the city through conspiracy and subterfuge (Daniel 11:21).

The blasphemous king: He will do according to his own will and exalt himself above God, denouncing both Judaism and Christianity and blaspheming God's name (Daniel 11:36).

The man of lawlessness: He will come in accordance with all the works of Satan and every evil that deceives those who have rejected the truth of the gospel (2 Thessalonians 2:3).

The man doomed to destruction: The Antichrist will arrive at a time of great rebellion on the earth, a time when many will reject the truth of the gospel and the law of God and live according to their own law. They will live immoral lifestyles, including idolatry – the worship of traditional idols in false religion, as well as the modern day worship of material gain, the worship of celebrities and the worship of the human body in pornography, the pursuit of materialism, the love of money and all the acts of the sinful nature as listed in Galatians 5:19 and spoken of by Jesus Christ in Matthew 15:19 (2 Thessalonians 2:3).

The man who proclaims himself to be God: He will sit in the newly rebuilt temple in Jerusalem demanding adulation and worship (2 Thessalonians 2:4).

A counterfeit miracle worker: He will perform supernatural miracles powerfully deluding those who have already been deceived by him and his world government (2 Thessalonians 2:9).

The beast from the sea: He will speak arrogantly and he will make war against the saints and be victorious over them and he will receive power over all people, tongue and nation and they will worship him (Revelation 13:2-10).

Hitler – the Antichrist Rises

The Bible prophesies in Daniel 7:25 that the Antichrist will blaspheme against God, persecute, or wear out the saints, and will have a plan to change their sacred festivals and laws.

'And he shall speak great words against the most High, and shall wear out the saints of the most High' (KJV). 'He will try to change their sacred festivals and laws, and they will be placed under his control for a time, times, and half a time' (NLT).

Hitler certainly spoke blasphemy against God. While referring to Christ, Hitler said, 'how terrific was His fight for the world against the Jewish poison. Today, after two thousand years, with deepest emotion I recognize more profoundly than ever before in the fact that it was for this that He had to shed His blood upon the Cross...' [23]

Hitler also likened himself to Christ saying, 'when I came to Berlin a few weeks ago and looked at the traffic in Kurfuerstendamm, the luxury, perversion, iniquity, wanton display, and Jewish materialism disgusted me so thoroughly that I was almost beside myself. I nearly imagined myself to be Jesus Christ when he came to his Father's temple and found it taken by money changers. I can well imagine how he felt when he seized a whip and scourged...out...the brood of vipers and adders.'

Later it is recorded that Hitler was seen striding up and down in the courtyard with his whip yelling, 'I must enter Berlin like Christ and drive out the moneylenders!' [24] Hitler even posed for a photograph with whip in hand, an allusion to the New Testament incident.

Other images designed to deify Hitler became commonplace in Nazi propaganda. One was a poster of Hitler standing amongst the masses with a shepherd-like staff in hand with heavenly beams of light emanating from the clouds, out of which a

144

bird approaches him from behind out of the light. One cannot help but wonder if this was an allusion to Christ's baptism. Matthew 3:16 reads, 'at that moment heaven was opened, and he saw the Spirit of God descending like a dove and lighting on him.' Whatever the intended message, the poster's religious overtones are plain to see.

The prophecy continues. He will wear out or persecute the saints of the most high. History records the horrors of the holocaust where Hitler specifically targeted and persecuted God's people – predominantly the Jewish people, but also Christians and other groups. Interestingly the prophecy is explicit in the use of the word often translated as 'persecute'. The original Hebrew word means to 'wear down' or 'wear out'. We have all seen the disturbing images of the concentration camp victims, gaunt and totally exhausted – literally worn out by the brutality of the Nazi regime.

Daniel goes on to detail that the Antichrist will attempt to change sacred festivals. In another fulfillment of Bible prophecy the Nazi Party through Heinrich Himmler replaced Christian festivals with state pagan holidays including Nazi Party holidays, Hitler's birthday, pagan Summer and Winter Solstices and secular wedding ceremonies for the sole purpose of undermining Judeo-Christian values and re-programming the German people. The prophecy continues to state that the Antichrist will also attempt to change laws. It is not widely known that the Nazi Party produced its own paraphrase of the New Testament entitled 'The Message of God.' It also rewrote the Ten Commandments and added two more, replacing 'honor your father and your mother' with 'honor your Fuehrer and master'. It eliminated all references to the Jewish race including such words as Hallelujah, Jehovah, Jerusalem and replaced Jesus' Jewish roots with Aryan ones in an attempt to Nazify Christianity. [25]

In fact part of the Nazi Party's official doctrine included what was known as Positive Christianity – a Nazified version of

Christianity which rejected any part of the Bible written by a Jew including the entire Old Testament. The Nazified 'New Testament' printed in 1941 was distributed to thousands of churches across Nazi occupied Europe.

These actions are a shadow of things to come. The prophesied one-world religion will have its own holy book which will include a lot of Judeo-Christian ideas in order to deceive the masses. It will contain a hotchpotch of doctrines from the world's religions.

The Bible offers a stark warning to those who dare to add or take away from the words of the bible: 'for I testify to everyone who hears the words of the prophecy of this book: If anyone adds to these things, God will add to him the plagues that are written in this book; and if anyone takes away from the words of the book of this prophecy, God shall take away his part from the Book of Life, from the holy city, and from the things which are written in this book.' Revelation 22:18-19

In Daniel 8:23-24 it is prophesied that the Antichrist will have a fierce expression, be able to understand sinister schemes, be a master of deception, gain great strength – but not on his own and he will persecute and kill the Jews. Hitler's fierce expression is clearly known by all who have watched any video archives of his Nazi speeches. His ability to understand sinister schemes and to be a master of deception is evidenced by his involvement in occultic groups where he gained his understanding regarding the plot hatched in the corridors of hell to eliminate the Jews. That Hitler could not go it alone to gain such power is also demonstrated by the fact that he needed the German people and axis countries such as Italy, Japan and others. Daniel 8:25 says the Antichrist will be known as the deceiver. A man who managed to sway an entire populace, and who in addition called himself a Christian but acted like the devil incarnate, certainly deserves the title of deceiver. Furthermore, so proud was he of his use of deceptive techniques that Hitler devoted two chapters to the subject in his book *Mein Kampf*.

The False Prophet – The Antichrist's Right Hand Man

According to Bible prophecy the Antichrist will not work alone in his totalitarian world government. Working closely by his side will be the False Prophet, described as the beast out of the earth. He will possess the same authority as the Antichrist. He will institute and be head of a one world religion intolerant to true Christianity and Judaism and will initiate global worship of the Antichrist, setting up graven images of the dictator around the world, ensuring that those who refuse to worship or pledge allegiance to the Antichrist be executed by beheading.

The False Prophet will also institute the infamous Mark of the Beast. This mandatory mark will be implemented worldwide on everyone, small and great, rich and poor, free and slave. This mark will become the only means whereby a person can buy or sell – the ultimate single 'currency', a digital currency in a cashless society. Those refusing the mark will be forced to find an alternative way to survive (Revelation 13:11-17).

In yet another uncanny fulfillment of Bible prophecy – which further reveals the spirit that embodied Hitler and his Nazi party was the end time spirit of the Antichrist – Hitler had his own false prophets by his side during his reign. Both Dietrich Eckart and Alfred Rosenberg believed themselves to be the prophets of Hitler. Eckart worked closely with Hitler and believed him to be the prophesied redeemer.[26] Such was the relationship between them that Hitler dedicated the second volume of his book *Mein Kampf* to Eckart. At the same time Rosenberg – who held important positions within the Nazi Party – rejected Christianity and played a pivotal role in the formation of Positive Christianity, the false religion of Nazism, a forerunner to the prophesied one world false religion presided over by the False Prophet. Equally disturbing however is that the introduction of the prophesied Mark of the Beast by the False Prophet began its journey of fulfillment in Nazi Germany, as we will see in chapter 14.

Continuing our gaze through the prophetic window of the activities of Hitler and his Nazi Germany yet more clues unfold regarding the future of our world and the journey leading up to the rise of the Antichrist and his alignment with the False Prophet.

In Hitler's end-time Satanic mandate he joined forces with the Islamic Grand Mufti of Jerusalem, Haj Amin al-Husseini, and signed an agreement with the Roman Catholic Church. This I believe reveals that a combination of a version of Islam and a kind of apostate Christianity (not exclusively Roman Catholic) will be directly involved in the activities of and the legitimization of the Antichrist and his global dictatorship.

Earlier in the previous chapter we looked at the prophetic dream of King Nebuchadnezzar which Daniel interpreted. Daniel saw the revived Roman Empire as the two feet of a great statue – representing the East and West respectively – the Eastern foot being the Byzantine Empire (with its center in Constantinople, modern Turkey) and the Western foot being the area covered by the European Union. According to Bible prophecy the Antichrist system will emerge from both these geographical areas.

It is vital that we understand this because it is all too often assumed that the Antichrist will rise from the Western European foot alone. While this is true, certainly in terms of its foundational roots as we have already seen, it is also clear that the prophecy includes the East which today is mainly Islamic. This reveals that the political entity of the Western foot will become heavily influenced by the spirit of Islam within the Eastern foot of modern day Turkey as the two rise together. The spirit of Nazism, (repackaged/rebranded/hidden, which is embodied within the ideals of the UN and the heritage of the European Union), will meet with Islam in a symbiotic relationship just as it did in the days of Hitler and Nazi Germany.

How could this be possible? They both appear to be quite different from one another.

However, when we strip away their religious and political ideologies it becomes evident that they are kindred spirits working towards the same ends.

Nazism (Repackaged)	Radical Islam
Dictatorial Totalitarian Government	Dictatorial Totalitarian Government
Aryan race = master race	Arab race = master race
Quest for world domination	Quest for world domination
Mission to exterminate the Jewish race	Mission to exterminate the Jewish race

Could it be then that the Antichrist rises from the Western foot and the False Prophet rises from the Eastern Islamic foot? Only time will tell, but whatever the details one thing is for certain, Islam will play a dominant role in the sequence of end-time events including the prophesied great apostasy spoken of by the Apostle Paul in 1 Timothy 4:1 and 4.16: 'now the Spirit expressly says that in latter times some will depart from the faith, giving heed to deceiving spirits and doctrines of demons...Take heed to yourself and to the doctrine. Continue in them, for in doing this you will save both yourself and those who hear you' (NKJV).

We should therefore guard our hearts and minds from being fooled by this pernicious ideology which continues to make inroads into western society and poisons an already corrupt and undemocratic political system.

As we consider the nature of Islam it is vitally important to make the distinction between the people of Islam and Islam itself. The two should always be separated. We must love with all our hearts our neighbor as we do ourselves – and that not in thought or word only but in actual deeds of kindness without even the slightest hint of discrimination. There is no room here for hatred towards our fellow man. Concerning the foreigner

God says, 'do not oppress...the foreigner... Do not plot evil against each other' (Zechariah 7:10, NIV): 'do not despise an Egyptian' (Deuteronomy 23:7 (NIV), and 'you shall love your neighbor as yourself' (Matthew 22:39, NKJV).

The Grand Mufti of Jerusalem was an ardent hater of the Jewish people, convicted by a military tribunal after he and his followers rampaged through the streets on April 4th, 1920 killing five Jews and injuring a further 211. He was nevertheless bizarrely appointed by the British government, who at the time had jurisdiction over Jerusalem, as the religious and political leader of the Palestinians. After Hitler rose to power the Grand Mufti met with Nazi leaders Adolf Eichmann and Herbert Hagen in a secret meeting in Palestine. Later he stayed in Berlin where he became a guest of the Nazis during the years of the Holocaust. Just two months after the Grand Mufti met with Hitler the Nazis held the Wansee Conference which initiated the Holocaust.[27] In an interview with the Grand Mufti on 30th November 1941 Hitler showed that his ambition to rid Europe of the Jews did not stop there. Hitler explained that 'Germany stood for uncompromising war against Jews. That naturally included active opposition to the Jewish national home in Palestine...' [28]

Furthermore minutes taken from the meeting between Hitler and the Grand Mufti provide additional information that Germany's objective would be to destroy the Jew living in Palestine. Hitler also promised that Husseini would become the most authoritative spokesman for the Arab World, the kind of status given by the Antichrist to the False Prophet at the time of the end! Coincidence? I do not think so. This further evidences the same end time spirit of the Antichrist working through Hitler.

A record of the conversation between Hitler and the Grand Mufti of Jerusalem was made on November 28, 1941, in the presence of Reich Foreign Minister and Minister Grobba in Berlin. Here is some of what was said at the meeting:

'The Fuhrer then made the following statement to the Mufti, enjoining him to lock it in the uttermost depths of his heart: "At the moment which was impossible to set exactly today but which in any event was not distant, the German armies would in the course of this struggle reach the southern exit from Caucasia. As soon as this had happened, the Fuhrer would on his own give the Arab the assurance that its hour of liberation had arrived. Germany's objective would then be solely the destruction of the Jewish element residing in the Arab sphere under the protection of British power. In that hour the Mufti would be the most authoritative spokesman for the Arab world. It would then be his task to set off the Arab operations, which he had secretly prepared..."'[29]

The Concordat between the Catholic Church and Hitler's government was signed on July 20th, 1933 – the same year that Hitler was given dictatorial powers through the Enabling Act. Under the terms of the agreement the church was given guaranteed autonomy but would be politically impotent with German bishops agreeing to swear an oath of loyalty to Nazi Germany.

Article 16 of the Concordat writes, 'before bishops take possession of their dioceses they are to take an oath of loyalty either to the Reich governor of the state (Land) concerned or to the President of the Reich respectively, according to the following formula: "Before God and on the Holy Gospels I swear and promise, as becomes a bishop, loyalty to the German Reich and to the State (Land) of...I swear and promise to honour the legally constituted government and to cause the clergy of my diocese to honour it. With dutiful concern for the welfare and the interests of the German state, in the performance of the ecclesiastical office entrusted to me, I will endeavor to prevent everything injurious which might threaten it.'[30]

The Concordat legitimized Hitler's dictatorial government in the eyes of the church and the world. This was a key component to the concealing of the truth and the advancement of the

151

Antichrist political system. The Catholic Church effectively made a pact with the devil – a pact that I believe will occur in a similar fashion between the one world religion – a form of Islam and an apostate church – and a dictatorial government in future end-time events.

Today Islam's influence and power is growing at an exponential rate across the western world. It is not difficult then to understand that Islam will feature extensively in the Antichrist system and the one world religion of the False Prophet.

Before we look at the rise of Islam though it should be pointed out that the Islamification of the west is being fostered by the globalists. The Hegelian Dialectic strategy of create or exploit a problem, evoke the required reaction, and then offer a solution is at work here.

The Rise of Islam

'As a rapidly growing Muslim population makes its presence felt in towns and cities across the continent, Islam is transforming the European way of life in ways unimaginable only a few years ago,' so said Soeren Kern, a Senior Fellow at the New York-based Gatestone Institute [31]. 'Turkey could become a great European power,' so said David Cameron, UK Prime Minister. [32]

Since 2005 Turkey has been in negotiations to become a member of the European Union, with the UK's Prime Minister David Cameron promising to fight for EU membership. Cameron said he wanted to 'pave the road' for Turkey's entry, stating that they could become a 'great European power' and help to build links with the Middle East. [33] Although it looks unlikely to happen immediately, when it does the ramifications will be significant and drastically alter the character of the EU. This powerful Muslim country will not only bring to the EU table a whole host of moral and social issues from an Islamic perspective, it will also bridge the gap between 'Christian' Europe and the Islamic world.

Brussels, home to the European Union parliament, is now the most Islamic city in Europe with over 300,000 Muslims in residence. It is predicted that by 2030 Muslims will be in a majority in Brussels. In October of 2012 two Muslim politicians, Lhoucine Aït Jeddig and Redouane Ahrouch, won municipal elections in Brussels and vowed to implement Islamic Sharia law in Belgium. At a press conference the elected councilors said, 'we are elected Islamists but above all we are Muslims. Islam is compatible with the laws of the Belgian people. As elected Muslims, we embrace the Koran and the tradition of the Prophet Mohammed. We believe Islam is a universal religion. Our presence on the town council will give us the opportunity to express ourselves.' [34] Considering that Brussels is the heart of the European Union this is a horrifying prospect.

France is home to the largest Muslim population in the European Union, at an estimated 6.5 million Muslims. In February 2012, the Persian Gulf Emirate of Qatar, which follows the Wahhabi sect of Islam, announced that it would be investing €50 million into the home of Muslim immigrants living in French suburbs. Shortly after this move Qatari Emir Sheikh Hamad bin Khalifa al-Thani vowed to spread the fundamentalist teachings of this sect of Islam across the entire world.

Further evidence of the influence Islam is having upon France is that all meat slaughtered in the greater Paris metropolitan area is now done in accordance with Islamic Sharia law.[35] The meat is known as halal, meaning in Arabic "permissible" or "lawful" – i.e. from an animal that has been slaughtered by having its throat cut while facing Mecca and reciting that Allah is great and greater than all the gods. One American pastor, Mark Biltz, while talking about the introduction of halal meat into American food stores, called the practice 'backdoor Sharia'.[36] 30% of all meat produced in France is now halal, while the Muslim population of France makes up around only 7%. The superfluous halal meat is then sold as non-halal, tricking French consumers into buying a product that they might not otherwise choose to eat.[37]

Furthermore according to the Gatestone Institute it was Muslims that cast the deciding votes which put Francois Hollande in power in the 2012 French election. During his election campaign Hollande promised amnesty to the 400,000 illegal Muslim immigrants living in France and a change in the electoral laws so that Muslims without French citizenship could vote in municipal elections in 2014.[38]

Finally in France it is clear the impact of Islam is gaining ground. A €22 million Grand Mosque with the capacity to hold 7,000 worshippers including an 82 feet high minaret, taller than any church steeple in the area and purposely designed to alter the suburb's skyline, has been given the go ahead despite opposition from local residents and businesses.[39]

Just across the border in Germany 25 million free copies of a German translation of the Quran were organized in April 2012 through a campaign called 'Project Read' run by a hard-line Islamic group known as Salafists, in an attempt to place a Quran in every household in the country. The Salafist mission is to establish a Sunni Islamic Caliphate throughout the Middle East, North Africa and Europe – a world governed by Sharia law imposed upon Muslim and non-Muslim alike. While in Hamburg, Germany's second largest city, the authorities have agreed to begin teaching Islam in public schools with the curriculum being developed by local Muslim leaders. According to experts who have been sounding the alarm for years a Salafist Caliphate could be on the horizon if the inroads made by Islam continue to be ignored.[40]

England is home to some 2.7 million Muslims. Anjem Choudary is one such Muslim residing in Ilford, London. He has also been called the face of radical Islam in Britain, holding frequent rallies calling for Sharia law to be imposed on the United Kingdom. Choudary says, 'I am 100 percent certain that the sharia will be implemented in America and in Britain one day. The question is, 'when?' and how it will come to fruition.'

According to Choudary it is currently not the time to fight, it is the time to propagate Islam. Once the balance is tipped however a Jihad against Britain is not ruled out. 'If we have enough authority and we have enough power, then we are obliged as Muslims to take the authority away from those who have it and implement sharia...' [41]

These treasonous sentiments should ring alarm bells to any sensible British citizen. Not so for Ken Livingstone a former mayor of London. Livingstone addressed Muslims at the Finsbury Park Mosque in March 2012. The mosque was formally controlled by the terrorist recruiter Abu Hamza but is now in the hands of the Muslim Association of Britain which apparently has links with the banned terrorist organization, Hamas. Livingstone said he would like to make London a beacon of Islam and if elected as mayor he would spend the next four years making sure that every non-Muslim in London knows and understands what Islam is truly about. [42] Presumably he was not talking about the part that involves a violent Jihad against the British people and the enforcement of Sharia law.

Yet more disturbing evidence of Islam's growing influence upon Britain is the fact that actions once associated with Islamic countries vehemently opposed to the existence of Israel have now found their way onto Britain's shores. British textbooks endorsed by the British Council have wiped Israel off the face of the map. The *Skills in English Writing Level 1* aimed at foreign students and immigrants to the UK displays a map with the words 'Occupied Palestine' in place of the Jewish State. [43] This further demonstrates the growing manifestation of anti-Semitic Nazi/Islamic ideology that we looked at previously. The textbook published by Garnet is one of the more popular and mainstream of English language publications. Garnet Education is run by the daughter of a pro-Syrian Arab nationalist Tahseen Khayat owner of a Lebanese media empire. [43]

Nothing can be more alarming though than the end time march of Islam across the Atlantic and onto the land of the most

influential country and number one superpower of the world
– the United States of America.

The fastest growing religion in America today is no longer
Christianity. Since 9/11 Islam has experienced explosive
growth. It has doubled in size and is rapidly changing the
continent. From 1 million in 2000 to a staggering 2.6 million
today Islam is showing little sign of abating. [44]

Chapter 9

America Beguiled

We do not consider ourselves a Christian nation
President Barack Obama [1]

If you actually took the number of Muslim Americans,
we'd be one of the largest Muslim countries in the world
President Barack Obama [2]

The Islamification of America can be mostly attributed to the influx of immigrants from Muslim countries, not through new converts. This is a form of Jihad – a 'holy Islamic war' – called Immigration Jihad. It is an attempt to subjugate the West to Islam through immigration. Once the percentage of Muslims rises in any given area Islamic ideology begins to influence and subvert Western culture and politics. Journalist Daniel Greenfield writes, 'several hundred years ago when the forces of Islam wanted to capture Vienna, they came with the sword and the cannon and laid siege to the city walls. Today they simply take a plane.' [3]

This continual influx of Muslims is literally reshaping America, with the number of mosques rising from 1,209 in 2000 to 2,106 in 2010. [4] In addition to this the call to Muslim prayer now sounds out over some US cities. It is clear that the Islamification of America is truly underway.

Dearborn, Michigan has one of the largest Muslim populations in America and is one such city where the call to prayer is broadcast over its loudspeakers. But while Muslim Arabs have found favor in Dearborn, Christian Arabs who want to share their faith have not. If they want to do so, it must be done from a small booth and not on the sidewalk. [5] While Islam has been allowed to flourish, Christianity has become more and more marginalized.

The insidious ideology of political correctness is one of the contributing forces here. It has silenced anyone who might dare to speak up against this rising tide in the fear that they might either offend someone, be accused of racism or worse be prosecuted. This so called tolerance, propagated through the mainstream media, has become a powerful weapon that has blinded citizens and politicians alike.

This has even found its way into our churches, attacking and redefining what true values, beliefs and morals are. It has left a culture bereft of any absolutes. Anything goes. The very fabric of Christian religion, morality and democracy upon which America has so prided itself is being eroded away piece by piece. While tolerance of all kinds is preached at every turn, little to no tolerance is given to those who value the Judeo-Christian way of life. Apparently it does not matter if they are offended.

In Seattle the shear madness of political correctness led to a school renaming Easter eggs 'spring spheres' so as not to offend those who would associate the word Easter with Christianity. [6]

Furthermore a town in Ohio recently dropped the name Easter Egg Hunt for its seasonal event in favor of 'The Spring Egg Hunt'. [7]

But it is not just Easter that is under attack but also Christmas too. Tolerance has led to 'Merry Christmas' being exchanged for 'Happy Holidays' and the Christmas tree becoming a 'holiday tree'. We should remember here that the Nazi party in accordance with Bible prophecy also replaced Christian festivals in their attempt to reprogramme the German people.

But who exactly is being offended here is a mystery. According to a recent poll 80% of Americans prefer to use the term 'Christmas tree' over 'holiday tree'.[8]

The war against Christianity has led to the removal of the Ten Commandments from governmental and educational institutions across America. But while Judeo-Christian laws are put away from public view, Islamic law advances throughout the land.

Harvard University founded in 1636 in Maasachusetts is one of the most prestigious institutions in the world. In January 2013 it placed a Quranic text in its entrance. The famed faculty described the verse as one of the greatest expressions of justice in history. The institution that also facilitates a Shariah-compliant gym[9], a Muslim chaplaincy and broadcasts the Muslim call to prayer (the Adhan in Arabic),[10] has provoked some groups to cite these actions as the 'Islamisation of the world's greatest university.' [11]

A recent report from the Center for Security Policy states, 'today, the United States faces what is, if anything, an even more insidious ideological threat: the totalitarian socio-political doctrine that Islam calls shariah. Translated as "the path," shariah is a comprehensive legal and political framework.'[12]

The very real concern that US law is being threatened by Islam is evidenced by a law signed in Kansas in 2012 aimed at blocking foreign laws. Stephen Gele, spokesman for the American Public Policy Alliance, said, 'this bill should provide protection for Kansas citizens from the application of foreign laws." Although the law does not specifically mention Shariah the alliance states on its website that it wants to protect Americans' freedoms from 'infiltration' by foreign laws and legal doctrines, 'especially Islamic Shariah Law.' [13]

As the White House continues to spout its war-against-Islamic-terrorism rhetoric, America is being purposely and systematically destroyed from within by the very threat that it is supposedly fighting against. Recently a leading Muslim cleric in Egypt vowed that the Islamic flag would eventually be raised above the White House. The Friday sermon captured on video before hundreds in Egypt and reported by The Arab World quoted the cleric's chilling words that should serve as a massive wakeup call not only to America but also to the rest of the world.

'I swear to Allah almighty Sharia will be implemented, I tell you, not only in Egypt. Sharia will be implemented in and govern the entire world.' The cleric went on to say, 'this is the word of Allah and his messenger [Muhammad]...I swear by Allah almighty, I swear, I swear the Islamic flag will be raised above the White House...I swear by Allah almighty – I swear by Allah almighty this will happen.'

The cleric told the followers of Islam to be patient and to keep working toward that goal. [14]

Let us not be mistaken here. These words are not empty threats spoken by a crazed fundamentalist. What this Muslim cleric is talking about here is the establishment of the Antichrist and False Prophet system that will govern our entire planet.

Tragically America does not hear the voice of this Muslim cleric because it is not listening. Indeed America cannot. It is unconscious. It has been taken in by the social engineering drug that has sent the entire Western world hurtling into the same comatose condition – the effects of which are the pursuit of self as the ultimate goal, expressed through the seeking after of pleasure through the entertainment industry in sports, music, movies and television, material gain, narcotics, alcohol and sexual gratification with whoever or whatever a person so desires. These worldly trappings are now the preeminent meaning of life. They have filled the hearts and minds of the people and they cannot see or hear the warning signs that are fast approaching. The Muslim cleric's words fall on deaf ears in this 'drug' addicted generation.

Let us not be fooled and think that the church is somehow immune to all of this. The church too has been seriously affected by the earthquake-like shift that has occurred in our culture. This social engineering has gradually snuck into the back of the church and now sits comfortably in the pews.

This ideology of political correctness has largely silenced the church into a one-sided gospel that is preached in a way so as to not upset or offend anyone. An inclusive gospel is preached where everyone is happy to live and do as they please.

Furthermore the church has become politically impotent. It has allowed the puppet masters over Washington to run amok with unconstitutional legislation time and again, which in turn has given rise to a literal police state and dictatorship that is ready at any point to enact a 'George Orwell 1984' type scenario.

This political silence is not just happenstance. No. It was orchestrated by government itself and agreed upon by the church in order to obtain tax relief.

In 1954 Senator Lyndon B Johnson, who later became President, added churches to the IRS tax code 501c3. This was part of his political agenda to silence the church from having any significant influence in shaping public policy. It was billed as a favor to the church. But in reality it was a weapon to silence it – and it worked. Certain restrictions are placed on a church in order to claim tax deductions on tithes and offerings. This is why the church refuses to take a stand against the rising tyranny and unconstitutional actions of Washington today. If they do they lose their tax deduction. They have been muzzled from expressing any political convictions.

Think about it. When was the last time a mega church pastor publicly spoke out about the encroaching police state, the loss of liberty, or dared to question the Obama administration? This silence has deceived God's people into believing that everything is okay.

Pastor Chuck Baldwin of Liberty Fellowship, liberty advocate and presidential nominee in the 2008 presidential elections has chosen for his church to opt out of the IRS tax deduction after having been under its control for many years. In a message to his congregation entitled 'The 501c3 Government Takeover of the Church' Baldwin stated, 'I didn't even realize the depth of the stranglehold that those tax codes hold over pastors...and the churches themselves until not too long ago...The depth of intimidation and evil that is held over the necks and the heads of churches relative to the 501c3 tax exempt status cannot be overstated. It's worse than you think it is, and it's worse than I thought it was. I'm just here to tell you by living testimonial that it is worse than you can possibly imagine...' [15]

This silencing of the churches should serve as a stark warning to us today. It happened before. Hitler silenced the church. He stated, 'we'll see to it that the Churches cannot spread abroad teachings in conflict with the interests of the State. We shall continue to preach the doctrine of National Socialism, and the young will no longer be taught anything but the truth.' [16]

This is exactly why the US government through Lyndon B Johnson has silenced the church – because its teachings expressed through the Bible conflict with the interests of Washington. However, not only did the evangelical church remain silent during the rise of Adolf Hitler, it openly supported him too. In like manner today many evangelical churches support Washington by their silence. They stand back without protest and allow tyrannical government to take root. Someone once said, 'all tyranny needs to gain a foothold is for people of good conscience to remain silent.' Is it time for the church, for those of good conscience, to rise up and speak out against this tyranny? To stand up and fight against the encroaching police state? To oppose the illegal and immoral actions being perpetrated in the name of freedom? If we do nothing the guilt will lay at our feet as it did in the days of Nazi Germany.

The US constitution lies in tatters, trampled by the globalists who are bent on dismantling America piece by piece. Why? Because it stands in the way of their fanatical quest – a new world order. America and all sovereign nations must ultimately fail and be rendered powerless. Then a world government can triumphantly rise from its ashes.

The allowance of Islam to prosper and grow in influence across America is no mistake. It is yet another opportunity in the hands of the globalists to bring America to its knees. Furthermore, the influence of Islam upon the White House itself has possibly never been as great as it is in this hour.

The Muslim cleric declared that in the future the Islamic flag would fly above the White House.

On the face of it this appears to be a preposterous declaration.

However, disturbing evidence suggests that it has been figuratively flying for some time now.

Chapter 10

Deception in the White House

A light will shine through that window, a beam of light will come down upon you, you will experience an epiphany, and you will suddenly realize that you must go to the polls and vote for Barack

Barack Obama [1]

When you listen to Barack Obama, when you really hear him, you witness a very rare thing. You witness a politician who has an ear for eloquence and a tongue dipped in the unvarnished truth

Oprah Winfrey [2]

Barack Obama to me, is a herald of the Messiah. Barack Obama is like the trumpet that alerts you something new, something better is on the way

Louis Farrakhan, Nation of Islam [3]

January 20th 2009 Barack Hussein Obama became the 44th president of the United States of America. Obama is the first president with Muslim roots and who sympathizes with the teachings of Islam. Such are his ties to Islam that many Muslims consider him to be a follower.

Muslim writer Asma Gull Hasan wrote in an article in Forbes entitled 'My Muslim President Obama', 'I have been part of more and more conversations with Muslims in which it was either offhandedly agreed that Obama is Muslim or enthusiastically blurted out. In commenting on our new president, 'I have to support my fellow Muslim brother,' would slip out of my mouth before I had a chance to think twice.' [4]

Nation of Islam leader Louis Farrakhan who heads up the Nation of Islam, an offshoot of Islam, also referred to Obama as a fellow brother in a 2008 message to his followers. 'I love that brother, and I want to see that brother successful. I don't want to say anything that would hurt that brother...' Farrakhan also said that when Obama talks 'the Messiah is absolutely speaking.' [5]

The Nation of Islam leader, who has been accused of black supremacy and anti-Semitism, kept quiet about his support for Obama during the 2008 presidential campaign. But that did not stop the connection between the two finding its way into the press. Obama's former church, the Trinity United Church of Christ, awarded the Nation of Islam leader the Trumpeter Award, saying that Farrakhan 'truly epitomized greatness.' [6]

This throws into question not only the legitimacy of Obama's former church but also exposes a relationship between them and the radical Nation of Islam movement. What kind of church would honor a man accused of racism and anti-Semitism? Indeed it was Farrakhan who said, 'The Jews don't like Farrakhan, so they call me Hitler. Well, that's a good name. Hitler was a very great man.' [7]

Furthermore, the church's pastor Reverend Jeremiah Wright, who claimed to have been Obama's close spiritual and political advisor and shaped the future president's worldview for more than 20 years, admitted that Obama possessed an 'Islamic background' and despite his conversion to Christianity had never abandoned his Muslim roots. [8]

The pastor said that he was like 'a second father' to Obama. If this is true then Jeremiah Wright should be quite an authority on Obama.

Ed Klein, author of *The Amateur: Barack Obama in the White House*, interviewed Jeremiah Wright and reveals how the future president's relationship with Wright went far beyond simply being a member at Trinity. According to Klein, 'Obama went to the Rev Wright at every stage of his career whenever things went wrong.' [9] Klein says that Wright was really a substitute father figure who guided Obama in the two major areas of his life, the first being Obama's identity and the second his political philosophy. 'Obama was steeped in Islam but knew nothing about Christianity,' Klein says. Klein asked Wright if he had been responsible for converting Obama from Islam to Christianity. Wright responded by saying that he made it easy for him to come to an understanding of who Jesus Christ is and not feel that he was turning his back on his Islamic friends and his Islamic traditions and his understanding of Islam. [10]

In fact, at Trinity it appears that Muslims are welcomed into membership without any need to change their faith. [11] Madeline Brooks, guest columnist for the Canada Free Press, writes that on a tip from a pastor she telephoned Trinity in February of 2010 to ask about requirements of membership. Brooks writes, 'the church receptionist transferred my call to the Director of Membership, who told me that baptism is optional and that Muslims who believe in the prophet Mohammed can be full members. In fact, she reassured me cheerfully, they have plenty of Muslim members.' [12]

If this is the case then it becomes easy to understand how Trinity felt able to give an award to the Nation of Islam leader Farrakhan and believed that he 'truly epitomized greatness.'

Despite the best efforts of the government controlled mainstream media to gloss over Obama's Islamic connections, the overwhelming evidence is there for anyone who wants to open their eyes and look past the mass of disinformation circulating concerning this. He attended a Muslim school in Indonesia [13] and studied the Quran.[14] His stepfather Lolo Soetoro was a Muslim.[15] He can recite the Muslim Arabic call to prayer in a first-rate accent and has commented that 'one of the prettiest sounds on earth at sunset' is the Muslim call to prayer.[16] He has referred to his 'Muslim faith' before being corrected 'your Christian faith' in an ABC News interview.[17] He bowed before the King of Saudi Arabia at a G20 Summit in 2009 which the Washington Times referred to as a 'shocking display of fealty to a foreign potentate.' The article went on to read, 'by bending over to show greater respect to Islam, the US president belittled the power and independence of the United States.' [18]

He has worn a ring for the last thirty years with the first tenet of the Islamic faith inscribed upon it, 'there is no god except Allah.' Egyptian-born Islamic scholar Mark A. Gabriel, Ph.D. and others confirmed this upon examination of photographs of the ring. Gabriel commented, 'there can be no doubt that someone wearing the inscription 'There is no god except Allah' has a very close connection to Islamic beliefs, the Islamic religion and Islamic society to which this statement is so strongly attached.' [19]

Obama has nominated a Muslim convert John Brennan as the new head of the Central Intelligence Agency. Ex-FBI agent John Guandolo says that Brennan is unfit to take charge of the CIA. He claims that US government officials based in Saudi Arabia during the time that Brennan served as CIA station chief in Riyadh between 1996 and 1999 'were direct witnesses to his growing relationships with individuals who work with the Saudi government and they witnessed his conversion to Islam.' [20]

But Brennan is not the only Muslim that Obama has working for him. According to an article that appeared in an Egyptian magazine six American Muslim leaders who work with the

Obama administration have ties with the radical Muslim Brotherhood. Although the Muslim Brotherhood is known to engage in political violence the White House has resisted naming them as a terrorist organization. Their stated aims are the introduction of Shariah law as the basis for controlling the affairs of state and society. Their creed states, 'Allah is our objective; the Quran is our law, the Prophet is our leader; Jihad is our way; and death for the sake of Allah is the highest of our aspirations.'

The Egyptian article names Arif Alikhan, assistant secretary of Homeland Security for policy development; Mohammed Elibiary, member of the Homeland Security Advisory Council; Rashad Hussain, U.S. special envoy to the Organization of the Islamic Conference; Salam al-Marayati, co-founder of the Muslim Public Affairs Council, or MPAC); Imam Mohamed Magid, president of the Islamic Society of North America, or ISNA; and Eboo Patel, a member of President Obama's Advisory Council on Faith-Based Neighborhood Partnerships. [21]

In further controversy Obama has been accused by many on the internet who claim that in 2006 he mocked the Sermon on the Mount and distorted Scripture. For instance, a simple Google search 'Obama mocks Christ' yields at least 1,890,000 results. Obama was speaking at the 2006 Call to Renewal conference. It has to be said that his comments are open to interpretation. However, James Dobson, psychologist and respected evangelical author commented, 'I think he's deliberately distorting the traditional understanding of the Bible to fit his own world view, his own confused theology.' [22]

Did Obama mock the Bible? If he did it is certainly cause for concern. But equally worrying is his apparent reverence for Islam. Obama describes Islam as a 'revealed' religion. 'I have known Islam on three continents before coming to the region where it was first revealed,' said Obama. Only Muslims speak about Islam in this way. A Bible-believing Christian would never describe Islam as a revealed religion. [23]

Then in 2008 Kenyan leader Raila Odinga claimed that he was a cousin of Barack Obama, that Obama's father was Odinga's maternal uncle.[24] Odinga is the former Prime Minister of Kenya who now shares leadership in a coalition government with President Mwai Kibaki. Odinga agreed upon re election to 'rewrite the Constitution of Kenya to recognize Shariah as the only true law sanctioned by the Holy Quran for Muslim declared religions.' [25] But when Odinga failed, according to ex-Odinga officials, he used tribal violence to regain the power he had lost. His followers went on a rampage. A mob numbering 2000 burned down approximately 800 churches and killed 1000 members of the Kikuyu tribe. In order to quell the unrest the Kenyan government stepped in and made Odinga Prime Minister and for all intents and purposes put him back into power.

Although the White House has denied the familial relationship between Obama and Odinga the connection between the two is unquestionable. An organization called 'Friends of Senator BO' (Barack Obama) donated $950,000 towards Odinga's election campaign.[26] Furthermore in 2006 Obama visited Kenya during which he campaigned on behalf of Odinga. The two travelled together throughout Kenya with Obama declaring, 'Kenyans are now yearning for change,' obviously referring to the change that Odinga would bring upon election. Obama had also previously met with Odinga in 2004, 2005 and 2006.[27]

The question has to be asked, why on earth would Obama back a man who agreed to implement Sharia Law upon re election? Is Obama really the person that the White House and media claim him to be?

Obama's Political Philosophy

As we have learned Obama was influenced for 20 years by his former pastor and father figure Jeremiah Wright and his politically driven black liberation theology church, the Trinity United Church of Christ. One piece of evidence highlighting the impact that the church had on Obama's political philosophy can be clearly seen by looking at the church's vision and mission statement.

As stated on their website's 10 point vision, Trinity is 'A congregation working towards ECONOMIC PARITY,' and their mission statement has a reference to 'God who is not pleased with America's economic mal-distribution!' [28]

Anthony B. Bradley, associate professor of theology and researcher for the 'Institute for the Study of Religion and Liberty', writes, 'the code language "economic parity" and references to "mal-distribution" is nothing more than channeling the twisted economic views of Karl Marx. Black Liberation theologians have explicitly stated a preference for Marxism as an ethical framework for the black church because Marxist thought is predicated on a system of oppressor class (whites) versus victim class (blacks).' [29]

Knowing this helps us to shape more of an understanding about the person of Obama. He is a man who is not only connected to Islam but one who has also sat for 20 years under the teachings of a pseudo-Christian theology intertwined with Marxist ideology.

But it was not Wright and his church that first introduced Obama to Marxist ideas. Obama himself in his book 'Dreams from my Father' refers to a man known only as 'Frank'. [30] Later upon release of the audio version of the book any references to Frank were removed altogether.

The man in question was Frank Marshall Davis. Frank was the young Obama's mentor throughout the 1970s. It was Obama's grandfather who introduced Davis to Obama who was seeking a mentor for his grandson. Davis was a full card-carrying Communist Party member. [31] Due to Davis' radical political antics he was placed on the Security Index of the federal government by the FBI. Davis wrote for Communist

171

publications The Chicago Star and Honolulu Record.[32] The Communist Davis was the man who indoctrinated Obama with his Marxist worldview during his formative years.

The late Manning Marable, prominent and lifelong black Marxist, confirmed Obama's Marxist connections writing, 'what makes Obama different is that he has also been a community organizer. He has read left literature, including my works, and he understands what socialism is. A lot of the people working with him are, indeed, socialists with backgrounds in the Communist Party or as independent Marxists.' [33]

It would come as no surprise then that Obama's new campaign slogan 'Forward' would be strongly associated with European Marxism. 19th and 20th century Communist and other left-wing publications are littered with this terminology. 'Forward' is the generic name of socialist publications – the German paper of the same name 'Vorwärts' (Forward), which backed the Russian Marxist economists, and Vladimir Lenin's Soviet publication 'Vpered', (Forward) to name but two. [34]

Cultural Marxism

However, Marxism has been on the rise in America well before Obama arrived on the scene. In 1923 an institute was set up at Frankfurt University in Germany by members of the Marxist Communist Party. It was called the Institute for Social Research and later became known as the Frankfurt School. After old Marxism was seen to have failed these new Marxists realized that it could only thrive and achieve its objective by moving through the cultural institutions and thus Cultural Marxism was born.

Italian Communist Antonia Gramsci wrote concerning the agenda of Cultural Marxism, 'the civilized world has been thoroughly saturated with Christianity for 2000 years. Any country grounded in Judeo-Christian values cannot be overthrown until those roots are cut. But to cut the roots – to change culture — a long march through the institutions is necessary. Only then will power fall into our laps like a ripened fruit.' [35]

For Cultural Marxism to take root it must breakdown cultural norms, specifically targeting Judeo-Christian values. It does this through the arts, through music, movies, soap operas and other television programming and advertising by introducing alternate or abnormal lifestyles as normal – by displaying immoral acts and immoral relationships as acceptable with little to no consequence, or through the glorification of violence, crime and murder. Today the entertainment industry has been hijacked by Cultural Marxism. It has become its most powerful advocate. This is psychological conditioning or brain washing as we discussed earlier. People are indoctrinated with Marxist ideology without even knowing it is happening. People today believe they are free thinkers. But it could not be further from the truth. They have become a product of the cultural engineers and like parrots they mimic their masters while arrogantly strutting about their cages as though they are free.

This cultural subversion by design leaves the masses bereft of any true beliefs or value system. The traditional family unit is destroyed. A vacuum is thus formed for Marxist ideology to fill and take root. Once rooted the people become reliant and subservient to the state – the ultimate aim of the Marxist agenda.

We do not have to look far to discover why Marxism harbors such hostility towards Christianity.

Karl Marx

Karl Marx (1818–1883) a Prussian-German philosopher and socialist, often called the 'Father of Communism' and writer of the Communist Manifesto, has been depicted as the founder of the greatest atheistic system in the world. One would conclude from this that Karl Marx therefore did not believe in God. The surprising truth however is that Karl Marx grew up in a Christian family and in his early years was actually a follower of Christ. Not only did Karl Marx write the Communist Manifesto, but also a book entitled 'The Union of the Faithful with Christ.' [36]

Marx wrote, 'through love of Christ we turn our hearts at the same time toward our brethren who are inwardly bound to us and for whom He gave Himself as sacrifice...' [37]

Again Marx writes, 'union with Christ could give an inner elevation, comfort in sorrow, calm trust, and a heart susceptible to human love, to everything noble and great, not for the sake of ambition and glory, but only for the sake of Christ.' [38]

On graduating from high school the following comments on Marx's graduation certificate under the heading of 'Religious Knowledge' read, 'his knowledge of the Christian faith and morals is fairly clear and well grounded...' [39]

After high school, however, something dramatic happened and Marx began to not only move away from his Christian faith but to denounce it and become an enemy of it. We do know that Marx joined an Illuminati organization known as the League of the Just in 1847. This group would heavily influence Marx and use him to penetrate the growing Socialist Labour movement for their own purposes in directing the course of Russia. It is possible that this group led Marx away from his Christian faith. [40]

Marx writes the following in a poem in which he confirms his aggressive agenda against God after his rejection of Christianity, 'I wish to avenge myself against the One who rules above.' [41]

In another poem Marx tragically describes his own spiritual condition. In 'The Pale Maiden' he refers to the biblical concepts of salvation, heaven and hell:

174

Thus Heaven I've forfeited,
I know it full well,
My soul, once true to God,
Is chosen for hell [42]

Then again Marx shows his anti-theistic agenda in his poem 'Human Pride.' Here we are also given a glimpse into the Antichrist spirit that had so gripped his soul:

With disdain I will throw my gauntlet
Full in the face of the world,
And see the collapse of this pygmy giant
Whose fall will not stifle my ardor.
Then will I wander godlike and victorious
Through the ruins of the world
And, giving my words an active force,
I will feel equal to the Creator. [43]

Marx's poem 'The Player' describes not only his spiritual descent into darkness but also the subsequent pact he made with the prince of darkness:

The hellish vapors rise and fill the brain,
Till I go mad and my heart is utterly changed.
See this sword?
The prince of darkness
Sold it to me.
For me he beats the time and gives the signs.
Ever more boldly I play the dance of death [44]

Karl Marx is not the man that history claims him to be. But more importantly then neither is Marxism. Marxism is a political ideology birthed out of a personal hatred for God. Marxism exists to overthrow morality, God and Christianity. What this reveals is that the political ideology of Marxism is merely a smokescreen to hide its true religious and Antichrist agenda. Much in the same way, although in reverse, Islam uses religion to shroud its true totalitarian socio-political Antichrist agenda.

These prevailing ideologies, along with Nazism, as we have already seen, embody the spirit of the Antichrist in this hour. Obama is both a product of Islam and Marxism, handpicked by the globalists, his skin color being the perfect distraction. As America and the world became caught up in the euphoria of the first ever black US president, were they blinded to what was really going on? Could it be that Obama is actually a puppet employed to take America ever closer into the nightmarish vision set out by the globalists?

Henry Kissinger – Bilderberger and key voice of the globalists – seems to confirm this. He gave his personal endorsement for Obama, saying 'he can give new impetus to American foreign policy partly because the reception of him is so extraordinary around the world. His task will be to develop an overall strategy for America in this period when, really, a new world order can be created. It's a great opportunity, it isn't just a crisis.' [45]

Obama's election solidified and advanced the globalist agenda. It established the perfect atmosphere for the rise of the Biblically prophesied Antichrist to enter onto the political world stage.

So it appears from the evidence that Obama might not be the Biblically orthodox Christian he and his propagandists claim. If this is true then he is a deceiver. Even his origins have been contested as false. Evidence abounds to suggest that Obama's birth certificate is a fabrication. If this was confirmed it would place his eligibility as president into question.[46] Has Obama, using the full repertoire of his communication skills, deceived the masses? If he has, then we should remember what the Bible says about the Antichrist. In like manner he will 'deceive the inhabitants of the earth' (Revelation 13:14).

Obama and his election are a shadow of things to come. Obama's celebrity style inauguration ceremony should have sent a chill down the spine of every person in America. Instead the chanting crowds, conditioned by hours of mindless entertainment, looked on spellbound as though a Hollywood star had just arrived for a movie premier.

The 'cult of personality' surrounding Barack Obama – disseminated through the controlled mainstream media – disturbingly shows how simple it will be for the Antichrist to arrive on the scene and be readily accepted by the masses. His policies do not interest people. As long as he is ushered in with celebrity hype, that is what really counts today.

The fact that the US constitution is held in total disregard – with many calling for it to be replaced altogether – shows just how far down the road to tyranny America has travelled. Louis Michael Seidman, a professor of constitutional law at Georgetown University, author of *On Constitutional Disobedience*, writes that the reason for America's economic crisis is 'our insistence on obedience to the Constitution, with all its archaic, idiosyncratic and downright evil provisions...we ought to try extricating ourselves from constitutional bondage so that we can give real freedom a chance.' [(47)]

This extrication from so called constitutional bondage has given rise to an American dictatorship. The most extreme kind of power is now in the hands of Barack Obama. If Obama wishes he can target his own citizens for assassination, without due process and far away from any battlefield. Obama holds 'Orwellian powers' to accuse, prosecute, judge and execute with zero transparency and zero accountability. The US Constitution states that no one may be deprived of life, liberty or property without due process of law. What Obama is doing is totally illegal and fundamentally contrary to the American constitution and way of life.

According to White House aides 'Terror Tuesday' is the weekly event the secret kill lists are proposed.[(48)] In September 2011 a drone strike in Yemen killed US citizens Anwar Awlaki and Samir Khan and two weeks later in another drone strike

16 year old Awlaki's American son Abdulrahman.[49] These executions were on foreign soil but according to US Attorney General Eric Holder the Obama administration believes that it can technically use military force to kill an American located within the United States too.[50] In January 2013 prominent American blogger Aaron Swartz, who was vocal in criticizing Obama's kill list, was found dead in his New York Apartment in an apparent suicide. His death prompted much speculation that executions on US soil had already begun.[51]

Under Obama, surveillance technology has risen to new heights. Police departments now deploy drones over American skies that were once used on the enemy in wars abroad. They also employ a state-of-art surveillance grid on the ground to monitor its citizens, installed without the knowledge of most Americans. 'Trapwire' as it is called picks up data from surveillance points every few seconds and instantaneously delivers it to a fortified central database.[52]

Obama now has full control over all water, all human and animal food, all transportation, all energy, all construction materials, all health resources, all farm equipment, all fertilizers, all fuels and much more. That's due to him signing Executive Order 13603 in March 2012. The Executive Order states that these powers are not merely to be claimed during war time or national emergency, but repeatedly states 'in peacetime and in times of national emergency' too.[53]

Despite the obvious signs to the contrary Obama has been likened to a kind of Christ figure. This is indicative of a dictatorship. One only has to think back to the days of the Roman Empire and Babylon where worship of the dictator was commonplace, or in recent history with Nazi Germany and Hitler's Messianic delusions, or today's worship of the Kim family in North Korea, to name but a few examples.

However, never before has a US president been alluded to in such messianic terms as now, with Barack Obama. The January

2013 edition of Newsweek's magazine front cover referred to Obama's second term as 'The Second Coming'.[54] A painting called 'Truth' on display at Boston's Bunker Hill Community College Art Gallery depicts Obama with arms outstretched in a crucified position, his head in downward pose and adorned with a crown of thorns.[55] Additionally, posters on sale at the Democratic National Convention displayed the praying face of Obama fading into an open Bible. The heading read 'Prophecy Fulfilled', with words explaining the Hebrew origin of Barack's name which means, 'flash of lightning.' [56] Not only that but T-shirts were on sale that used a verse from Psalm 110:1, 'the Lord said unto my Lord, 'Sit Thou at My right hand until I make Thine enemies Thy footstool.'" [57]

Calendars were also available. The month of August (Obama's birth month) had a photo of Obama and his short-form birth certificate with the words 'Heaven Sent' and the Bible verse John 3:16, 'God so loved the world that he gave his one and only Son, that whoever believes in him shall not perish but have eternal life.' [58]

Then in 2013 a YouTube video emerged of a young boy praying to Obama. The video immediately sparked controversy with people labeling it as blasphemous. The boy, called Stephen, prayed, 'Barack Obama, thank you for doing everything and all the kind stuff. Thank you for all the stuff that you helped us with. Thank you for taking the courage and responsibility for everything you have done for us. And God has given you a special power and you are going to handle it just fine. You are good, Barack Obama and you are great and when you get older, you will be able to do great things. Love, Stephen. Barack Obama!' [59]

One article that appeared in the Huffington Post read, 'Commentators have furiously weighed in, labeling the video blasphemous...' One commenter wrote, 'praying TO Barack Obama? Wonder how the Lord God Almighty is taking that...' while another said, 'idolatry. That sounds more like a prayer To Obama, not FOR him. How sad – and even sadder that you are proud of the poor kid doing this.' [60]

Fox News Radio reporter Todd Starnes even suggested that the boy was breaking one of the Ten Commandments, asking, 'what kind of parent would allow their child to blaspheme God?' [61]

The Huffington Post article further went on to note comments previously made by the Reverend Jesse Lee Peterson regarding the presidency of Obama. Peterson said, 'President Obama is the most divisive man to ever occupy the White House – period! Yet, 95 percent of black Americans worship him as if he's the messiah.' [62]

The messianic and religious fervor surrounding the cult of Obama is really quite extraordinary and serves to show the prophetic age in which we are living.

During the run-up to Obama's election Jamie Foxx, Oscar-winning actor, referred to Obama as 'our lord and savior.' Foxx said, 'it's like church over here. It's like church in here. First of all, give an honor to God and our lord and savior Barack Obama. Barack Obama.' [63] Foxx is not the only person that has deified Obama. Barbara A Thompson, a Florida professor, believes that Obama, or Apostle Barack as she calls him, has been sent to create 'heaven here on earth.' Claiming that she was given the message in a dream, Thompson believes that Obama needed re-election so he could continue to accomplish his work to perfect political union here on earth. [64]

It is interesting to note here that the extravagant stage created for Obama's 2008 acceptance speech bizarrely resembled the famed Pergamon Altar of Zeus, known in the Bible as the seat where Satan dwells or the Seat of Satan, as we discussed earlier. This is the Altar that Hitler had built as an exact replica and from which he announced his final solution to the Jewish question. This is the same Altar that the current European Union president gave his first speech of Europe in 2010 in which he said that powerful forces were driving them. Is this coincidental? Or are the same demonic forces and personalities which brought Hitler to power back in 1933 orchestrating events today?

Obama is being used, just as the Bible says that the Antichrist will be used. The Antichrist will be the ultimate tool of the globalist puppet masters. He will be created by them to do their bidding. His election to office will be celebrity style. It will be completely false and played out like a Hollywood blockbuster movie, with televised special effects and signs to deceive the masses, who will be whipped up into a media frenzy, weeping for joy at the coming of their 'savior'. 'The coming [of...the antichrist]...will be attended by great power and with all sorts of [pretended] miracles and signs and delusive marvels – [all of them] lying wonders – And by unlimited seduction to evil...' 2 Thessalonians 2:9-10 (AMP).

It was not too long ago that Hitler, who dabbled heavily in satanic practices, became possessed by the spirit of the Antichrist. But could it really happen again today? Could a high ranking politician become possessed with this spirit and bring about the complete fulfillment of the prophesied Antichrist?

One only needs to create the right atmosphere. Firstly Christianity must be sidelined. As the Communist Gramsci said, 'any country grounded in Judeo-Christian values cannot be overthrown until those roots are cut.' Secondly, satanic practices must be purposely engaged in.

This is gathering pace today. We are seeing a serious marginalization of Biblical Christianity right across the Western world. This is not by chance but according to an orchestrated plan. We are seeing more and more persecution against Christian people and evidence of an angry spirit that wishes to stifle and shut the mouths of those professing godly and moral values.

Once Christianity is stifled ideologies such as Nazism, Islam and Marxism gain a foothold which in turn opens the doorway for Satan to come and dwell.

But what of satanic practices?

Is there any evidence to suggest that, just like Hitler, politicians are engaging in such wicked activities today?

Chapter 11

The Secret Satanic Practices of the Global Elite

The very word "secrecy" is repugnant in a free and open society; and we are as a people inherently and historically opposed to secret societies, to secret oaths and secret proceedings

John F Kennedy [1]

All secret, oath-bound political parties are dangerous to any nation

Ulysses S. Grant, 18th President of the United States

Cursed is every man who makes a god or something to look like a god, the work of the hands of the able workman, and sets it up in secret. It is hated by the Lord

Deuteronomy 27:15 (NLV)

Outside the city are the dogs. They are people who follow witchcraft and those who do sex sins and those who kill other people and those who worship false gods and those who like lies and tell them

Revelation 22:15 (NLV)

The prophesied Antichrist world system is being advanced through many processes. One of those ways is through the secret meetings of the elites. We have already looked at the secretive

Bilderberg Group which brings together world leaders, royalty and other people of influence in yearly pseudo-parliamentary type gatherings. Operating outside of the system of democracy they appoint men into key leadership roles and plot the next course of events that will bring their vision of the world one step closer into being.

But besides Bilderberg the elite gather in other secretive groups and societies. Unlike Bilderberg however these groups are overtly evil in origin and practice. Just as Hitler engaged with the dark forces of hell in order to achieve his objective for global domination, so too do the elites. The fact that they participate in such sinister practices reveals one thing. In order to gain global control of the planet one must first tap into the spiritual powers of darkness.

This is because Satan currently has jurisdiction over our planet. This took place at the time of the fall, when Adam was deceived by Satan and lost his authority over the earth. John 12:31 says that Satan is the 'ruler of this world', and again in 2 Corinthians 4:4 he is called the 'god of this world', and in Ephesians 2:2 Satan is referred to as 'the prince of the power of the air.' In Ephesians 6:12 we read that our struggle is against the powers of this dark world and the spiritual forces of evil in the heavenly realm.

The kinds of rule which Satan works in order to lure men into serving him is perfectly illustrated in the temptations of Christ. When Jesus was tested in the wilderness Satan took him to a high mountain and showed him all the kingdoms of the world and their splendor. Satan said, 'all this I will give you if you will bow down and worship me.' What Satan was offering to Jesus here was the Antichrist system that would govern the entire planet under a Satanic dictatorship – Satanic because Jesus would have become subservient to Satan.

Jesus answered, 'Worship the Lord your God and serve him only.' (Matthew 4:10) Although Satan had the authority to offer

Jesus the earth, for the transaction to take place Jesus had to first bow down and worship Satan. This is the mistake that Adam and Eve made on that fateful day at the beginning of time. Satan told them that if they were to eat from the forbidden fruit they would become like God (Genesis 3). They believed him, and in so doing gave Satan authority.

Importantly when man does not bow, Satan has NO power.

This moment in Christ's life reveals some vital and salient points. Firstly, in order to obtain global control a person must first bow down and worship Satan. Where the devil failed with Christ because of His sinless nature he will succeed with man because of his corrupt nature.

Secondly, world power is as much a spiritual position as it is a political one. This is why the globalists are drawn to and bow down to Satanic powers. Satan beckons them, 'bow to me and I'll give you the world. You will become like God.' By worshipping Satan they receive in return the spiritual mantle, albeit temporary, that will enable them to control the entire planet. This will ultimately fulfill the end-time prophecy when the Antichrist takes his position.

This is why the tyrants of old believed themselves to be gods. This is particularly notable in ancient Babylon where kings like Nebuchadnezzar built a great golden statue of himself which the people worshipped by decree; or in ancient Egypt where the Pharaohs were considered to be an incarnation of the god Horus or later Isis; or in ancient Rome where the Roman emperor was worshipped as a god.

In more recent times it is interesting to note that Saddam Hussein built giant statues and displayed massive images of himself when he ruled modern day Babylon. In fact he also attempted to rebuild the Great Walls of Babylon and was convinced that he was the reincarnation of Nebuchadnezzar.

It was this same spirit that lay behind Karl Marx's words when he felt compelled to say, 'I wander Godlike and victorious...I feel equal to the Creator.'

Hitler's messiah complex was borne out of this bowing to Satan, and finally the cult of personality surrounding Barack Obama is a manifestation of this. Cleverly orchestrated through the controlled mainstream media, Obama has been exalted to an otherworldly position. This is evidenced particularly throughout his 2008 campaign for presidency as we saw earlier.

In the following examples we will see that without question the elites today are bowing down to Satanic powers in order to achieve their quest for global control of the planet.

But before we do it is worth mentioning here that while some globalists might recognize that it is Satan to whom they bow, others do not. The Scriptures declare, 'Satan himself transforms himself into an angel of light.' (2 Corinthians 11:14 NKJV) These people have been sorely deceived and following after their own evil desires have succumbed to the temptation for power.

Bohemian Grove

Every July deep in the redwood forests of San Franscisco some of the world's most powerful men meet together. This secret gathering of the global elite is known as Bohemian Grove. Over the years the Bohemian Grove has played host to some of the most influential politicians in history. Former attendees include Presidents Ronald Reagan, Richard Nixon, George W Bush and his father Bush Senior and Jimmy Carter. [2] Also former British Prime Minister John Major and Prince Philip have attended.[3] Others have included Donald Rumsfeld, Newt Gingrich, German Chancellor Helmut Schmidt, Henry Kissinger, Alan Greenspan, David Rockefeller and Colin Powell, media presidents from CNN, Associated Press, executives from Time-Warner[4], military contractors Lockheed Martin, the Federal Reserve Bank, Halliburton and other powerful groups.

The strictly men-only Bohemian Grove founded in 1872 is today replete with restaurants, bars, stages and lodges. It caters for around 2000 plus members making it a much bigger event than Bilderberg. However, what makes it stand out from Bilderberg is not the size, but rather the unorthodox activities reported by ex-employees or by those who have managed to sneak into the heavily guarded event.

The reported immoral and hedonistic antics at the Grove reveal the true nature of this annual gathering, with stories of excessive alcoholic drinking, wild parties, male prostitution and a male porn star on site.[5] In 1999 the National Archives released for the first time a 1971 taped Oval Office conversation where President Richard Nixon said, 'the Bohemian Grove, which I attend from time to time...It is the most faggy g** d***** thing you could ever imagine with that San Francisco crowd. I can't shake hands with anybody from San Francisco.' [6]

As the Grove is strictly men-only female prostitutes are apparently flown in from around the world and made available in the neighboring town.[7] Furthermore sexually perverse entertainment has also been alleged, including bestiality, lesbian sex, incest and even a 'Necrophilia' theme room.[8]

Bohemian Grove is a Satanic manifestation of what the globalists are truly about. The activities of the 'Grovers' or 'Bohos' as they are called reveal the utter darkness behind what drives their spiritual quest for world hegemony. What takes place at Bohemian Grove serves to show how the Antichrist and his system are being established today.

In 2000 radio talk show host and documentary film maker Alex Jones and TV producer and author Mike Hanson teamed up with British television station Channel 4 to infiltrate the Grove. Jones and Hanson were successful and became the first people to secretly film the ritualistic ceremony known as 'The Cremation of Care' which takes place annually at the event.

At the site a 40ft stone owl idol stands ominously amongst the redwood trees across from a lake where the male attendees look on as a ceremony takes place after darkness has fallen upon the forest. A bound body is drawn on a wagon by what Jones describes as 'someone dressed like the Grim Reaper' with a group of priests carrying torches of fire. Jones writes that as this happened all was silent except for the cries of some of the old men who shouted, 'burn that b*****d! Kill him! That's what he deserves!' Jones said he was uncertain whether the body used in the ceremony was real or an effigy. Moments later, the same 'grim reaper' figure travelled by boat across the lake with the sacrificial body to where a High Priest stood at the foot of the great owl. The bound body begging for its life over the loud speaker system was shown no mercy. Then the owl commanded the priests to burn the body which is known in the ceremony as 'Dull Care'. As the body continued to beg for mercy small metal crosses dotted along the lake edge burst into flames.[9]

Jones writes, 'so, I was there witnessing something right out of the medieval painter Hieronymus Bosch's Visions of Hell: burning metal crosses, priests in red and black robes with the high priest in a silver robe with a red cape, a burning body screaming in pain, a giant stone great-horned owl, world leaders, bankers, media and the head of academia engaged in these activities. It was total insanity.'[10]

The High Priest spoke in a deep and resonating voice to the globalists who watched from across the lake. The deeply occultic language of the High Priest was recorded by Jones' concealed camera and further reveals the Satanic nature of the ceremony. (The full transcript can be read at the end of this chapter.)

Alex Jones is not the only person to have snuck into the elitist club. Philip Weiss spent seven days posing as a guest back in 1989. Weiss who also witnessed the 'Cremation of Care' concurs with Jones' description of what he saw and the video footage captured.

'The cremation took place at the man-made lake that is the center of a lot of Grove social activity. At 9:15 p.m. a procession of priests carrying the crypt of Mr. Dull Care came out of the trees on the east side, along the Grove's chief thoroughfare, River Road. They wore bright red, blue and orange hooded robes that might have been designed for the Ku Klux Klan by Marimekko. When they reached the water, they extinguished their torches. At this point some hamadryads (tree spirits) and another priest or two appeared at the base of the main owl shrine, a 40-foot-tall, moss-covered statue of stone and steel at the south end of the lake, and sang songs about Care. They told of how a man's heart is divided between "reality" and "fantasy," how it is necessary to escape to another world of fellowship among men. Vaguely homosexual undertones suffused this spectacle, as they do much of ritualized life in the Grove. The main priest wore a pink-and-green satin costume, while a hamadryad appeared before a redwood in a gold spangled bodysuit dripping with rhinestones. They spoke of "fairy unguents" that would free men to pursue warm fellowship, and I was reminded of something Herman Wouk wrote about the Grove: "Men can decently love each other; they always have, our women never quite understand." Then the crypt of Care was poled slowly down the lake by a black-robed figure in a black gondola, accompanied by a great deal of special effects smoke. Just as the priests set out to torch the crypt, a red light appeared high in a redwood and large speakers in the forest amplified the cackling voice of Care: "Fools! When will ye learn that me ye cannot slay? Year after year ye burn me in this Grove.... But when again ye turn your feet toward the marketplace, am I not waiting for you, as of old?" With that, Care spat upon the fires, extinguishing them. The priests turned in desperation to the owl. "Oh thou, great symbol of all mortal wisdom, Owl of Bohemia ... grant us thy counsel!" [11]

In 2005 Chris Jones, an employee at the Grove, captured daylight video footage of the owl idol and also obtained footage of effigies and stole a membership list.[12] Jones also confirmed the homosexual activity citing that on numerous occasions he was propositioned for sex by several of the so called 'Grovers'. Then in 2009 Vanity Fair reporter Alex Shoumatoff was arrested for entering the Grove. In an article for the magazine Shoumatoff listed events from a 2008 program including the 'Cremation of Care' ceremony. The entry read, 'Saturday, July 12, 9:15 p.m – Owl Shrine – Cremation of Care. Come join us as we raise the battle banners in the name of beauty, truth, peace and fellowship. Oh, Beauty's Vassals, let us together seek the counsel of the Great Owl of Bohemia so that we may rediscover the wisdom needed to banish Dull Care once again! 'Hail, Fellowship's Eternal Flame!'" [13]

Then in March 2013 former UK Prime Minister Tony Blair was linked to the secretive gathering when a computer hacker obtained personal emails from former Secretary of State Colin Powell. According to Russia Today, Andrew Knight News Corp executive allegedly sent an email to Powell requesting him to ask Blair to attend Bohemian Grove in 2012.

The email stated, 'Dear Colin...Might you be able gently/firmly to point out to Tony that you rank the Bohemia Middle Weekend in your diary before allowing any other duties to get in the way?! Lack of exposure suggests that Tony has not yet got his priorities straight...Warm best – Andrew' [14] The importance the globalists place on attending this event is clear.

That the elite meet together annually at Bohemian Grove and attend a macabre ceremony to banish their cares involving incantations, high priests, a gigantic stone owl idol and the burning of a human sacrifice effigy is disturbing to say the least – not to mention the drunkenness, debauchery and sexual perversions that are alleged to go on inside the Grove. As an aside we should understand here that this banishing of oneself from care is an attempt by the globalists to rid themselves from the guilt within. This is a demonic substitute for the real thing. Only Christ can banish care! 1 Peter 5:7 tells us plainly, because God cares for us we must cast all our cares upon him.

But it gets worse. What is possibly more shocking is the imagery used on the 'Cremation of Care' program that Alex Jones and Mike Hanson obtained when they gate crashed the event back in 2000. The program featured the owl idol with the burning sacrifice of an infant at its feet. Although the image used was likely photoshopped and not a real baby it serves to show how morally destitute and deceived are those who attend the Grove. Who in their right mind would feel comfortable with attending a ceremonial event depicting infant sacrifice on its program cover?

The bible tells us what kind of people would go along with this. The Scriptures prophetically say that 'in the latter times some will abandon the faith and follow deceiving spirits and things taught by demons.' Such teachings it says 'come through hypocritical liars, whose consciences have been seared as with a hot iron.' (1 Timothy 4:1-2) Another version translates it, 'their consciences are dead.' (NLT) This is what the global elite have done. They have abandoned the faith upon which the western world was once built. They have followed after deceptive spirits and things taught by demons. Their consciences have been seared.

By engaging in this mock sacrificial ceremony the global elite are sanctioning the ancient and ritualistic act of infant sacrifice, the kind that was active in ancient Babylon. As shocking as this may seem, in many ways it should come as no surprise that the elite busy themselves with such wicked behavior. Does the Bible not predict that the Antichrist ruler and his religious henchman the False Prophet will reign over the earth? How else will they surface and rise to power? They will not just arrive on the scene, out of the blue so to speak, without having been first groomed from a place of utter darkness and contempt. They will be the product of a political and religious system that long ago abandoned the truth of the Judeo-Christian faith in a Holy God, and one that has bowed down to and embraced the lord of darkness, Satan himself.

Jones had wondered if the body used during the 'Cremation of

191

Care' ceremony was real or an effigy. It is not possible to know what he witnessed being sacrificed on that night in July 2000. However, Jones had every good reason to wonder.

Cathy O'Brien a former mind control abuse victim reveals her experiences at the Bohemian Grove in the disturbing book *Trance Formation of America – The True Life Story of a CIA Mind Control Slave*. According to O'Brien her mission was to take part in porn being filmed at the Grove and to entertain the guests in the live sex rooms. According to O'Brien's testimony real ritual sacrifice at the Grove has taken place before. O'Brien writes:

'As an effective means of control to ensure undetected proliferation of their perverse indulgences, slaves such as myself were subjected to ritualistic trauma. I knew each breath I took could be my last, as the threat of death lurked in every shadow. Slaves of advancing age or with failing programming were sacrificially murdered "at random" in the wooded grounds of Bohemian Grove, and I felt it was "simply a matter of time until it would be me". Rituals were held at a giant, concrete owl monument on the banks of...the...River.

My own threat of death was instilled when I witnessed the sacrificial death of a young, dark-haired victim at which time I was instructed to perform sexually "as though my life depended upon it". I was told, "...the next sacrifice victim could be you. Anytime when you least expect it, the owl will consume you. Prepare yourself, and stay prepared." Being "prepared" equated to being totally suggestible, i.e., "on my toes" awaiting their command.'" [15]

Bohemia's Owl

The owl deity is central to the Bohemian Grove. In fact it is the emblem of their Bohemian Club, adorning the sides of the shuttle buses that ferry members and guests throughout the complex. Members too wear an owl ring upon their finger with the Grove's motto, 'Weaving Spiders Come Not Here', a reference to leaving all business dealings outside the Grove. The owl can be seen set into a wall on Taylor Street, San Francisco, California, where the club's headquarters are based.

Owl symbolism is not only unique to the Bohemian Club though and can be seen in other places too. It has also found its way onto the one dollar bill. Next to the large '1' on the upper right of the bill a tiny owl can be seen hidden in amongst the design. We will discuss further hidden messages within the one dollar bill later. The original National Press Club emblem also featured an owl. It was at a National Press Club speech that David Rockefeller bragged about his family conspiring with others around the world to build a more integrated global political and economic structure. The owl also featured heavily in the Harry Potter fantasy novels and movie franchise. The books chronicle the adventures of Harry Potter at Hogwarts School of Witchcraft and Wizardry. In fact the so called Wizarding Examinations authority in the series administers a test known as O.W.L – Ordinary Wizarding Level. Finally the original insignia of the Bavarian Illuminati included the Roman goddess, the Owl of Minerva, within its design.

But why the owl? In his book *Bohemian Grove: Cult of Conspiracy,* Mike Hanson notes the significance of the owl in an interview between radio host Alex Jones and occult expert Texe Marrs. Marrs quotes from *The Woman's Dictionary of Symbols and Sacred Objects* by Barbara Walker. 'The wise owl appears with witches at Halloween, the Celtic feast of the Dead. It has a past association...with many forms of the Chrome Goddess. Also it is associated with Lilith, Athena, Minerva, and the owl-eyed Goddess, Marie...[These goddesses] often were said to take the owl's shape as their own...the owl was known as a bird of death...to the Babylonians, the owls (the hooting owls) were ghosts of women who died in childbirth, calling for their offspring...In medieval times the owl was sometimes called the Night Hag, like the daughters of Lilith who were possessed by demonic succubi [a female spirit]. Female spirits with owl wings were feared as potential kidnappers of infants.' [16]

As we can see owl symbolism has dark roots. Traditionally it is connected with witchcraft, the occult, demon spirits and its origins can be traced right back to the goddesses of ancient Babylon itself. This is the stone idol that features at Bohemian Grove – a Babylonian owl deity. In Babylon there were many gods, but one that fits the description of the Bohemian owl is the Babylonian goddess known as Lilith. *The ABC of Witchcraft* by Doreen Valiente lists Lilith as a 'patroness of witches'. Valiente describes Lilith as 'the enticing sorceress, the beautiful vampire, the femme fatale. Her loveliness is more than human; but her beauty has one strange blemish. Her feet are great claws, like those of a giant bird of prey.'

A Mesopotamian terracotta plaque that depicts a nude goddess is displayed in London's British Museum. The relief is known as the 'Queen of the Night'. Dating from the old Babylonian period the nude goddess is winged, with the feet of a bird of prey. She is flanked by twin owls. Many consider this to be a depiction of the goddess Lilith.

More importantly though, let us take a look at what the Bible has to say concerning the identity of the Bohemian owl.

Firstly it is noteworthy that the Bible lists the owl as an abomination among the birds. 'And these you shall regard as an abomination among the birds...the short-eared owl...the little owl, the fisher owl, and the screech owl; the white owl...' Leviticus 11:13-18 (NKJV)

But there is more. The book of Isaiah offers some important insights regarding the meaning of the owl. The owl is mentioned in a prophecy concerning the future judgment of the nations.

In chapter 34 we read that the land has been laid waste because of the abominable practices of the people there. It reads, 'the desert owl and screech owl will possess it; the great owl...will nest there." (Isaiah 34:11 NIV) Further clues of the owl's identity can be found when cross referencing this verse with an apocalyptic proclamation to be found in the book of Revelation: 'With a mighty voice he shouted: 'Fallen! Fallen is Babylon the Great!' She has become a dwelling for demons and a haunt for every impure spirit, a haunt for every unclean bird, a haunt for every unclean and detestable animal.' (Revelation 18:2) In Revelation we can see that the owl, or unclean bird, is synonymous with demons and detestable things.

Returning to the prophecy of Isaiah the identity of the owl becomes clearer especially when cross referencing these verses with other Bible translations. We read in verse 14, 'the screech owl also shall rest there, and find for herself a place of rest.' (KJV) Other translations render it, 'And demons and monsters shall meet, and the hairy ones shall cry out one to another.' (Douay-Rheims Bible) Or again, 'the night-monster shall settle there, and shall find her a place of rest.' (ASV) The Message Bible reads, 'the night-demon Lilith, evil and rapacious, will establish permanent quarters. Scavenging carrion birds will breed and brood, infestations of ominous evil.' Finally the Orthodox Jewish Bible renders the verse, 'and lilit (night creature) dwells there and finds for itself a mano'ach (place of rest).'

The commentary from Barnes' Notes on the Bible helps us to understand more: 'the screech-owl – 'Night-monster.' The word properly denotes a night-specter – a creature of Jewish superstition. The rabbis describe it in the form of a female elegantly dressed that lay in wait for children at night – either to carry them off, or to murder them.' And *Gill's Exposition of the Entire Bible* comments, 'by the name "Lilith", it appears to be a night bird, which flies and is heard in the night. The Jews call a she demon by this name, which, they say has a human face, and has wings, and destroys children as soon as they are born.'

The Scriptures give a clear definition of what the screech owl means. It is not a literal owl but a metaphor for an evil spirit, a night monster, a night creature, a female demon called Lilith. The Scriptures describe perfectly the Bohemian owl. The Bohemian owl is worshipped at night and is a symbolic (or literal) night murderer of infants, new born babies and adults.

The Bible says that those who worship idols become like them (Psalm 115:8). Hosea 9:10 says, 'they consecrated themselves to that shameful idol and became as vile as the thing they loved.'

The globalists have and continue to tragically fulfill Scripture with exact precision.

Is it really any wonder that as politicians worship at the feet of the demon child killer 53 million babies have been brutally murdered in America since 1973 [17], and between 1968 and 2003 nearly 6 million in Britain? [18] In the name of abortion the sadistic killing of the innocent and defenseless has been sold to the masses through clever marketing strategies. What can only be described as a deplorable and sickening act has become a morally acceptable and normal practice. This is yet another example of mind-manipulating propaganda techniques employed through the mass media. So conditioned has the populace become that now experts are confidently beginning to take this genocide to the next level.

An article in the Journal of Medical Ethics claimed in 2012 that newborn babies are not 'actual persons' and do not have a 'moral right to life' and parents should be able to have their child killed when it is born.[19] Furthermore John Holdron, the senior advisor to President Obama on science and technology has openly acknowledged that he has been influenced by Geochemist Harrison Brown. In 1986 Holdren co-edited the book *Earth and the Human Future: Essays in Honor of Harrison Brown*.[20] Brown advocated the use of government-mandated eugenics to prevent overpopulation. Brown who referred to humans as 'a pulsating mass of maggots' wrote concerning a solution to overpopulation, 'all excess children could be disposed of much as excess puppies and kittens are disposed of at the present time.' [21] In 2007 Holdren referred to Brown as one of his 'several late mentors' to whom he was thankful for 'insight and inspiration.'

It is the acceptance of abortion by the manipulated masses that has led to this next disturbing phase in eugenics. The question is how many times will the 'experts' redefine who has the 'moral right to life'?

It is also worth remembering that in the Old Testament the god known as Molech was worshipped by sacrificing children in the fire. The Lord God strictly forbids this practice. 'and you shall not let any of your descendants pass through the fire to Molech, nor shall you profane the name of your God: I am the Lord.' (Leviticus 18:21 NKJV) Again the Lord God says, 'I will cut him off from his people, and all who prostitute themselves with him to commit harlotry with Molech.'" (Leviticus 20:5 NKJV). What does this verse mean concerning our leaders today? Has God cut them off for their acceptance of these wicked practices?

The High Priest of Bohemian Grove honors Babylon and Tyre during the incantation. Babylon and Tyre were places where Baal worship was practiced. Baal worship involved human sacrifice, orgies, prostitution, sexually perverse behavior and the worship of nature. According to reports this is the kind of activity that goes on at the Grove.

Remember that for the early Christians Rome was 'Babylon'. Babylon to them was a metaphor for every kind of abomination that was manifesting itself in Rome. Just as the Bible predicted, the Roman Empire with all the abominations of Babylon, is once again being restored in these last days. Through Bohemian Grove the prophecy is being fulfilled now. Even the name Bohemia is prophetically linked to the Holy Roman Empire – Bohemia being an historic kingdom within central Europe's Holy Roman Empire.

Finally the Bohemian Grove's motto 'Weaving Spiders Come Not Here' is a reference to leaving business dealings outside the camp. However, this is not adhered to as is evidenced by one particularly disturbing occasion that happened at the Grove some decades ago. In September of 1942 a planning meeting for the Manhattan Project took place there. This project was for the research and development that led to the creation of the first atomic bomb. [22] The Manhattan Project was led principally by the United States with the help of the United Kingdom and Canada. Just three years after the Bohemian Grove meeting on 6th August 1945 the first bomb was dropped over Hiroshima, Japan killing approximately 80,000 people and injuring a further 70,000. Three days later the second bomb was dropped over Nagasaki, Japan. 35,000 were killed and 60,000 injured. One has to question what other evil events have been plotted there and if Armageddon will be hatched at Bohemian Grove.

What further evidence do we need to realize that great evil dwells at the Bohemian Grove? The atomic bomb was birthed out of there – two weapons of mass destruction that caused utter devastation and such terrible loss of life. But then the globalists, true to Scripture, were behaving according to the requirements of the owl deity that they worship – principally human sacrifice. No wonder the first two commandments that God gave to mankind through Moses were to worship the one true God and serve Him only! He was trying to protect His people. Look at what happens when His laws are disregarded.

Skull and Bones

Skull and Bones is a society shrouded in the utmost secrecy. Founded in 1832 at Yale University, New Haven, Connecticut by William Huntington Russell and Alphonso Taft. The society continues at Yale to this day. The prestigious Yale University has educated many US presidents and government officials. The Boston Globe summed up the influence of Yale, 'if there's one school that can lay claim to educating the nation's top national leaders over the past three decades, it's Yale.' [23]

Notable Yale graduates have been William Howard Taft, Gerald Ford, Prescott Bush, George H.W. Bush, George W. Bush, Bill and Hilary Clinton, John Kerry, Dick Cheney, Joe Lieberman and others.

It is no coincidence that Skull and Bones operates out of a university that educates those who later move into positions of great power. The hall was built in three stages over a period between 1856 and 1911. It is a large imposing windowless stone structure with Neo-Gothic towers and a Greco-Egyptian style facade. A massive triple padlocked iron door protects the secrets hidden inside this building otherwise known as the 'tomb'. But that didn't stop a group of Yale students breaking in on the night of September 29th 1876. They documented everything they saw. An old pamphlet describing the break-in reads, 'as long as Bones shall exist the night of September 29th (1876) will be to its members the anniversary of the occasion when their temple was invaded by neutrals, their rarest memorabilia confiscated and their most sacred secrets unveiled to the eyes of the uninitiated.' [24]

Inside the so-called tomb is a sacred room named 322. Above the door reads, 'who was the fool, who the wise man, beggar or king? Whether poor or rich, all's the same in death.' The slogan though does not appear in English but the German language. Surrounded by Masonic symbols the text can be traced back to the Bavarian Illuminati of the 1700s. Like Skull and Bones they also used skeletal remains in their rituals. Bavaria, located in Germany, is one of the oldest states in Europe. In the 17th century, the Duke of Bavaria became Prince-elector of the Holy Roman Empire of the German Nation. It is of prophetic significance that Skull and Bones was born out of The Holy Roman Empire of the German Nation.

The pamphlet describes the walls of the tomb, 'The walls are adorned with pictures of the founders of Bones at Yale and of the members of the Society in Germany when the Chapter was established here in 1832...Bones is a chapter of a corps in a German University. It should properly be called, not Skull & Bones Society but Skull & Bones Chapter. General R------ (Russell), its founder, was in Germany before Senior Year and formed a warm friendship with a leading member of a German society. He brought back with him to college, authority to found a chapter here. Thus was Bones founded.' [25]

In Nuremburg, Germany the altar room of a Masonic lodge offers the perfect example of the use of bones within Freemasonry too. Down an aisle of hanging skeletons a coffin is surmounted with a skull and crossbones – just like the official Skull and Bones emblem. [26]

It is a chilling thought to remember here that Adolf Hitler, fascinated with the occultic Thule Society, of which its founder Rudolf Von Sebottendorff was an initiate of Freemasonry, used the skull and crossbones insignia (the Totenkopf, German for "dead man's head") on the Nazi SS peaked caps and elsewhere. Was the Nazi idea to use the skull and crossbones inspired by similar German secret orders on which the Yale fraternity was based?

The use of bones in rituals is widespread amongst secret societies, witchcraft and the voodoo religions too. It is not unique to Skull and Bones which serves to show the true nature and root of this secret group. Sarah Lawless author and a practitioner of witchcraft describes the meaning of bones in paganism:

'Bones are a type of fetish. A fetish is "an object regarded with awe as being the embodiment or habitation of a potent spirit or as having magical potency". The word fetish originates from the French fétiche which stems from the Portuguese word feitiço meaning "charm" or "sorcery"... Skulls and bones have an appeal to witches who perform spirit work and are a necessary and simple way to connect with spirits of the dead and of animals. Working with bones is not just for necromancers and black magicians. Practitioners who work with bones are a wide range of healers, diviners, shapeshifters, rootworkers, witches, shamans, druids, and pagans.' [27]

The Odd Fellows secret society, also linked to Freemasonry, offers another example of the use of bones. In 2001 Paul Wallace was repairing some overloaded circuits in an old brick building belonging to the Warrington Lodge fraternity, when he came across a small door in the wall. On further investigation Wallace discovered a black wooden box. To his surprise inside the box were human remains. Wallace said, 'it was like a Dracula movie...The top of the skull was covered, but you could see the rib cage and the sinew.' But this was not an isolated incident. Skeletons like the one found by Wallace have been found nationwide in Odd Fellows lodges. [28]

With death being the central theme surrounding Skull and Bones this is no ordinary fraternity. In fact their morbid obsession has led it to acquire the skulls of the famous deceased.

Reported to reside in the Skull and Bones 'tomb' is the skull of Geronimo, the Apache leader who fought against US expansion into the Apache tribal lands. A letter written in 1918 by one of the society members reads, 'the skull of the worthy Geronimo the Terrible...exhumed from its tomb at Fort Sill by your club... is now safe inside the tomb and bone together with his well worn femurs, bit and saddle horn.' [29]

This skull was allegedly stolen by none other than the grandfather of George W. Bush who was a member of the secret fraternity. In 2009 the great-grandson of Geronimo filed a lawsuit against Skull and Bones claiming that its members stole the remains and have kept them ever since. [30]

Members join by invitation only and are aptly known as Bonesmen. The exclusive society admits just 15 Yale seniors each year. Entry into the Order involves Satanic initiation rites which involve the confession of sexual secrets, the kissing of a skull and the shouting of sexual obscenities. Members take a vow of secrecy concerning the Order and are given a secret name.

Journalist Ron Rosenbaum and former Yale classmate of George W. Bush became the first person to secretly witness and film the initiation ceremony. Rosenbaum who lived close to the 'tomb' said, 'I had passed it all the time. And during the initiation rites, you could hear strange cries and whispers coming from the Skull and Bones tomb.'[31] Rosenbaum described some of what he caught on video. 'A woman holds a knife and pretends to slash the throat of another person lying down before them, and there's screaming and yelling at the neophytes.'[32] The name neophyte is also used in Freemasonry to describe its initiates.[33][34]

Rosenbaum also obtained a dossier on the bones rituals of 1940 that read, 'new man placed in coffin – carried into central part of the building. New man chanted over and 'reborn' into society. Removed from coffin and given robes with symbols on it. A bone with his name on it is tossed into bone heap at start of every meeting...'[35]

This is without question a Satanic practice. Founder of the Church of Satan and author of the *Satanic Bible*, Anton LaVey describes the coffin ritual in his book *The Satanic Rituals*. Its similarity to what is alleged to take place inside Skull and Bones is unmistakable. Writes LaVey, 'there is blatant pornography and sexism throughout The Satanic Rituals...the altar is often a naked woman. Sexual acts are common: 'The (L'air Epais) ceremony of rebirth takes place in a large coffin.'

The late Pat Pulling, who lectured police departments on the occult and Satanism noted that there is a considerable amount of ritual abuse during Satanic ceremonies. Pulling claimed that rituals may include amongst others the placing of the victim into a coffin and 'sexual abuse aimed at confusing a recruit and destroying his/her moral foundation.'[36] Furthermore, Lawrence Pazder, an expert on ritualistic abuse defines ritual abuse as a tool to turn a person against itself, family and society through the use of repeated physical, emotional, mental and spiritual assaults combined with a systematic use of symbols and secret ceremonies.[37] Is this the purpose of the Skull and Bones initiation ceremony?

The Satanic activities that are alleged to go on at the so-called tomb on the grounds of the prestigious Yale University are indeed shocking to say the least. But really what is more disturbing than this is the fact that Washington has been greatly infiltrated by this evil group. The world's superpower is literally awash with these 'Bonesmen'.

From the fraternity's inception many US politicians, presidents and other influentials have been Bonesmen. William Howard Taft (1878), 27th US president, Charles Seymour (1908), founding member of The Council on Foreign Relations, Percy Rockefeller (1900) director of Standard Oil and Remington Arms, George Leslie Harrison (1910), Prescott Bush (1917), Brown Brothers Harriman & Co., US Senator (who allegedly stole the skull of Geronimo), President of the Federal Reserve Bank of New York, George Herbert Walker Jr (1927), financier and co-founder of New York Mets, John Rockefeller Prentice (1928), lawyer and cattle breeder, Tex McClary (1932), political strategist to President Eisenhower and George H. W. Bush (1948), 41st US president, 11th Director of Central Intelligence (son of Prescott Bush and father to George W. Bush) Incidentally his Skull and Bones secret name was curiously the apocalyptic title of 'Magog'. These are just a few names of which there are many others.

More recently members have been George W. Bush, 43rd US President, and John Kerry, 68th US Secretary of State under the current Obama administration, and Austan Goolsbee, chief economist for President Obama.

In fact George W. Bush appointed many Bonesman officials during his time as President. Other recent Bonesmen were Evan G. Galbraith, NATO Advisor, William H. Donaldson, Chairman Securities Commission, George H. Walker III, US

Ambassador to Hungary, Jack E. McGregor, Member Saint Lawrence Corporation, James E. Boasberg, Judge Superior Court of the District of Columbia, Victor Ashe, Director Fannie Mae, Roy Leslie Austin, US Ambassador to Trinidad and Tobago, Robert McCallum, Jr. Attorney General Civil Division, Rex Cowdry, Director Economic Council, Edward E. McNally, President of Homeland Security, David B. Wiseman, Attorney Justice Department.

In the run up to the 2004 presidential elections both nominees Bush and Kerry were challenged on TV's 'Meet the Press' regarding their membership of the secretive order. Bush looked obviously taken aback and somewhat embarrassed to be asked. Kerry flippantly shrugged off the question as it was posed by Tim Russert. Below are parts of the transcript from the interviews, which took place on two separate occasions:

Bush Interview

Russert: You were both in Skull and Bones the secret society.

President Bush: It's so secret we can't talk about it.

Russert: What does that mean for America? The conspiracy theorists are going to go wild.

President Bush: I'm sure they are. I don't know. I haven't seen the (unintel) yet. (laughing, red faced)

Russert: Number 322.

President Bush: (stutters obviously embarrassed) First of all, he's not the nominee... (changes subject) [38]

Kerry Interview

Russert: You both were members of Skull and Bones a secret society at Yale. What does that tell us?

Kerry: Er, not much, cos it's a secret (smirks and laughs it off)

Russert: Is there a secret handshake or secret code

Kerry: (shuffles uncomfortably from side to side) I wish there were something secret I could manifest (smiles embarrassed)

Russert: 322? A secret number?

Kerry: (no eye contact, looks down in denial and shakes head) There are all kinds of secrets, but one thing that's not a secret, (changes subject) I disagree with this president's direction that he's taking the country... [39]

Austan Goolsbee represented one of the newest generation of Bonesmen in the White House. He was Chairman of Obama's Council of Economic Advisors from September 2010 to August 2011. According to *Buzzfeed*, Goolsbee invited eight Yale Bonesmen to the White House for a secret meeting. According to White House records the students met with Goolsbee in room 234 of the Eisenhower Executive Office Building at around 4pm on March 4th, 2011. The meeting was not publicized at the time and what they discussed remains unknown. [40]

It is certainly disturbing to consider that people who are trusted to run the world's superpower and other influential bodies in America could have taken Satanic oaths of secrecy and engaged in wicked practices, the roots of which can be traced back to Germany and the Bavarian Illuminati and groups like the Thule Society that influenced Adolf Hitler.

But what of the Skull and Bones influence over America? Has the group wielded any power since its inception in 1832? Has it affected any change upon American Society?

Antony C Sutton, historian and expert on Skull and Bones believes this to be the case. In his book, *An Introduction to the Order of Skull and Bones,* Sutton writes:

'The Order has either set up or penetrated just about every significant research, policy, and opinion making organization in the United States, in addition to the Church, business, law, government and politics. Not all at the same time, but persistently and consistently enough to dominate the direction of American society. The evolution of American society is not, and has not been for a century, a voluntary development reflecting individual opinion, ideas and decisions at the grass roots. On the contrary, the broad direction has been created artificially and stimulated by The Order.'

Sutton observed that Skull and Bones is the initial impetus behind the start of a new influential organization. For example, they install the first Bonesman president or chairman with the strategy to steer the group, and when everything is up and running he moves into obscurity. Sutton cites the examples of various associations that are key for the conditioning of society that were started by members of Skull and Bones or by those closely linked to the Order. These are the American Historical Association, the American Economic Association, the American Chemical Society, and the American Psychological Association.

Think about it – the American History Association founded by unscrupulous men. Does this not throw into question the established version of historical events? Have they been manipulated to hide the truth? Sutton writes that 'the official line always assumes that events such as wars, revolutions, scandals, assassinations, are more or less random unconnected events. By definition, events can NEVER...result from premeditated planned group action.' But as we have seen so far nothing could be further from the truth.

It is also telling to note that Sutton discovered a link between the Skull and Bones Order and the United Nations. Sutton writes, 'the FIRST Chairman of an influential but almost unknown organization established in 1910 was also a member of The Order. In 1920 Theodore Marburg founded the American Society for the Judicial Settlement of International Disputes, but Marburg was only President. The FIRST Chairman was member William Howard Taft. The Society was the forerunner of the League to Enforce the Peace, which developed into the League of Nations concept and ultimately into the United Nations.' [41]

206

Other areas the Skull and Bones Order influenced in this way and documented by Sutton are the church, law, communication, industry, the Federal Reserve and of course the White House[42], with both Bush Senior and Junior being the most recent Bonesmen to be installed at the very top, each having given new impetus to the Order's vision to control and influence the world's superpower – the impact of which is seen on a global scale every day.

Cremation of Care full transcript

Cremation of Care – full transcript from the year Alex Jones and Mike Hanson secretly recorded the ceremony for the first time in 2000. [43]

> The Owl is in His leafy temple
> Let all within the grove be reverent before Him.
> Lift up your heads oh ye trees
> And be lifted up ye everlasting spires
> For behold here is bohemia's shrine
> And holy are the pillars of this house.
>
> Weaving spiders come not here!
>
> Hail, Bohemians!
> With the ripple of waters
> The song of birds
> Such music as inspires the sinking soul
> Do we invite you into Midsummer's joy.
>
> The sky above is blue and sown with stars
> The forest floor is heaped with fragrant grit
> The evening's cool kiss is yours
> The campfire's glow
> The birth of rosy fingered dawn.
>
> Shake off your sorrows with the city's dust
> And cast to the winds the cares of life.
>
> But memories bring back the well-loved names of gallant friends
> Who knew and loved this grove
> Dear boon companions of a long ago
> Aye! Let them join us in this ritual!

And not a place be empty in our midst.
All of his battles to hold
In this gray autumn of the world
Or in the springtime of your heart.

Attend our tale
Gather ye forest folks!
And cast your spells over these mortals!
Touch their world-blind eyes with carrion
Open their eyes to fancy
Follow the memories of yesterday
And seal the gates of sorrow.

It is a dream
And yet, not all a dream
Dull Care in all of his works
Harbored it
As vanished Babylon and goodly Tyre
So shall they also vanish
But the wilding rose blows on the broken battlements of Tyre
And moss rends the stones of Babylon

For beauty is eternal
And we bow to beauty everlasting
For lasting happiness we turn to one alone,
And She surrounds you now,
Great nature. Refuge of the weary heart,
And only found Her breasts that have been bruised.

She has cool hands for every fevered brow
And dreadless silence for the troubled soul.
Her counsels are most wise
She healeth well
Having such ministries as calm and sleep
She is ever faithful
Other friends may fail
But seek ye Her in any quiet place
Smiling, She will rise and give to you Her kiss

So must ye come as children
Little children that believe don't ever doubt Her beauty or Her faith
Nor deem Her tenderness can change or die
Bohemians and Priests!
The desperate call of heavy hearts is answered!

By the power of your fellowship, Dull Care is slain!

His body has been brought yonder to our funeral pyre
To the joyous pipings of a funeral march
Our funeral pyre awaits the corpse of Care!

O thou, thus ferried across the shadowy tide
In all the ancient majesty of death
Dull Care, ardent enemy of beauty
Not for thee the forgiveness or the restful grave
Fire shall have its will of thee
And all the winds make merry with thy dust
Bring fire!

Fools!
Fools!
Fools!
When will ye learn
That me ye cannot slay?
Year after year ye burn me in this grove
Lifting your puny shouts of triumph to the stars.
When again ye turn your faces to the marketplace
Do you not find me waiting, as of old?
Fools!
Fools!
Fools to dream ye conquer care.

Say Thou mocking spirit!
It is not all a dream
We know thou waitest for us
When this our sylvan holiday has ended
We shall meet thee and fight thee as of old
And some of us prevail against thee
And some Thou shalt destroy
But this, too, we know
Year after year within this happy grove
Our fellowship bans Thee for a space
Thine malevolence which would pursue us here
Has lost its power under these friendly trees.
So shall we burn Thee once again this night
And, with the flames that eat Thine effigy
We shall read the sign
Midsummer sets us free!

Ye shall burn me once again?
Not with these flames
Which hither ye have brought
From regions where I reign

Ye fools and priests
I spit upon your fire!

Oh Owl! Prince of all mortal wisdom
Owl of Bohemia, we beseech Thee
Grant us Thy counsel
No fire, no fire, no fire
Unless it be kindled
In the world where care is nourished on the hates of men
And drive Him from this grove.
One flame alone must light this fire
One flame alone must light this fire
A pure, eternal flame
A pure, eternal flame
At last, within the lamp of fellowship
Upon the altar of Bohemia.

Oh, Great Owl of Bohemia!
We thank Thee for Thy adoration!
Be gone detested Care!
Be gone!
Once more, we banish Thee!
Be gone Dull Care!
Fire shall have its will of Thee!
Be gone Dull Care!
And all the winds make merry with Thy dust!
Hail fellowship's eternal flame!
Once again, Midsummer sets us free!"

Chapter 12

Freemasonry, the Illuminati and the Symbology of the New World Order

*It is high time that the Church of Christ was awake
to the character and tendency of Freemasonry*

Rev Charles G Finney, evangelist,
revivalist and ex-Freemason, 1869 [1]

*From the days of...Weishaupt [founder of the Illuminati]
to those of Karl Marx...this worldwide conspiracy for
the overthrow of civilization and for the reconstitution of
society on the basis of arrested development, of envious and
impossible equality, has been steadily growing. It has been the
mainspring of every subversive movement during the
19th century*

Winston Churchill [2]

*The Freemason has no way of reaching any of the esoteric
teachings of the Order except through the medium of legend or
symbol*

Albert Mackey, 33rd Degree Freemason [3]

211

Freemasonry is a massive fraternal organization that exists in various forms around the world, with an estimated six million in membership. The origins of Freemasonry can be traced to the medieval stonemasons who built the great cathedrals and castles.

Today, however, it is no longer a fraternity for master builders. Freemasons can be found across every strata of society, from politicians to Prime Ministers to hundreds of UK judges, with over a 1000 UK magistrates owning up to being Freemasons[4] – not to mention lawyers, bankers and royalty. British Prime Minister Winston Churchill[5] was a Freemason as were British kings Edward VIII and George VI and other kings of England. Today the Duke of Kent is the Grand Master of the United Grand Lodge of England [6] and his brother Michael of Kent is a Mason too. [7] Royal connections run deeper however. In 2008 a lodge was formed at Buckingham Palace for members of the royal household. [8] There is also a Bank of England lodge.[9]

In 2011 a national Masonic lodge was set up by top British police officers. Founding members included the senior officials from the Police Federation, officers from the Metropolitan Police, Essex Police, Thames Valley Police and other forces from Northumbria, Dyfed Powys, South Wales, South Yorkshire and Royal Gibraltar Police. The lodge is based at the headquarters of the Supreme Council of the 33rd Degree, the highest and most mysterious degree within Freemasonry. According to a report the lodge was opened despite a Parliamentary inquiry warning that 'freemasonry can have an unhealthy influence on the criminal justice system.'[10]

Freemasonry has also been felt across the English Channel and had a direct impact in influencing the European Union. According to The Brussels Journal in 2008 the European Commission President José Manuel Barroso met with the French Federation of Le Droit Humain, one of France's Masonic lodges. The report stated, 'this meeting constitutes a major event regarding the place of Freemasonry in the construction of Europe.' [11]

According to the report Barroso assured the delegation of Freemasons that the EU would uphold the principles of separation of religion and state. The delegation stressed that the history of the Enlightenment in Europe should be on equal footing with its religious roots. Finally the article noted in the near future the Masonic order will propose 'a recommendation concerning the principle of emancipation that ought to form the basis of all European education systems, in direct relation to a recognition of the contribution of the Enlightenment to the common culture of the peoples that compose Europe, and in accordance with the principles of the Charter of Fundamental Rights.' [12] The report also noted that the anti-Christian delegation was concerned about the return of religious fundamentalism in Europe. [13]

The influence of Freemasonry has also spread to America. Many US presidents have been Freemasons – Presidents George Washington, James Monroe, Andrew Jackson, James Polk, James Buchanan, Andrew Johnson, James Garfield, William McKinley, Theodore Roosevelt, Howard Taft, Warren Harding, Franklin Roosevelt, Harry Truman and Gerald Ford. Abraham Lincoln intended to become a Freemason although postponed his membership. Other US presidents associated with Freemasonry have been Ronald Reagan, Bill Clinton, who was a member of the Order of DeMolay (Freemasonry for youth) [14], and George W Bush, to name but a few.

When exactly Freemasonry was founded is difficult to date because it has developed gradually over time. However, the oldest Masonic document known as the 'Regius Manuscript' is dated at approximately 1390. The 'Regius Manuscript' is a poem, the contents of which give fascinating and helpful insights into the earlier Masons.

The poem begins with a history of Masonry describing Euclid of Alexandria – the Father of Geometry. It continues with the spread of geometry through various lands until it arrived in England. But what is most interesting about the document is the sound Christian doctrine used within its text, as well as the references to the code of Christian conduct that should be adhered to as a Mason. Some of the relevant parts of the 'Regius Manuscript' can be found at the end of this chapter.

According to the evidence, original Masons were men of good Christian standing. At some point however, as with many institutions, the biblical principles as set out in the 'Regius Manuscript' gradually waned and the fraternity moved away from its Christian roots and it became corrupted by men who had little regard for moral values.

Later the Masons would become infiltrated by what was known as the Order of the Illuminati. The Illuminati was a product of the Age of Enlightenment, when traditionally held Judeo-Christian beliefs were rejected.

The Order was founded between 1775–1776 in Bavaria by Adam Weishaupt. It was apparently quashed just eleven years later in 1786 after it was discovered that they had plans to circumvent government.

However, evidence abounds that the Order continued under different guises.

John Robison, a man of high standing, (who invented the siren and worked on the steam car with James Watt), obtained original documents concerning the activities of the Illuminati and published *Proofs of a Conspiracy* in 1798.

Robison writes concerning the Illuminati and its subsequent infiltration of Freemasonry,

'The Association of which I have been speaking, is the Order of ILLUMINATI, founded in 1775, by Dr. Adam Weishaupt, professor of Canon law in the university of Ingolstadt, and abolished in 1786 by the Elector of Bavaria, but revived immediately after, under another name, and in a different form, all over Germany. It was again detected, and seemingly broken up; but it had by this time taken so deep root that it still subsists without being detected, and has spread into all the countries of Europe. It took its first rise among the Free Masons, but is totally different from Free Masonry. It was not, however, the mere protection gained by the secrecy of the Lodges that gave occasion to it, but it arose naturally from the corruptions that had gradually crept into that fraternity, the violence of the party-spirit which pervaded it, and from the total uncertainty and darkness that hangs over the whole of that mysterious Association.'

Robison disclosed a letter from Weishaupt that stated he had no plans to allow his Order to be destroyed and that he had carefully devised a plan to ensure its continuation. The letter also reveals the Illuminati's utter contempt for humanity, the violent way in which it would implement control of the masses, and the fact that it would in secret influence all politics.

'By this plan we shall direct all mankind. In this manner, and by the simplest means, we shall set all in motion and in flames. The occupations must be so allotted and contrived, that we may, in secret, influence all political transactions...I have considered everything, and so prepared it, that if the Order should this day go to ruin, I shall in a year re-establish it more brilliant than ever.' [15] So wrote Weishaupt.

We should take note here that the Illuminati agenda discussed in Weishaupt's letter not only perfectly describes the plans of the prophesied Antichrist but also what is happening today all around us. The Antichrist will control all mankind. He will set the world in flames. He will, in secret, supplant all state affairs.

Furthermore a letter dated October 24th 1798, just thirteen years after the supposed end of the Illuminati, George Washington confirmed that the Illuminati were still in existence and had spread in the United States. Additionally Washington discussed the infiltration of the Illuminati into Freemasonry.

Washington writes, 'It was not my intention to doubt that, the Doctrines of the Illuminati, and principles of Jacobinism had not spread in the United States. On the contrary, no one is more truly satisfied of this fact than I am. The idea that I meant to convey, was, that I did not believe that the Lodges of Free Masons in this Country had, as Societies, endeavored to propagate the diabolical tenets of the first, or pernicious principles of the latter (if they are susceptible of separation). That Individuals of them may have done it, or that the founder, or instrument employed to found, the Democratic Societies in the United States, may have had these objects; and actually had a separation of the People from their Government in view, is too evident to be questioned.' [16]

The fact that Washington wrote concerning the Illuminati's infiltration into Freemasonry shows the serious consideration of the matter at the time. Although Washington stated that he did not believe that it had occurred Freemasonry itself documents to the contrary.

Today Adam Weishaupt is revered by Freemasons.

Albert G. Mackey, a 33rd Degree Freemason and prominent scholar of Freemasonry writes of Weishaupt, 'he is celebrated in the history of Masonry as the founder of the Order of Illuminati of Bavaria...At first, it was totally unconnected with Masonry, of which Order Weishaupt was not at that time a member. It was not until 1777 that he was initiated in the Lodge Theodore of Good Counsel, at Munich. Thenceforward, Weishaupt sought to incorporate his system into that of Masonry, so that the latter might become subservient to his views, and with the assistance of the Baron Knigge, who brought his active energies and genius to the aid of the cause, he succeeded in completing his system of Illuminism.' [17]

We can see then that Freemasonry was drastically impacted by

216

the Illuminati and as a result a very different kind of fraternity came into being.

Robison observed the following transformation of Freemasonry,

'I saw that the Jesuits had several times interfered in it...I saw it much disturbed by the mystical whims of J. Behmen and Swedenborg – by the fanatical and knavish doctrines of the modern Rosycrucians – by Magicians – Magnetisers – Exorcists...I observed that these different sects reprobated each other, as not only maintaining erroneous opinions, but even inculcating opinions which where contrary to the established religions of Germany, and contrary to the principles of the civil establishments. At the same time they charged each other with mistakes and corruptions, both in doctrine and in practice; and particularly with falsification of the first principles of Free Masonry, and with ignorance of its origin and its history; and they supported these charges by authorities from many different books which were unknown to me...[18]

There, and more remarkably in France, I found that the Lodges had become the haunts of many projectors and fanatics, both in science, in religion, and in politics...These projectors had contrived to tag their peculiar nostrums to the mummery of Masonry, and were even allowed to twist the Masonic emblems and ceremonies to their purpose; so that in their hands Free Masonry became a thing totally unlike, and almost in direct opposition to the system (if it may get such a name) imported from England; and some Lodges had become schools of irreligion and licentiousness. [19]

It has accordingly happened, that the homely Free Masonry imported from England has been totally changed in every country of Europe, either by the imposing ascendancy of French brethren, who are to be found everywhere, ready to instruct the world; or by the importation of the doctrines, and ceremonies, and ornaments of the Parisian Lodges. Even England, the birth-place of Masonry, has experienced the French innovations;

and all the repeated injunctions, admonitions, and reproofs of the old Lodges, cannot prevent those in different parts of the kingdom from admitting the French novelties, full of tinsel and glitter, and high-sounding titles.' [20]

Today various degrees exist within Freemasonry. This is key to understanding how Freemasonry works. The degrees are: Entered Apprentice, Fellow Craft and Master Mason, the Master Mason being the highest degree. Importantly though, within this top level, a Master Mason can be promoted by degrees numbering from 4 to 33. The degrees separate the member from what lies above them. They are not privy to what goes on there – they are kept in the dark.

The Freemason publication Morals and Dogma explains this, 'the Blue Degrees are but the outer court or portico to the Temple. Part of the symbols are displayed there to the Initiate, but he is intentionally misled by false interpretations. It is not intended that he shall understand them, but it is intended that he shall imagine he understands them. Their true explication is reserved for the Adepts, the Princes of Masonry.' [21]

These lower level Freemasons, who make up the majority, have not engaged in the overtly satanic practices of those in the highest degrees. It is these men at the highest levels that have become the minions of the Illuminati agenda as prescribed by Adam Weishaupt and do its bidding. These 'Illuminised' Freemasons, empowered by the spirit of the Antichrist, hold great sway within government and organizational bodies on a local and national level.

Gary H. Kah, a former high level government liaison and occult expert puts it like this,

'The hierarchy uses millions of innocent people as dupes to serve as a shield between the public and themselves. These people who devote countless hours to establish hospitals, to help the crippled, and to do other good works unwittingly provide a cover under which the adepts operate – a perfect public relations ploy. Who would ever suspect a good works organization to be instead one massive conspiracy to usher in an occult New World Order?' [22]

The Scriptures declare, 'Satan himself transforms himself into an angel of light' (2 Corinthians 11:14, NKJV).

In fact John Robison in his book *Proofs of a Conspiracy* discloses an Illuminati letter describing how the group would hide themselves and influence the public mind by stealth:

'The great strength of our Order lies in its concealment; let it never appear in any place in its own name, but always covered by another name, and another occupation. None is fitter than the three lower degrees of Free Masonry; the public is accustomed to it, expects little from it, and therefore takes little notice of it. Next to this, the form of a learned or literary society is best suited to our purpose, and had Free Masonry not existed, this cover would have been employed; and it may be much more than a cover, it may be a powerful engine in our hands. By establishing reading societies, and subscription libraries, and taking these under our direction, and supplying them through our labors, we may turn the public mind which way we will. In like manner we must try to obtain an influence in the military academies (this may be of mighty consequence) the printing-houses, bookseller's shops, chapters, and in short in all offices which have any effect, either in forming, or in managing, or even in directing the mind of man...'

We can see then that Freemasonry is much more than meets the eye. According to Robison hidden behind it is a sinister plot that has an agenda to overturn governments. On the outside it is a benevolent organization but deep on the inside it is at work manipulating the masses through taking control of the media and even the military. But this is not all. Over time Freemasonry has also developed into a religion, despite Freemasonry's claim to the contrary, it is obvious for all to see.

In order to become a Freemason one must first undergo a series of ceremonial rituals. Some of the known initiation rituals of the Freemasons involve exposing the left breast and right knee of the candidate. Others include being blindfolded and a hangman's noose placed around the neck. Freemasonry is very clear that the blindfold ritual is a spiritual experience: 'Blindfolding a candidate in any rite is not for practical but spiritual reasons. The temporary blinding is a symbol of present darkness, which will be displaced by light when and if the initiate succeeds in penetrating the mysteries before him.' [23]

Freemasonry has its own version of the bible. Many of these bibles use imagery and references contrary to the teachings of the bible. For example some Masonic bibles display images of the upturned occultic pentagram. Also a coffin and skull and bones illustration can be found in some. Possibly the use of the bible and Judeo-Christian references is a throwback to its earlier Christian origins. Or else it is an attempt to deceive the initiate into believing that he has joined a society based on Christian beliefs.

Other religious themes surround the Masonic elements of consecration. The Freemason's Lodge is called a temple. Their buildings are considered to be holy places and Masons make offerings to consecrate them. *Mackey's Encyclopedia of Freemasonry* writes, 'Corn, wine, and oil are the Masonic elements of consecration...Freemasons' Lodges, which are but temples to the Most High, are consecrated to the sacred purposes for which they were built by strewing corn, wine, and oil upon the Lodge, the emblem of the Holy Ark.' [24]

One has to ask the question though, what 'Most High' god are the Masons referring to here? Initially from the terminology it sounds like the God of the bible. But let us take a closer look.

Firstly it is important to know that today Freemasonry acknowledges all gods. In fact a Freemason is required only to profess belief in a deity, it matters not which one. On this point alone then we can say that the 'Most High' in Freemasonry is not the God of the bible. It is whichever god a person happens to believe in.

Christopher Haffner describes the Masonic concept of God in his book *Workman Unashamed*. Haffner, who says he is both a Freemason and a Christian, writes that Allah, Vishnu and the Christian God are one and the same:

'They are praying to the same God as I, yet their understanding of His nature is partly incomplete (as indeed is mine...)' [25]

A true Christian would know that the bible strictly does not teach this.

However, apart from this we can confidently say that the Freemason's belief about God is not derived from the bible, even though it may initially appear to be biblical.

This is also clearly illustrated in one of the main symbols of Freemasonry – the 'All-Seeing Eye,' often set within a triangle with light emanating from behind it.

In Freemasonry the use of symbols are of great and vital significance. Albert Mackey explains the power that symbols hold over a Freemason in his book *The Symbolism of Freemasonry*.

'The Freemason has no way of reaching any of the esoteric teachings of the Order except through the medium of legend or symbol...At one time, nearly all the learning world was conveyed in symbols...Freemasonry still cleaves to the ancient method, and has preserved it in its primitive importance as a means of communicating knowledge...the symbol relates to dogmas of a deep religious character...To study the symbolism of Masonry is the only way to investigate its philosophy. This is the portal of its temple, through which alone we can gain access to the sacellum* where its aporrheta** are concealed.'

So what is the deep religious character of the 'All-Seeing Eye' used in Freemasonry? Firstly according to Freemasonry it represents the Supreme Being or the Grand Architect.

The Symbology of the New World Order

Albert Mackey states that the All-Seeing Eye is derived from both the Hebrew and the Egyptian cultures. However, this is incorrect. The Hebrews never used the All-Seeing Eye symbol to denote God. In fact the Jews of the Old Testament were strictly prohibited from creating any images of God lest it become idol worship to them. Exodus 20:4 reads, 'you shall not make for yourself a carved image – any likeness of anything that is in heaven above, or that is in the earth beneath, or that is in the water under the earth' (NKJV).

It is also worth noting that the reason the Jews were told not to create any image was because they had never seen God appear in any form.

'Therefore watch yourselves very carefully. Since you saw no form on the day that the Lord spoke to you at Horeb out of the midst of the fire, beware lest you act corruptly by making a carved image for yourselves, in the form of any figure.' (Deuteronomy 4:15, NKJV).

For the Jewish people there was NO image used for God – it was prohibited by God himself. Of course when the Jews disobeyed God and created graven images, God's anger burned against them.

Mackey bases his idea of the Jew's usage of the 'All-Seeing Eye' on two bible verses.

Mackey writes, 'the open eye was selected as the symbol of watchfulness, and the eye of God as the symbol of Divine watchfulness and care of the universe. The use of the symbol in this sense is repeatedly to be found in the Hebrew writers.

Thus, the Psalmist says, Psalm 34:15: "The eyes of the Lord are upon the righteous, and his ears are open unto their cry," which explains a subsequent passage (Psalm 121:4), in which it is said: "Behold, he that keepeth Israel shall neither slumber nor sleep."' [26]

The first point here is that these verses are not talking about the use of a symbol. They are merely stating God's action of looking upon the righteous at all times. Secondly the Psalm reads 'eyes' – plural. This claim of Mackey holds no credibility whatsoever.

In fact the opposite is true. For the Jew the symbol of the eye has a sinister meaning. This idea however did not stem from the Jewish scriptures (the Torah). In Jewish folklore the symbol of the eye became known as the Evil Eye. It was alleged the Evil Eye could curse a person or a new born infant.

The Encyclopedia of Judaism interestingly links the Evil Eye to the demon god Lilith – the owl deity of Bohemian Grove. The encyclopedia states, 'the concept of the evil eye does not appear in Jewish literature until the third century C.E. The belief was strongest in Babylonia, whose culture contained similar images and concepts. By the Middle Ages, when many Jews were living in Europe...the evil eye found its way into Jewish custom and thought as well...Healthy children were considered magnets for the evil eye...A demon named LILITH...was commonly thought to cast the evil eye upon newborn babies...' [27]

However, Mackey's suggestion that the 'All-Seeing Eye' had usage in the ancient mystery religions of Egypt is accurate. Mackey writes, 'the Egyptians represented Osiris, their chief deity, by the symbol of an open eye, and placed this hieroglyphic of him in all their Temples.' [28]

Osiris was the Egyptian god of the dead and ruler of the underworld. The 'All-Seeing Eye' symbolism of the Supreme Being or the Grand Architect must surely be depicting the god of the dead. Is this the god of Freemasonry?

The bible says regarding these things;

'Their idols are silver and gold, The work of men's hands...Eyes they have, but they do not see...Those who make them are like them; So is everyone who trusts in them.' (Psalm 115:4,5,8 NKJV)

Osiris was related to the goddess Isis. Both display an 'eye' hieroglyph in their names – just like the eye of Freemasonry. In ancient Egypt the sun and the moon were considered to be the eye of various gods including Horus and Ra. Furthermore from these gods were derived symbols of protection, known as "The Eye of Horus" and "The Eye of Ra". God specifically warned the people not to worship these Egyptian gods.

'And beware lest you raise your eyes to heaven, and when you see the sun and the moon and the stars, all the host of heaven, you be drawn away and bow down to them and serve them...' (Deuteronomy 4:16-18)

The All-Seeing Eye of Freemasonry is depicted most notably on the reverse of the Great Seal of the United States and also on the US one dollar bill. Interestingly it is also the emblem used by the World Union of Deists. It was Deism that Adam Weishaupt, founder of the Illuminati embraced.

'Christian' Deism, which gained prominence during the Age of Enlightenment, rejected the foundational doctrines of the Christian faith as revealed in the Bible, while holding on to

---

* In ancient Roman religion, a sacellum is a small shrine.
** Greek, meaning forbidden, secret, mystical, not to be spoken (things); secret instructions delivered to a candidate for initiation in the Mysteries. More importantly, facts of nature of rigidly esoteric character learned by adepts through initiation and improper to divulge to the uninitiated; hence spoken of as forbidden.

224

a form of Christianity – a Christianity devoid of revelation, miracles, the supernatural and with Christ demoted to a mere human. As we discovered earlier, this is specifically defined in scripture as Antichrist teaching.

Furthermore, it is noteworthy that Freemasonry and Deism both identify God as the 'Supreme Being'. The title of 'Supreme Being' is a definition of God from a philosophical point of view. It is from this perspective that beliefs such as Theosophy and Rosicrucianism were born. These are esoteric philosophies (esotericism), that believe there are hidden mysteries to be revealed in order to obtain divine knowledge and wisdom, and in so doing find God.

It was the Theosophist Helena Blavatsky, co-founder of the Theosophical Society, who inspired Alice Bailey. Bailey founded the Lucifer Publishing Company, now called Lucis Trust – an influential United Nations NGO. Later Bailey's husband, a 32nd Degree Freemason, became the National Secretary of Blavatsky's society. It was Blavatsky who wrote in the 'The Secret Doctrine' the blasphemous statement that 'Lucifer is divine and terrestrial light, the "Holy Ghost" and "Satan," at one and the same time.' This belief is known as Luciferianism. In Luciferianism, Lucifer is considered to be good as opposed to the biblical teaching of Lucifer as being the devil or Satan. The name Lucifer means 'light-bringer', Lucis means 'of light' and Illuminati means 'enlightened' which is from the words 'to shine' or 'light'. So we can clearly see the links here with the person of Lucifer in these organizations. What is more sinister though is the fact that the upper echelons of Freemasonry also teach that Lucifer is good.

Albert Pike, a prominent Freemason and Sovereign Grand Commander of the Scottish Rite's Southern Jurisdiction for 32 years devoted his time to developing the rituals of Freemasonry. In 1871 Pike published Morals and Dogma of the Ancient and Accepted Scottish Rite of Freemasonry. Pike wrote,

'Lucifer, the Light-bearer! Strange and mysterious name to

225

give to the Spirit of Darkness! Lucifer, the Son of the Morning! Is it he who bears the Light, and with its splendors intolerable blinds feeble, sensual, or selfish Souls? Doubt it not!' [29]

The bible clearly tells us who Lucifer is, or more accurately who Lucifer was. According to the bible Lucifer was originally the 'son of the morning', the 'shining one' or 'morning star'. However, we read in Isaiah 14:12-13;

'How you are fallen from heaven, O Lucifer, son of the morning! How you are cut down to the ground, You who weakened the nations! For you have said in your heart: 'I will ascend into heaven, I will exalt my throne above the stars of God.' (NKJV)

And again we read,

'You were the anointed cherub who covers; I established you; you were on the holy mountain of God; you walked back and forth in the midst of fiery stones. You were perfect in your ways from the day you were created, till iniquity was found in you... Your heart was lifted up because of your beauty; you corrupted your wisdom for the sake of your splendor; I cast you to the ground...' (Ezekiel 28: 14-15, 17)

Lucifer was a cherub that God cast out of heaven because iniquity was found in him. At this time there was a rebellion in heaven and many angels followed Lucifer. After this Lucifer became known as Satan or the devil and the angels that followed him became demon spirits. New Testament references to this event can be found in Revelation 12:9: 'The great dragon was hurled down – that ancient serpent called the devil, or Satan, who leads the whole world astray. He was hurled to the earth, and his angels with him.' In Matthew 10:18 Jesus also refers to this incident. Jesus tells his disciples that He actually saw the event take place: 'I saw Satan fall like lightning from heaven.'

It is a sobering thought to realize that when a foundational doctrine such as the divinity of Christ is rejected, teachings like

Luciferianism (the worship of Satan as the light) spring up. No wonder Christ himself and the apostles, inspired by the Holy Spirit, warned the early saints about this erroneous teaching and called it Antichrist. Let us be warned not to enter into the same folly of denying the divinity of Christ during this pivotal moment in time, when deceiving spirits are particularly in a heightened pursuit of this goal.

'Now the Spirit expressly says that in latter times some will depart from the faith, giving heed to deceiving spirits and doctrines of demons.' (1 Timothy 4:1, NKJV)

Just how far Freemasonry has embraced a doctrine of demons is clear. The Reverend Charles G Finney, evangelist, revivalist and an ex-freemason himself, wrote the following two accounts of which are printed here from his book *The Character, Claims and Practical Workings of Freemasonry*, published in 1869.

'In the degree of Templar and Knight of Malta, as found in the seventh edition of "Light on Masonry," page 182, in a lecture in which the candidate is giving an account of what he had passed through, he says: "I then took the cup (the upper part of the human skull) in my hand, and repeated, after the Grand Commander, the following obligation: 'This pure wine I now take in testimony of my belief in the mortality of the body and the immortality of the soul – and may this libation appear as a witness against me both here and hereafter – and as the sins of the world were laid upon the head of the Savior, so may all the sins committed by the person whose skull this was be heaped upon my head, in addition to my own, should I ever, knowingly or willfully, violate or transgress any obligation that I have heretofore taken, take at this time, or shall at any future period take, in relation to any degree of Masonry or order of Knighthood. So help me God?'

'On the 185th page of the same book, we find a note quoted from the work of Brother Allyn, who renounced Masonry and published on the subject...Mr. Allyn says of the fifth libation,

227

or sealed obligation,..."When I received this degree I objected to drink from the human skull, and to take the profane oath required by the rules of the order. I observed to the Most Eminent that I supposed that that part of the ceremonies would be dispensed with." The Sir Knights charged upon me, and the Most Eminent said: 'Pilgrim, you here see the swords of your companions drawn to defend you in the discharge of every duty we require of you. They are also drawn to avenge any violation of the rules of our order. We expect you to proceed." A clergyman, an acquaintance of mine, came forward, and said: "Companion Allyn, this part of the ceremonies is never dispensed with. I, and all the Sir Knights, have drank from the cup and taken the fifth libation. It is perfectly proper, and will be qualified to your satisfaction." I then drank of the cup of double damnation.' [30]

Finney comments, "now, can any profanity be more horrible than this? And yet there is nothing in Masonry, we are told, that is at all inconsistent with the Christian religion!'"

Finney details the following description of the ceremony relating to the Royal Arch Degree in which he writes how Freemasons blasphemously use the Holy Scriptures.

'The following is found in the Royal Arch degree, pp. 126, first edition, 137, eighth edition:

Question. – "Are you a Royal Arch Mason?" Answer. – "I am that I am." [Note. "I AM THAT I AM, is one of the peculiar names of the Deity; and to use it as above, is, to say the least, taking the name of God in vain. How must the humble disciple of Jesus feel when constrained thus to answer the question, "Are you a Royal Arch Mason?"] Light on Masonry, seventh edition.

On pp. 154, 155, we have a description of a ceremony in the same degree, as follows: "The candidates next receive the obligation, travel the room, attend the prayer, travel again, and are shown a representation of the Lord appearing to Moses from the burning bush. This last is done in various ways. Sometimes an earthen pot is filled with earth, and green bushes set around the edge of it, and a candle in the center; and sometimes a stool is provided with holes about the edge, in which bushes are placed, and a bundle of rags or tow, saturated with oil of turpentine, placed in the center, to which fire is communicated. Sometimes a large bush is suspended from the ceiling, around the stem of which tow is wound wet with the oil of turpentine. In whatever way the bush is prepared, when the words are read, 'He looked and behold the bush burned with fire,' etc., the bandage is removed from the eyes of the candidate, and they see the fire in the bush; and at the words, 'Draw not nigh hither, put off thy shoes,' etc., the shoes of the candidate are taken off, and they remain in the same situation while the rest of the passage to the words, 'And Moses hid his face; for he was afraid to look upon God,' is read. The bandage is then replaced and the candidates again travel about the room while the next passage of Scripture is read."

[Note. "This is frequently represented in this manner: When the person reading comes to that part where it says, 'God called to him out of the midst of the bush, and said.' etc., he stops reading, and a person behind the bush calls out, 'Moses, Moses.' The conductor answers, 'Here am I.' The person behind the bush then says: 'Draw not nigh hither; put off thy shoes from off thy feet, for the place whereon thou standest is holy ground.' His shoes are then slipped off. 'Moreover, I am the God of Abraham, and the God of Isaac, and the God of Jacob.' The person first reading then says: 'And Moses hid his face, for he was afraid to look upon God.' At these words the bandage is placed over the candidate's eyes."] And, if any himself will examine, and read the books through for themselves, in which these revelations are made, they will find that the higher degrees are replete with the same shocking and monstrous perversion of the Scriptures. Many of the most solemn passages in the Bible are selected, read in their lodges, repeated by their candidates, and applied in a manner too shocking to read.

Here you observe the candidate taking the Royal Arch degree, when asked if he is a Royal Arch Mason, replies: "1 am that 1 am;" which is represented in the Bible as being said by Jehovah himself. This answer was given by God to Moses when he inquired after the Divine name. God answered, "I AM THAT I AM." Just think! a Christian, when inquired of if he is a Royal Arch Mason, affirms of himself "I am that I am," taking to himself the name of the God of Israel.

Again, in this representation of the burning bush, the candidate is told to take off his shoes from off his feet, for the place on which he stands is holy ground; and then the Master of the lodge claims to be the God of Abraham, of Isaac, and of Jacob. Now how awfully profane and blasphemous is this!

Again, observe that that most solemn scene, depicted in the ninth chapter of Ezekiel, is misapplied in the most profane manner. Reader, the chapter is short; will you not take your Bible and read it?

So again, in those chapters in Revelation, the opening of the seals by the Son of God is misapplied, and profanely misrepresented. Just think! Four aged men, with bladders filled with wind, are made to represent the four angels that hold the four winds from desolating the earth till the servants of God were sealed in their foreheads. What a shocking misapplication and misrepresentation do we find here! And the cases are numerous in which, as I have said, the most solemn passages in the Word of God are used in their mummeries and childish ceremonies, in so shocking a manner that we can hardly endure to read them. I beg my Christian readers to examine these books for themselves, and then see what they think of the assertions of so many professors of religion, and even of professed Christian ministers, that "there is nothing in Freemasonry inconsistent with the religion of Jesus Christ!" I cannot imagine anything more directly calculated to bring the Word of God into contempt, than such a use of it in Masonic lodges. It is enough to make one's blood curdle in his veins to think that a Christian minister, or any Christian whatever, should allow himself to pass through such an abominable scene as is frequently represented in the degrees of Masonry: – multiplying their horrid oaths, heaping one imprecation upon another, gathering up from every part of the Divine oracles the most solemn and awful sayings of Jehovah, and applying them in a manner so revolting, that the scene must make a Christian's heart tremble, and his whole soul to loathe such proceedings. [31]

Finally, Gary H. Kah, in his book, *En Route to Global Occupation* recounts details of a Masonic ceremony described from Reverend James Shaw, an ex 33rd degree Freemason who turned to Christ. Shaw writes how he was invited by the Secretary of the Scottish Rite to attend and conduct the Maundy Thursday services prior to Easter. Shaw comments, "I can tell you that the Lodges always make a mockery of Christian Holy Days." Shaw writes, 'We were all in our places...each dressed in black robes...I began to speak, "My brothers, we meet this day to commemorate the death of our most wise and perfect Master – NOT as inspired or divine, but at least the greatest of all humanity." ...The next speaker said his part and lit a candle on the menorah. All spoke and lit candles...We had the Black Mass, drinking wine from a skull and eating a piece of bread – passing it around the table–saying to each man, "Take, drink, and give to the thirsty. Take, eat and give to the hungry."...I stood and began to recite the closing words. "We now close this commemoration of the death of our master. MOURN! LAMENT!! CRY ALOUD!! HE IS GONE!! NEVER TO RETURN!! MOURN!! LAMENT!!"'

Shaw writes, 'during my 19 years as a Mason, I witnessed and participated in numerous disturbing events, but the single most important reason causing me to leave was the fact that Jesus Christ was not the one being worshipped. Many gods in the Scottish Rite are revered and many religions taught, but never is the Blessed Name of Jesus Christ allowed. One is not even allowed to close a prayer in the name of Jesus, but instead must use vague references to God, which could mean anyone or anything. Teachings of the Kabbalah, Zend Avesta, and the Gnostics are used along with astrology and the doctrines of ancient gods Brahma, Vishnu, and Shiva are also given reference as deities. But whenever Christ was mentioned, it was only in the form of a mockery.' [32]

Returning back to the Great Seal, we can see that Deism and the Illuminati infiltrated Freemasonic lodges undoubtedly had their hand in the decision making for its design. Let us have a look at some more details in the design here.

The Eye on the seal is surrounded above, by the Latin words 'Annuit Cœptis', which means literally, 'He approves of our beginnings', or 'He has approved of the undertakings' – 'to nod' – 'to approve'. The leading question here must be – who is the one approving of their beginnings?

Below is written the words in Latin 'Novus Ordo Seclorum' which means 'New Order of the Ages' or 'New World or Secular Order'. It is from this point of reference that many politicians have used the term 'New World Order', to mean the new political order of a global government.

President George H. W. Bush, a great proponent for world government, defined the Great Seals reference to the 'new world order' vision when he said,

'Out of these troubled times, our fifth objective – a new world order – can emerge: a new era – freer from the threat of terror, stronger in the pursuit of justice, and more secure in the quest for peace. An era in which the nations of the world, East and West, North and South, can prosper and live in harmony. A hundred generations have searched for this elusive path to peace, while a thousand wars raged across the span of human endeavor. Today that new world is struggling to be born, a world quite different from the one we've known. A world where the rule of law supplants the rule of the jungle. A world in which nations recognize the shared responsibility for freedom and justice.' [33]

Only months later Bush referred to the new world order again. This time however he chillingly and unashamedly proclaimed to congress how this new world order would be implemented.

'Until now, the world we've known has been a world divided – a world of barbed wire and concrete block, conflict and cold war. Now, we can see a new world coming into view. A world in which there is the very real prospect of a new world order. In the words of Winston Churchill, a "world order" in which "the principles of justice and fair play...protect the weak against the strong...A world where the United Nations, freed from cold war stalemate, is poised to fulfill the historic vision of its founders.' [34]

We know from bible prophecy that this order will be the New World Order of the Antichrist. We have also learned that the United Nations actively embraces and encourages the spirit of the Antichrist within its workings.

The Eye itself is set inside a capstone hovering above an Egyptian pyramid. Light emanates from behind it. This is unusual imagery to use for the Great Seal of the United States. The first settlers were from Europe not Egypt. But herein lies further proof that within America at that time the Illuminati had already begun working behind the scenes.

Let us look in more detail at the hidden meaning of the Great Seal.

At the base of the pyramid in Roman numerals is inscribed the year 1776. This is of course the date that America officially began its nationhood. But also note it is the same year that the Illuminati was founded. Possibly of greater significance however is the capstone itself. The All-Seeing Eye of Horus hovers above the pyramid. Note that the pyramid, like the actual great pyramid in Egypt, is unfinished. Many historians agree that the great pyramid was never completed. Normally a pyramid would be topped with a capstone of precious stone or gold. The absent capstone has led many groups to believe that there will come a time when it will be put in place and that this ceremony will symbolize the completion of the globalist vision for a new world order – or one world government as symbolised on the Great Seal.

In fact to celebrate the new millennium an elaborate event was organized in Egypt that would involve the capping of the Great Pyramid. A massive music and laser show commissioned by New Ager Jean-Michel Jarre drew upon the occultic themes of ancient Egypt. According to reports in an Egyptian newspaper, Al Shaab, headlined 'Devil worship at the millennium party profanes the sanctity of Ramadan', Jarre intended to project the All-Seeing Eye onto the Great Pyramid. The newspaper denounced the event as a 'Masonic stunt'. Eventually however, the culture minister was forced to scrap the controversial plans that would see the Great Pyramid capped by helicopter at midnight. [35]

It is also of interest that a 7 foot high stone pyramid memorial complete with capstone is dedicated to the founder of the Jehovah Witnesses, Charles Taze Russell. The memorial, erected in 1921, replete with Freemason symbology stands in the cemetery where Russell is buried in Pittsburgh. Adjacent to the memorial is the Greater Pittsburgh Masonic Center. Did the Jehovah's Witnesses believe that its founder was the man to complete the new world order vision? Whatever their reasoning for the memorial it clearly shows a relationship between the Jehovah Witnesses and the Antichrist agenda upheld in the activities of the Illuminati.

The Illuminati inspired symbol on the Great Seal combines the missing capstone with its own occult interpretation. The All-Seeing Eye of Horus becomes the mysteriously missing capstone, coming down to complete the unfinished pyramid.

Edgar Cayce was a well known American psychic who lived from 1877-1945. Dubbed the sleeping prophet, Cayce was sympathetic to the cause of Freemasonry. Cayce who had 'prophesied' that the capping of the Great Pyramid would symbolize the return of 'Christ' believed that the principles upon which Freemasonry is based will one day rule the world. Cayce wrote:

'For with those changes that will be wrought, Americanism with the universal thought that is expressed and manifest in the Brotherhood of man into group thought as expressed in the Masonic Order, will be the eventual rule in the settlement of affairs in the world. Not that the world is to become a Masonic Order, but the principle that are embraced in the same will be the basis upon which the new order of peace is to be established.' [36]

Henry Wallace, prominent Freemason and US Vice-President to Roosevelt from 1940 to 1944 was a great believer in the message behind the Great Seal. Wallace stated:

'It will take a more definite recognition of the Grand Architect of the Universe before the apex stone [capstone of the pyramid] is finally fitted into place and this nation in the full strength of its power is in position to assume leadership among the nations in inaugurating 'the New Order of the Ages.' [37]

The Eye of Horus comes into yet more focus for us. The ancient god of the mystery religions is synonymous with the globalists themselves. They will inaugurate the new world order through a global government, a global financial system and a global religion.

Remember that when Satan tempted Adam and Eve in the Garden of Eden they were deceived into believing they would become like gods. The globalists today have been deceived by that serpent of old. They too believe they are like gods. This is the ultimate deception. This is the spirit of the Antichrist. This is what the Antichrist himself will believe – that he is God! He will set himself up in the Temple in Jerusalem and decree that he be worshipped in the sickening and diabolical one world religion or the new world order.

Regius Manuscript

The Regius Manuscript is the oldest Masonic document known and is dated at approximately 1390. Parts of the poem that refer to Christianity are copied below.

> For this you must know needs,
> But much more you must know,
> Than you find here written.
> If thee fail therto wit,
> Pray to God to send thee it;
> For Christ himself, he teacheth us
> That holy church is God's house,
> That is made for nothing else
> But for to pray in, as the book tells us;
> There the people shall gather in,
> To pray and weep for their sin.
> Look thou come not to church late,
> For to speak harlotry by the gate;
>
> Then to church when thou dost fare,
> Have in thy mind ever more
> To worship thy lord God both day and night,
> With all thy wits and even thy might.
> To the church door when thou dost come
> Of that holy water there some thou take,
> For every drop thou feelest there
> Quencheth a venial sin, be thou sure.
> But first thou must do down thy hood,
> For his love that died on the rood.
> Into the church when thou dost go,
> Pull up thy heart to Christ, anon;
>
> Upon the rood thou look up then,
> And kneel down fair upon thy knees,
> Then pray to him so here to work,
> After the law of holy church,
>
> For to keep the commandments ten,

That God gave to all men;
And pray to him with mild voice
To keep thee from the sins seven,
That thou here may, in this life,
Keep thee well from care and strife;
Furthermore he grant thee grace,
In heaven's bliss to have a place.

In holy church leave trifling words
Of lewd speech and foul jests,
And put away all vanity,
And say thy pater noster and thine ave;
Look also that thou make no noise,
But always to be in thy prayer;
If thou wilt not thyself pray,
Hinder no other man by no way.
In that place neither sit nor stand,
But kneel fair down on the ground,
And when the Gospel me read shall,

Fairly thou stand up from the wall,
And bless the fare if that thou can,
When gloria tibi is begun;
And when the gospel is done,
Again thou might kneel down,
On both knees down thou fall,
For his love that bought us all;
And when thou hearest the bell ring
To that holy sacrament,
Kneel you must both young and old,
And both your hands fair uphold,
And say then in this manner,

Fair and soft without noise;
Jesu Lord welcome thou be,
In form of bread as I thee see,
Now Jesu for thine holy name,
Shield me from sin and shame;
Shrift and Eucharist thou grand me both,
Ere that I shall hence go,
And very contrition for my sin,
That I never, Lord, die therein;
And as thou were of maid born,
Suffer me never to be lost;
But when I shall hence wend,

Pray to God with heart still,
To give thy part of that service,
That in church there done is.
Furthermore yet, I will you preach
To your fellows, it for to teach,
When thou comest before a lord,
In hall, in bower, or at the board,
Hood or cap that thou off do,
Ere thou come him entirely to;
Twice or thrice, without doubt,
To that lord thou must bow;
With thy right knee let it be done,

Christ then of his high grace,
Save you both wit and space,
Well this book to know and read,
Heaven to have for your reward.
Amen! Amen! so mote it be!
So say we all for charity.

Chapter 13

One World Religion

*Humanity stands at a critical juncture in history, one that
calls for strong moral and spiritual leadership to help set
a new direction for society. We, as religious and spiritual
leaders, recognize our special responsibility for the well-being
of the human family and peace on earth*

World Council of Religious Leaders [1]

*Love your God; love your neighbor as yourself. These simple
admonitions are the guiding light of our faith. They give us
the possibility of 'A Common Word.' When we lose our way,
Christians or Muslims, this is the light by which we
re-discover our true path*

Tony Blair [2]

*One of the aims of the Tony Blair Faith Foundation will be
that of remaking the major religions, just as his colleague
Barack Obama will remake global society...The religions will
have to be reduced to the same common denominator, which
means stripping them of their identity...In the case of the Tony
Blair Faith Foundation, this is also a matter of promoting one
and only one religious confession, which a universal, global
political power would impose on the entire world*

Professor Michel Schooyans [3]

Then I saw another beast [False Prophet] coming up out of the
earth, and he had two horns like a lamb and spoke like a dragon.

239

And he exercises all the authority of the first beast [Antichrist] in his presence, and causes the earth and those who dwell in it to worship the first beast. (Revelation 13:11-12 NKJV)

As we have seen, global control of the planet is being implemented through various systems and structures. These systems – or building blocks – are being erected incrementally and over a period of time so as to avoid notice and concern amongst the masses. They make up the main architecture for the globalist new world order.

These pivotal structures, amongst other lesser ones, involve the amalgamation of all governments through political bodies such as the United Nations, the European Union and the North American Union. They also involve the merger of the world's economies through organizations like the International Monetary Fund, the World Bank and the European Central Bank. It is from these, or hybrids of these banking institutions, that the Mark of the Beast will become operational. This mandatory mark, controlled through the banking system, will be imposed via the one world religion (Rev: 13:16). It will be as much a mark used for financial control as it will be a religious mark to denote affiliation to the Antichrist system (Rev 13:17; 14:9; 19:20).

The final structure and possibly the most arduous to unite will be that of religion. However, in spite of the seemingly insurmountable obstacles, we will see that this unification is gaining a startling momentum today.

Once these three structures are firmly fixed into place and become fully operational, it will be checkmate for the peoples of the world. Total people control will ensue. Like caged animals trapped inside the pyramidical tomb of the new world order, the peoples of the world will descend into abject darkness as the capstone descends over them and locks into place.

The final push that completes the unification of all religions will ultimately see the incarnation of the Biblically prophesied Antichrist and his diabolical henchman the False Prophet. They will arrive onto the world stage where religion and state will unite in a caliphate-style, Nazi-like governmental dictatorship, with its epicenter in the heart of Jerusalem (Dan 11:31; 2; Matt 24:15; 2 Thessalonians 2:3-4). This system will be given great impetus and credence as a result of its orchestration and constitution of the long awaited peace in the Middle East (Dan 9:27). This will be seen as one of the greatest miracles of all time. The masses, including many church groups, will be in awe of this astonishing wonder. As ever they will be duped through the mainstream media. In addition, Bible prophecy reveals that the global acceptance of the world religious system will come through the administration of mind-altering chemicals and pharmaceuticals. The people will therefore readily submit to the new politico-religious system without question.

In Revelation 18:23 we read that the Antichrist world order engages in what it calls sorcery – 'for by your sorcery all the nations were deceived' (NKJV).

The word sorcery used here has often been taken to mean only witchcraft, black magic or the casting of spells. While this is most certainly an accurate translation, there is more to its meaning. The word 'sorcery' in Greek is the word pharmakeia. This comes from the word pharmakeuo, which means to 'administer drugs'.

The English words Pharmacy, Pharmacist and Pharmaceuticals are derived of course from this Greek noun and verb.

The Strong's Exhaustive Concordance of the Bible defines pharmakeia as 'the use of medicine, drugs, spells, then poisoning, then witchcraft...In sorcery the use of drugs, whether simple or potent, was generally accompanied by incantations and appeals to occult powers, with the provision of various charms, amulets, etc., professedly designed to keep the applicant or patient from the attention and powers of devils, but actually to impress the applicant with the mysterious resources and powers of the sorcerer.'

On a side note, it is interesting to learn that in 2010 the British Medical Association actually likened the practice of homeopathy to that of witchcraft. Deputy Chairman of the BMA's junior doctors committee said, 'homeopathy is witchcraft. It is a disgrace that nestling between the National Hospital for Neurology and Great Ormond Street [in London] there is a National Hospital for Homeopathy which is paid for by the NHS.' [4]

The BMA's opinion lines up with the Bible. Homeopathy is more based on hocus-pocus than medical science. For example, to facilitate the preparation of homeopathic remedies, its founder, Samuel Hahnemann, had a wooden striking-board constructed with leather on one side and horse hair on the other. In this superstitious practice the homeopathic substance was hit against the board ten times in order to achieve its efficacy. Today this idea continues through automation in homeopathic factories.

A list of unusual homeopathic agents such as ovary extract from a cow, toad poison, hair from a horse, dog saliva, [5] and 'thunderstorms' collected from rain water do sound more akin to a witch doctor's potion. Some techniques even include 'paper remedies' where the substance is written on a piece of paper. It is then pinned to the patient's clothing, put in their pocket, or placed under a glass of water that is then given to the patient. [6]

Bible prophecy specifically describes how medicines, drugs and potions will be part of the process which leads the entire global population into deception during the end times.

In other words the prophecy could also be read, 'the whole world was deceived through the use of pharmaceuticals.'

This great deception will be administered through the pharmaceutical industry, or what has commonly become known as Big Pharma. That 'Big Pharma' features in end time Bible prophecy should come as no surprise. The companies that make up the pharmaceutical industry are among the largest and most powerful corporations on the planet.

A 'Centers for Disease Control and Prevention' report reveals just how far Bible prophecy is being played out today. In America alone nearly half the population now takes prescription drugs. One third use two or more and one in ten use five or more prescription drugs regularly. The total cost of all these drugs in 2008 was a staggering $234 billion. In England the use of ADHD drugs increased by 50% in just six years. National Health Service prescriptions for psychotropic drugs including Ritalin rose from the already staggering figure of 420,000 in 2007 to 657,000 in 2012. [7]

On being asked about the dangers of taking these kinds of drugs, consultant psychiatrist Professor Tim Kendall commented, 'I think there's also increasing evidence that it precipitates self-harming behavior in children...' Shockingly the professor went on to say, 'we have absolutely no evidence that the use of Ritalin reduces the long-term problems associated with ADHD.' [8]

It is a disturbing fact that some of the most commonly used drugs today are mind-altering psychotropics, administered not only to adults but also children. (9) By 2014 global sales of pharmaceuticals are expected to reach $1.1 trillion. [10]

Mike Adams of Natural News wrote, 'America has become a nation of druggies. The seniors are being drugged for nearly every symptom a doctor can find, children are being doped up with (legalized) speed, and middle-aged soccer moms are popping suicide pills (antidepressants).' [11]

Adams chillingly believes that 'the mass medication of American citizens has reached a disturbing tipping point where the future of the nation itself is at risk. That's because pharmaceuticals cause cognitive decline, and once you get to the point where over 50 percent of the voters can't think straight, you're trapped in a crumbling Democracy.' [12]

The accuracy of Bible predictions is confirmed. In a drugged up stupor the American populace, along with the rest of the planet, will sacrifice its freedoms to follow the Antichrist system.

The multi-billion dollar pharmaceutical industry uses, manipulates and in some instances creates illness for capital gain. Creating illnesses is otherwise known as 'disease mongering'. In her book 'Disease-Mongers: How Doctors, Drug Companies, and Insurers Are Making You Feel Sick' Lynn Payer defines disease mongering as 'trying to convince essentially well people that they are sick, or slightly sick people that they are very ill.' [13]

According to Dr. Larry Dossey, disease mongering began in 1879 with the invention of Listerine, which was originally a surgical antiseptic. It was then sold in its concentrated form as a floor cleaner. In 1895 it was marketed to dentists for oral care and then later in 1914 it became the first over-the-counter mouthwash. In order to sell it they first needed a disease – so they created one and called it 'halitosis', in other words 'bad breath'. Before then 'halitosis' was an obscure medical term that practically no one had heard of. Advertisers began to promote the 'disease' and the 'cure'. The rest is history. [14]

But it gets more sinister than mouthwash. In the 1960s clinical depression was a rare condition. In fact it was so rare that there was little profit in the marketing of a new antidepressant known as amitriptyline. The solution to the lack of uptake was to increase diagnosis. In order to achieve this, a leading pharmaceutical company purchased fifty thousand copies of the book 'Recognizing the Depressed Patient' by Frank Ayd and sent them out free to doctors all over America. Prescriptions for amitriptyline took off immediately. [15]

The term pharmakeia can be found also in Revelation 9:20-21 where it says that the people did not repent of their false religion and their pharmakeia. Again in Revelation 21:8 it lists pharmakeia amongst whore-mongering, idolatry and lying as abominable practices. In Revelation 22:15 we read that outside God's Kingdom are those who practice pharmakeia and prostitution. The Apostle Paul lists pharmakeia as one of the acts of the sinful nature;

Now the works of the flesh are evident, which are: adultery, fornication, uncleanness, lewdness, idolatry, sorcery (pharmakeia), hatred, contentions, jealousies, outbursts of wrath, selfish ambitions, dissensions, heresies, envy, murders, drunkenness, revelries, and the like; of which I tell you beforehand, just as I also told you in time past, that those who practice such things will not inherit the kingdom of God (Galatians 5:19-21, NKJV).

It is noteworthy that we consistently see in Scripture that the term pharmakeia is used in conjunction with prostitution, adultery and idolatry. This is significant. As we will learn, these three behaviors are an integral part of the one world religious system.

Importantly not all pharmaceutical drugs will be guilty of leading the nations into deception. Many pharmaceuticals have no doubt helped countless millions. However we should not blindly accept every offering prescribed by our GPs without first seriously researching the drug and its side-effects. It is sobering to consider that contrary to bringing health and wholeness prescription drugs cause the deaths of 100,000 Americans every year. What is more shocking however is that this figure is taken only from those people who died through taking a prescribed drug exactly as the doctor had ordered.[16]

It is mostly drugs that have psychotropic effects on the mind that will be harnessed in this massive end time deception.

Psychotropic drugs are used for a variety of psychiatric disorders. They act upon the central nervous system's brain functions and are known to alter a person's mood, consciousness and behavior. It takes little imagination to consider the power that a person or government could hold over the mind of an individual that has been subjected to psychotropic drugs. A user's normal thought processes are without question seriously compromised. This is evidenced by the US government covert MK-Ultra CIA experiments conducted between 1950s-70s that originated in Nazi Germany. These experiments involved the use of psychotropic barbiturates, amphetamines, temazepam and LSD related drugs.

These drugs are effective tools of manipulation because they can create feelings of euphoria or a heightened sense of awareness. Psychotropic drugs are prescribed for a whole host of psychological issues such as anxiety, depression, bipolar disorder, attention deficit disorder (ADD) attention deficit hyperactivity disorder (ADHD) and schizophrenia, to take just a few examples.

In recent years the dangers of prescription-based psychotropic drugs have been cited by various professionals in the field.

Grace E. Jackson, psychiatrist and author of *Drug-Induced Dementia – a Perfect Crime*, shows that psychotropic drugs cause significant brain damage in patients. Jackson proved that any of the five classes of psychotropic drugs administered to psychiatric patients – antidepressants, antipsychotics, psychostimulants, tranquilizers and anti-seizure 'mood-stabilizer' drugs – have shown 'microscopic, macroscopic, radiologic, biochemical, immunologic and clinical evidence of brain shrinkage and other signs of brain damage, especially when used long-term. Long-term use can result in clinically diagnosable, probably irreversible dementia, premature death and a variety of other related brain disorders that can mimic mental illnesses "of unknown cause."' [17]

According to the Citizen's Commission on Human Rights

International the following mind-altering side-effects have been documented for the following psychotropic drugs:

Anti-anxiety drugs – such as Xanax, Valium, Halcion, Klonopin, Ambien, Ativan (also known as Benzodiazepines) – result in abnormal behavior, agitation, ironically anxiety, cognitive impairment, delusional thinking, hallucinations, hostility, insomnia, memory loss, aggression, homicidal thoughts, suicidal thoughts and violence.

Antidepressant drugs – such as Paxil, Prozac, Zoloft, Celexa, Luvox, Wellbutrin, Cymbalta, Effexor, Lexapro, Elavil, Remeron, Sarafem, Trazodone – result in agitation, anxiety, hallucinations and delusional thinking, homicidal thoughts, self-harm, suicidal thoughts, violence, akathisia (agitation, distress and restlessness), mania and psychosis.

ADHD drugs – such as Ritalin, Concerta, Adderall, Metadate, Vyvanse, Provigil – result in aggression, agitation, anxiety, depression, hallucinations, hostility, mania, psychosis, suicidal thoughts, violence, delinquency, emotional outbursts and homicidal thoughts.

Antipsychotic drugs – such as Abilify, Clozaril, Geodon, Invega, Risperdal, Seroquel, Zyprexa, Fanapt – cause severe restlessness, cognitive and motor impairment, violence, delusional thinking, psychosis and confusion.

Think about how easy it will be for the Antichrist world order to deceive and manipulate people who are experiencing drug-induced hallucinations, delusional thinking and paranoia, or how easy it would be to coerce them into engaging in acts of violence or terrorism.

Consider also how these drugs are known to cause a dumbing down of the subject through brain damage, dementia and reduced intelligence.

Dumbing down through Fluoride

One of the most commonly used of such drugs is Fluoxetine, otherwise known as Prozac, Sarafem or Fontex. This drug is so named because it contains small amounts of fluoride. [18]

Fluoride is well known for its dumbing down effects. Studies of the relationship between fluoride and human intelligence show that those exposed to fluoride had a reduced IQ. According to the study fluoride exposure in children caused brain damage. As a result of the studies Harvard scientists concluded that fluoride's effect upon a child's brain should become a 'high research priority.' [19]

But the fluoride drug is not confined to Prozac alone; it is well known as being the active ingredient in toothpaste too. In fact the makers of Colgate toothpaste, Procter & Gamble, reportedly admitted that a small tube of toothpaste 'theoretically at least contains enough fluoride to kill a small child.' [20]

Non-pharmaceutical grade fluoride is also regularly poured into many water supplies around the world as a form of mass medication. In the United States 65% of people are subjected to the chemical in an apparent battle to fight tooth decay.

However according to reports the worst tooth decay occurs in areas that have been fluoridated for decades.

The chemicals used to fluoridate drinking water are hydrofluorosilicic acid, sodium fluorosilicate, and sodium fluoride. These chemicals are unpurified industrial by-products that do not undergo any purification procedures. Consequently they have been found to contain various contaminants, particularly the deadly poison arsenic. Once collected the chemicals are shipped in liquid or dry powder form and dumped into the water supply.

Fluoride has been linked to debilitating brain diseases such as Alzheimer's and other serious diseases like cancer. In only small doses fluoride has been shown to cause genetic damage. Fluoride causes skin, muscle, ligaments and bone to disintegrate. Ironically in recent years the fluoridation of water has been the cause of damage to children's teeth.

The poisoning of the fresh water supply is in accordance with end time prophesied events. Revelation 8:11 records what the Apostle John saw in his visions, 'a third of the water turned bitter, and many people died from the poisoned water.' (MSG) According to the Bible this water poisoning event will specifically affect the fresh water supply and will occur after an object from the sky 'blazing like a torch' impacts the earth.

Revelation 8:10 reads, 'and a great star fell from heaven, burning like a torch, and it fell on a third of the rivers and on the springs of water.'

There are two possibilities regarding the identity of this great star. One is that the Apostle John saw a meteorite; the other that he saw a guided chemical weapons missile.

The Apostle John could never have known 2000 years ago how such a terrible event could occur and cause the pollution of a third of the world's fresh water supply. But this only serves to show the truth of his revelations.

Today an international study has been carried out on groundwater quality around the ancient Lake St. Martin meteorite crater north of Winnipeg in Canada.

For years scientists have been trying to find out why the water quality in the communities around Lake St. Martin was so poor.

According to the study a meteorite that slammed into prehistoric Canada found that its impact caused a shattering of the subsurface granite. This in turn allowed for naturally occurring fluoride to seep into the groundwater. A researcher said, 'the possibility that a meteor impact could devastate modern human civilization is a real concern...However, meteors may affect human populations through more subtle routes in addition to these commonly recognized, catastrophic events.'

Furthermore scientists have theorized that the Canadian site has sister craters in France, Quebec, North Dakota and Russia which were all created within hours of each other. [21]

Could a future meteor strike across the earth release harmful amounts of fluoride into a third of the fresh water supply?

Another possible interpretation of the prophecy is that the Apostle saw the detonation of a guided chemical weapon missile of some description. Sarin is a man-made fluorinated nerve gas. Sarin is part of a G-series of nerve agent chemical weapons first developed in Nazi Germany. It consists of four common chemical compounds: dimethyl methylphosphonate, phosphorus trichloride, sodium fluoride and alcohol. Hitler's chemists discovered that 'fluoride could dramatically boost the toxicity of nerve gases.' Saddam Hussein also used Sarin gas on the Kurds of Halabja. [22]

It is also disturbing to note that in the summer of 1943 a group of New Jersey farmers reported that something was 'burning up' their peach trees, maiming their horses and cattle and killing their chickens. It was found that the source of the mystery came from a nearby factory that was producing millions of pounds of fluoride for use in the atomic bomb program, the Manhatten Project. A lawsuit was filed. In response to the bad press concerning fluoride, Professor Harold C Hodge, chief of fluoride toxicology studies of the project asked his superiors if there 'would be any use in making attempts to counteract the local fear of fluoride through lectures on fluoride toxicology and perhaps the usefulness of fluoride in tooth health?' [23]

Robert Carton, Ph.D. former US EPA scientist said, 'fluoridation is the greatest case of scientific fraud of this century, if not of all time.' [24]

Carton's words resonate precisely with the prophecy, 'for by your sorcery (pharmaceuticals) all the nations were deceived' (Revelation 18:23 NKJV).

Considering the amount of scientific evidence relating to the dangers of fluoride it is really quite remarkable that for decades it has been poured into many drinking water supplies as a health benefit. Once again this serves to show the power of propaganda over the masses.

Psychotropic pharmaceuticals linked to US mass shootings

Tragic shootings across America are strongly connected to prescribed psychotropic drugs. Consider the following examples.

In 1986 14 year old Rod Matthews beat a classmate to death. He was put on Ritalin in the third grade.

In 1988 19 year old James Wilson went on a shooting rampage in South Carolina. Two children died and seven other children and two teachers were wounded. From 14 onwards Wilson had been on a mixture of psychotropic drugs. He was withdrawing from Xanax at the time of the shooting.

In 1998 Kip Kinkel went on a shooting spree in Oregon, after killing his own parents, he went on to kill two more, and injure a further 22 other people. He was reportedly taking Prozac and Ritalin.

In 1999 Shawn Cooper from Idaho intended to shoot a school secretary and students but surrendered. Cooper was on Ritalin.

Again in 1999 Eric Harris masterminded the killing of 12

students and a teacher at Columbine High School in Colorado. He was taking the antidepressant Luvox.

In 2001 Elizabeth Bush shot and injured a fellow student. She was on Prozac.

In 2001 Jason Hoffman wounded one teacher and three students in El Cajon. Hoffman was on Effexor and Celexa.

In 2005 16 year old Jeff Weise shot dead his grandparents and then went to his school and killed a further 9 before killing himself. He was taking Prozac.

In 2007 Asa Coon, 14, shot and wounded four people before killing himself. Coon was on Trazodone.

In 2008 27 year old Steven Kazmierczak killed 5 and wounded 16 others. According to his girlfriend Kazmierczak was taking Prozac, Xanax and Ambien. [25]

In 2012 the 'Batman' shooter James Holmes killed 12 people and injured a further 58 others in a movie theatre in Colorado. Holmes was taking Zoloft and Clonazepam (Klonopin). [26]

Again in 2012 Adam Lanza, 20, Shot and killed his mother. Shortly after he shot and killed 20 children and six staff members at Sandy Hook Elementary School in Connecticut.[27] Louise Tambascio, a family friend of the shooter and his mother said, 'I know he was on medication.' [28]

While guns are cited as being the main culprit behind these tragedies, the question of whether psychotropic drugs have any involvement is largely ignored. But that is because it suits the policy-makers to cloud the issue.

To quote Rahm Emanuel, 'never let a serious crisis go to waste. And what I mean by that it's an opportunity to do things you think you could not do before.'

These crisis moments provide a perfect opportunity to continue chipping away at the Second Amendment, the 'right to keep and bear arms', and enact an eventual and total gun ban on the American people. The amendment's purpose amongst others is to deter tyrannical government. Hitler and other dictators banned guns before they took total control of the populace. Germany enacted gun control in 1938. Thirteen million Jews and others were rendered powerless to defend themselves. They were then rounded up and executed in cold blood.

Hitler said, 'the most foolish mistake we could possibly make would be to allow the subject races to possess arms. History shows that all conquerors who have allowed their subject races to carry arms have prepared their own downfall by so doing. Indeed, I would go so far as to say that the supply of arms to the underdogs is a sine qua non for the overthrow of any sovereignty. So let's not have any native militia or native police. German troops alone will bear the sole responsibility for the maintenance of law and order throughout the occupied Russian territories, and a system of military strong-points must be evolved to cover the entire occupied country.' [29]

This new world religion will be presided over by a man second only to the president of the new world order. He will have been groomed from out of the darkness of the Illuminati-controlled secret societies and will be a religious extremist, well versed in the occult practices and rites of Luciferianism (Rev 13:11-15). He will claim that all religions lead to god and, like the Antichrist, deny both the Father and the Son – Jesus Christ. The new world religion will absorb the basic tenets of the established Abrahamic faiths while specifically distorting and twisting key Christian doctrines to its own delusional advantage. This distinct targeting of Christianity will be borne out of the Antichrist's ardent hatred for God; like Karl Marx he will wish to 'avenge himself against the One who rules above.' Evidence suggests that the predominant and overarching faith within this new world religion will be that of Islam, with an eclectic mix of the mystery religions of ancient Babylon, Rome and the later esoteric and Luciferian philosophies adopted by the likes of Blavatsky, Bailey, Aleister Crowley and others – with which Adolf Hitler became so enthralled in his own quest to become the final Antichrist (Rev 17:5).

World peace will be the highest doctrine of the faith. It is this doctrine that will be used as one of the devices to deceive the masses into readily accepting it. Those who reject it will be considered agitators and haters of the world, not only by the system but also by the masses who have given themselves over to it. These people, whether Christians or liberty advocates, will be hunted down as terrorists, bigots and blasphemers. They will be framed, wrongly accused, imprisoned and beheaded by the new religious system (Rev 13:10; 14:12; 17:6; 20:4).

The prophesied one world religion is described in Revelation 13:8 where it reads that ALL the inhabitants of the earth will worship the Antichrist. This is also referred to in Revelation 13:3; 13:4; 13:12. In Revelation 13:14 we read that the whole earth was forced into and seduced into worship and the setting up of idols in honor of the Antichrist. This event will most likely be administered through the ten regionalized areas of global government (Daniel 7:7, 20, 24; Rev 12:3; 13:1; 17:3, 12, 16), in which each regional area leader will have given themselves completely over to the religious system (Rev 17:2).

This one world religion in the Bible is accorded the title of 'Mystery Babylon, the Mother of Harlots', or 'The Great Harlot', and in other translations 'The Great Whore' or 'The Great Prostitute'. The Amplified version reads:

[She] with whom the rulers of the earth have joined in prostitution (idolatry) and with the wine of whose immorality (idolatry) the inhabitants of the earth have become intoxicated... And on her forehead there was inscribed a name of mystery [with a secret symbolic meaning]: Babylon the great, the mother of prostitutes (idolatresses) and of the filth and atrocities and abominations of the earth (Revelation 17:2 & 5 AMP).

The New King James translates this same passage as follows: Come, I will show you the judgment of the great harlot who sits on many waters, with whom the kings of the earth committed fornication, and the inhabitants of the earth were made drunk with the wine of her fornication... And on her forehead a name was written: MYSTERY, BABYLON THE GREAT, THE MOTHER OF HARLOTS AND OF THE ABOMINATIONS OF THE EARTH.

The term 'harlot' is predominantly metaphorical in its application and is used throughout the Bible to denote false religion. In Exodus 34:15 we read that the inhabitants of the land played the harlot with their gods and made sacrifice to them. We also read in Leviticus 20:5 that God will cut off those who prostitute themselves and commit harlotry with the god Molech, and in Judges 8:33 the people 'played the harlot' with Baal. In Deuteronomy 31:16 the peoples are again described as playing the harlot with the gods of the foreigners.

However, as we have learned, those who engage in false religious practices invariably also engage in sexual acts with prostitutes too (evidenced by the alleged activities of the Bohemian Grove annual event, to cite just one example). The worship of both Molech and Baal involved the use of male and female temple prostitutes. In ancient Rome prostitutes featured in religious practices and festivals. Offerings for example were made to the goddess Venus who is associated with love, beauty and sex and was also considered to be the goddess of prostitution. This offering coincided with the wine festival known as Vinalia held in honor of both Venus and Jupiter. This is why the Apostle Paul was so adamant: 'do not get drunk on wine, which leads to debauchery' (Ephesians 5:18 NIV).

It is here that we also begin to see at work the literal application of the term harlotry in the Bible prophecy. It is important to see that a partial fulfillment of the 'great harlot' prophecy occurred in the 10th century when the Roman Catholic Church became literally entrapped by harlotry. Their rule during this time has been described by historians as 'pornocratic' government, or 'the Rule of the Harlots'. Between 904 and 964 the Popes were under the control of the Theophylacti, an aristocratic family. Pope Sergius III became completely under the spell of one female member of this family who used sex to exert her power over the religious affairs of Rome.

It was this pornocratic rule that tellingly brought about the 'Saeculum obscurum' – Latin for the Dark Age. As the ruling power engaged in harlotry a time of great darkness descended upon the land. A terrible tribulation ensued for the Christians of the day who where martyred. Many were beheaded for their unyielding faith in Jesus Christ. Both tribulation and beheadings of the saints follow the prophesied 'great harlot' end-time system.

From this event we can understand the reality, power and workings of the 'great harlot' religious system of which the Apostle John prophesied would rise from Rome and dominate the globe in the end times.

Additional prophetic insights can be obtained by looking at the etymology of the word pornocracy. 'Pornocracy' comes from Greek – pornokratia, meaning 'prostitute rule'. It is derived from the Greek word pornai which means 'to sell' and the word porni meaning 'prostitute'. It is the word from which the English word 'porn' is derived.

In these end-times we are living in an age that is literally awash with pornography, the viewing of prostitutes performing sexual acts, where people bow down and worship the graven images of other people. Porn has become embedded in our culture. Accelerated by the information age, porn has found its way into all streams of media. What was once only obtainable in secret from 'under the counter' is now readily available at the click of a mouse in every internet-enabled home across the globe.

Significantly, today a bronze idol called 'Belle' stands in full public view in Europe's Sodom – Amsterdam. [30] Installed in March of 2007 the statue honors the prostitutes of the world. This international symbol of the harlot system reveals just how acceptable the destructive sex trade has become and will continue to be in the new world order of the Antichrist.

Conversely the Bible says, 'for a harlot is a deep pit, and a seductress is a narrow well. She also lies in wait as for a victim, and increases the unfaithful among men' (Proverbs 23: 27-28 (NKJV)). 'For the lips of an immoral woman drip honey, and her mouth is smoother than oil; her feet go down to death, her steps lay hold of hell.' 'For why should you, my son, be enraptured by an immoral woman?' 'His own iniquities entrap the wicked man, and he is caught in the cords of his sin. He shall die for lack of instruction, and in the greatness of his folly he shall go astray' (Proverbs 5: 3, 5, 20, 22-23, NKJV).

This harlotry through the medium of pornography is not a random perversion within our culture today. No, it is intrinsically linked to the prophesied 'great harlot' religious system. This form of idol worship is not only one of the vices that will aid in the religious system's rise to power, but also one that will ultimately result in the worship of a man – the Antichrist.

And he [the False Prophet] exercises all the authority of the first beast [Antichrist] in his presence, and causes the earth and those who dwell in it to worship the first beast... (Revelation 13:12, NKJV).

The Bible exhorts humanity to flee from all sexual immorality (1 Corinthians 6:18). If those who engage in these practices do not heed the warning it will be impossible for them to withstand the wiles of the devil in this late hour. They will, without resistance, succumb to the deception of the Antichrist and give themselves over completely to his system. 'And he [the False Prophet and head of the great harlot world religion] deceives those who dwell on the earth' (Revelation 13:14, NKJV).

The Apostle Paul confirms that fornication which is adultery is synonymous with the religious act of idolatry. 'Therefore put to death...fornication...which is idolatry' (Colossians 3:5). Again in Ephesians 5:5 he writes, 'for this you know, that no fornicator... who is an idolater, has any inheritance in the kingdom of Christ and God' (NKJV).

This is why Jesus charged that looking upon the female form lustfully was akin to the act of adultery (Matthew 5:28). because it is idolatry – worship of the human form. In Romans 1:25 we read they 'exchanged the truth of God for a lie, and worshipped and served the creature rather than the Creator'. Romans 1:26-27 goes on to describe the fruit this kind of worship brings:

For this reason God gave them up to vile passions. For even their women exchanged the natural use for what is against nature. Likewise also the men, leaving the natural use of the woman, burned in their lust for one another, men with men committing what is shameful, and receiving in themselves the penalty of their error which was due. (Romans 1:26-27, NKJV).

As men and women exchange what is natural for unnatural we see yet another fulfillment of end time Bible prophecy. Today the sanctity of traditional marriage between a man and a woman hangs in the balance. It is under vehement attack by amoral groups and western governments. The Bible declares the silencing of marriage in its description of the end-time doom of the religious world system. Revelation 18:23 reads, 'the voice of bridegroom and bride shall not be heard in you anymore' (NKJV).

The false worship of people is also evidenced in the music industry. Today many recording artists dress and perform in a blatantly sexual and pornographic manner – in ways that in former years were reserved only for the strip clubs.

Miley Cyrus' sexually debauched performance perfectly demonstrated this at the 2013 MTV Video Music Awards.

Cyrus a former child star of the Disney Channel and adored by millions of young girls continues to be a role model under this new guise. Her performance in hair-twisted devil horns and flesh-coloured latex bikini, Cyrus wagged her tongue, touched her crotch with a giant foam finger and gyrated with Robin Thicke.

This is nothing less than prostitution for the masses.

It is this kind of conduct which has caused fans to literally idolise these aptly named divas. This adulation is a form of religious-style worship. Pastor Keith Hudson, father of Katy Perry the pop music star, who reportedly called his daughter a 'devil child' in his sermons and requested that his congregation 'pray for Katy' said, 'I was at a concert of Katy's where there were 20,000. I'm watching this generation and they were going at it. It almost looked like church. I stood there and wept and kept on weeping and weeping. They're loving and worshipping the wrong thing.' [31]

Furthermore, Madonna, whose very name is sacrilegious, has been described as being largely responsible for erasing the line between music and pornography.[32] She has also been depicted as being 'an almost sacred feminist icon'[33] and a 'porn rock star'. Her controversial music video and number one hit 'Like a Prayer' (1989) prophetically portrayed the end time fusion between sexual and religious idolatry. Madonna cavorts in a skimpy dress amid a satanic backdrop of blazing crosses of fire. With lyrics laden with hidden sexual references, the statue of a Roman Catholic saint miraculously comes to life inside a church and kisses Madonna. At one point the saint appears to be dressed in the clothes of Christ. Madonna also receives stigmata, a phenomenon usually associated in Catholicism with that of sainthood.

We can see then that the prophesied world religious system will be one that is engaged in whoredom both religiously and sexually. These two adulterous acts are idolatry – the act of worship in false religion – and the worship of the human form that will eventually lead to the worship of the Antichrist world leader.

World Peace

The ideology of world peace is the single most powerful tool that will see a unification of the world religions. World peace is and will be the highest doctrine of the one world religious system. But in God's Law, as well as in end-time prophecy, the Bible makes it very clear that this goal will be impossible to achieve, even through the best and well meaning efforts of humanity. We read in Leviticus that if the people walk in accordance with God's Law then peace will come to the land. It is as simple as that. World peace is achievable only through obeying God's Law for life. The one world religious system by its very nature is opposed to the Biblical Law of God. In fact it does not recognize the God of the Bible let alone the Bible.

The Scriptures declare:

If you walk in My statutes and keep My commandments, and perform them...you shall...dwell in your land safely. I will give peace in the land, and you shall lie down, and none will make you afraid; I will rid the land of evil beasts, and the sword will not go through your land (Leviticus 26:3,5b,6, NKJV).

The opposite occurs for those who choose to disobey God's Law:

But if you do not obey Me, and do not observe all these commandments, and if you despise My statutes, or if your soul abhors My judgments, so that you do not perform all My commandments, but break My covenant...you shall be defeated by your enemies. Those who hate you shall reign over you (Leviticus 26:14-15,17, NKJV).

As we have seen the globalist vision for a new world order and new world religious system is completely contrary to the commands of God as laid out in the Bible. Through these systems therefore world peace is an utterly false and unobtainable goal.

The Antichrist, when he arrives and is received by the religious and political bodies, will use the prospect of peace as one of his main strategies to be received by the masses. The Antichrist will become the de facto leader of the peace movement. By signing a seven year peace treaty with Israel concerning a land dispute (Daniel 9:27, 11:39) the Antichrist will solidify the peace movement and bring it into full effect.

However, this 'master of deception' (Daniel 8:25) will not intend to keep his promise, and after three and a half years of peace, will break it (Daniel 9:27). When the people feel secure he will wage war killing many (Daniel 8:25). Jeremiah and the Apostle Paul spoke of false prophets who claimed peace when there was none. Jeremiah wrote about false prophets proclaiming 'peace, peace!' When there is no peace, (Jeremiah 6:13-14, NKJV) and the Apostle Paul said, concerning the day of the Lord, 'for when they say, "Peace and safety!" then sudden destruction comes upon them...' (1 Thessalonians 5:3, NKJV).

World peace amongst other schemes of the Antichrist will be a 'delusive marvel' a 'lying wonder' and an 'unlimited seduction to evil and with all wicked deception for those who are perishing because they did not welcome the Truth but refused to love it that they might be saved [the true gospel of Jesus Christ]...[they were given] a working of error and a strong delusion to make them believe what is false...[false religion]' (2 Thessalonians 2:9-11, AMP).

This will be in stark contrast to Jesus Christ who will follow directly after the Antichrist. Christ, also prophetically called the Prince of Peace (Isaiah 9:6), has – unlike the Antichrist – made a covenant that he will never break. The peace that is being offered today is through worldly means. But Jesus made it clear that true peace is not of this world, 'My peace I give to you; not as the world gives do I give to you...' (John 14:27, NKJV).

The United Nations is predominantly at the heart of the world peace movement today. The UN emblem itself symbolically depicts its mission and vision for world peace by using a map of the earth surrounded by olive branches.

Alongside the UN working to achieve this goal is the interfaith movement. One such interfaith group is The World Council of Religious Leaders which works with the United Nations in the quest for world peace. It was founded between 12th-14th June 2002 in Bangkok at Buddhamonthon and also at the United Nation's Economic and Social Commission for Asia and the Pacific (UNESCAP) [34].

The stated aims of the organization serve to show that the ideal of a one world religious system is intertwined with both the United Nations and world peace:

The World Council of Religious Leaders aims to serve as a model and guide for the creation of a community of world religions. It seeks to inspire women and men of all faiths in the pursuit of peace and mutual understanding. It will undertake initiatives that will assist the United Nations...by uniting the human community for times of world prayer and meditation, the Council seeks to aid in the development of the inner qualities and external conditions needed for the creation of a more peaceful, just and sustainable world society...The role of religious leaders has never been more important in helping to set a new direction for the human community. The World Council will encourage the religious traditions and the United Nations to work in closer cooperation in building a community of the world's religions to work for the benefit of the global family. [35]

The World Council of Religious Leaders was borne out of The Millennium World Peace Summit of Religious and Spiritual

Leaders which was hosted in the General Assembly chamber at the United Nations headquarters in August of 2000. The summit brought together 1000 religious leaders from around the world, and was announced after media mogul and globalist elite Ted Turner, founder of CNN, and the then UN Secretary-General Kofi Annan had met in conversations. It is disturbing that Turner, who is known for his anti-Christian rhetoric, was one of the influencing minds behind the summit and it really serves to show its true nature and anti-Christian agenda. Turner has said of Christianity that it is a 'religion for losers' and commented that anti-abortionists were 'Bozos.' [36]

Ted Turner, who also serves on the board of directors for the United Nations Foundation – a charity set up in order to broaden UN support – donated a staggering $1 billion to the support of the United Nations. According to reports, Turner who addressed the 1000 peace summit delegates, denounced Christianity commenting that it was 'intolerant because it taught we were the only ones going to heaven.' Turner continued 'that confused the devil out of me since that would have left heaven a very empty place.' [37]

The response of the delegates was apparently one of high approval. But one has to wonder what acceptance the crowd would have given if Turner had condemned Islam in such a way.

Some of the funding for the event came from fellow globalists and United Nations supporters, the Rockefeller Brothers foundation. [38] Remember it was the Rockefellers who originally donated the land for the United Nations complex that stands on the Manhattan River today.

The World Council of Religious Leader's UN-approved emblem has adopted the exact same earth artwork from the UN emblem, but replaces the olive leaves with thirteen religions icons. The religions represented are; Bahai, Buddhism, Christianity, Confucianism, Hinduism, Indigenous Religions, Islam, Jainism,

Judaism, Shintoism, Sikhism, Taoism, Zoroastrianism.

'Indigenous Religions' is an all encompassing term, but can be defined simply as Paganism. Pagan religions include beliefs such as the following: polytheism (the belief in many deities), shamanism (the contact of spirits through altered states), animism (the belief that all things, including living things and inanimate objects, possess a spirit) and pantheism (where God and the universe are one and the same). Other indigenous religious practices include divination, magic, witchcraft, sorcery, secret societies and Satanism.

All these practices are strictly prohibited in God's Law. Deuteronomy 18:10-13 reads:

There shall not be found among you anyone...who practices witchcraft, or a soothsayer, or one who interprets omens, or a sorcerer, or one who conjures spells, or a medium, or a spiritist, or one who calls up the dead. For all who do these things are an abomination to the Lord, and because of these abominations the Lord your God drives them out from before you. You shall be blameless before the Lord your God (NKJV).

Furthermore the Bible declares that anyone who practices witchcraft cannot know peace. 'What peace, as long as the harlotries of your mother Jezebel and her witchcraft are so many?' (2 Kings 9:22, NKJV)

The religious faiths will not be able to co-exist with one another without compromising their core beliefs. For some of course will not need to as their belief systems accommodate many ideas and possess no strict articles of faith. However for the Abrahamic religions such as Judaism, Christianity and Islam a drastic departure from their foundational doctrines will need to take place. For example, all three Abrahamic religions attest that there is only one God, that idol worship is strictly prohibited and that witchcraft, divination and the like are abominable practices.

264

This is really where world peace will operate as the main factor in unifying the world religions. The peace plan will ultimately find its fulfillment first in the Middle East when the Antichrist signs the peace treaty with Israel. However, a very significant event will need to take place to initiate this. Could it be a false-flag terrorist attack upon the Temple Mount area that results in the destruction of the Dome of the Rock, or the al-Aqsa mosque, or a heightened and very real threat of nuclear war in the region? Whatever the circumstances we know from Bible prophesy that peace will be declared.

At some point in the near future according to Bible prophecy a third Jewish temple will be built on the mount. Whether or not it will co-exist alongside the Islamic holy site remains to be seen. What is clear though is that the idea for the third temple is fast looking like it will become the vehicle to bring about the prophesied false peace.

The Temple Institute whose aim is to rebuild the third temple in our time writes, 'of all the issues we confront today, there is only one which holds the key. The key to peace, prosperity, security, and fulfillment – the rebuilding of the Holy Temple in Jerusalem, the place that G-d has chosen.'[39] Once the temple is built the Antichrist, 'the man of peace', will according to prophecy desecrate it. The true key to peace is the Prince of Peace Jesus Christ (Isaiah 9:6) – not a physical temple (Hebrews 9:11).

As peace is achieved and declared in the Middle East the ripple effect will go out to the nations and in effect solidify the fledgling one world religion.

The Middle East Peace Quartet exists for the purpose of bringing peace to the Israeli-Palestinian conflict. This group is the embryo or forerunner that will see the signing of the prophesied peace treaty. The Quartet is so named due to the four political entities that are involved in the peace process. These are the United Nations, the United States, the European Union and Russia.

The former Prime Minister of the United Kingdom Tony Blair is its Special Envoy.

Since leaving Downing Street Tony Blair has become influential on the economic, political and religious world stage. In 2009 Blair was in the running to become the first President of Europe. Although he failed to make the post it did not deter him from taking his eyes off the prophetic continent. In 2012 Blair called for a directly elected President of Europe. 'A Europe-wide election for the presidency...is the most direct way to involve the public. An election for a big post held by one person – this people can understand.' In issuing this call, Blair alluded to the very post he himself wanted. [40]

While Blair was in power his spin chief Alastair Campbell famously declared 'we don't do God.' [41] Today however Blair is now a convert to Roman Catholicism and ironically the founder of the Tony Blair Faith Foundation. This foundation is a highly influential interfaith organization that also happens to operate its US office out of Yale University, where the notorious Illuminati Skull and Bones Order is based. One has to wonder if this is purely coincidental. From a spiritual perspective it is certainly not by chance. Jesus declared that in the time of the end where many are claiming true religion that 'wherever the corpse is, there the vultures will gather' (Matthew 24:28, NSAB).

Blair's foundation is aggressively pushing forward the interfaith agenda and works with other interfaith groups such as The Coexist Foundation and Abraham House, which seek to bring the Islamic, Jewish and Christian faiths into harmonious relationship with each other.

Michel Schooyans, a doctor in philosophy and theology, believes that 'one of the aims of the Tony Blair Faith Foundation...will be that of remaking the major religions...With this purpose, the foundation in question will try to expand the "new rights," using the world religions for this end and adapting these for their new duties. The religions will have to be reduced to the same common denominator, which means stripping them of their identity.'[42]

Blair's Faith Foundation also participates and promotes the United Nations World Interfaith Harmony Week. The Harmony Week whose stated multi-faith commandments are 'Love of God, and Love of the Neighbor' has also created multi-faith prayer beads in support of the interfaith event. Hand made from the Holy Land's finest olivewood, the 'Harmony beads' have been specifically designed for people of all faiths.

Blair's appointment as Special Envoy in the Middle East Peace Quartet itself echoes prophecy. Blair is more associated with war than he is with peace. His role in the Iraq invasion of 2003 and the subsequent weapons of mass destruction scam has left many demanding that he be indicted for war crimes. In like manner so the Antichrist and the False Prophet will speak peace, but in reality will be men of war.

In further prophetic overtones, Blair – who has often been accused in the press as having a Messiah complex – was at one point preparing to move into a palace in Jerusalem.[43] The residence stands on 'The Hill of Evil Counsel' and is the place where Judas betrayed Christ.[44] The palace home would have given Blair a daily view over the contested Temple Mount area, where the al-Aqsa mosque and the Dome of the Rock currently stands, and according to Bible prophecy where the Third Temple will be built. Due to much criticism however the move never took place. Eerily though Blair still seems to consider Jerusalem his home. Upon visiting the British Embassy in Washington in 2009 Blair strangely entered 'Jerusalem' as his place of residence in the VIP guest book. [45]

Although Blair does not live in Jerusalem, he does however spend at least one week a month in the Holy Land. In a bid to broker the prophesied peace deal Blair operates out of his highly secure purpose built offices in Sheikh Jarrah, the millionaires' row of East Jerusalem. [46] Speaking from his Jerusalem offices

Blair spoke of his renewed hope in reaching such a settlement upon the re-election of Obama. 'I think President Obama's re-election gives us the chance to go back into it with a renewed sense of momentum and a plan to move it forward. I think, expect, hope that this is what will happen.' [47]

Prophetic undercurrents continue within the relationship between Blair and Obama. These shadows or types serve to reveal the intense spiritual climate that is leading towards the fulfillment of Bible prophecy today.

Obama lavished praise on Blair at the 2009 National Prayer Breakfast in Washington when Blair was the principle speaker. 'I want to thank my good friend Tony Blair for coming today, somebody who did it first and perhaps did it better than I will do. He has been an example for so many people around the world of what dedicated leadership can accomplish. And we are very grateful to him.' [48]

Blair's adulation of Obama is also clear. In his memoirs Blair wrote, '[Obama's]...personal character is clear: this is a man with steel in every part of him.' [49]

Blair's relationship with Obama extends further though and in 2012 it emerged that he even helped Obama in his re-election campaign. [50]

The relationship between the two men is certainly an interesting one. Both have found a certain affinity and that is likely wrapped up in their mutual high profile leadership roles, but also and more importantly in their significant religious convictions.

What with Obama's Islamic persuasions and his role as dictatorial head of the world's superpower (thereby ostensibly the leader of the world), and with Tony Blair's Roman Catholic faith (acting as leader of the fledgling one world religion through his Faith Foundation, and coupled with that his peace role in the religious capital of the world), this certainly makes for a very interesting alliance indeed. One could be forgiven for believing that the combined credentials of these two men had been pulled right out of the pages of an end time novel.

The archetypal connection of the Antichrist and the False Prophet at work here in the relationship between Blair and Obama is impossible to deny.

The Antichrist will lead the world in a dictatorial world government while his religious aid – the False Prophet – will lead the one world religion.

Blair, in keeping with his interfaith convictions, does not adhere to Biblical Christianity. His faith is more of a smorgasbord of different religious ideas. Blair, who has praised Islam as being 'beautiful' [51] and said its prophet Mohammed had been 'an enormously civilizing force' [52], is also an avid reader of the Quran. 'I read the Quran every day. Partly to understand some of the things happening in the world, but mainly just because it is immensely instructive.' [53]

Moreover, in 2006 Blair said of the Quran that it was a 'reforming book, it is inclusive. It extols science and knowledge and abhors superstition. It is practical and way ahead of its time in attitudes to marriage, women and governance.' [54]

Presumably Blair has not read the Quran's marital advice for wives: 'but those [wives] from whom you fear arrogance – [first] advise them; [then if they persist], forsake them in bed; and [finally], strike them.' (Quran 4:34)

It is certainly disturbing that Blair has claimed the Quran to be a reforming book, but it is a claim with which his counterpart Obama would likely agree.

The governance that Blair believes is ahead of its time can surely only refer to governance by Sharia law. After years of examination by great imams through the interpretation of the

Quran, Hadith (sayings of Mohammed) and Mohammed's life the legal system known as Sharia came into being.

Sharia is well known for its discrimination against women.

Human rights activist Nahla Mahmoud from Sudan writes concerning Islam's attitude towards women: 'a woman's testimony is worthy half a man's in Islam. She gets half the inheritance of her male siblings; a woman's marriage contract is between her male guardian and her husband. A man can have four wives and divorce his wife by simple repudiation using the word "Talig", whereas a woman must give specific reasons, some of which are extremely difficult to prove...Another issue is marital rape, honor killings and domestic violence: in Pakistan, there are 300 cases of acid burnt women with no charges pressed against their husbands.'

Mahmoud continues, 'under Sharia law, a girl is eligible for marriage as soon as a girl begins her first period. This makes it difficult to maintain a minimum age for girls to be married. Considering there were at least five cases recorded in the London Borough of Islington (including girls of only 9 years old), I wouldn't bother to count the number of child marriages in Islamic states where it is legal...Moreover, little girls are often taught from birth that they are 'lesser' human beings, which results in lower self-esteem and lack of confidence later in life.' [55]

Under Shariah a Muslim woman's entire body is considered to be 'Awrah,' a sexual organ. She must therefore cover it completely and in many instances her face also. To prove rape a woman must have four male witnesses. If a man catches his wife in the act of adultery and murders her he is forgiven. However, the opposite is not true for the woman, since he could also be married to the woman he was caught with. If a wife is considered to be rebellious on her husband's part he has permission to beat and imprison her in the home. A man can have sex with women captured in battle. If the woman happens to be married, her marriage is annulled. (56)

These distorted views towards women are not only demeaning but they also echo again the connection between the lusts of the flesh and the end-time religious system. Further evidence of this can also be seen in the Islamic idea that a Muslim martyr will receive between 70 and 72 virgins in the hereafter. But actually the idea of a sex crazed paradise extends to all Muslim men whether martyr or not. The Islamic paradise is described in full wanton detail in the Quran. The men are waited on by immortal youths with an endless supply of wine while dark eyed beautiful virgins tend to their every need for all eternity, (Quran 56:12-39). The Quranic commentator and polymath Al-Suyati (1505) wrote that men will be in a constant state of sexual excitement and the 70 women they marry will have 'appetizing vaginas.' (57)

In direct contrast to this the Bible emphatically declares that those who engage in the practices described in the Islamic paradise will have no place in God's holy kingdom: 'the acts of the sinful nature are obvious: sexual immorality, impurity and debauchery...drunkenness, orgies, and the like. I warn you as I did before, that those who live like this will not inherit the kingdom of God;' 'do not get drunk on wine, which leads to debauchery' (Galatians 5:19-21; Ephesians 5:18, NIV). 'Wine is a mocker... and whoever is led astray by it is not wise;' 'he who loves pleasure will be a poor man; he who loves wine...will not be rich' (Proverbs 20:1; Proverbs 21:17).

Further examples of what governance under Sharia looks like include its attitude towards homosexuality. Homosexuality is punishable by public flogging, imprisonment or the death penalty. Conversion to another religion leaves a person an apostate, which is often also punishable by death. Free thinking and free speech are treated as a crime, as is blasphemy. Perpetrators are subject to public flogging, imprisonment or execution.(58)

It is possible that Blair's ideas concerning Islamic women and governance by Sharia law have arisen from the influence of his sister-in-law rather than from his reading of the Quran. Lauren Booth, Cherie Blair's sister, converted to Islam in 2010. Booth had what she recounted as a 'holy experience.' After visiting an Islamic shrine, Booth claimed she 'felt this shot of spiritual morphine, just absolute bliss and joy.'

Booth said that she hoped her conversion would help change Blair's views about Islam. It appears that it did just that.[59]

Whatever the reasons for Blair's attitude towards Islam, the influence of this religion upon his Faith Foundation cannot be underestimated. It is a matter of grave concern. This is because Islam is fundamentally not content peacefully to co-exist with its non-Islamic religious neighbors. Blair's vision here is naïve. While Christianity and other faiths compromise their belief systems and embrace one another in so called harmony, Islam, by stealth, moves in for the kill.

The West's interfaith movement, political correctness and its complete indifference to the encroaching danger of Islam is opening the door to total religious subjugation. Muslims are taking full advantage of the apathetic tide that has swept across the West.

While Muslims demand and receive permission to build Saudi-funded mosques throughout Britain, Europe and America, the Saudi government bans Christian churches in Saudi Arabia![60]

Furthermore our leaders bizarrely tell us that Muslims who slay people on the streets of Britain – while crying Allahu Akbar, 'Allah is greater' – have absolutely nothing to do with Islam. Muslim clerics must stand back and laugh as more ground is claimed in their fight to subdue the West.

Consider the horrific killing of soldier Lee Rigby on the streets

272

of Britain in May 2013. The assailants screamed 'Allahu Akbar' while hacking their victim to death and decapitating him. One of the killers, Michael Adebolajo, declared on video moments after the attack: 'the only reason we have killed this man today is because Muslims are dying daily by British soldiers.'[61] Rigby had served in Afghanistan.

Prime Minister David Cameron responded by saying that the attack was 'a betrayal of Islam' and that those responsible had 'sought to justify their actions by an extremist ideology that perverts and warps Islam...There is nothing in Islam that justifies acts of terror...'[62] While the London mayor Boris Johnson exclaimed, 'it is completely wrong to blame this killing on Islam.'[63]

However, contrary to both Cameron and Johnson's claims, Adebolajo seemed to think otherwise. He went on to state, 'we are forced by the Quran, in Sura At-Tawba, through many ayah in the Quran, we must fight them as they fight us. An eye for an eye, a tooth for a tooth.'[64]

Adebolajo specifically made reference to At-Tawba, chapter nine of the Quran. This chapter is basically one long call to jihad. Let us be clear here, Adebolajo stated, 'we are forced by the Quran.' Adebolajo knew what he was talking about. Adebolajo was obeying the Quran.

At-Tawba 9:5 reads: 'and when the sacred months have passed, then kill the polytheists wherever you find them and capture them and besiege them and sit in wait for them at every place of ambush.'

The term polytheist is a reference to those who are of the Christian religion. Islam teaches that a Christian worships more than one God – the Father and the Son.

Furthermore, the Quran specifically justifies the reason for such murders and explicitly details how they should be carried out.

'The punishment of those who wage war against Allah and His messenger and strive to make mischief in the land is only this, that they should be murdered or crucified or their hands and their feet should be cut off on opposite sides or they should be imprisoned; this shall be as a disgrace for them in this world, and in the hereafter they shall have a grievous chastisement.' (Quran 5:33)

'I will cast terror into the hearts of those who disbelieve. Therefore strike off their heads and strike off every fingertip of them.' (Quran 8:12)

Jihad is the religious duty of all true Muslims. In Arabic it literally means 'struggle.' This struggle refers to the fight against those who do not adhere to the beliefs of Islam. The purpose and goal of jihad is to establish Islamic rule – both religious and political – over the entire planet.

Mawlana Abul Ala Mawdudi one of Islam's best known scholars, writers and thinkers concerning modern jihad comments:

'Islam is not a normal religion like the other religions in the world, and Muslim nations are not like normal nations. Muslim nations are very special because they have a command from Allah to rule the entire world and to be over every nation in the world.

Islam is a revolutionary faith that comes to destroy any government made by man... Islam doesn't care about the land or who owns the land. The goal of Islam is to rule the entire world and submit all of mankind to the faith of Islam. Any nation or power in this world that tries to get in the way of that goal, Islam will fight and destroy.
In order for Islam to fulfill that goal, Islam can use every power available every way it can be used to bring worldwide revolution. This is jihad.' [65]

How then is jihad carried out?

274

It is practiced in three stages. Mark A. Gabriel PH.D a former professor of Islamic history identifies these stages as the 'weakened stage', the 'preparation stage' and the 'jihad stage'. This carefully strategized process of gradual intensification explains why in some instances Islam can appear benign and peaceful.

The 'weakened stage' is when Muslims are in the minority, as is the case in many Western nations. It is in this stage that Muslims are peaceful and more tolerant. Quranic verses are used such as, 'you shall have your religion and I shall have my religion,' (Quran 109:6) and, 'there is no compulsion in religion' (Quran 2:256).

The 'preparation stage' is when Muslims still form a minority but are growing in influence. It is at this stage that they make preparation for the final confrontation in the jihad stage. Quran 8:59-50 reads: 'let not the Unbelievers think that they can get the better (of the godly): they will never frustrate (them). Against them make ready your strength to the utmost of your power, including steeds of war, to strike terror into (the hearts of) the enemies, of Allah and your enemies.'

Quran 8:60 reads – with additional commentary – 'and make ready against them all you can of power, including steeds of war (tanks, planes, missiles, artillery) to threaten the enemy of Allah.'

The 'jihad stage' is when Muslims continue to be a minority but now have influence and power. It is at this point that they are commanded to engage in full jihad in a non-Muslim land and attempt to establish Islamic rule.
As Quran 9:5 states: 'fight and slay the Pagans wherever you find them, and seize them, beleaguer them, and lie in wait for them in every stratagem (of war).'

Then again in Quran 9:29 it says, 'fight those who believe not in Allah nor the Last Day, nor hold that forbidden which hath been forbidden by Allah and His Messenger, nor acknowledge the Religion of Truth, from among the People of the Book, until they pay the Jizyah (non-Muslim citizen tax) with willing submission, and feel themselves subdued.'

This verse is significant. Here Muslims are not ordered to fight only the oppressor but to fight those who do not believe in Islam. Once the jihad stage is active Jews and Christians therefore become the enemies of Islam too.

The following teachings of Mohammed reveal Islam's true attitude towards both Christians and Jews:

'O you who believe! do not take the Jews and the Christians for friends; they are friends of each other; and whoever amongst you takes them for a friend, then surely he is one of them; surely Allah does not guide the unjust people.' (Quran 5:51)

'And the Jews say: Uzair is the son of Allah; and the Christians say: The Messiah is the son of Allah; these are the words of their mouths; they imitate the saying of those who disbelieved before; may Allah destroy them; how they are turned away!' (Quran 9:30)

'Those who reject (Truth), among the People of the Book and among the Polytheists, will be in Hell-Fire, to dwell therein. They are the worst of creatures.' (Quran 98:6)

'Muhammad said: "I will expel the Jews and Christians from the Arabian Peninsula and will not leave any but Muslim."' (Sahih Muslim 4366)

'Muhammad said: "Do not give the People of the Book the greeting first. Force them to the narrowest part of the road."' (Al-Bukhari, Al-Adab al-Mufrad 1103)

So far in this chapter we have seen that a one-world religion will be the final building block in the globalist takeover of the planet. We have seen that this religious system will be headed by the False Prophet, that the nations will be duped in a massive end-time deception both through the media and pharmaceutical drugs, that the one world religion is called the 'The Great Harlot' and that it will be a religious system engaged in whoredom both religious and sexual, that world peace will be the highest doctrine to deceive the masses into accepting it, that the United Nations and interfaith groups and particularly Blair's Faith Foundation are working towards unifying the religions. We looked at the attitude of the West towards the growing threat of Islam. Finally we saw how Tony Blair's vision to bring the world religions together in harmony is inherently flawed; Islam does not desire to live in peace with its religious neighbors, but rather has a mandate to dominate the entire world.

Now let us look at the evidence to suggest that the prophesied one world religion could indeed be a form of Islam.

By looking at both Christian and Islamic eschatology (study of the end times) side by side, a startling picture begins to emerge.

In Islamic eschatology Muslims are waiting for the coming of a man called 'the Mahdi' or 'al-Mahdi,' which literally means in Arabic 'the Guided One.' The coming of the Mahdi is central to all Islamic end-time teaching.

The Mahdi is Islam's savior. According to Islamic tradition, the Mahdi will bear the name of Mohammed. It is important to note that when Muslims say they are waiting for Mohammed they do not mean the prophet Mohammed, but rather a relation of him and one who bears his name.

'The world will not come to pass until a man from among my family, whose name will be my name, rules over the Arabs.'[66] 'Allah will bring out from concealment al-Mahdi from my family.'[67]

277

When the former president of Iran, Mahmoud Ahmadinejad, addressed the United Nations General Assembly he always opened by asking God to 'hasten the arrival of the Imam Mahdi.'

According to Islamic teaching the Mahdi will rule the entire world. He will lead a vast army and conquer Israel and reach the 'Baitul Maqdas' in Jerusalem, which means in Arabic 'the holy house' or 'the Dome of the Rock' on the Temple Mount.

'No power will be able to stop them and they will finally reach Eela (Baitul Maqdas in Jerusalem).' [68]

It is Jerusalem that Islam teaches will be the centre of Islamic rule.

At some point during the Mahdi's reign he will institute a seven year peace treaty between the Arabs and the West.

'Rasulullah [Muhammad] said: "There will be four peace agreements between you and the Romans [Christians]. The fourth agreement will be mediated through a person who will be from the progeny of Hadrat Haroon [Honorable Aaron – Moses' brother] and will be upheld for seven years.' [69]

The actions of the Mahdi in Islamic tradition resemble exactly the actions of the Antichrist as recorded in the Bible.

The Antichrist will rule the entire world, 'and authority was given him over every tribe, tongue, and nation' (Revelation 13:7b NKJV).
He will gather a vast army, 'it was granted to him to make war with the saints and to overcome them. (Revelation 13:7a NKJV)'

He will take himself to the Temple Mount (Islam's 'holy house') in Jerusalem. He will set himself up in the Third Temple and rule from it.

'Therefore when you see the 'abomination of desolation,' spoken of by Daniel the prophet, standing in the holy place (whoever reads, let him understand),' Matthew 24:15 (NKJV). See also Daniel 9:27 and 2 Thessalonians 2:4.

He will sign a seven year peace treaty with Israel. 'And he shall enter into a strong and firm covenant with the many for one week [seven years]' Daniel 9:27 (AMP).

During this time the Antichrist will deceive the Jews into believing that he accepts their religion. We know this because he allows them to perform their animal sacrifice. This false acceptance is a further evidence of Islam's involvement, since Islamic law allows lying to the Jewish people. The Islamic philosopher Ibn Taymiyah (1263-1328) wrote, 'believers should lie to people of the book (the Jews) to protect their lives and religion.' [70]

Furthermore, Mark A. Gabriel writes, 'there's a simple Islamic proverb that says, "If you can't cut your enemies' hand, kiss it."' Interestingly Gabriel goes on to say that Muslims are known for lying about peace agreements. 'Muslim groups will use peace talks or peace agreements to buy time so they can make new plans, prepare and position themselves for victory. Muslim military leaders will tell the other side whatever it wants to hear in order to buy time, but when it comes time to deliver what it agreed on, you will see a different story.' [71]

We know that when the Antichrist manifests evil incarnate he will break the peace treaty, abolish the sacrifices and desecrate the Temple. In Scripture this event is called the 'abomination that causes desolation'. It is spoken of by the prophet Daniel, by Jesus Christ himself and the Apostle Paul (Daniel 9:27; 11:31; 12:11; Matthew 24:15-16; 2 Thessalonians 2:4).

As if all this wasn't enough, Islamic eschatology also teaches about the second coming. Muslims actually believe in the second coming of Jesus, or to be more accurate, the second coming of their version of Jesus. Don't forget that Islam teaches that Jesus did not die upon the cross and that he is not the Son of God. Islam's Jesus is not the real Jesus.

According to Islamic tradition the second coming of Jesus is linked with that of the coming of the Mahdi. Jesus will meet with the Mahdi who will invite Jesus to pray. Jesus will however decline.

'Jesus Son of Mary will then descend and their (Muslims') commander (Al Mahdi) will invite him to come and lead them in prayer.' [72]

According to Islamic tradition, Jesus will institute Sharia law. While the Mahdi will be the political world leader, Jesus will be the religious world leader and enforce Sharia law. He will abolish Christianity, destroying their crosses and leading Christians to convert to Islam.

'Muslims will follow him as their leader. According to Shalabi, the Mahdi will lead the Muslims in prayer, and Jesus will rule the Muslims according to the Divine Law (Shariah).' [73]

'Jesus will descend from heaven and espouse the cause of the Mahdi. The Christians and the Jews will see him and recognize his true status. The Christians will abandon their faith in his godhead.' [74]

'The Prophet said: There is no prophet between me and him, that is, Jesus. He will descend (to the earth)... He will break the cross...Allah will perish all religions except Islam.' [75]
Jesus will then kill the Islamic version of the Antichrist called the 'Dajjal' along with his followers, the Jewish people.

'The Yahudis (Jews) of Isfahaan will be his (The Dajjals) main followers.' [76]

280

'His followers the Yahudis, will number 70,000... (Then) Hadrat Isa (honorable Jesus) kills the Dajjal at the Gate of Hudd, near an Israeli airport, in the valley of "Ifiq." The final war between the Yahudi's will ensue, and the Muslims will be victorious.'[77]

What are we to make of that?

This is what we are to make of it. The Jesus of Islam is the False Prophet in Biblical eschatology. The False Prophet will be the religious world leader.

'And he (False Prophet) exercises all the authority of the first beast (Antichrist) in his presence, and causes the earth and those who dwell in it to worship the first beast...' (Revelation 13:12, NKJV).

Furthermore, according to Bible prophecy, apostates who refuse to follow the world religion will be beheaded.

'Then I saw the souls of those who had been beheaded for their witness to Jesus and for the word of God, who had not worshiped the beast or his image...' (Revelation 20:4, NKJV).

Islam is well known for beheading apostates under Sharia law today.

In August 2012 a Christian man was beheaded by Muslims. The execution allegedly took place in Tunisia. During the video of the murder, the victim is seen calmly mouthing a prayer while a background speaker is heard condemning Christianity: 'let Allah be avenged on the polytheist apostate'; 'Allah empower your religion, make it victorious against the polytheists'; 'Allah, defeat the infidels at the hands of the Muslims'; 'There is no god but Allah and Muhammad is his messenger. Allahu Akbar!' [78] (God is greater).

It appears there is a serious case of mistaken identity within Islam. The Madhi of Islam sounds exactly like the Antichrist, while the Islamic Jesus is a perfect description of the Biblical False Prophet!

It is sobering to think that Islam's counterfeit Jesus will proclaim himself to be the true Christ. This could be one of the most powerful deceptions during the end times.

In light of this, Jesus' words regarding false prophets in the last days carry even more significance. Jesus warned, 'then if anyone says to you, 'Look, here is the Christ!' or 'There!' do not believe it. For false christs and false prophets will rise and show great signs and wonders to deceive, if possible, even the elect. See, I have told you beforehand' (Matthew 24:23-25, NKJV).

The 'Dajjal' or 'Al-Maseeh' in Islamic eschatology is the Islamic Antichrist. 'Dajjal' means 'the liar or Deceiver', and 'Al-Maseeh' means 'The Messiah'.

The Dajjal will claim to be both Jesus Christ and divine. He will be Jewish and the Jews will follow him.

'The Jews await the false Jewish messiah, while we await, with Allah's help... the Mahdi and Jesus, peace be upon him.' (79)

Could it be that the Muslim's Anti-Christ is really the true Jesus of the Bible? It sounds like it could be!

We can see that the likelihood of an Islamic dominant religious system is highly likely in the end times. 'Who's who' is going to be one of the biggest questions. It will involve a massive case of mistaken identity.

In summary —

The Jesus of Islam is the False Prophet of the Bible
The Mahdi of Islam is the Antichrist of the Bible
The Antichrist of Islam is the Jesus Christ of the Bible

Christians will need to know their Bible and hold fast to the truths contained within it, lest they be swept away by every wind of teaching. We will need to become more and more biblically literate so 'that we should no longer be children, tossed to and fro and carried about with every wind of doctrine, by the trickery of men, in the cunning craftiness of deceitful plotting' (Ephesians 4:14, NKJV).

There is however a more chilling piece of evidence that a form of Islam could be the world religious system during the end times.

In the next chapter, we will examine this clue.

Chapter 14

The Mark of the Beast

*They want a one world government, controlled by them,
everybody being chipped, all your money in those chips, and
they control the chips, and they control the people, and you
become a slave, you become a serf to these people*

Aaron Russo [1]

Some 2000 years ago the Apostle John, while imprisoned on
the island of Patmos, received a prophecy – a prophecy which
at that time would have been impossible to comprehend fully.
John wrote about a mark that would be applied to the hand or
the forehead of everyone on the planet – a device that would
become the ultimate surveillance tool and the only means
whereby a person could buy or sell. John wrote, 'he causes all,
both small and great, rich and poor, free and slave, to receive
a mark on their right hand or on their foreheads, and that no
one may buy or sell except one who has the mark or the name
of the beast, or the number of his name' (Revelation 13:16,17
– other Bible references to the 'Mark of the Beast' can be found
in Revelation 14:11; 15:2; 16:2; 19:20; 20:4) .

The original Greek word used for 'mark' in the book of Revelation
is revealing. The word is charagma. It means a 'stamp', 'etching',
'scratch'. It also means to 'brand' – as a farmer brands cattle.

Many people are familiar with the Bible verses in Revelation
which warn people not to accept the Mark of the Beast. But also

285

worthy of note is a verse in the Old Testament given to Moses in the book of Leviticus: 'you shall not make any cuttings in your flesh for the dead, nor tattoo any marks on you: I am the LORD' (Leviticus 19:28). God's laws are set in place to protect us and it is for this reason that He decreed that we should neither make cuts in our flesh nor receive tattoos on our bodies. When the mark of the beast is implemented worldwide those who have not heeded God's warning and have tattoos and piercings will likely offer the least resistance to this invasive proceedure.

Hitler and the Mark of the Beast

As we mentioned earlier the prophecy concerning the Mark of the Beast began its latter-day fulfillment in Nazi Germany. Hitler, fuelled by the anti-Semitic ideas propagated by his occultic gurus, persecuted and exterminated Europe's Jews and anyone who had converted to Christianity. But in order to achieve this colossal task he needed to first identify them. Once they had been identified only then could they be targeted. Today this would be an easy task in our technological and computerized world, but not so in 1933. When Hitler came to power computers were non-existent. However IBM had invented what was called the Hollerith punch-card machine. This would prove to be an invaluable tool for the Nazis in cataloguing and designating their victims for persecution and extermination. Each prisoner was assigned a five digit IBM Hollerith number for tracking purposes. Shockingly IBM supplied to Hitler's program of Jewish extermination the technological assistance he needed to accomplish this unprecedented act of genocidal murder. These machines where not only sold to Hitler's regime but disturbingly IBM even custom designed them for the task. [2]

After 1941 the five digit number was tattooed on the prisoners of Auschwitz concentration camp, the largest death camp in Europe, using a special stamp composed of needles. Later the number was tattooed using a single needle. As I showed earlier, the Greek word for 'mark' is charagma meaning to 'stamp', 'etch' or 'scratch'. What the Nazis implemented in Auschwitz was a dress rehearsal for the way the Mark of the Beast will be applied in the future. Its future use however will go far beyond simple identification. It will also complete the prophecy concerning commerce and the new global financial system.

The idea of tracking and numbering people did not die away with Nazi Germany. On the contrary, today in our technologically advanced world the idea has developed to a degree Hitler could not have dreamed.

For the first time ever it is now possible to control everyone on the planet, just as the Apostle John saw in his vision of the future. Without the Mark no one will be able to buy or sell. This is total people control. Now the technology exists. The next step is the implementation.

The Human Barcode

The microchipping of animals and pets has become standard practice. In England by 2016 it will become illegal to own a dog that has not been microchipped.[3] What about the microchipping of human beings?

In 2010 the residents of Virginia, Georgia and Tennessee states became concerned that they were being forced into accepting the prophesied Mark of the Beast. CBS News ran an article entitled, 'Va. Lawmakers Oppose Forced Microchip Implantation, and the Antichrist'. The article went on to read, 'the Virginia House of Delegates on Wednesday approved a measure that could protect Virginia residents from overbearing employers, and possibly the apocalypse. The law would make it illegal to implant an identification or tracking device into a person's body without their written consent. As the use of implanted microchips becomes more common – people use them to track pets and could possibly use them for purposes such as securing one's medical history...Others...are also concerned the use of microchips could be the "mark of the beast" – or the coming of the Antichrist. My understanding – I'm not a theologian – but there's a prophecy in the Bible that says you'll have to receive a mark, or you can neither buy nor sell things in end times,' Del. Mark L. Cole, the bill's sponsor, told the Post. 'Some people think these computer chips might be that mark.' [4]

Other news sources quoted, 'Human Microchips seen As 'Device of Antichrist' By Some in Virginia' [5], while another headlined, 'Apocalyptic Talk Stokes Microchip Implant Debate' [6]

You might think this kind of controversy would halt companies advancing the idea for human micro-chipping. But it has not. The VeriChip marketed by the VeriChip Corporation is a human RFID microchip for implantation into the human body which received approval from the US Food and Drug Administration in 2004. The microchip encased in a silicate glass rice sized tube contained an RFID transponder (Radio-frequency Identification) with a unique ID number that could be linked to an external database containing a variety of information such as personal identification and contact details, health records and medications of the implantee. However, in 2007 a damning blow was dealt to the VeriChip when it was found that similar implants had caused cancer in hundreds of lab animals.[7] The VeriChip Corporation now known as PositiveID therefore decided to discontinue marketing the product in 2010.

It is interesting by way of an aside that according to Bible prophecy, 'malignant sores broke out on everyone who had the mark of the beast and who worshiped his statue' (Revelation 16:2 NLT). Could the prophecy be referring to the side-effects of receiving an implantable microchip?

The mainstream media was quick to herald the demise of the VeriChip – also taking the usual opportunity to deride so-called conspiracy theorists too. In a piece entitled, 'Down With the Chip: PositiveID Axes Its Scary Medical Records Implant', we read that 'in a huge disappointment to bloggers and conspiracy theorists everywhere, PositiveID (PSID) CEO Scott Silverman says his company has stopped marketing its medical records microchip implant for humans. The reason: No one wants it.'[8]

You would have thought that this had sounded the final death knell for the beleaguered chip. But not so! Just two years later in a bizarre twist in January 2012 the very same Scott Silverman – now owner of the VeriTeQ Acquisition Corporation – acquired the VeriChip implantable microchip that apparently 'no one wants'! This begs the question, why acquire and market an unwanted product?

On the acquisition of the VeriChip, Silverman stated, 'I have always been a believer in the broad range of potential applications stemming from implantable RFID technology... implantable RFID microchips can provide an important link for patients, their medical records, vital signs and other important data.'[9] The controversy surrounding the implantable device does not seem to have stemmed Mr Silverman's enthusiasm.

In fact VeriTeQ is actually quite proud of its acquisition, stating on its website home page, 'welcome, VeriTeQ is a leader in implantable, radio frequency identification ("RFID") for humans and animals. VeriTeQ develops and markets innovative, implantable RFID technologies for humans...VeriTeQ's Unique Device Identifier (UDI) is the first human-implantable passive RFID microchip cleared for medical use by the U.S. Food and Drug Administration.' [10]

Let's read the last part of that sentence again, 'the first human-implantable passive RFID microchip cleared for medical use by the U.S. Food and Drug Administration.'

This raises yet another but disturbing question. Why has the US Food and Drug Administration not retracted its clearance for the implantable microchip amid the evidence of cancerous tumors found in animals implanted with similar devices?

The answer could be found in a startling interview conducted in 2007 with the late Hollywood director and documentary film maker Aaron Russo who produced the documentary 'America – From Freedom to Fascism' in which he exposed the criminality of the Federal Reserve, the central banking system of the United States.

According to Russo he was befriended by Nick Rockefeller who shared with him the secret goals of the elite. In the interview Russo said, 'the whole agenda is to create a one world government where everybody has an RFID chip implanted in them, all money is to be in those chips, right, there'll be no more cash, and this is given me straight from Rockefeller himself... all money will be in the chips and so instead of having cash any time you have money in your chip, they can take out whatever they want to take out, whenever they want to. If they say you owe us this much money in taxes they just deduct it out of your chip digitally...total control...and if you're like me or you, and you're protesting with what they're doing they can just turn off your chip, and you have nothing, you can't buy food, you can't do anything. It's total control of the people. Everything is in there. So they want a one world government, controlled by them, everybody being chipped, all your money in those chips, and they control the chips, and they control the people, and you become a slave, you become a serf to these people. That's their goal, that's their intension.' [11]

According to Russo, upon asking Rockefeller what was the point of doing all this, he replied, 'the end goal was to get everybody chipped, to control the whole society. To have the bankers, the elite people...controlling the world.'

What Rockefeller described to Russo was without doubt the fulfillment of the Mark of the Beast prophesied by the Apostle John 2000 years ago:

'He causes all, both small and great, rich and poor, free and slave, to receive a mark on their right hand or on their foreheads, and that no one may buy or sell...'

Daniel Estulin, author of *The True Story of the Bilderberg Group*, also describes this elitist plan. Estulin comments, 'one of the reasons they are trying to create a cashless society, because as long as you and I have cash, we can eat and as long as we can eat, we're free, at least we can defend ourselves. When you take the cash away, you create credit cards, and then you create microchips. What you're doing is, suddenly we become the whim of the powerful people. They can punish us by pressing delete three times on the computer screen and suddenly $10,000 turns into $10.' (12)

Of course VeriTeQ's implantable microchip is at this time being marketed mostly as a health tool so in this restricted capacity it does not fulfill the prophesied Mark of the Beast. However, the aspirations of Scott Silverman, VeriTeQ's owner, do. In 2003 Silverman, then Chief Executive of Applied Digital Solutions, said in a speech at the ID World 2003 Conference in Paris that they had developed a "VeriPay" technology and were hoping to find partners in financial service firms. The article on CNET News, entitled 'Chip implant gets cash under your skin', revealed, 'Applied Digital Solutions...is hoping that Americans can be persuaded to implant RFID chips under their skin to identify themselves when going to a cash machine or in place of using a credit card.' The article ends quoting MasterCard's Vice President Art Kranzley who told USA Today, 'it could be in a pen or a pair of earrings. Ultimately, it could be embedded in anything – someday, maybe even under the skin.' Finally, in a special promotion, Applied Digital Solutions urged Americans to 'get chipped' with the first 100,000 recipients to sign up for chipping to receive a $50 discount. (13)

Not long after the conference the exclusive VIP Baja Beach Club in the Catalan city of Barcelona adopted the ultimate membership card – the VeriChip implantable microchip, a payment device whereby members could purchase drinks without cash using simply a swipe of the hand. BBC Science producer Simon Morton, who received the microchip at the exclusive beach club, said, 'the idea of having my very own microchip implanted in my body appealed. I have always been an early adopter, so why not.' [14]

Then in 2005 another VIP club followed suit, Bar Soba in Glasgow. Brad Stevens, owner of Bar Soba, said, 'there are a number of advantages from instant access to...not having to carry money or credit cards...' [15]

Despite the issues and concerns surrounding the implantable microchip it is gaining a slow but sure level of acceptance.

This is being achieved in three principal ways.
These are:

1. A strategy of fear
2. Convenience and a cashless society
3. The technological enhancement of the human body

1. A strategy of fear

Using the 'problem, reaction, solution' paradigm we can quickly see that the implantable chip is being marketed by feeding on the fears of the consumer.

The chip, it is claimed, will save your life in an emergency – that is according to a VeriChip Health Link television advertisement which added somewhat emotively regarding the chip, 'when every second counts in the emergency room.' [16]

Every parent is concerned for the safety of their child. The chip will allegedly stop children from being abducted and murdered. Scientist Kevin Warwick from Reading University, west of London, says parents can keep track of their children by having them implanted with a microchip. Such a chip could prevent an abduction from becoming a murder, he says. [17]

Microchips can also monitor stress levels, inflammation, diseases, nutrition needs, and more in soldiers on the frontline.[18] In the wake of 9/11 most Americans valued safety over freedom and the microchip implant received a new lease of life. Digital Angel's CEO Sullivan said, 'today's security measures don't work very well...' noting that in five years he could see the chips being used in children, the elderly, prisoners, and by employers at facilities such as airports and nuclear plants. Society in general could use them instead of ATM or credit cards.[19]

2. Convenience and a cashless society

If it means shorter lines at the supermarket, a quarter of Germans would be happy to have a chip implanted under their skin, read an article reporting on a technology exhibition held in the city of Hanover, Germany in 2010. Professor August Wilhelm Scheer, speaking to an audience including Germany's Chancellor Angela Merkel, said that implanting chips into humans was going to become commonplace this decade. During the speech Scheer remarked, 'we just carried out a survey and one out of four people are happy to have a chip planted under their skin for very trivial uses – for example to pass gates more quickly at a discotheque and to be able to pay for things more quickly in the supermarket.' [20]

To a large degree cash is already dead and the prophesied cashless society is upon us. Therefore, it is vital to understand that with the advent of this cashless society the mark of the beast ebbs ever closer into actualization. That is because the mark of the beast and the cashless society are intrinsically linked together. Once cash is phased out and everyone is transferring money electronically, more and more convenient ways to make electronic payments will become available, the most significant of which will be contactless payment. This form of payment enables the consumer to wave their device over a point of sale reader. It is already in common use today in places like Japan, Singapore and South Korea, but will gain widespread use globally in the coming months and years.

At this point in time contactless payment uses a host of devices ranging from credit cards, debit cards, 'Coin' – which allows you to load up to eight credit cards onto a single plastic device, key fobs, smartcards and most significantly the cell phone – significant firstly because of their widespread use and secondly because it is quicker, simpler and more secure than other methods.

In 2011 Google launched the Google Wallet which allows for storage of all personal credit and debit cards onto a cell phone – all this while eBay's PayPal has teamed up with four Australian merchants to introduce a cashless payment system in Australia via a cell phone PayPal application, and in Amsterdam QR codes (a two dimensional version of the now common barcode) – gaining slow but sure popularity – are being rolled out. Here shoppers can scan the QR code fixed in a shop window using their cell phone, which automatically takes the user to the products displayed in the window. A product can then be selected and purchased using PayPal.[21] Thus the cell phone evolves into an electronic wallet, which can then be used to make purchases at stores by simply positioning the phone on a contactless payment terminal.

The cell phone will therefore provide the momentum to take contactless payment to a universally accepted norm. Once this has been established the transition to an even more convenient and secure method will become globally acceptable. Imagine a microchip implanted or attached in or tattooed on the hand becoming a popular option at the supermarket checkout, eliminating the need to rummage through pockets and handbags and speeding up the payment process. Just simply swipe your hand over the contactless payment terminal and you're good to go.

The general public has offered little resistance to contactless payment. This is due in part to its gradual roll out and clever marketing strategy. Today most people no longer carry cash. When cash is used it is usually for very small purchases like drinks and snacks, with large purchases being made using a debit or credit card, or online through payment systems like PayPal. In fact today it is not possible to make cash purchases in some stores as Diane Campbell from the US found when she went to purchase an iPad with a wad of cash. She was refused. 'Sorry, we don't take cash,' said the clerk. [22]

More and more the use of cash is being discouraged. In Britain utility companies are known for penalizing customers who do not pay with direct debit and are charged up to £100 extra a year over and against Direct Debit users. Furthermore, research conducted for a Channel 4 program – 'Dispatches' – found that anyone paying for a holiday using cash or check could see an increase in their bill of up to £400.[23] Many US airlines' domestic flights have now declared their cabins to be cash-free zones in order to simplify the in-flight transaction process.[24] But in what might possibly be one of the most significant leaps towards the planned cashless future – one which may create an avalanche of other retailers following suit – is that McDonald's restaurants in the United Kingdom and across Europe will be outfitting their fast food franchise locations with touch screen technology where customers will order and pay for their food with a credit card. Again convenience is the hook, with the claim that the average transaction is going to be three to four seconds faster. The machine's only method of payment will be debit or credit, with cash in McDonalds' restaurants being completely eliminated. [25]

3. The technological enhancement of the human body

The technological enhancement of the human body has been popularized in science fiction novels and Hollywood for decades. Movies like Star Wars, Robocop, Universal Soldier and Iron Man explore and even exalt the idea of humankind merging with technology. The danger of movies like these, particular for the young and impressionable, is that they can subconsciously create a fascination and desire to be like the heroic character portrayed in the story – especially if they have undergone technological enhancement. This subtly contributes towards a breakdown of resistance and can encourage a belief that the human body is somehow deficient in its natural God-given state. The conditions are then created in which the prospect of receiving an implantable microchip in the real world becomes an exciting and desirable idea rather than something to be feared and shunned.

In the lead-up to the eventual mass roll-out and marketing push for the implantable microchip in the western world we should expect to see Hollywood incorporating the chip into movie storylines as either incidental or as a part of the main storyline, and in a positive way.

The desire to modify the human body with technological enhancements is evidenced by the creation of the Cyborg Foundation in 2010. The foundation came about as a result of the amount of people around the world who were interested in becoming a cyborg. The Cyborg Foundation was the world's first organization dedicated to aiding humans to become a cybernetic organism – a union of biological with electronic, mechanical or robotic parts. The foundation's aim is the enhancement of the human anatomy by creating cybernetic extensions to the body, to promote human cybernetics and to defend cyborg rights. This technological union with humanity is also known as transhumanism – an ideology which disturbingly believes that in time humanity will have the ability through technological enhancement to transform itself far beyond what it considers to be the limitations of the human body into a superhuman, a posthuman or transhuman.

We are a long way off from the outlandish ideas of Transhumanism. However it is these kinds of concepts which open the door to accepting the technology today that will lead humanity into the trap known as the Mark of the Beast tomorrow.

Already we can see evidence that the microchip implant agenda

296

is gaining slow but sure ground. Acceptance and popularity of the implantable device is beginning to rise.

Amal Graafstra author of *RFID Toys* is one of the first 'do it yourself' implantees boasting an RFID implant in both hands. Graafstra recalls how he posted photos of his implant procedure on the internet which resulted in a barrage of emails including some from concerned Christians and even his own mother anxious that what he was doing was linked to the Mark of the Beast.[26] Graafstra builds and customizes devices that enable interaction with cell phones, cars and houses via an implantable chip. On his website Graafstra has an online shop ironically called 'Dangerous Things' selling a whole range of items from the implantable microchip to a DIY implantation kit for those who want to undergo the implant procedure themselves. In August of 2012 Graafstra attended ToorCamp, a summer camp for electronics enthusiasts in which he had his own RFID Implantation Station at which attendees could receive an implantable chip there and then.

The idea of having an implantable device in the hand is becoming more and more widespread with many suppliers available on the internet. It is now even possible to purchase a microchip, also known as an RFID glass tag on eBay for as little as £7.00. Although it is recommended that these are not implanted under the skin. Such is the enthusiasm of those wishing to be implanted with the device that they do it anyway. A company called SparkFun, who sell the RFID glass tags on their online shop, makes it clear that their microchips are not for human implantation, stating, 'please don't implant this thing into yourselves.'[27] However, comments left on the site by enthusiastic customers reveal how they ignore the warning:

'I had one of these implanted in my right hand today. So if you're wondering if it works, well it does...'

'I have a different one; the one I had implanted is a HiTagS 2048 it has a EM4100...'

'This can be implanted in humans, I have one but I don't know the long term consequences, though there shouldn't be any'

'These look fine for implanting...I've had one...in my hand for almost a decade. I had mine put in by a guy that did subdermal implants'

'I've had one of these chips in my hand for close to a year now. No problems so far'

Of course for many the idea of an implantable device under the skin will remain a squeamish concept and something to be evaded at all costs. This is where the RFID invisible chip-less tattoo will become the preferred alternative to the implantable device. This technology has the potential to greatly advance the agenda to control humanity. Unlike the invasive implantable microchip, tattoos are now widely accepted and popular in western society. No longer associated with bikers and tribes, the tattoo expresses a person's individuality and can range from all kinds of designs from as small as a few stars on the ankle, or a motive on the lower back, to tattoos covering the entire body.

In 2007 Somark Innovations announced that they had successfully developed a biocompatible chip-less RFID ink which could be tattooed within the skin of an animal for the purposes of identification and tracking. Secondary target markets amongst others would include military personnel.[28] Highlighting the planned use to go beyond cattle tracking, Mark Pydynowski, co-founder of Somark Innovations, remarked that the RFID ink is fully biocompatible and safe for use in humans and that the RFID ink tattoo could be used to track and rescue soldiers. 'It could help identify friends or foes, prevent friendly fire, and help save soldiers' lives,' said Pydynowski.[29] This tattoo technology paved the way for other electronic devices such as the brain-machine interface announced in August 2011 – a thin flexible, skin-like temporary tattoo mounted to the forehead. This is yet another shadow of the prophesied future

– a future in which the Mark of the Beast will also be applied to the forehead (Revelation 13:16, 17). The forehead tattoo interface, utilizing tiny electronic components, is capable of transmitting brain waves wirelessly to a computer. Professor Todd Coleman, who co-led the team that developed the device, envisions endless applications for use in the worlds of military, gaming, education and consumer electronics.[30]

Remember that the original Greek word used for 'mark' in the book of Revelation is the word charagma, meaning to either 'stamp', 'etch' or 'scratch'. The word also means to 'brand' as a farmer brands cattle. Does this not sound like a perfect description of the application used by Somark's RFID tattoo?

It is important to recall again that the Bible expressly warns us not to make any cuttings in our flesh or receive a tattoo on our bodies. 'You shall not make any cuttings in your flesh for the dead, nor tattoo any marks on you: I am the LORD.' (Leviticus 19:28) Both are necessary for the implantation of the microchip and for Somark's chip-less tracking technology.

God did not warn us because He is some kind of killjoy who wants to remove our personal freedoms. On the contrary, He gave this warning to set us free from the approaching tyranny that will eventually lead us down a pathway towards spiritual destitution, causing an inability to turn to God for help and salvation. The terrible fate of those who receive the Mark is prophesied in Revelation 14:11: 'if anyone worships the beast and his image, and receives his mark on his forehead or on his hand, he himself shall also drink of the wine of the wrath of God, which is poured out full strength into the cup of His indignation. He shall be tormented with fire and brimstone in the presence of the holy angels and in the presence of the Lamb. And the smoke of their torment ascends forever and ever; and they have no rest day or night, who worship the beast and his image, and whoever receives the mark of his name.' (NKJV)

But how could such a material device cause such a wretched

spiritual condition resulting in eternal separation from God? Let us have a look at some reasons why this might be so.

You cannot serve two masters

Jesus gave a stark warning to his followers concerning the storing up of earthly riches:

'Do not lay up for yourselves treasures on earth, where moth and rust destroy and where thieves break in and steal; but lay up for yourselves treasures in heaven, where neither moth nor rust destroys and where thieves do not break in and steal. For where your treasure is, there your heart will be also. The lamp of the body is the eye. If therefore your eye is good, your whole body will be full of light. But if your eye is bad, your whole body will be full of darkness. If therefore the light that is in you is darkness, how great is that darkness! No one can serve two masters; for either he will hate the one and love the other, or else he will be loyal to the one and despise the other. You cannot serve God and mammon (money).' (Matthew 6:19-24, NKJV)

Let us look at these words of Christ in the context of the Mark of the Beast. Although Jesus was not talking about this subject here, His lesson to us is illuminating. His words will serve to protect anyone from being deceived into receiving the fatal Mark of the Beast.

What are treasures on earth? They can represent the love of material luxuries such as holidays, cars, houses, clothes, shoes, the latest gadgets, or they can point to worrying about the material things we need in order to survive such as food, water, shelter, clothes, warmth, and electricity. These are all earthly treasures and concerning ourselves with them by either obtaining them or worrying about them is the storing up of treasures on earth. Jesus exalts us to love the things of heaven, setting our hearts on things above where Christ is seated at the right hand of God (Colossians 3:1). The Bible urges us to focus on whatever is true, noble, right, pure, lovely, admirable and anything that is excellent or praiseworthy (Philippians 4:8), and not to worry about anything, what we will eat or drink or wear, because our heavenly Father knows of everything that we need (Matthew 6:25-35). If we are focused on material things then that is where our desire and affections will be.

Jesus said here that it is our physical eyes that bring light into our souls. What we see and desire with our physical eyes will penetrate into our soul and either illuminate it with the holiness of God or fill it with the utter darkness of sin. So if we look at and desire or focus on worrying about material things, that we either want or even need, then our souls become filled with great darkness. We have to make a choice, to either be concerned with Godly things or to be concerned with material things, because Jesus said materials things and Godly things are masters. We become a servant to either one or the other. We either worship one or the other. We cannot serve two masters. We either hate one or love the other. It is not possible to have affections towards both masters. According to Jesus those who focus on desiring these material things have become a servant, a slave, a lover or a worshipper to the master of the material and by default a hater of God and flooded with absolute darkness. The master is of course money.

It is vital to understand that the Mark of the Beast is fundamentally a monetary reality. Without the Mark no one will be able to buy or sell. It will be the universal payment system adopted by a corrupt world bank and controlled by the money masters – the Antichrist and the false prophet. Those who are taken up with the cares and pleasures of this world will be flooded with the darkness that Jesus spoke of and will be unable to discern evil. They will consider material wellbeing above the spiritual. These people, including some who profess to be Christians, will take the Mark of the Beast with little to no resistance, since without the Mark they will not be able to continue serving their materialistic master – money. Having become slaves to money, they will now become slaves to the Antichrist. A person cannot serve both Antichrist and Christ.

No wonder Jesus became so upset when he entered the Temple in Jerusalem and overturned the tables of the money changers who were buying and selling (Mark 11:15). He knew where the love of money would eventually lead – the rejection of God and damnation of the soul to hell. The insidious hold that money can have on an individual must never be underestimated. The Bible records that a rich young ruler who had kept all of the commandments approached Jesus and asked what he must do to gain eternal life. Jesus replied, 'sell what you have and give to the poor, and you will have treasure in heaven.' But such was the grip of the money master upon him that the rich young man went away with great sorrow – he was unable to serve both God and money. After the man left Jesus said to His disciples, 'assuredly, I say to you that it is hard for a rich man to enter the kingdom of heaven. And again I say to you, it is easier for a camel to go through the eye of a needle than for a rich man to enter the kingdom of God' (Matthew 19:23-24, NKJV).

Mind Control

It is sobering to realize that the Mark of the Beast could have the capacity to do more than control a person's ability to buy and sell. Experiments with chip implantation have shown that a person's mind can be controlled by such a device, making a person do and think things that they would otherwise not do. Under the Antichrist rule, who is to say what modifications might be made to a forehead microchip, including mind manipulative technologies?

Professor Jose Delgado pioneered the brain chip, an electronic device designed to manipulate the mind. Delgado implanted the radio-equipped electrode array into the brains of humans and showed that it was possible to control their minds and bodies at the flick of a switch. The implanted chip was able via remote control to stimulate the motor cortex and produce physical reactions. One person who had received the implant, upon stimulation of the motor cortex, clenched his fist, even when trying to resist such an action. In a rather disturbing response the patient revealed the power that could be wielded over a person with such a device, saying, 'I guess, doctor, that your electricity is stronger than my will.' In 1963 Delgado performed his most famous experiment in Cordoba, Spain. Several fighting bulls received the implant into the brain. The professor stood in the bullring and controlled the movement of each animal by pressing buttons on a handheld transmitter. In a most dramatic moment of the experiment Delgado was able to force a charging bull which was charging at him to skid to an abrupt stop, just a few feet away from him.[31]

However Delgado found that it was not only possible to control physical responses but also emotional ones by sending signals to the limbic system, the area of the brain that supports emotion, behavior and motivation. Through his experiments Delgado was able to induce fear, rage, lust, euphoria, excessive talking and other emotional reactions. Delgado wrote about one experiment conducted on a female patient suffering from crippling attacks of anxiety. Upon stimulation of the thalamus, the area of the brain that relays sensory and motor signals to the cerebral cortex and also regulates consciousness and sleep, the patient experienced intense feelings of fearfulness.

Delgado wrote 'stimulation...induced a typical fearful expression and she turned to either side, visually exploring the room behind her. When asked what she was doing, she replied that she felt a threat and thought that something horrible was going to happen. This fearful sensation was perceived as real, and she had a premonition of imminent disaster of unknown cause. The effect was reliable on different days...'[32]

While additional patients became anxious and restless upon stimulation of other areas of the brain, Delgado wrote that 'a few reported a "vital anxiety in the left chest," and screamed anxiously if the stimulation was repeated. Intense emotional reactions have been evoked by stimulation of the amygdaloid nucleus, but responses varied in the same patient even with the same parameters of stimulation. The effect was sometimes rage, sometimes fear. One patient explained, "I don't know what came over me. I felt like an animal". The sensation of fear without any concomitant pain has also been observed as a result of ESB of the temporal lobe. This effect may be classified as "illusion of fear" because there was obviously no real reason to be afraid apart from the artificial electrical activation of some cerebral structures.' [33]

Delgado also wrote that stimulation of the amygdaloid part of the brain, whose primary role is memory and emotional reactions, was discovered by other investigators. He cited the story of a woman suffering from depression and alienation: 'with an extremely flat tone of voice and a facial expression which was blank and unchanging during interviews, who upon stimulation of the amygdala with 5 milliamperes had greatly altered vocal inflections and an angry expression. During this time she said, "I feel like I want to get up from this chair! Please don't let me do it! Don't do this to me, I don't want to be mean!" When the interviewer asked if she would like to hit him, the patient answered, "Yeah, I want to hit something...and just tear it up. Take it so I won't! "She then handed her scarf to the interviewer who gave her a stack of paper, and without any other verbal exchange, she tore it into shreds saying, "I don't like to feel like this." When the level of stimulation was reduced to 4 milliamperes, her attitude changed to a broad smile, and she explained, "I know it's silly, what I'm doing. I wanted to get up from this chair and run. I wanted to hit something, tear up something-anything. Not you, just anything. I just wanted to get up and tear. I had no control of myself." An increase in intensity up to 5 milliamperes again resulted in similar aggressive manifestations, and she raised her arm as if to strike.' [34]

Not only anxiety and anger were elicited, but also pleasure. Delgado wrote:

'Studies in human subjects with implanted electrodes have demonstrated that electrical stimulation of the depth of the brain can induce pleasurable manifestations, as evidenced by the spontaneous verbal reports of patients, their facial expression and general behavior, and their desire to repeat the experience...the patients became relaxed, at ease, had a feeling of well-being, and/or were a little sleepy."..."the patients were definitely changed...in a good mood, felt good. They were relaxed, at ease, and enjoyed themselves, frequently smiling. There was a slight euphoria, but the behavior was adequate." They sometimes wanted more stimulations... when "the euphoria was definitely beyond normal limits. The patients laughed out loud, enjoyed themselves, and positively liked the stimulation, and wanted more."...Finally...ESB [electrical brain stimulation] produced unpleasant reactions including anxiety, sadness, depression, fear, and emotional outbursts. One of the moving pictures taken in this study was very demonstrative, showing a patient with a sad expression and slightly depressed mood who smiled when a brief stimulation was applied to the rostral part of the brain, returning quickly to his usual depressed state, to smile again as soon as stimulation was reapplied. Then a ten-second stimulation completely changed his behavior and facial expression into a lasting pleasant and happy mood.' [35]

Finally Delgado found that it was also possible to evoke hallucinations when the depth of the tip of the left temporal lobe was electrically stimulated. He wrote: 'the following phenomena have been observed in patients: 1) illusions (visual, auditory, labyrinthine, memory or déjà vu, sensation of remoteness or unreality, 2) emotions (loneliness, fear, sadness), 3) psychical hallucinations (vivid memory or a dream as complex as life experience itself, and 4) forced thinking (stereotyped thoughts crowding into the mind). The first three groups of phenomena have been induced by different intra-cerebral stimulations.'[36]

These brain implant experiments were conducted over forty years ago. Imagine what further advancements have been made since then and are available today.

The Defense Advanced Research Projects Agency (DARPA) is an agency of the United States Department of Defense. It is responsible for the development of new technologies for military use. DARPA, which pioneered the internet back in the 1960's[37], has turned the imagined into the real.

Since 2009 DARPA has been working on project 'Silent Talk'. This project will allow for synthetic telepathic communication between troops on the battlefield[38] by 2017.[39] The technology detects word-specific neural signals in the mind before they are vocalized. It then transmits them to the intended recipient.

Other more disturbing uses, beyond the battlefield communication between troops, are indicated by research designed to make the enemy obey commands. So writes the National Research Council and the Defense Intelligence Agency in a report published in 2008: 'although conflict has many aspects, one that war fighters and policy makers often talk about is the motivation to fight, which undoubtedly has its origins in the brain and is reflected in peripheral neurophysiological processes. So one question would be "How can we disrupt the enemy's motivation to fight? Other questions raised by controlling the mind: How can we make people trust us more? What if we could help the brain to remove fear or pain? Is there a way to make the enemy obey our commands?'[40]

Imagine these kinds of modified microchips in the hands of a totalitarian government. Imagine how it could be used to elicit certain emotional responses in high-tech psychological torture of religious and political dissidents, or how anger and rage could be produced to harm oneself or others, or how manufactured depression could bring a person to commit suicide, or create hallucinations in order to confuse and deceive, or to obey on command. If anyone received a device that wielded such control over their mind they would very likely be unable to see clearly in order to turn to God for help and salvation.

One example of the microchip implant modification comes

from a Saudi Arabian inventor, who applied for patent under the German Patent Law in 2009. Although it does not relate specifically to the kind of mind control we have been discussing here, this device would certainly bring about a control of the mind through fear. It also illustrates how modifications to the original microchip implant are already taking place for more sinister purposes. His model would consist of a GPS transceiver for tracking purposes, used to track terrorists, criminals, fugitives, illegal immigrants, political dissidents, domestic servants and foreigners overstaying their visas – with the added functionality of a dose of cyanide in order to remotely kill the implantee, should the authorities deem them a threat to society.[41] Needless to say the patent was denied. However, it does illustrate what is now technologically available and the kinds of ideas that are being developed for people control across the planet. When a world leader arises in the form of the prophesied Antichrist, this application of the microchip would be the perfect tool to instill the worst kind of fear in a person – the fear of sudden death on refusal to obey commands.

The Worship of other Gods and Idol worship

Finally the Mark of the Beast is associated directly with the new one world religion imposed and headed by the false prophet. All who take the Mark align themselves with this false religious system and are coerced into worshiping the Antichrist as God and bowing down to his image in idol worship.

One of the Ten Commandments given to Moses reads, 'you shall have no other gods before Me. You shall not make for yourself a carved image – any likeness of anything that is in heaven above, or that is in the earth beneath, or that is in the water under the earth; you shall not bow down to them nor serve them. For I, the Lord your God, am a jealous God, visiting the iniquity of the fathers upon the children to the third and fourth generations of those who hate Me, but showing mercy to thousands, to those who love Me and keep My commandments' (Exodus 20:1-6, NKJV).

Those who worship the false god of the Antichrist and his idolatrous image automatically become God-haters because they become like the god they bow to and worship. The Antichrist hates God with every fiber of his being. The Bible says concerning those who bow to and worship idols, 'those who make them are like them; so is everyone who trusts in them' (Psalm 115:8 NKJV). Again, Jesus confirmed this saying, 'no one can serve two masters; for either he will hate the one and love the other' (Matthew 6:24 NKJV).

As these devices gain more and more widespread acceptance in our culture, those protesting against them will become marginalized.

And there will come a day when the gradual optional roll-out will end. According to prophecy the Mark of the Beast will not be an optional extra but it will be enforced by law.

The Mark, The Name, and The Number – An Unholy Trinity

Biblical prophecy specifically states that the Mark is synonymous with the name of the beast, that is the Antichrist, and that the Antichrist's name is synonymous with a number. This means that the MARK, THE ANTICHRIST and the NUMBER are synonymous – an unholy trinity if you like. The Bible says this requires wisdom. Whoever is intelligent can figure out the meaning of the number of the Antichrist because the number stands for a certain man. The Bible gives the number of the Antichrist – 666. Here is the verse in full.

'The beast forced all the people, small and great, rich and poor, slave and free, to have a mark placed on their right hands or on their foreheads. No one could buy or sell without this mark, that is, the beast's name or the number that stands for the name. This calls for wisdom. Whoever is intelligent can figure out the meaning of the number of the beast, because the number

308

stands for the name of someone. Its number is 666' (Revelation 13: 16-18 GNT).

The Bible prophecy declares that the meaning of the numbers 666 can be understood. It is not an unsolvable mystery. By understanding the number we can identify a certain person. Walid Shoebat former Islamic terrorist for the Palestinian Liberation Organization (PLO), who converted to Christianity in 1994, believes he has found its meaning.

Shoebat, after having looked at the infamous translated '666' Greek letters (Chi Xi Stigma), in one of the oldest existing manuscripts of the Greek Bible known as the Codex Vaticanus – named after its place of conservation since the 15th century in the Vatican Library – commented, 'when I first saw the Codex Vaticanus I was literally shocked. Because I could read the text. It was Arabic!'

The Greek characters used to denote '666' are Chi Xi Stigma.

Here are the words Chi Xi Stigma (666) from the original Greek manuscripts:

And here are some symbols that look remarkably similar. Shoebat immediately saw the striking similarity.

The meaning of the Arabic word is 'Bismillah' reading from right to left, the first symbol meaning 'in the name of' and the second symbol, the middle symbol, meaning 'Allah', followed by two crossed swords used commonly throughout the Muslim world. Looking at both the Greek words and the Arabic words side by side the resemblance is clear to see. The only difference is that the word for Allah is at a different angle. But upon flipping the 'Allah' symbol and putting them side by side with the Greek or vice-versa the similarities are uncanny to say the least.

And now side by side with the 'Allah' symbol, flipped in right hand symbols, from the Codex Vaticanus,

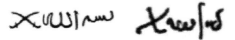

Walid Shoebat's findings are certainly a compelling hyphothesis especially when considering that the false prophet who instigates the Mark could be from the Islamic foot of the revived Roman Empire as discussed in chapter 8. Further support for this idea is the fact that Islamic eschatology is remarkably similar to Christian eschatology as we saw in chapter 13 – on the One World Religion.

Could it be that the Apostle John not only saw that the Mark of the Beast would be a device implanted under or etched onto the skin for the purpose of buying and selling, but that he also identified the religious system from which it would rise?

We cannot be sure of the details but what we do know is that the Bible prophesies it will be a mark applied to either the hand or forehead. It will be the mark of the Antichrist. It will be a device used for the new monetary system run by a world bank, that if a person does not have the mark, he will neither be able to buy or sell, that the Mark of the Beast is total control of the people, and that it will be forced on the global population by the false prophet of the Antichrist.

One final thought: even if the devices discussed within this chapter do not turn into the prophesied Mark of the Beast, the fact is that there is an agenda to implement global micro-chipping of humans. Once complete these devices will be used by a totalitarian government to enslave the global populace. At best the idea is demonically inspired, conceived in the corrupt minds of a godless and Antichrist system, a system that will make subservient anyone receiving that 'mark'. It should therefore be avoided by all freedom-loving people at all costs, whether Christian or otherwise. Remember, God in His loving kindness has already forewarned us in order to set us free from earthly or spiritual bondage: 'you shall not make any cuttings in your flesh for the dead, nor tattoo any marks on you: I am the LORD' (Leviticus 19:28).

If we obeyed this verse alone we would be rescued from governmental enslavement.

Chapter 15

Surveillance Society

Always eyes watching you and the voice enveloping you.
Asleep or awake, indoors or out of doors, in the bath or bed –
no escape. Nothing was your own except the few cubic
centimeters in your skull

George Orwell, 1984

We live in a surveillance society. The nightmarish future envisioned by George Orwell back in 1949 has today become a disturbing reality. But Orwell's surveillance idea has not only been reached; it has also been vastly exceeded.

Even more shocking is the fact that people have come to accept this invasion into their private lives. Actually, people have given such a level of consent to this invasion that it is now of little real concern.

Aldous Huxley, author of *Brave New World*, wrote in 1932 that due to the level of governmental manipulation people would actually come to love their enslavement. For the most part this is what has happened with surveillance today.

Huxley wrote: 'a really efficient totalitarian state would be one in which the all-powerful executive of political bosses and their army of managers control a population of slaves who do not have to be coerced, because they love their servitude.'

What is even more worrying is that through TV shows like 'Big Brother' and social networking platforms like Facebook and Twitter, surveillance has now become a form of entertainment. Surveilling people 24 hours a day eat, sleep, wash and even engage in immoral activity is what Big Brother is all about. While on Facebook what once was a private email to a friend is now sent via a person's 'wall' for everyone to read; even private family photo albums can be looked at by practically any stranger around the world.

All the while our boundaries of privacy are broken down and we cease to care that we are being watched.

While the masses engage in these apparently trivial pastimes the surveillance grid steadily grows. Governments, banks and corporations across the world are empowered more and more by the very people they are spying on.

Twenty four hours a day global intelligence agencies are monitoring every communication we make. All phone calls, all emails and all internet activity, including Google searches, are recorded and analyzed. Absolutely nothing is private.

In June of 2013 Yahoo announced an upgrade to their latest platform. The upgrade allowed Yahoo to scan and analyze all email sent and received through it. Privacy expert Katherine Albrecht commented, 'emailing through Yahoo means surrendering your privacy, whether it's your own account or your friend's. It's time we start paying attention to these policies, because they're growing more shockingly abusive every day.' [1]

Through whistleblowers like Julian Assange and Edward Snowden, the threat of the rising global surveillance grid has become more public. But the truth is the surveillance society has been incrementally taking shape across the globe for many years.

Richard Thomas, Information Commissioner for the United Kingdom between 2002-2009, said back in 2006, 'two years ago I warned that we were in danger of sleepwalking into a surveillance society. Today I fear that we are in fact waking up to a surveillance society that is already all around us.'[2]

The evidence is visible everywhere today. We only have to step outside our homes or visit the major cities of the world to see the spiraling mass surveillance state that we now tolerate. It is estimated that 420,000 CCTV cameras operate in London alone, while a further 1.85 million operate around the United Kingdom as a whole, making the UK the largest surveillanced society in the world. [3]

The sustained threat of terrorism propagated through the mainstream media has further fuelled an acceptance of surveillance. As I have written earlier, the fear of death leads people to give up their freedoms readily.

After the events of 9/11 the surveillance agenda significantly shifted gear and went into hyperdrive. The US Patriot Act signed into law by President Bush on 26th October 2001 was as a direct result of September 11th.

However, former Republican Congressman, Ron Paul said of the act, 'the Patriot Act was written many, many years before 9/11.' The attacks simply provided 'an opportunity for some people to do what they wanted to do.'[4]

The Patriot Act vastly expanded the US government's authority to spy on its own citizens. As a direct result, the FBI can legally enforce anyone at all, including professionals and internet service providers, to turn over records of client and customer information – even if they don't have any evidence of illegal activity. Astonishingly surveillance orders can be enacted based upon a person's choice of books and their internet browsing. Furthermore these searches are carried out in secret. The individual or organization that has been forced to hand over the information is prohibited from disclosing the search to anyone. The person is therefore completely unaware that they have been or continue to be under surveillance.[5]

In all of this it is vital for us to realize that the Patriot Act is actually illegal under the US constitution. It is a direct violation of the Fourth Amendment which states:

'The right of the people to be secure in their persons, houses, papers, and effects, against unreasonable searches and seizures, shall not be violated, and no Warrants shall issue, but upon probable cause, supported by Oath or affirmation, and particularly describing the place to be searched, and the persons or things to be seized.'

Under the guise of protecting the people, governments around the world have intensified their surveillance of everyone.

It should come as no surprise that the most surveilled nation on the globe is also home to the largest electronic monitoring station in the world. Located in the United Kingdom, the Royal Air Force base in North Yorkshire at Menwith Hill contains an array of ominous looking radoms that are linked to orbiting satellites encircling the earth, while deep in the ocean a massive transatlantic cable monitors all internet and email communications.

Menwith Hill is also a ground station for a number of satellites operated for the US National Security Agency (NSA). The base is a part of the Echelon surveillance program. Echelon is a signals intelligence network operated by the five nations that signed up to the 1946 UKUSA Security Agreement (Australia, Canada, New Zealand, the United Kingdom, and the United States).

The Echelon eavesdropping station – which also comprises other bases dotted around the world – intercepts and monitors all communication's traffic. The Echelon system automatically flags up keywords from the billions of streams of daily chatter. In June 2013 it was reported that similar programs, such as the NSA's previously top secret Prism system, were being used with the assistance of the companies involved to access the servers of Google, Apple, Facebook and others. The system allows for the collection of internet search histories, email content, file transfers and live chat.[6] The companies denied the knowledge of any such program.

Google said in a statement, 'Google cares deeply about the security of our users' data. We disclose user data to government in accordance with the law, and we review all such requests carefully.'[7]

However, Google is known for its spying activities and so for them to claim that they care deeply about the security of their users is very questionable. In 2010 it was discovered that Google spied on British households by stealing and recording passwords and private emails from home computers. The theft occurred when Google sent out a fleet of specially equipped cars in 2008 fitted with 360 degree cameras in order to photograph every road in Britain for its Google Earth map program.[8] Google was later threatened in 2013 with legal action when it was found that the data they had pledged to destroy had "accidentally" been retained on additional discs.[9] Furthermore Google also works for US intelligence agencies supplying a customized search technology called 'Intellipedia'. The highly secure online system is used by the CIA, FBI, the National Security Agency and others.[10]

We need also to recognize that Facebook and Twitter are more than just friendly social networking sites. In an industrial area in Virginia the CIA studies thousands of Facebook posts and Twitter feeds. The agency's Open Source Center was set up in response to a recommendation by the 9/11 Commission for the primary purpose of monitoring terrorist activity. Facebook and Twitter posts are cross-referenced with intercepted phone conversations. The CIA analysis ends up in President Obama's daily intelligence briefings. The center interestingly highlighted the fact that social media could be a game-changer and a threat to governments in places like Egypt.[11]

In light of this we need to ask whether the CIA considers social media to be a possible threat to Washington. A further CIA connection with Facebook is Greylock Venture Capital. Greylock invested $27.5 million into the social networking giant. One of Greylocks senior partners is Howard Cox who is also on the board of In-Q-Tel. In-Q-Tel happens to be the venture capital wing of the CIA. Did the CIA indirectly fund Facebook?

Wikileaks founder Julian Assange said of people using Facebook, 'when they add their friends to Facebook they are doing free work for United States intelligence agencies.' [12]

The 2013 surveillance leaks are nothing new. The civilian population has been spied on for years. Back in 1999 the BBC reported on the Echelon system, whose existence both Britain and America officially denied at the time.

The report read, 'imagine a global spying network that can eavesdrop on every single phone call, fax or e-mail, anywhere on the planet. It sounds like science fiction, but it's true. Two of the chief protagonists – Britain and America – officially deny its existence. But the BBC has confirmation from the Australian Government that such a network really does exist and politicians on both sides of the Atlantic are calling for an inquiry.' [13]

In 2001 the European Parliament investigated the existence of the Echelon surveillance system and its purpose to intercept private communications. The report was subtitled 'the existence of a global system for intercepting private and commercial communications (the ECHELON interception system)'. It stated:

'Whereas the existence of a global system for intercepting

communications, operating by means of cooperation proportionate to their capabilities among the USA, the UK, Canada, Australia and New Zealand under the UKUSA Agreement, is no longer in doubt; whereas it seems likely, in view of the evidence and the consistent pattern of statements from a very wide range of individuals and organizations, including American sources, that its name is in fact ECHELON...there can now be no doubt that the purpose of the system is to intercept, at the very least, private and commercial communications, and not military communications...' [14]

The truth is that today the intelligence services no longer have to bug a person's home. The amount of internet enabled gadgets surrounding our lives do the job for them. Take, for example, the British company Gamma International, who in 2010 offered Egypt's Hosni Mubarak's government "IT intrusion" technology to covertly spy on Skype conversations and other internet connected communications while he was in power. [15] The world has literally been turned into a massive surveillance grid, from which it has become impossible to escape. Try it. Even a passport today has an RFID chip embedded into it. The biometric passport contains the personal data of the holder and can be utilized as a tracking device if need be – with RFID chips now even concealed in clothing and shoes. Even what we eat is going under surveillance too. The plan to add edible RFID chips into food is already underway. [16]

We are literally being watched all the time. Governments, banks and businesses pull together details about our movements, financial transactions and purchases, building up a detailed portrait of everyone, as we leave our daily digital trail behind.

We are already a marked society just as the apostle John prophesied over 2,000 years ago. This is the surveillance society that leads humanity directly into the trap of the prophesied Mark of the Beast – the end game of surveillance. The encroaching surveillance grid is the very spirit of the Beast.

From the latest smart TVs, personal computers, cell phones and other gadgets, homes across the globe are being set up for the biggest surveillance nightmare in the history of the world. Even as far back as 1999 special access codes were prepared by the US National Security Agency (NSA) and secretly built into the Windows operating system.[17] With the advent of cloud computing however the risks to snooping on personal data becomes unequalled. At some point soon cloud computing will replace all personal hard drives. As computers will have little to no storage space, everyone will be forced into storing their personal data on a cloud owned by one of the major corporations.

Steve Wozniak who co-founded Apple with Steve Jobs said;

'I really worry about everything going to the cloud...I think it's going to be horrendous...I think there are going to be a lot of horrible problems in the next five years...with the cloud, you don't own anything. You already signed it away. I want to feel that I own things...A lot of people feel, 'Oh, everything is really on my computer,' but I say: the more we transfer everything onto the web, onto the cloud, the less we're going to have control over it.'[18]

But it doesn't stop with computing. Even TVs are becoming increasingly more sinister. In the past, what concerned us used to be what we watched. While that is certainly still an issue – with all the mind-numbing programming and endless propaganda on TV today – what should now concern us is the fact that your television is watching you. The latest smart TVs have transformed the TV into a literal surveillance device. While you watch it, it watches you.

It has been discovered that Samsung's Smart TVs can give a hacker access to all a user's personal data stored on their TV. Even more worrying is the access given to its built-in camera and microphones, allowing the hacker to watch and listen to everything happening in front of it[19] – and all this while 'back door' access has been given to the US government to control a cell phone. In the event of a national emergency, 'PLAN' (Personal Localized Alerting Network) allows for the government to take control of a cell phone. Today some people fear that the controversial government alerts are in reality a part of the federal government's takeover of the communications networks.[20]

If that was not enough, the NSA has openly spoken about their development of code for Google's Android operating system.

Bloomberg Business Week reported, 'through its open-source Android project, Google has agreed to incorporate code, first developed by the agency in 2011, into future versions of its cell phone operating system, which according to market researcher IDC runs on three-quarters of the smartphones shipped globally in the first quarter. NSA officials say their code, known as Security Enhancements for Android, isolates apps to prevent hackers and marketers from gaining access to personal or corporate data stored on a device. Eventually all new phones, tablets, televisions, cars, and other devices that rely on Android will include NSA code, agency spokeswoman Vanee' Vines said in an e-mailed statement. NSA researcher Stephen Smalley, who works on the program, says, "Our goal is to raise the bar in the security of commodity mobile devices." [21]

Are Americans really expected to believe that the NSA is generously providing the source code for every Android-based system for their own security? In reality of course these 'security enhancements' will give government access to spy on and monitor all Android system devices used in phones, tablets, TV's and even cars.

Coupled with this it is important to know that a cell phone can be used to track a user's every move. A cell phone can also be turned into a listening device to eavesdrop on a conversation while the phone is not even in use.

Furthermore cell phones and other smart gadgets are now being used to activate home lights, central heating, open and lock a front door, open an elevator, make payment for groceries and start a car engine.

Nowadays it is even possible to remotely seize control of a car. Richard Clarke, former National Coordinator for Security, Infrastructure Protection and Counter-terrorism said, 'it's relatively easy to hack your way into the control system of a car, and to do such things as cause acceleration when the driver doesn't want acceleration, to throw on the brakes when the driver doesn't want the brakes on, to launch an air bag... You can do some really highly destructive things now, through hacking a car, and it's not that hard.'

Clarke was commenting on the mysterious car crash that killed journalist Michael Hastings when his car exploded into a fireball in June 2013. Hastings was investigating the CIA at the time, in what he said was 'going to be the biggest story ever.' Moments before the crash Hastings sent a panicked email to a friend saying, 'need to go off the radar for a bit.'[22]

Once the masses have become completely dependent upon these kinds of technologies they become an open target for total control.

Think about it. In the near future, when the totalitarian regime is fully unleashed, this technology will be used against the people to quell religious gatherings and political dissent. Imagine being forcibly locked and imprisoned within your own home or trapped inside an elevator. Or your car being disabled remotely, stopping you from traveling to or from a destination, or worse being used as a weapon to assassinate you. Imagine having a private conversation with a friend and while your cell phone innocently lies on the coffee table beside you, someone is using it to listen in on your conversation. What was once the realm of science fiction is now a terrifying reality.

Furthermore, cloud computing offers a unique opportunity which dictators in the past couldn't even begin to imagine. Today many computer services that once resided on a company or organization's server are now hosted on the cloud. Take for example a church database system. These systems hold detailed information about church members. Their age, photo ID, address, contact details and even their activities within the church community can be recorded.

When the Antichrist decides to round up all the Christians from any given church, where will he go first? Of course, he will go to the church database systems. Most certainly Hitler would have utilized this most obvious and powerful tool. Shockingly the churches themselves will become responsible for aiding the Antichrist in their own persecution.

Today civilization is teetering on the brink of a new world order. Once it is fully revealed the complete surveillance nightmare will unfold.

The statement is often made that if a person has nothing to hide then there is nothing to fear. But the problem is that surveillance itself is manifestly evil, because its core purpose is the enslavement of mankind. Apart from the fact that a human being possesses a basic innate God-given right to freedom and privacy, there is another reason why surveillance is so sinister.

Surveillance silences those who speak for liberty and truth.

The activities of Christians, liberty advocates and those opposed to encroaching government are being monitored even at this very moment. In the near future though, it will become a relentless activity. Those deemed by government as terrorists will be persecuted, hunted down, imprisoned and executed.

Dictatorial regimes are renowned for not tolerating free expression and speech. It is for this reason that surveillance systems are put into place. Dictatorships are paranoid political systems that see everyone as a threat. They are ever on the look out to know what people are talking about and crush any inkling of dissent that will threaten their rule. It is also important to understand that the very knowledge of being spied on leads to a subconscious silence through fear of being caught.

Surveillance states are nothing new. Secret police forces were used in Elizabethan England, pre-revolutionary France, Tsarist and Soviet Russia and of course Nazi Germany, to name but a few.

The secret police of the Nazi regime, the Gestapo (Geheime Staatpolizei) was used to spy on religious groups, political subverters and to quell dissent. During its time in power the Nazi police state arrested thousands of people every year, including Jews, priests, church pastors, Christians, Jehovah's Witnesses, Communists, trade unionists and others.

But surveillance is as old as civilization itself. Even in the days of the Roman Empire an ancient 'Gestapo' known as the Frumentarii engaged in intelligence gathering and utilized informers and spies.

Jesus and the early Christians lived through Roman occupation and must have had a good understanding of what it meant to be under surveillance. But it was not only Roman surveillance they had to be mindful of. Jerusalem's high-priestly rulers, the Pharisees who collaborated with the Romans, exercised incredible surveillance over Jesus and his disciples.

'So the scribes and Pharisees watched Him closely...that they might find an accusation against Him' (Luke 6:7, NKJV).

Evidence that after Jesus' death Christians operated in secrecy to avoid exposure can also be seen by the use of the fish symbol. The fish symbol was used by Greeks, Romans and pagans alike. It made for an unlikely and therefore perfect code to be used by the early persecuted believers. The symbol was used to secretly identify themselves to other Christians. According to one story, when a Christian met a stranger he would draw one arc of the fish outline in the sand. If the stranger was also a Christian he would respond by drawing the other half. Both then knew it was safe. Also Greek-speaking Jews would sometimes use the Greek name Jason, (meaning healer), instead of the more conspicuous Jewish name Jesus, as a means of disguising who they were really referring to.

It is also interesting to consider Jesus' and his followers' actions in the context of being under surveillance.

For example Jesus often taught his disciples privately. In Luke 9:10 we read, 'then He took them and went aside privately into a deserted place....'

Then again we read in Luke 10:23-24, 'then He turned to His disciples and said privately, "Blessed are the eyes which see the things you see; for I tell you that many prophets and kings have desired to see what you see, and have not seen it, and to hear what you hear, and have not heard it"' (NKJV).

In John 7:10 Jesus even disguised himself to keep his identity a secret: 'but when His brothers had gone up, then He also went up to the feast, not openly, but as it were in secret.' Furthermore Jesus also traveled in secret, and at one time wished to keep secret the house in which he was staying (Mark 7:24).

The disciples sometimes came to Jesus in private. We read in Matthew 17:19, 'then the disciples came to Jesus privately...' and in Matthew 24:3, as Jesus sat on the Mount of Olives, 'the disciples came to Him privately.' On the occasion of the death of Lazarus Mary called her sister privately and whispered to her saying, 'the teacher is close at hand and is asking for you' (John 11:28, AMP). Did Mary whisper because she did not want others to know he was on his way?

Jesus often desired that the miracles He performed were also kept a secret too.

There are many possible reasons for this. But one could have been that He was aware of the Romans and the religious leaders who were watching Him and he wanted to avoid early exposure. We know that the Pharisees watched Jesus perform miracles so that they might accuse him (Luke 6:7, NKJV).

For example Jesus healed two blind men. 'And their eyes were opened. And Jesus sternly warned them, saying, "See that no one knows it"' (Matthew 9:30, NKJV).

Again Jesus healed a man with leprosy. We read, 'And He strictly warned him and sent him away at once, and said to him, "See that you say nothing to anyone"' (Mark 1:40-45, NKJV).

When Jesus raised Jairus daughter back from the dead we read that 'he commanded them strictly that no one should know it' (Mark 5:43 NKJV).

Jesus also healed a man that was deaf and mute. Jesus told the people 'they should tell no one' (Mark 7:36).

As was often the case however the healed person went about excitedly proclaiming what had happened. Indeed, after a leper was healed Jesus was unable to openly enter that city and was forced to go out into the deserted places to minister, possibly away from the city authorities and the prying eyes of the Pharisees. (Mark 1:45)

The fact is that Jesus and his disciples and also the early Christians were subject to extreme persecution and even death at the hands of those who watched their every move.

This brings us back to the present day.

The prophesied revived Roman Empire will operate much in

the same way as it did back then. It will depend heavily upon surveillance to control and track the people. Surveillance will be a key strategy used against Christians and the Church in what the Bible describes as the Great Tribulation. End-time Christians would do well to consider adopting the evasive tactics of Christ.

Today the global surveillance grid monitors all communications. One of the ways it does this is by isolating keywords. In 2011 the US Department of Homeland Security was forced to release its keywords after a freedom of information lawsuit. At the time some of the DHS keywords – of which there are hundreds – were:

FEMA, (Federal Emergency Management Agency), Secret Service, Homeland Defense, CIA, FBI, TSA, National Guard, United Nations, Assassination, Attack, Dirty bomb, Homeland Security, Militia, Evacuation, Hostage, Explosion, Police, National security, Threat, Lockdown, Emergency landing, incident, facility, Suspicious package/device, Collapse, Computer infrastructure, Grid, Power, Smart, Body Scanner, Cancelled, Delays, Service disruption, Violence, Decapitated, Terrorism, Al Qaeda (all spellings), Terror, Attack, Environmental terrorist, Eco terrorism, Conventional weapon, Target, IRA (Irish Republican Army), Car bomb, Jihad, Taliban, Suicide bomber, Extremism, Radicals, Homegrown, Plot, Nationalist, Recruitment, Fundamentalism and Islamist.[23]

For example, Michele Catalano was looking online for information about pressure cookers while at the same time her husband was conducting a Google search for backpacks. Later six men from the joint terrorist task force showed up at the house to see if they were terrorists.[24]

Tomorrow the surveillance system will monitor all Christian content. For instance keywords such as, evangelical, Baptist, Pentecostal, Christian, church, fellowship, missionary, prayer meeting, God, Jesus, Christ, Holy Spirit, pastor and Bible etc will be flagged up and those found to be responsible for 'religious chatter' will be considered enemies of the state and dealt with accordingly.

The ultimate surveillance grid is now set. As soon as the Antichrist system reaches full maturity the all-seeing eye of surveillance will be used to its most horrifying degree.

There is however another reason why surveillance is so intrinsically evil. It is surveillance that leads directly to the prophesied Great Tribulation.

Chapter 16

Tribulation Rising

*Countless people...will hate the new world order...
and will die protesting against it*

H.G. Wells [1]

*Then you will be arrested, persecuted, and killed.
You will be hated all over the world because you are
my followers*

Jesus Christ [2]

*For then there will be great tribulation (affliction, distress,
and oppression) such as has not been from the beginning of the
world until now – no, and never will be [again]*

Jesus Christ [3]

From the evidence I have provided so far, it is hard not to conclude that humanity is careering headlong towards the prophesied Great Tribulation. According to the Bible, this will be a time when the planet will fall into complete turmoil – a turmoil the like of which the world has never known.

Jesus spoke of the Great Tribulation, referring to it as 'the beginning of sorrows'. He said:

'Then they will deliver you up to tribulation and kill you, and you will be hated by all nations for My name's sake. And then many will be offended, will betray one another, and will hate one another' (Matthew 24:9-10, NKJV). Much of the Book of Revelation is also devoted to this critical time period. Even some of the Old Testament prophets speak concerning this future event. In fact, it is the prophet Daniel who gives us a specific time frame for the Tribulation. He tells us that it will last for a total of seven years.

A Severe Constraining

Looking at the etymology of the word 'tribulation' opens the doors onto some revealing insights.

According to the New Bible Dictionary, the root meaning of the word for tribulation is 'narrow' or 'compressed'. This leads to the figurative connotation, 'straitened circumstances', and hence, affliction, distress or tribulation. The basic idea here is 'severe constriction', or 'severe constraining'.

To 'constrain' means to 'force, coerce, pressure, restrict, restrain, limit or curb.'

It is hard not to think of today's surveillance state when reading those words. Human beings are nowadays severely restricted, coerced and limited by the enslaving spirit that lies behind surveillance. Surveillance then is a fundamental characteristic of tribulation.

An incident in the Apostle Paul's life further reveals this link. Paul records that one time while he was ministering in Damascus the governor under King Aretas had his people surveilling the city in order to arrest him. On this occasion Paul and his friends devised an ingenious escape from the authorities. They lowered him in a basket from a window in the city wall (2 Corinthians 11:32-33).

For Paul, being under surveillance was part of experiencing tribulation.

This highlights the fact that Christians are called to suffer in tribulation. The Christian is asked to follow in the footsteps of Christ, who endured great tribulation. All tribulation then must stand in the light of Christ Jesus who was 'despised and rejected by men, a man of sorrows and acquainted with grief. Smitten by God, and afflicted' (Isaiah 53).

However, this important aspect of Christian doctrine is sorely missing in our churches today. The absence of this theology of suffering is to the detriment of the believer living in the end times. Without it they are left unarmed and powerless to stand in the face of tribulation.

For many, all suffering must be avoided at all costs and prayed away. Many churches today are responsible for creating a sugar coated gospel. But this version of the gospel bears little relation to what the Bible, Jesus and the early church taught. The Bible teaches that a true Christian will not only enjoy the power of Christ's resurrection; they will also have to embrace a fellowship with his sufferings.

This is why the subject of the end times is often met with a fearful expectation, because it does not fit with the believers understanding of suffering.

The Bible clearly teaches that suffering for the name of Christ, however tough, should be embraced, just like Christ embraced it.

In the garden of Gethsemane he cried, 'O My Father, if it is possible, let this cup pass from Me; nevertheless, not as I will, but as You will' (Matthew 26:39, NKJV). When he spoke of 'the cup', Christ was speaking of his impending suffering – including his subsequent arrest, capture and crucifixion at the hands of his religious persecutors.

Christ therefore gives us an example to follow.

But we are not only to look upon the sufferings of Christ as a mere example. No, we are exhorted to 'share in Christ's sufferings' and to carry in our bodies the death of Jesus. The Apostle Paul tells us what his life's mission is: 'that I may know Him and the power of His resurrection, and the fellowship of His sufferings, being conformed to His death' (Philippians 3:10, NKJV). Again in 2 Corinthians 4:8-10, Paul teaches that by carrying in our bodies the death of Jesus, His life is revealed in us: 'We are hard-pressed on every side, yet not crushed; we are perplexed, but not in despair; persecuted, but not forsaken; struck down, but not destroyed – always carrying about in the body the dying of the Lord Jesus, that the life of Jesus also may be manifested in our body' (NKJV).

We can see then that relationship with Christ and suffering for him, and therefore with him, are inseparably connected. This suffering is not as the world knows. In fact by conforming to Christ's sufferings, the very resurrection power that raised Christ's body from the dead is activated so that the believer can be transformed into the likeness of Christ himself (Philippians 3:10). Paul further teaches concerning the divine relationship through suffering. 'We are children of God, and if children, then heirs – heirs of God and joint heirs with Christ, if indeed we suffer with Him, that we may also be glorified together.' (Romans 8:16-17)

The early church knew this, as Hebrews 11:35 clearly attests when it says that Christians in the first century 'were tortured to death with clubs, refusing to accept release [offered on the terms of denying their faith], so that they might be resurrected to a better life' (AMP). The earliest Christians knew that their sufferings allowed them to experience a heavenly, inexpressible joy. This was true for Jesus. We read in Hebrews 12:2, 'He, for the joy [of obtaining the prize] that was set before Him, endured the cross' (AMP). What was it that caused Christ such joy? It was the realization not only of his own joyful reunion with the Father, it was also the indescribable joy of knowing that through his selfless death on the Cross, believers would be reunited with the Father too!

Tribulation Joy

As it was with Christ, so it is with the believer. Joy surrounds the Christian who is going through tribulation. We can see this in the story surrounding Stephen, the first Christian martyr. As Stephen shared the gospel, the crowds became more and more hostile. They began by hurling insults at him until eventually they dragged him out of the city and stoned him to death. 'But he,' the Bible says, 'being full of the Holy Spirit, gazed into heaven and saw the glory of God, and Jesus standing at the right hand of God, and said, "Look! I see the heavens opened and the Son of Man standing at the right hand of God!"' (Acts 7:54, NKJV). Stephen was so caught up in this heavenly joy that before his death he cried out in compassion for his murderers! 'Lord', he cried, 'do not charge them with this sin' (Acts 7:60, NKJV). These words sound just like the cry of his master Jesus moments before his death. Jesus said. 'Father, forgive them, for they do not know what they do' (Luke 23:34, NKJV).

Notice how Luke, who wrote this account, likens Stephen's death to 'falling asleep' (Acts 7:60). This description reveals further the peace and joy that overwhelmed Stephen during his final moments. Who would ever describe the violent death of a man at the hands of an angry mob as 'falling asleep'? This is impossible to imagine unless that person had witnessed something unique in the apostle's death – the paradox of joy in suffering.

Even in death Stephen was empowered by God to lay down in green pastures! His soul was restored! Even though he walked through the valley of the shadow of death HE FEARED NO EVIL, GOD WAS HIS COMFORT. (Psalm 23)

This is a powerful lesson for the end time believer. We need to understand that we will not be facing tribulation in our own strength. We will have the Holy Spirit, the one promised by Jesus. He is the Comforter – literally, the one who draws alongside us to comfort and defend us.

Through tribulation in all its forms God will work his comforting and fearless power in us.

As the Apostle Paul writes in 2 Corinthians 1:5: 'for just as we share abundantly in the sufferings of Christ, so also our comfort abounds through Christ' (NIV).

And don't forget the power of this kind of testimony. Remember that at the scene of the first Christian martyrdom stood a certain man named Saul, a staunchly religious man and ardent persecutor of the church. Later he would receive a miraculous visitation of Christ and undergo a radical conversion to Christianity.

God heard the dying prayer of Stephen! God did not hold Saul's sins against him.

Saul, or course, became known as Paul. Paul went on to write some thirteen books of the New Testament, which contain powerful revelations concerning the subject of tribulation and suffering.

We must never therefore underestimate God's power – not only to save the fiercest of opponents to the Christian faith, but also to turn them into great champions for the cause. This is why it is so important, like Christ and Stephen, to adopt a heart of love and compassion towards those who persecute us.

Returning then to the theme of joy through tribulation, this is a critical teaching of Scripture. To reiterate, tribulation should not be feared but rather embraced.

There can be no greater preparation for the coming days ahead than to have a revelation regarding this.

What the Bible says concerning persecution is revolutionary. Indeed James writes to us that we should consider trials as pure joy. 'Consider it pure joy, my brothers and sisters, whenever you face trials of many kinds, because you know that the testing of your faith produces perseverance. Let perseverance finish its work so that you may be mature and complete, not lacking anything' (James 1:2-4, NIV). James also writes that those who persevere through these trials are not only blessed but also receive the ultimate prize. 'Blessed is the one who perseveres under trial because, having stood the test, that person will receive the crown of life that the Lord has promised to those who love him' (James 1:12, NIV).

So what is the prize? It is the promise of union and friendship with Christ today and forever!

We can see then that just as Christ had that joy set before him, we too have that same joy set before us.

The Apostle Paul experienced this 'tribulation' joy too. He wrote: 'I am filled with comfort. I am exceedingly joyful in all our tribulation' (2 Corinthians 7:4).

What a comfort it is to know that as the storm clouds of persecution begin to loom large over the end-time church, it will become overwhelmed by joy, and therefore empowered to face its most terrible hour.

When we are severely constrained, we will experience the joy of the Holy Spirit.

The Apostle Paul exhorts us to 'glory in our tribulations' because they produce in us perseverance; and perseverance, character; and character, hope. (Romans 5:3) Tribulation then has a refining work on the character of the believer. It emboldens us to face the Antichrist government and persecution from those around us who have given themselves over to godless living.

Paul was speaking from experience here. He tells us that many times he was in danger of death for the sake of the gospel. On five separate occasions he was whipped across the back thirty-nine times, three times beaten with sticks, once stoned, three times shipwrecked with one time spending a day and a night in the water. He was in danger from high waters on rivers, danger from robbers, danger from his fellow Jews, danger in the cities and the desert, danger from false apostles and many times Paul went without sleep, food, water and clothing (2 Corinthians 11:23-28).

Christian tradition holds that Paul was eventually martyred for his faith by being beheaded at the orders of Nero around AD 68.[4] No doubt as Paul readied himself for death, thoughts of Stephen flashed through his mind; and he like him became encapsulated in the risen Christ. As the sword came down upon his neck an inexpressible joy and comfort overwhelmed this hero of the faith and he too fell asleep.

In fact it is written that all of Jesus disciples went through tribulation, and all but John were martyred for their faith.

John however did not escape persecution. He spent the latter years of his life in a labor camp on the island of Patmos, sent there by the Roman emperor Domitian. John of course went on to receive the most startling revelations concerning the coming tribulation while imprisoned there.

James (son of Zebedee) was beheaded in AD 44.

Philip was scourged, thrown into prison and afterwards crucified in AD 54.

Matthew was slain with a halberd in the city of Nadabah, AD 60.

James, at the age of ninety-four was beat and stoned by the Jews, and had his brains dashed out by a fuller's club.

Matthias, who replaced Judas, was stoned and then beheaded. Andrew was crucified in Edessa.

336

Mark was dragged to his death by the people of Alexandria.

Peter was crucified upside down, because according to Jerome, Peter said he was unworthy to be crucified in the same manner as Christ.

Jude was crucified at Edessa in AD 72.

Bartholomew was beaten and then crucified in India.

Thomas was also martyred in India, being thrust through with a spear.

Luke was said to have been hanged on an olive tree in Greece.

Simon was, according to church history, crucified in Britain in AD 74.

Finally Barnabas was martyred in Cyprus around AD 73.[5]

Suffering was the apostolic way. In every case, the martyr knew the joy of the Lord in their suffering. And this has been true for persecuted believers ever since. Consider the following accounts.

Thomas Hudson was condemned by the vicar of Aylesbury in the 1500s.

'The spot of execution was called Lollard's Pit, without Bishopsgate, at Norwich. After joining together in humble petition to the throne of grace, they rose, went to the stake, and were encircled with their chains. To the great surprise of the spectators, Hudson slipped from under his chains, and came forward. A great opinion prevailed that he was about to recant; others thought that he wanted further time. In the meantime, his companions at the stake urged every promise and exhortation to support him. The hopes of the enemies of the cross, however, were disappointed: the good man, far from fearing the smallest personal terror at the approaching pangs of death, was only alarmed that his Savior's face seemed to be hidden from him. Falling upon his knees, his spirit wrestled with God, and God verified the words of His Son, "Ask, and it shall be given." The martyr rose in an ecstasy of joy, and exclaimed, "Now, I thank God, I am strong! and care not what man can do to me!" With an unruffled countenance he replaced himself under the chain, joined his fellow-sufferers, and with them suffered death, to the comfort of the godly, and the confusion of Antichrist.'[6]

Now consider Robert Samuel, martyred 1555.

'When Robert Samuel was brought forth to be burned, certain there were that heard him declare what strange things had happened unto him during the time of his imprisonment; to wit, that after he had famished or pined with hunger two or three days together, he then fell into a sleep, as it were one half in a slumber, at which time one clad all in white seemed to stand before him, who ministered comfort unto him by these words: "Samuel, Samuel, be of good cheer, and take a good heart unto thee: for after this day shalt thou never be either hungry or thirsty."

This blessed Samuel, the servant of Christ, suffered the thirty-first of August, 1555. The report goeth among some that were there present, and saw him burn, that his body in burning did shine in the eyes of them that stood by, as bright and white as new-tried silver.' [7]

Mrs Cicely Ormes of Norwich was burned at the stake in 1557.

'After declaring her faith to the people, she laid her hand on the stake, and said, "Welcome, thou cross of Christ." Her hand was sooted in doing this, [It was the same stake that had previously martyred other Christians] and she at first wiped it; but directly after again welcomed and embraced it as the "sweet cross of

Christ." After the tormentors had kindled the fire, she said, "My soul doth magnify the Lord, and my spirit doth rejoice in God my Savior." Then crossing her hands upon her breast, and looking upwards with the utmost serenity, she stood the fiery furnace. Her hands continued gradually to rise until the sinews were dried, and then they fell. She uttered no sigh of pain, but yielded her life, an emblem of that celestial paradise in which is the presence of God, blessed forever.'[8]

So we can see then that for the believer, tribulation is not to be feared but rather joyfully embraced. For in persecution or martyrdom we know that the powerful outworking of Christ in us is a guaranteed certainty. The end result of which will gain us the crown of life – union with Christ now and forever.

So as we look at the coming tribulation, let's do so with hope and joy in the Holy Spirit, not with fear and trembling.

The Gathering Storm

What will the Great Tribulation look like?

The catalyst for the Great Tribulation will most likely be the total collapse of the global financial infrastructure. The current financial crisis is only the beginning. Out of the ashes of the economic ruins a new global financial system will rise. We can see this taking shape today. Cash will be consigned to history and the only means to buy and sell will be through a digitized system – the prophesied Mark of the Beast.

Martial law – the imposition of military rule to maintain order – will be instituted. The burgeoning surveillance grid will facilitate the military takeover and implementation of the Mark. The people, desperate for food, will do anything in order to survive. All concerns that the new monetary system might be evil will be silenced through the relief that the people can once again return to a 'normal life', once again feed themselves and their families.

As armies control the masses, the world government will take advantage of the crisis, tightening its grip and consolidating its power. Those who refuse to accept the new world order and its economic system will be deemed enemies of the state. They will be apprehended, imprisoned or executed.

According to Daniel's prophecy the Great Tribulation will last seven years (Daniel 9:27). At some point around this tumultuous time the 'rapture' of the church will occur. The rapture is referred to in 1 Thessalonians 4:17. This is when the true followers of Christ will be 'caught up in the air' to meet 'the Lord in the air.' The word 'rapture' is derived from Latin 'raptus' meaning 'seized' or 'carried away.' The Greek rendering of the word is harpagisometha which literally means 'caught up' or 'taken away.'

One of the key questions for many believers concerns the timing of the rapture. Some believe that through the rapture the church will escape the Great Tribulation entirely, while others believe the church will experience only half of it, and still others hold that the church will go through the entire Great Tribulation. All agree though that at some point the church will be taken away from the earth in a supernatural event.

However, in many ways the timing of the rapture has become a distraction. While it is undoubtedly an important eschatological fact, one point is seldom discussed – that the Great Tribulation will not just happen overnight, but there will be a lead up to it in which the hour will grow darker and darker. A tribulation then will precede the Great Tribulation and seamlessly merge into it. Just as the persecution of the Jews in Nazi Germany evolved from 1933 into the Final Solution, so it will be for God's people during the end times. Tribulation will grow and expand into the Great Tribulation. The Great Tribulation then will be the most intense and turbulent part in a time where a tribulation has already begun. The church will go through this preceding, preparatory phase of trouble. In light of this at what point the church escapes through the rapture during Daniel's seven years becomes a matter of lesser importance.

Believers would therefore do better to prepare for what is soon to come than be preoccupied with debating the timing of the rapture.

Signs of the Times

It is difficult to imagine how the West could ever arrive at a place of such tribulation. But the warning signs are all around us. They are in fact staring us in the face.

The unabated deluge of media manipulation vomited out upon the masses is paving the way for the persecution that is to come. The all-out assault brought about by decadence and the derision of godly values has left a culture for dead, totally bereft of any true and lasting morality. The church has been impacted by this onslaught too, leaving many dysfunctional and complacent believers in its wake. All this comes from the media and its ardent preachers of secular amorality, who are by default haters of true religion. As the Apostle Paul wrote, they are actually 'haters of God'. According to Paul these people have debased minds and are filled with all manner of unrighteousness. They are full of deceit, maliciousness and gossip. They are slanderers, boastful, heartless, ruthless and inventors of evil (Romans 1:28-32). These character traits embody the spirit behind persecution. It rests upon lawless persecutors and is directed against believers.

But why do such people hate Christianity so vehemently? Because it exposes their lifestyle for what it really is. Jesus clearly explained this. He said, '[the world] hates Me because I testify of it that its works are evil' (John 7:7). Jesus Christ and authentic Christianity shine with the light of true righteousness. They expose the works of sinful human beings as utterly wicked.

341

In rejecting Christianity, the West is now beginning to move into the next stage – the persecution of the church. We can see this happening all around us today. The following are just a few of many examples.

In June of 2013 a group of Christians sang Amazing Grace during a peaceful protest against a proposed abortion law in Austin, Texas. The pro-abortion lobby however was having none of it. As they attempted to drown out the Christian worship they chanted 'Hail Satan, Hail Satan.'[9]

In another incident a street preacher was knocked to the ground and repeatedly punched and kicked by homosexuals at a gay pride event in Seattle. The preacher was carrying a sign that said 'Jesus saves from sin.'[10] This kind of persecution is not isolated. In August 2012 a pro-gay activist opened fire inside the headquarters of a Christian lobbying group, the Family Research Council in Washington, D.C. because the group opposed gay marriage.[11]

Churches have also been vandalized. A group called 'Angry Queers' hurled stones through the stain glass windows of Mars Hill Church in Portland, Oregon, stating, 'Mars Hill is notoriously anti-gay.' Gay rights protestors have also shouted profanities at the congregation's children, telling them they were 'homophobes' and that they would 'burn in hell.' [12]

While in November 2013 a violent 7000 pro-abortion mob attacked praying pro-lifers. The group of men and women attempted to storm the Cathedral of John the Baptist in San Juan de Cuyo, Argentina. In response 1500 young catholic men formed a human shield around the cathedral to prevent the mob from storming it. Topless feminists spray painted the faces of the praying men, fixed Nazi swastikas to their clothing, spat upon them and engaged in lesbian sexual acts in front of them. All this while the police said they were powerless to act because the protestors were women. [13]

These occurrences are on the rise. They will only become more widespread as the Antichrist spirit intensifies across the earth. Another example of this outright rejection and hatred of Christianity was displayed in St. Peters Cathedral, Cologne, Germany in December 2013. During the Christmas mass feminist Josephine Witt ran out from the congregation and jumped upon the altar naked from the waist up screaming and with the words 'I am God' daubed across her breasts. [14]

This kind of persecution is inevitable in cultures that abandon authentic Christianity. And we have abandoned true Christianity in the West. The decision to make no mention of God in the EU 'constitution', the removal of Christian crosses throughout Italian schools as part of a European Union directive, the Ten Commandments being removed from government and educational buildings across the US, are just some examples we have covered in previous chapters.

Silencing Free Speech

This abandonment of Christianity by increasingly secularized cultures has led to widespread disdain for those who hold to the teachings of the Bible. Although Western democracies proclaim the value of free speech, in reality political correctness silences large numbers of Christians from sharing confidently what the Bible unequivocally teaches about traditional marriage, homosexuality, or the right to life for an unborn child.

Free speech no longer really exists. The European Union 'Equal Treatment' directive illustrates this. An article in 'Evangelical Now' newspaper described the directive as a 'frightening threat to free speech and free exercise of religious conscience in the UK'.[15] The article went on to say that if the Directive is executed in its current form, religious liberty experts 'expect an exponential increase in persecution of the faithful.'[16] It is these kinds of equality laws and policies enacted by governments across the EU that compel Christians to act against their consciences.

Possibly the most disturbing part of the Directive is the harassment provision. This would allow an individual to accuse someone of violating the law just because they perceive that what the individual or group is expressing is offensive, or creating an offensive environment. This means that a Christian or a Christian organization without any intent to offend or harass could be prosecuted. Litigations could arise from a simple chat in a Christian bookstore. The employee could state she believes that Jesus is the only way, or that she did not agree with abortion. The customer could allege offence and sue. The Directive empowers anyone with an anti-Christian agenda and the litigation possibilities would be innumerable. Furthermore, according to the report, the Directive also lacks exceptions necessary to protect expressions of religious conscience. Religious liberty experts warn of further problems within the Directive, namely the infringement on the right to associate and meet together.

The report sums up the Directive as having the potential to 'extinguish Christian expression' and to 'inflict cultural genocide' in Europe. 'Armed with arbitrary provisions and draconian penalties, the Directive emerges as an instrument holding the potential to inflict cultural genocide. Christian Concern For Our Nation' (CCFON) warns that those with an anti-Christian agenda will wield a weapon capable of extinguishing Christian expression in Europe.'[17]

This end to free speech is indicative of the anti-democratic path our governments have taken. It is proof that we are no longer living in a democratic society. Today people who march in protest against perceived evils are herded into non-populated zones. Those wishing to have their say are either relocated to another place where their voice cannot be heard, or they are simply told to move on, or arrested for breaking the law.

In fact since 2011 unprecedented powers have been given to restrict peaceful protest around the British Parliament in Westminster. These have been granted to the authorities through the Police Reform and Social Responsibility Act. This draconian law was showcased in the story of a young lady who stood near Downing Street wearing a T-shirt displaying the words, 'Rogue State Britain.' She was approached by a police officer who told her, 'you can't wear that here, it is a demonstration.' Others have been arrested for simply reading out a list of names of people who have died in Iraq, and still others have received warning letters for carol singing at Christmas.[18] This repressive law allows an authorized person to demand the name and address of a person if there is 'reasonable ground for belief' that 'a person has contravened' one or more of the laws. It even allows for the seizure of a person's property.

In 2004 Michael Marcavage of Repent America and Steve Lefemine of Columbia Christians for Life attended the Republican National Convention in Madison Square Garden to address the large number of pro-abortion speakers at the event. While the two stood on the public sidewalk holding signs they were approached by police who told them they could not stand there because it had been marked as a 'no demonstration' zone. The men responded by asking where they could engage in free speech and the officers directed them to a free speech zone located a block away. As Marcavage and Lefemine walked with the police they questioned the purpose of the zone. They were then both arrested. Marcavage explained, 'they took us to an abandoned warehouse where they funneled hundreds of people into cages that they had set up for this purpose. They treated us like cattle.' The two men were released twenty four hours later.[19]

These exclusion zones are a total affront to democracy. Without free speech there is no democracy. Democracy is now all but an illusion, bolstered only by the perpetual propaganda techniques disseminated through the mainstream media.

A Strategy of Vilification

However, more disturbing than all of this is the government stance toward Christianity and civil liberty groups. Christians are not only being silenced, they are also being criminalized by government bodies. This in itself serves to show the Antichrist spirit that is pervading western government today. It also reveals the accuracy of Jesus words concerning the final days, 'then you will be arrested, persecuted, and killed. You will be hated all over the world because you are my followers' (Matthew 24:9, NLT).

It is a disturbing fact that today US government papers describe Bible believing Christians as right wing extremist terrorists. According to a US Department of Homeland Security paper entitled 'Rightwing Extremism' published in 2009, a right wing extremist terrorist is someone who is against abortion, against same sex marriage and believes in end time Bible prophecy.

Further disturbing definitions of a right wing extremist terrorist contained within the document show that right wing terrorists are those who are:

- conspiracy theorists, namely those who are concerned about the 'declaration of martial law, impending civil strife...suspension of the U.S. Constitution, and the creation of citizen detention camps'
- concerned about the US government's role in the formation of a One World Government
- concerned about antigovernment conspiracy theories
- concerned about illegal immigration
- concerned about increasing federal power
- against firearms restrictions
- concerned about the loss of U.S. sovereignty
- a returning war veteran
- against government policy

The war on terror strategy has even shifted focus to accommodate the vilification of Christianity. Once only the focus of Arab Muslims, today the DHS focus on white middle class

Americans too. This is further evidenced by a video released by the Department of Homeland Security's 'See Something, Say Something' campaign in 2011. The video characterized white middle class Americans as being the most likely terrorists, with those reporting on them as being either black, Asian or Arab.

The belief promoted by the DHS that Christianity is somehow dangerous is taking root. In 2013 during an Army Reserve briefing based in Pennsylvania, a US Army training instructor listed under the heading 'Religious Extremism' Evangelical Christianity, Catholicism, and other Christian denominations, alongside terrorist groups Al Qaeda and Hamas.[20] The material went on to define religious extremism as those who held beliefs, attitudes, feelings or actions that were far removed from the ordinary, such as the belief that their faith is the only right way and that all other beliefs are wrong. Col. Ron Crews, executive Director of the Chaplain Alliance for Religious Liberty said that he was astounded soldiers were taught that a key foundation of the Christian faith is now considered extreme and that Christians are now compared to those who want to implement Shariah law. 'The idea of salvation being exclusively through Christ is a key doctrine of the Christian faith,' Crews said. [21]

But it is not only the Department of Homeland Security that has set its sights on the persecution of the faithful.

A report published in 2009 by the Missouri Information Analysis Center (MIAC) entitled 'The Modern Militia Movement' labeled supporters of presidential candidates Ron Paul, Pastor Chuck Baldwin, and Bob Barr as a terrorist threat. The report further instructed Missouri police to be on the lookout for anyone displaying 'Constitutional Party, Campaign for Liberty, or Libertarian material' associated with these men, including car bumper stickers. All three men are self-confessed Christians.

The report states; '[Militia] members are usually supporters of former Presidential Candidate: Ron Paul, Chuck Baldwin, and Bob Barr. Anti-Government Propaganda: Militia members commonly display...bumper stickers that contain anti-government rhetoric...Additionally...anti-immigration, and anti-abortion, material may be displayed by militia members.'

Other potential terrorists include those who are against;

- Gun control
- The Federal Reserve
- The United Nations
- The North American Union
- The New World Order
- Income tax
- Radio frequency identification
- Abortion
- Illegal immigration

Furthermore, books and documentaries including Aaron Russo's warning to the American people *America: Freedom to Fascism* are also considered to be terrorist material, highlighted as 'Literature and Media Common to the Militia.'[22] The question has to be asked, how long will it be before the Bible is highlighted as literature common to the militia?

Prohibiting so called subversive books and material is nothing new. Again it is indicative of a dictatorship, echoing the Third Reich and Communist Russia's censorship of literature.

It seems that the process of labeling and vilifying Christians has therefore begun.

Christians as Terrorist Threats

Labeling Christians as extremist terrorists would of course be nothing new. As far back as 1999 the Federal Bureau of Investigation (FBI) produced a startling report entitled *Project Megiddo* which amounted to no less than a contingency plan for dealing with the Second Coming of Christ. The document's central thesis was concerned with the rising tide of so called conspiracy theorists and end-time Bible prophecy followers who believed that Armageddon was approaching, and how law enforcement would prepare and respond in the wake of civil disobedience.

The report reads, 'many extremist individuals and groups place some significance on the next millennium, and as such it will present challenges to law enforcement at many levels. The significance is based primarily upon either religious beliefs relating to the Apocalypse or political beliefs relating to the New World Order (NWO) conspiracy theory. The challenge is how well law enforcement will prepare and respond.'

This report, while stating that it is not possible to define exactly what a terrorist group is, leaves the door wide open to include a spectrum of religious and Christian groups under the label 'terrorist threat.'

The document's wording is clever too, consistently undermining real and known threats and labeling them as examples of conspiracy theory.

The report reads, 'the NWO conspiracy theory holds that the United Nations (UN) will lead a military coup against the nations of the world to form a socialist or One World Government. UN troops, consisting mostly of foreign armies, will commence a military takeover of America. The UN will mainly use foreign troops on American soil because foreigners will have fewer reservations about killing American citizens. U.S. armed forces will not attempt to stop this invasion by UN troops and, in fact, the U.S. military may be "deputized" as a branch of the UN armed forces. The American military contingent overseas will also play a large part in this elaborate conspiracy theory, as they will be used to help conquer the rest of the world. The rationale for this part of the theory is that American soldiers will also have less qualms about killing foreigners, as opposed to killing their own citizens.

Under this hypothetical NWO/One World Government, the following events are to take place: 1) private property rights and private gun ownership will be abolished; 2) all national, state and local elections will become meaningless, since they will be controlled by the UN; 3) the U.S. Constitution will be supplanted by the UN charter; 4) only approved churches and other places of worship will be permitted to operate and will become appendages of the One World Religion, which will be the only legitimate doctrine of religious beliefs and ethical values; 5) home schooling will be outlawed and all school curriculum will need to be approved by the United Nations Educational, Scientific and Cultural Organization (UNESCO); and 6) American military bases and other federal facilities will be used as concentration camps by the UN to confine those patriots, including the militias, who defy the NWO. Other groups beside the UN that are often mentioned as being part of the NWO conspiracy theory are...the Council on Foreign Relations, the Bilderbergers and the Trilateral Commission.'

'Religious motivation and the NWO conspiracy theory are the two driving forces behind the potential for millennial violence. As the end of the millennium draws near, biblical prophecy and political philosophy may merge into acts of violence by the more extreme members of domestic terrorist groups that are motivated, in part, by religion. The volatile mix of apocalyptic religions and NWO conspiracy theories may produce violent acts aimed at precipitating the end of the world as prophesied in the Bible. When and how Christ's second coming will occur is a critical point in the ideology of those motivated by extremist religious beliefs about the millennium. There is no consensus within Christianity regarding the specific date that the Apocalypse will occur. However, within many right-wing religious groups there is a uniform belief that the Apocalypse is approaching. Some of these same groups also point to a variety of non-religious indicators such as gun control...the NWO, the banking system, and a host of other "signs" that the Apocalypse is near. Almost

350

uniformly, the belief among right-wing religious extremists is that the federal government is an arm of Satan. Therefore, the millennium will bring about a battle between Christian martyrs and the government. At the core of this volatile mix is the belief of apocalyptic religions and cults that the battle against Satan, as prophesied in the Book of Revelation, will begin in 2000.'

In the document, Bible-believing Christians are repeatedly classified as a potential domestic terrorist threat.

It is chilling to consider that a person is classified as such if they believe

- the Book of Revelation and its description of the battle of Armageddon
- end-time Bible prophecy
- that God will overcome the enemies of Christianity
- the Second Coming of Christ
- that there will be a United Nations takeover of America presided over by the Antichrist
- that people will be forced to wear the Mark of the Beast to participate in business and commerce

The question has to be asked then, are all Bible believing Evangelical Christians seen as potential terrorist threats by the US government? If so, we have a serious problem and the church should wake up.

Learning from History

Here we must take a lesson from history. Hitler's campaign against the Jews living in Germany began by alienating them from their neighbors. He adopted the same strategy I am describing here, labeling them as extremists. In so doing he conditioned the people against them. This in turn enabled the government to forcibly have them removed and sent off to internment camps.

When both Christians and liberty advocates are regarded as threats to society, persecution in the West will begin at an unprecedented level. Just as we saw in Nazi Germany, hundreds of thousands of people will be forcibly removed from their homes and herded into internment camps.

If this sounds too difficult to believe, look back in history and realize that it would not be the first time internment camps have been set up and used on American soil to detain American citizens.

In 1942 during World Two internment camps were set up and over 110,000 people of Japanese desent, 62% of whom were American citizens, were rounded up and rail-roaded to them.[23] The internment was authorized by President Franklin D. Roosevelt after the attack on Pearl Harbor. After two and a half years of imprisonment the interns were finally released, to return home – if they still had one.

Years later in 1988 President Ronald Reagan signed legislation that apologized for the internment camps on behalf of the US government. Importantly the legislation stated that the government's actions were based upon three criteria:

- Racial prejudice
- Wartime hysteria
- And a failure of political leadership [24]

It is also important to remember, as previously mentioned, that today President Obama currently holds the unconstitutional power to detain a US citizen or foreigner suspected of being a terrorist under the National Defense Authorization Act of 2012. This means that the US government can detain a person indefinitely on the grounds that it believes they could be a threat. In a democratic society a person must be considered innocent until they have been proven guilty of wrongdoing. Importantly, a person cannot be incarcerated for thought crime.

In addition we should not forget about the existence of the deplorable US military prison at Guantanamo Bay in Cuba. This notorious place allows for American citizens to be arrested on US soil and incarcerated there without Habeas Corpus. Stories of ill treatment and torture abound. The camp resonates chillingly with Hitler's Nazi concentration camps.

A study led by Physicians for Human Rights found evidence of torture and other abuses that resulted in serious injury and mental disorder at the Guantanamo Bay detention camp and also Abu Ghraib prison. (Abu Ghraib prison was used for detention purposes by the US led coalition occupying Iraq).

According to the report those examined reported of being tortured or abused sexually, of being shocked with electrodes, beaten, shackled, stripped naked, deprived of food and sleep, and spat and urinated on. Although US President George W. Bush claimed in 2004 after the prison torture was revealed that it was the work of 'a few American troops who dishonored our country and disregarded our values,' it was found in once secret documents that the Pentagon and Justice Department allowed for a time the torture of the prisoners, through forced nakedness, isolation, sleep deprivation and humiliation at both Guantanamo Bay and Abu Ghraib.

Dr Allen Keller, one of the doctors who conducted the study said 'the findings on the physical and psychological exams were consistent with what they reported.'

Former detainees reported being subjected to:

- Stress positions, including being suspended for hours by the arms or tightly shackled for days
- Prolonged isolation and hooding or blindfolding, a form of sensory deprivation
- Threats against themselves, their families or friends from interrogators or guards

- Ten said they were forced to be naked, some for days or weeks
- Nine said they were subjected to prolonged sleep deprivation
- At least six said they were threatened with military working dogs, often while naked
- Four reported being sodomized, subjected to anal probing, or threatened with rape [25]

In another report Moazzam Begg a former detainee at the camp claimed, 'I was subjected to the sounds of a woman screaming. I was led to believe that my wife was being tortured.' Begg also spoke of being cavity searched and given directions on how to commit suicide, having his hair shaved off, being punched, kicked and spat upon. [26]

To summarize:

- The US government has detained US citizens in internment camps on US soil before

- Obama holds the right to detain a US citizen indefinitely because they might be a terrorist (i.e. they have not committed a crime, but are for example 'guilty' of being a Pastor Chuck Baldwin supporter, against abortion, against same-sex marriage, believe in end-time Bible prophecy, or possess material such as Aaron Russo's documentary 'Freedom to Fascism'. Importantly the definition of a terrorist has broadened to include Bible believing Christians and liberty advocates. In short according to the US government a Bible believing Christian is a terrorist).

- According to evidence the Guantanamo Bay internment camp is no less evil than a German Nazi concentration camp.

With this information in mind the notion that the US

government could round up and indefinitely detain en masse individuals for no crime whatsoever, except that is for being a Bible believing Christian or liberty advocate, becomes a disturbing possibility. Under the Obama administration all the 'legal' framework is now set in place to allow this to happen.

Preparing for Civil Unrest

Coupled with these facts, it is alarming to learn that in 2012 US government domestic agencies purchased two billion rounds of ammunition [27] and according to some reports the Department of Homeland Security is obtaining thousands of heavily armored vehicles for urban use within the United States. [28]

Furthermore the DHS is under investigation for purchasing large stockpiles of ammunition, just days before legislation was introduced to restrict the amount a government agency could legally purchase. Despite the fact that DHS officials repeatedly deny stockpiling ammunition, reports claim to the contrary. According to the Associated Press the agency plans to buy more than 1.6 billion rounds of ammunition over the next four to five years. This amount is the equivalent of a 24-year Iraq War. Americans are obviously concerned with what purpose these rounds would serve the DHS domestically. Of further concern the Social Security Administration has reportedly already purchased 360,000 rounds of hollow point bullets. Hollow rounds are forbidden under international law for use in war. These rounds explode on impact for maximum damage. [29] It has been claimed by law enforcement officials that the purchases are for training purposes, but as former Marine Richard Mason pointed out, hollow-point bullets are not the best choice for training purposes because they are more expensive than standard rounds. Furthermore, Mason said, 'we never trained with hollow points, we didn't even see hollow points my entire four-and-a-half years in the Marine Corps.' [30]

Congressman Timothy Huelscamp said the DHS has refused to answer questions from multiple members of Congress about the stockpiling. 'They have no answer for that question. They refuse to answer that,' said Huelscamp. [31]

If this is not enough the discovery of over 500,000 plastic coffin liners in a field in Madison, Georgia, has led to questions being asked. Just why are tens of thousands of burial vaults stacked in a field there, and who are they intended for?

The plastic coffin liners that stretch down the field stacked one on top of the other are a product called 'Burial Vault' made by the company PolyGuard Vaults. As described by the company. 'a Burial Vault is an outside receptacle or container, in which the casket and remains are placed, at the time of burial.' According to reports the US government has been buying Burial Vaults from PolyGuard Vaults for years.[32]

Stories abound that the burial vaults are the property of FEMA, the Federal Emergency Management Agency.

FEMA was created in 1979 under President Jimmy Carter. Upon creation of FEMA several government organizations with responsibility for the civil defense of the USA were amalgamated into it.

Seven years later in 1986 Army Regulation 210–35, Civilian Inmate Labor Program, was set up secretly. For over a decade it remained concealed until in 1997 it was declassified by the Clinton administration. The regulation listed twelve camps built by the US Army to hold American citizens, some of which already hold US citizens today.

Since then the number of camps has doubled from twelve to twenty four. The government's stated purpose for these labor camps is to

- provide aid during a natural disaster
- provide support after a terrorist attack

356

- combat the threat of illegal aliens
- USE DURING PERIODS OF CIVIL UNREST *(emphasis mine)*

These camps eerily resemble the concentration camps of Nazi Germany in that they come replete with inward facing barbed wire fencing (to keep people from getting out, rather than getting in) and guard towers. Just weeks after the DHS report on who is a right wing extremist, the US Army ran an ad campaign seeking those who would be interested in being an 'Internment/Resettlement Specialist.' The ad stated successful candidates will 'provide external security to...detention/ internment facilities' and 'provide counseling and guidance to individual prisoners within a rehabilitative program.' [33]

Detention Camps

In 2003 President Bush placed FEMA under the Department of Homeland Security. FEMA's directives are:

- National Emergency Recovery
- Continuity of Government
- Combating perceived threats to the existing social and political order

Ever since 9/11 and the introduction of the Patriot Act the fundamental liberties protected by the U.S. Constitution have been dismantled piece by piece.

Under the Patriot Act American citizens can be arrested, or held without being arrested, and incarcerated without even being charged with a crime.

The Act authorizes police to perform searches and seizures of private property without a warrant.

Later in 2009 a bill riding off the back of these wide and

sweeping powers was introduced by congress entitled the 'National Emergency Centers Establishment Act' (HR 645). This bill allocates military bases to be converted into FEMA emergency centers complete with educational and medical facilities similar to the Japanese internment camps of the 1940s. Judging by a leaked US Army document in 2012 entitled 'FM 3-39.40 Internment and Resettlement Operations', the educational facilities will be used to re-educate amongst others, political activists. The shocking plans involve a Psychological Operations Officer whose team's task will be designed to:

- Develop PSYOP products that are designed to pacify and acclimatize detainees or DCs to accept U.S. I/R facility authority and regulations

- Gain the cooperation of detainees or DCs to reduce the number of guards needed

- Identify malcontents, trained agitators, and political leaders within the facility who may try to organize resistance or create disturbances

- Develop and execute indoctrination programs to reduce or remove antagonistic attitudes

- Identify political activists

- Provide loudspeaker support (such as administrative announcements and facility instructions when necessary)

- Help the military police commander control detainee and DC populations during emergencies

- Plan and execute a PSYOP program that produces an understanding and appreciation of U.S. policies and actions

The term PSYOP is an abbreviation for Psychological

Operations. These are operations to convey selected information to influence emotions, motives and objective reasoning to an intern. The ultimate objective is to induce or reinforce behavior favorable to US objectives.

The document that outlines policies for the processing of detainees inside and outside the United States is linked to partner organizations such as the United Nations, Red Cross, the Department of Homeland Security and FEMA. Importantly the document does not only pertain to foreign combat operations but also applies domestically to US citizens. The wording in the document makes this perfectly clear, using many references to the DHS and FEMA to implement policies within US territory as a part of civil support operations.

Under the subheading 'Support to Civil Support Operations' the document reads: '2-39. Civil support is the DOD support to U.S. civil authorities for domestic emergencies, and for designated law enforcement and other activities. (JP 3-28) Civil support includes operations that address the consequences of natural or man-made disasters, accidents, terrorist attacks and incidents in the U.S. and its territories. 2-40. The I/R [Internment/Resettlement] tasks performed in support of civil support operations are similar to those during combat operations, but the techniques and procedures are modified based on the special OE associated with operating within U.S. territory and according to the categories of individuals (primarily DCs) to be housed in I/R facilities.' [34]

Also under the subheading 'Agencies Concerned with Internment and Resettlement', domestic application is confirmed:

'External involvement in I/R missions is a fact of life for military police organizations. Some government and government-sponsored entities that may be involved in I/R missions include:

- Department of Homeland Security
- U.S. Immigration and Customs Enforcement (ICE)
- Federal Emergency Management Agency' [35]

Clearly there are plans in place for detaining non-conformist US Citizens in centers across the country.

The time is coming when Bible believing Christians, political dissidents and liberty advocates will either have to remain silent or risk the actions of tyrannical government. It is happening right under the noses of the American people. But blinded by mainstream media few know what is happening.

Closed Hospitality Centers

What about the European Union? Has it escaped this madness? Or is it under the same spell?

Internment camps have never really disappeared in Europe. In fact Rivesaltes in the South of France, which was one of the largest French internment camps for Jews in World War II, was used to intern migrants up until its closure in 2007. The smallest centers hold a few dozen while the largest hold more than 1,000. The centers are fitted with surveillance cameras and coils of barbed wire. The worst are infested with rats, have little medical care and according to studies are subject to riots, arson attacks and suicides. A detention center that was finally closed on the Greek island of Samos was nicknamed 'Guantanamo' by the community surrounding it. Here arrivals were assaulted with the stench of vomit, urine and sweat. Sewage seeped into the dormitories and severe overcrowding meant people slept on the floor. Entry to the camps is often denied to reporters and governments are reluctant to even admit their existence. [36]

These detention centers however are being rebranded. Today they are being called 'closed hospitality centers'. In 2012 it was reported that Greece was to open thirty of these camps on disused military sites across the country in what was described as a 'desperate bid' to contain the social chaos prompted by the economic crisis.[37]

The Minister for Citizen Protection, Michalis Chrisohoidis said of the camps: 'we have a commitment to start operating these closed-hospitality centers, and we will keep to that commitment...it will act as a model to show Greek citizens that these facilities are safe for the public and will operate to high standards of health and hygiene.'

Former European MP Richard Cottrell wrote an article and expressed his concern about the wording used by Chrisohoidis and asked:

'Am I alone in detecting some singularly inappropriate language here? After all, was it not the Nazis who indulged in 'health and hygiene' as a constant reprise, particularly when it came to the 'closed-hospitality' camps established for the benefit (and 'hygiene') of European Jews? Can we ever forget the horrific deception of the gas chambers as fumigators?' [38]

It is time to get ready!

In this chapter we have discussed the Biblical idea of suffering and tribulation. We have looked at how the church will be called to endure persecution whether the rapture occurs before, during, or after the Great Tribulation.

We have looked at how the deluge of media filth has created a society devoid of any true morality.

We have discussed how society has now turned away from Christianity and become hateful of it, and how haters of religion are now persecuting the faithful.

We have seen too how governments have begun to vilify Christians and liberty activists, labeling them 'Right Wing Extremist Terrorists' in such government publications as the

'Megiddo Report', the DHS's 'Rightwing Extremism,' and the MIAC report on 'The Modern Militia Movement'.

We have also seen how the US government appears to be readying itself for massive social unrest – likely precipitated by the next phase of economic crises – through the purchase of massive amounts of ammunition, armored vehicles to be used on US streets, the strange anomaly of tens of thousands of coffin liners discovered in places like Madison, Georgia, and finally the creation of internment camps on both US and European soil.

It is just as Jesus prophesied: 'then you will be arrested, persecuted, and killed. You will be hated all over the world because you are my followers.'

Friends, let there be no doubt, tribulation is coming. At what point the rapture takes place is somewhat irrelevant in light of this. Tribulation is right at the door. The church will not escape this, just as the church did not escape the tyranny of Rome, or the Jews did not escape the tyranny of Nazi Germany, or the underground Chinese church has not escaped the tyranny of Communism.

Why do we believe we will somehow escape? God did not intend that we escape such calamity but that through it our faith in Him, which is more important than life itself, would be found genuine even to the salvation of our souls.

The Apostle Peter who was crucified under a tyrannical government revealed this to us. He said, 'in this you greatly rejoice, though now for a little while, if need be, you have been grieved by various trials, that the genuineness of your faith, being much more precious than gold that perishes, though it is tested by fire, may be found to praise, honor, and glory at the revelation of Jesus Christ, whom having not seen you love. Though now you do not see Him, yet believing, you rejoice with joy inexpressible and full of glory, receiving the end of your faith – the salvation of your souls.'

The West is about to be shaken as never before. The question is, are we ready? Are we ready both practically and spiritually? Are our hearts ready before the Lord? Are we ready to stand our ground like those who have gone before us? Are we prepared to refuse the direction in which our governments dictate we should go? Will we refuse to bow to ungodly government as Daniel, Shadrach, Meshach, and Abednego refused to bow despite the consequences? Will we defiantly stare our pharoanic leaders in the face as Moses did in his day – and declare LET MY PEOPLE GO? Will we stand up and expose the immoral lifestyles of our leaders just like John the Baptist did, despite the threat of a lawsuit or imprisonment?

Chapter 17

World War III

For nation will rise against nation, and kingdom against kingdom. And there will be famines, pestilences, and earthquakes in various places

Matthew 24:7

And there will be signs in the sun, in the moon, and in the stars; and on the earth distress of nations, with perplexity, the sea and the waves roaring; men's hearts failing them from fear and the expectation of those things which are coming on the earth, for the powers of the heavens will be shaken. Then they will see the Son of Man coming in a cloud with power and great glory. Now when these things begin to happen, look up and lift up your heads, because your redemption draws near

Luke 21:25-28

Wars, famines, epidemics, earthquakes and tsunamis in various places – these are the events described in the prophecy of Jesus Christ concerning the closing chapters of world history.

Jesus said that even the heavenly bodies would be affected with fearful sights in the sky.

Jesus' words offer a fascinating and detailed insight into not only the chronology of end-time events but also the correlation between the devastating perils that will befall the nations of the earth during this cataclysmic and climactic period of history.

Failing Hearts

Jesus said that the events at the end of history would be of such a magnitude that men's hearts would fail them. (Luke 21:26)

A medical report has revealed how the human heart can indeed fail due to fear. The study in question was interestingly based around people's reactions to earthquake and war, confirming the accuracy of Jesus' words.

Dr Robert Kloner, a cardiologist at the Good Samaritan Hospital in Los Angeles, found with his team that on the day of the 1994 Los Angeles earthquake five times more sudden cardiac deaths occurred than would ordinarily be expected. The study noted that this had nothing to do with people physically exerting themselves as they escaped the rubble.[1]

Dr Kloner said, 'the typical story was that a patient clutched his chest, described chest pain, and dropped over dead.'[2]

Such catastrophic heart failure was also observed during the 1991 Iraqi missile strike on Israel during the Gulf War. 147 deaths were recorded during the early hours of 18th January. Most of these were caused by heart attack and not by the missiles themselves.[3]

According to medical studies intense fear can stimulate organs by causing nerves to discharge catecholamines (adrenaline) directly into them. The brain responds in this way to ready the body for what might follow. It is this sudden injection of adrenaline into the heart that can sometimes trigger a deadly reaction.

What then is the antidote to this deadly fear?

For Christians it is the perfect love of God.

'There is no fear in love; but perfect love casts out fear' (1 John 4:18, NKJV).

366

How wonderful it is to realize that the love of God in the human heart has a very practical application too. As our hearts are made free from fear, God's love protects us from deadly cardiac arrests.

Natural Disasters

Other apocalyptic passages tell us that at the end the moon will turn blood-red because of the events being played out on the earth below (Joel 2:31, Acts 2:20, Revelation 6:12).

Reasons for a red moon are known today. According to astronomers the perception of a red moon can be caused by a forest fire or a volcanic eruption. If the air is filled with a large amount of dust it can partially obscure light from the sun and moon. These particles scatter blue and green light leaving red to pass through more easily.[4]

In 2011 a red moon was observed for this very reason. Sky watchers looked on at a stunning lunar eclipse as ash in the atmosphere from a Chilean volcano turned it blood red.[5]

The Apostle John describes burning forests and what sounds like a volcanic eruption (Revelation 8:7-8). In fact according to prophecy such will be the widespread intensity of the fires on the earth that a third of humanity will perish in plagues of fire, smoke and sulphur. These three elements could also be indicative of volcanic activity. Besides this, the fresh water supply will become poisonous and kill many. Ash from volcanic eruptions is known to poison water. In fact a deadly chemical fluoride can be found in the affected water. One such example was from the volcano Hekla situated in the south of Iceland. In a 1970 eruption, the Smithsonian Institute's Global Volcanism Program recorded that 'local groundwater is measuring high amounts of fluorine, which is toxic to sheep and horses. Fluorine concentration in creek water has been measured at 10 mg/liter.' It was also reported that fluoride contamination of the pastures caused major stock losses.[6]

Interestingly the Apostle John also saw in his visions what Jesus prophesied. John wrote, 'and behold, there was a great earthquake; and the sun became black as sackcloth of hair, and the moon became like blood. And the stars of heaven fell to the earth' (Revelation 6:12, NKJV).

There are various end-time earthquakes mentioned in Revelation, but one stands out from them all. This devastating earthquake is of global proportions. A gigantic lightning and thunderstorm will signal the approaching disaster. The power of the quake will be such that it will level the cities of the world and the island nations will be totally wiped off the face of the earth. Freak weather conditions will then ensue and deal another fatal blow to the already disorientated survivors. Giant hailstones weighing in at a hundred pounds each will rain down upon them.

These catastrophic events follow directly after the gathering together of the nations at the place called Armageddon.

Manmade Catastrophes

It is noteworthy that the Book of Revelation states that the war-mongering nations will be drawn to the battleground through demonic deception. According to prophecy demons will come forth through the lies spoken by the Antichrist, the political arm of the world government, and from the lies spoken by the False Prophet, the head of the religious arm. These lying spirits seduce world leaders into gathering at the infamous location for what will likely be the third World War. (Revelation 16:13-21)

This gives us valuable insight. We should not think that this demonic activity is reserved only for the near future. Today this serves to show us that it is through the mouths of lying politicians that nations are gathered together and demons of war are made manifest.

We can see shadows of this prophecy actively at work in our time. In 2002 Bush and Blair urged NATO (an alliance of nations) to invade Iraq on the basis of what is now known to be lies. More recently Obama played a lead in the US/NATO campaign against Libya in 2011. The rationale was freedom and democracy but in reality it was to seize Libya's vast oil reserves.[7] These are just two of many examples of nations going to war because of lies.

So it will be at Armageddon.

To help gain further understanding of Jesus' end-time prophecies it is important to consider the correlation between war and the natural disasters that follow. It is interesting that all these catastrophic disasters unfold immediately after the nations gather together for battle at Armageddon. This is often missed, leaving the reader with a list of seemingly random and unconnected events. Famine and pestilence often follow war, after all. But there may also be an even closer link than this.

Could it be for instance that as nation rises against nation, famine, pestilence, freak weather, volcanic eruptions, earthquakes, tsunamis and the like are unleashed as a result of the use of a high-tech weapons arsenal?

Never before in history has Jesus prophecy so perfectly fitted with the technological possibilities of our time. Jesus could well have been describing the high-tech warfare that is feasible today.

Many advancements in weapons technology have been made since the last world war. In fact the theatre of war is now a very different one than any other in history. Today all manner of weapons and warfare are possible.

One example is what is known as 'weather warfare.' Weather warfare is the ability to control weather conditions through techniques such as cloud seeding. Cloud seeding disperses chemical substances such as silver iodide into the air. This action alters the microphysical workings of a cloud. The result can either produce or prevent rain, snow, hail and fog. Cloud seeding is widely used today in airports and other non military applications around the world.

From 1949-1955 the RAF conducted artificial rainmaking experiments over Britain. RAF navigator Group Captain John Hart commented of the experiments, 'we flew straight through the top of the cloud, poured dry ice down into the cloud. We flew down to see if any rain came out of the cloud. And it did about 30 minutes later, and we all cheered.'

Operation Cumulus was conducted over southern Britain in 1952. On August 15th 1952 one of the worst flash floods occurred in Britain and swept through the Devon village of Lynmouth. Thirty five people lost their lives as an unusual downpour of rain and thousands of tons of rock from Exmoors hilly moorland came crashing into the village destroying homes, bridges, shops and hotels.

The meteorological office had previously denied that any rainmaking experiments were conducted before 1955 and reported that flights undertaken were for the purpose of collecting cumulus cloud data only. But an unearthed 50-year-old radio broadcast told a different story. Alan Yates an aeronautical engineer and glider pilot involved in Operation Cumulus at that time described his experience. Yates who sprayed quantities of salt over Bedfordshire was thrilled to learn from scientists that it had led to torrential rainfall 50 miles away in Middlesex. Yates said, 'I was told that the rain had been the heaviest for several years – and all out of a sky which looked summery...there was no disguising the fact that the seedsman had said he'd make it rain, and he did. Toasts were drunk to meteorology and it was not until the BBC news bulletin [about Lynmouth] was read later on, that a stony silence fell on the company.'

370

Decades later silver residue from iodide was found in the waters of the river Lyn and stories persist to this day that planes were seen circling the skies before the deluge.

Declassified minutes from an RAF air ministry meeting dated November 3rd 1953 revealed a list of possible uses for cloud seeding including, bogging down enemy movement, increasing water flow in rivers and streams to hinder or stop the enemy, and for clearing fog from airfields. More shocking than this however is that the document also discussed rainmaking having a potential 'to explode an atomic weapon in a seeded storm system or cloud. This would produce a far wider area of radioactive contamination than in a normal atomic explosion.'[8]

During the Vietnam War the US military used cloud seeding from 1967-1972 as a weapon of war in what was called Operation Popeye. The operation seeded clouds with silver iodide. The compound deployed by C-130 Hercules and F-4C Phantom aircraft was for the purpose of prolonging the monsoon season. The 54th Weather Reconnaissance Squadron that carried out the operation was successful in their objective. The excess rain water greatly inhibited the use of the roads by Vietnamese enemy supply trucks.[9]

Other weather modification mechanisms include the ability to create typhoons and hurricanes. The Wall Street Journal reported in 1997 that in attempts to tackle smog problems over Malaysia the government had approved a plan to use man-made cyclones to eradicate the haze. Datuk Law Hieng Ding, minister for science, technology and the environment said, 'we will use special technology to create an artificial cyclone to clean the air.' According to the report the cyclones would be produced by a Russian government owned company.[10]

Knowing that weather modification exists and have been readily used must raise serious questions for us today. What about the freak weather conditions and hurricanes which are gathering pace around the world today? Are they all naturally occurring or could some of them be part of an experimental program or stealth weather warfare being waged between nations?

Professor Gordon J F MacDonald author of *Unless Peace Comes*, wrote in a chapter entitled 'How to wreck the environment', 'among future means of obtaining national objectives by force, one possibility hinges on man's ability to control and manipulate the environment of his planet. When achieved, this power over his environment will provide man with a new force capable of doing great and indiscriminate damage...these weapons are peculiarly suited for covert or secret wars.' The book was published back in 1968. Just imagine the advances in weather weapons technology that must have been made since then.

In 2012 Iran accused the West of using weather weapons to influence the nation's climate. The head of Cultural heritage and tourism Hassan Mousavi said that he was 'suspicious about the drought in the southern part of the country.' Mousavi went on to say that 'the drought is an acute issue and soft war is completely evident...This level of drought is not normal.' '[The West] are influencing Iran's climate conditions using technology.' [11]

Weather modification through the process of cloud seeding has been going on for decades. Today weather modification continues under the name of geoengineering. The science of geoengineering is man's intervention in earth's climatic system. Shrouded behind the guise of saving the planet from global warming the globalists are implementing a plan that will lead to the eventual and total control of the geosphere.

It is easy to see what is going on here. Again we see the Hegelian dialectic at work. Create or exacerbate a problem, prepare the masses by creating fear and then rush in to save the world with a solution. The manipulated masses give the globalists what they want every time – in this case 'full spectrum dominance' of the geosphere.

They will do this through a variety of schemes including putting chemical dust into the atmosphere to reflect the sun's rays back into space.

Obama's chief scientific advisor John Holdren an advocate of the science said, 'it's got to be looked at. We don't have the luxury of taking any approach off the table.'[12] Holdren outlined the idea of shooting either sulphur dioxide particles, aluminum oxide dust or specially designed aerosols into the stratosphere – just like the military secretly did over Britain in the 50's. Holdren admitted the scheme could have grave side effects but said, 'we might get desperate enough to want to use it.' [13]

Poisoning the Planet

As we learned earlier, Holdren is also a chief proponent of government-mandated eugenics to prevent overpopulation. With a man who is on the record for holding little regard for human life it would surely not take too much desperation on his part to implement the full plan.

It is important to understand here that long ago many scientists exchanged the truth of a Creator God for the Darwinian lie. Consequently human beings have been reduced to mere beasts and are therefore treated as beasts. The extermination of human beings is akin to the culling of wild animals for these godless scientists.

The health effects of aluminum on the human body are clear and documented in what became known as one of Britain's worst cases of mass poisoning. In July of 1988 a lorry driver added 20 tons of aluminum sulphate to the drinking water supply at the Lowermoor treatment works near Camelford in Cornwall. Apart from the immediate short-term health problems of urinary complaints, skin problems, stomach cramps, joint pain, diarrhea and fatigue reported by residents who drunk the water, the more concerning longer-term problems were memory loss and brain malfunction. In fact a 1999 report in the British Medical Journal concluded that people had suffered 'considerable damage' to their brain function. Carole Cross a resident who had drunk from the poisoned water later died in 2004 from a rare and aggressive form of Alzheimer's. Cross's brain was found to contain unusually high levels of aluminum.[14]

Professor Exley, a world-renowned expert on aluminum said, 'hundreds of publications demonstrate that aluminum is not safe.' The professor explained, 'when the amount of aluminum consumed exceeds the body's capacity to excrete it, the excess is then deposited in various tissues, including nerves, brain, bone, liver, heart, spleen and muscle... We call it the 'silent visitor' because it creeps into the body and beds down in our bones and brain.'[15]

But this 'silent visitor' will not only rain down upon the masses in the future. Francis Mangels, former US Department of Agriculture scientist and present researcher in geoengineering, has solid evidence that the proposed plan is already underway. Mangels' research shows that normal soil samples in Sugar Pine Canyon Cr. Redding should read 15,000 ppb of aluminum, but lab reports show a staggering 4,600,000 ppb in upper and lower stream. Subsequently fish have been observed as 'losing scales' and being 'sick looking.'[16] Also snow samples off side the Mount Shasta, California tested 61,000 ppb. Mangels commented, 'this is just ordinary snow water and people are drinking this stuff when they're hiking on the mountain...government action is required at a 1,000. This is 61 times over the government limit and our hikers are drinking this poisonous water on Mount Shasta.'[17]

Dane Wigington, solar expert and climate researcher said, 'we've seen in five years soil pH's in this area that have escalated 10 to 12 times. We can prove that conclusively. This is not speculation...we have duplicate samples.'[18]

Wigington also asked, 'why would we not believe that it's

happening when what we see in the sky matches exactly the express goal of numerous geoengineering patents, about 160 or more? Why would we not believe this is happening when every element showing up in the rain tests are the primary elements named in those geoengineering patents? Why would we not believe this is happening when we have escalating levels in very short time frames, as much as five years, we see rain levels of aluminum, for example, escalating as much as 50,000%?"[19]

Two of the many patents that Wigington refers to are patents 3,899,144, August 12, 1975 and 5,003,186, March 26, 1991 which state:

'Light scattering pigment powder particles...are dispensed from a jet mill deagglomerator as separate single particles to produce a powder contrail having maximum visibility or radiation scattering ability for a given weight material.'[20]

'A method is described for reducing atmospheric or global warming resulting from the presence of heat-trapping gases in the atmosphere...The method includes the step of seeding the layer of heat-trapping gases in the atmosphere with particles of materials characterized by wavelength-dependent emissivity. Such materials include Welsbach materials and the oxides of metals which have high emissivity.'

'The method of claim 1 wherein said material comprises aluminum oxide...particles are dispersed by seeding the stratosphere with a quantity of said particles at altitudes in the range of seven to thirteen kilometers above the earth's surface.

A method for reducing atmospheric warming due to the greenhouse effect resulting from a greenhouse gases layer, comprising the following step: seeding the greenhouse gases' layer with a quantity of tiny particles of a material characterized by wavelength-dependent emissivity or reflectivity...The method... wherein said material comprises aluminum oxide."[21]

However aluminum is also being ingested by the populations through many other processes today. It is used in vaccines, cosmetics, deodorants, sunscreens, aspirin, cakes and biscuits that need raising agents, sweets, tea, cocoa, some wines, carbonated drinks and most processed foods to name but a few examples. Even high levels of aluminum which exceeded the legal amount permitted in water were found in infant formula, according to studies. Professor Exley said, 'we know aluminum can be toxic, yet there is no legislation to govern how much of it is present in anything, apart from drinking water.' [22]

Geoengineering will enable the globalists to utilize the geosphere for waging war against countries by, for example, inhibiting rain and thereby inducing drought and famine, as was alleged to have taken place in Iran. According to end-time prophecy, 'they were given power over a fourth of the earth to kill by...famine...' (Revelation 6:8, NIV). This prophecy could easily be fulfilled through geoengineering.

Controlling the Heavens

If this kind of warfare sounds too incredible to be true, irrefutable evidence exists that there are plans underway to control the heavens. A document published for the US military entitled, *Weather as a Force Multiplier: Owning the Weather in 2025* details the strategy.

The document boldly quotes, 'the technology is there, waiting for us to pull it all together. In 2025 we can "Own the Weather."'

'In 2025, US aerospace forces can "own the weather" by capitalizing on emerging technologies and focusing development of those technologies to war-fighting applications. Such a capability offers the war fighter tools to shape the battlespace in ways never before possible. It provides opportunities to impact operations across the full spectrum of conflict and is pertinent to all possible futures. The purpose of this paper is to outline a strategy for the use of a future weather-modification system to achieve military objectives...While some segments of society will always be reluctant to examine controversial issues such as weather-modification, the tremendous military capabilities that could result from this field are ignored at our own peril. From enhancing friendly operations or disrupting those of the enemy via small-scale tailoring of natural weather patterns to complete dominance of global communications and counterspace control, weather-modification offers the war fighter a wide-range of possible options to defeat or coerce an adversary.'[23]

The document discusses 'degrading enemy forces' through denial of fresh water and the inducement of drought, and states that the US, in partnership with NATO, will likely include weather modification as a part of their national security policy and use rain, fog, thunder and lightning as part of its weapons arsenal.

On discussing the harnessing of lightning as a weather weapon the document states:

'One area of storm research that would significantly benefit military operations is lightning modification...offensive military benefit could be obtained by doing research on increasing the potential and intensity of lightning. Concepts to explore include increasing the basic efficiency of the thunderstorm, stimulating the triggering mechanism that initiates the bolt, and triggering lightning such as that which struck Apollo 12 in 1968. Possible mechanisms to investigate would be ways to modify the electropotential characteristics over certain targets to induce lightning strikes on the desired targets as the storm passes over their location.' [24]

But it does not stop there. The Antichrist-aligned agricultural biotech corporations will benefit greatly from geoengineering. When natural crops die off due to drought, aluminum and other poisonous toxins, genetically modified tolerant versions will replace them.

Monsanto, a world leader in genetically engineered seed and

herbicide is one such company producing these super crops. For example Monsanto's 'Genuity DroughtGard', drought-tolerant corn comprises germplasm selected for its drought-tolerant characteristics. The GM corn plant uses less water in drought conditions.[25]

The International Food Policy Research Institute also confirmed the use of aluminum tolerant crops: 'ongoing trends such as climate change and population growth will likely exacerbate binding stresses. A new generation of genetically engineered (GE) crop research aims to alleviate these pressures through the improvement of subsistence crops...that incorporate traits such as tolerance to drought, water, and aluminum in soils...'[26]

Through these kinds of processes agricultural biotech corporations will gain control of the global food supply and the price of crops will increase. To quote the military document 'Owning the Weather', 'the ability to modify the weather may be desirable both for economic and defense reasons.'[27] This is also in line with end-time Bible prophecy where a loaf of wheat or three loaves of barley will cost a day's pay (Revelation 6:5-6, NLT).

Ultimately the Antichrist system will dominate most of earth's geosphere in the end-times. This will give the Antichrist and the False Prophet the appearance of having supernatural and god-like abilities as they will be able to 'predict' drought and famine, and also create wonders in the sky above – for example by 'stimulating the triggering mechanism that initiates... lightning.' [28] As the prophecy declares, 'he performs great signs, so that he even makes fire come down from heaven on the earth in the sight of men. And he deceives those who dwell on the earth by those signs which he was granted to do' (Revelation 13:13-14, NKJV). In the 1960's scientists launched rockets into the atmosphere to trigger lightning discharges in what was prophetically called Project Skyfire.[29]

Controlling the Earth

Monsanto is known as a leader in genetically engineered seed. This form of crop production is fast being heralded as a key to the survival of humanity. (30) But this tampering with God's creation is unleashing a devastating impact not only to the biosphere but upon humanity itself. Already Monsanto's GM crops are contaminating natural crops in nearby farms. Monsanto claimed that the outbreak of GM wheat on an Oregon farm was an 'isolated incident', but Kansas wheat farmers said Monsanto 'knew there was a high risk that the genetically modified wheat could contaminate other varieties of wheat'. Warren Burns, a partner of Houston's Susman Godfrey, who are leading a lawsuit against Monsanto, said: 'we fully expect we will see future episodes in other parts of the country...The potential here is this is the tip of the iceberg.'[31]

It surely will not be too long before all foods have been irreparably contaminated by genetic modification, and it will become impossible to eat any natural product at all. Genetic modification is out of control and for the first time in history man has begun a process that will irreversibly corrupt all plant life on the planet leaving humanity with no other choice but to eat of its poison.

The health risks to GM products are well documented. The American Academy of Environmental Medicine says that 'there is more than a casual association between GM foods and adverse health effects' and 'the strength of association and consistency between GM foods and disease is confirmed in several animal studies.' Multiple animal studies show significant immune dysfunction including increases in asthmatic, allergic and inflammatory disorders. Studies also show an altered structure of the liver, kidney, pancreas, spleen as well as cellular changes that could lead to accelerated aging. Infertility was also linked to GM corn-fed mice and intestinal damage and disruption of the intestinal immune system was also found. Russian biologist Alexey V. Surov and his colleagues, after feeding hamsters for two years on a GM diet, discovered horrifying results. Most GM soy-fed hamsters lost the ability to reproduce and some were even found to have hair growing inside their mouths. Babies born to GM fed hamsters were also smaller and could not reproduce at all. When male rats were fed GM soy their testicles turned from pink to dark blue. Italian scientists also confirmed this change including damaged young sperm cells.[32]

If this does not sound bad enough Gilles-Eric Séralini, professor of molecular biology at Caen University in France, reported the results of a €3.2m study. Rats fed on a diet of Monsanto's Roundup-tolerant GM corn for a total of two years developed abdominal cancer tumors. This was the first time GM maize had been tested on rats for a period of two years, as opposed to the 90-day trials currently demanded by regulators. [33]

In further GM outbreaks Monsanto's herbicide resistant plants have found their way into the wild and even mutated along the way, producing a new never-before-seen third crop of GMO plants, resistant to major weed killers.[34] But also 'superweeds' are causing a problem for thousands of farmers across the US too, with up to 15 million acres of American crops affected by giant ragweed. Farmer Jeremy Leech, who grows corn and soybean in Nebraska, is under constant threat from the resistant weeds which tower above and strangle his crops. The culprit is Monsanto's glyphosate chemical weed killer marketed as Roundup which the crops were engineered to survive. After years of spraying Roundup, the ragweed has acquired such resistance that now 24 times the recommended dose fails to kill them.

What then is the solution? Yet another strain of genetically modified crop! The new GM product will be created to withstand a virulent chemical component of the Vietnam War defoliant codenamed Agent Orange.[35] The US Department of Agriculture is yet to give clearance for the controversial new crop but if it does the threat to the environment will be devastating. The extremely toxic chemical herbicides known as 2,4-D and dicamba will likely destroy nearby trees, plants, and crops. 'Save our Crops Coalition' a group of farmers, food companies and concerned citizens formed to petition its approval by the USDA said, '2,4-D and dicamba are known to drift and volatilize, causing damage to plants over 10 miles away from the point of application.'[36]

What then of Agent Orange? Operation Ranch Hand was a US military chemical warfare program. It was one of the worst chemical warfare attacks ever committed in history. The lethal herbicide codenamed Agent Orange composed of 50% 2,4-D was manufactured by Monsanto and Dow Chemical for the US Department of Defense. It is indeed an unsettling thought to discover that one of the foremost providers of GM foods today was complicit in such a heinous crime. But it would not be the first time. Monsanto was also involved in the creation of a far more destructive and wicked weapon of mass destruction – the atom bomb.

Charles Allen Thomas, an executive of Monsanto, coordinated the Dayton Project, the research program involved in the construction of the first atomic bombs that decimated Japan's cities Hiroshima and Nagasaki in 1945.[37]

The spirit of war that bedevils Monsanto is clear for all to see. Monsanto's attack against the biosphere, their involvement in both chemical warfare and the creation of the atom bomb is a disturbing reality. We need to ask ourselves a vital question before we continue. How can we trust Monsanto with our food when it has consistently shown itself to have no regard whatsoever for human life?

During the Vietnam War, planes loaded with the deadly herbicide sprayed over 43 million liters of the chemical over central and southern Vietnam from 1962-1970 in order to clear foliage that was providing the enemy with cover.[38] Other uses were for forced draft urbanization and deprivation of the food supply by destroying crops.

It is estimated that 400,000 people were killed or maimed, and a further 500,000 children were born with terrible deformities or multiple health problems as a result of chemical attack. Also high rates of miscarriage have been recorded. Today it is estimated that over 3 million people are either disabled or suffer from serious health issues directly related to the atrocity[39] and deformed babies continue to be born even to this day.

Tong Van Vinh, a 26 year old truck driver for the North Vietnamese military witnessed the program first hand. The white powder that fell from the skies remained a mystery to the soldiers: 'the whole earth was covered with it,' commented Vinh. 'We thought they were dropping smoke bombs on us. We didn't know it was a chemical.' It was not until a few weeks later that they came to understand the horror of the ominous clouds that appeared above them. Vinh said, 'the trees died. Even the grass died. When we went to collect branches and leaves to disguise our trucks, there were none left.'[40]

End-time prophecy predicts that a third of the trees and grass will be destroyed by what it describes as a mixture of hail, fire, and blood coming down from the sky (Revelation 8:7) Could this have something to do with a future global GM crop disaster either through the spraying of the deadly chemical to destroy super weeds, or in an attempt to control GM crops gone awry? It wouldn't be the first time GM crops have been set on fire. In 2013 Hungary announced that 1,200+ acres of its GM corn was purposely destroyed by fire in an attempt to eradicate the crop over concerns that they were harming the natural environment. [41] Or worse, could the prophecy relate to a large scale chemical attack similar to Operation Ranch Hand?

Whatever the reasons for this massive attack upon the biosphere, one thing looks sure from Bible prophecy – thousands of planes and helicopters will be used to deploy weapons of mass destruction.

The Apostle John saw what he described as locusts coming out of the smoke and descending from the sky. These locusts wore iron armor and roared like an army of chariots rushing into battle. At their front they had human faces and in their tails they were able to sting mankind (Revelation 9:3-12).

On the face of it this might sound like John was describing some kind of flying mutant creatures. While this might not be outside the realms of possibility through the advancements made in future genetic engineering programs, it is more likely that what John saw were planes or helicopters. His description certainly fits with this idea.

These 'locusts' were armor plated with iron. This suggests that they were not organic. Their roar was likely the sound of many engines, and the human faces could easily have been the men piloting them. They came out of smoke and poison issued from their tails. It is easy to see how this could be a reference to the deployment of some kind of chemical or biological weapon.

Video footage of the roaring planes flying over Vietnam with the toxic chemicals pouring out from what appears to be their tails certainly echoes themes within some of the Apostle John's visions.

John saw in one particular vision a non-deadly but torturous poison being released that targeted only the people. Specifically it does not harm the grass, plants or trees. 'They were told not to harm the grass or plants or trees, but only the people...' (Revelation 9:4). This could refer to a biological weapon of some description. Today it is possible to deploy a biological weapon that singles out people and even whole ethnic groups. An ethnic bio-weapon could wipe out whole people groups or render them incapacitated through disease, leaving plant life unharmed. According to the British Medical Association report entitled 'Biotechnology, Weapons and Humanity II' published in 2004, the construction of genetic weapons 'is now approaching reality' and 'genetic bombs' could contain anthrax or bubonic plague tailored to activate only when genes showed the infected person was from a particular group.[42]

Jesus' words two thousand years ago seem more relevant today than they have ever been in human history:

'There will be...pestilences (plagues: malignant and contagious or infectious epidemic diseases which are deadly and devastating); and there will be sights of terror and great signs from heaven' (Luke 21:11, AMP).

Was Jesus talking about weather warfare here? The sight of terror and great signs in the sky could easily be an army of planes unleashing the deadly toxins of cancer producing chemicals and infectious diseases. The spreading of the prophesied plagues could be through the techniques of cloud seeding, or through similar spraying methods used in Vietnam, or through the dropping of biological warheads upon densely populated areas.

Of the three techniques, cloud seeding is the most surreptitious and therefore the most likely initial step. Remember that the Antichrist and the False Prophet are portrayed as masters of illusion and proclaimers of a false peace. Their war against the masses will proceed covertly long before more obvious weapons are employed.

It should not be ruled out that part of this strategy could also be part of a government-mandated eugenics program to depopulate the earth as backed by people like John Holdren, Obama's chief science advisor. Consider also that according to documented evidence cloud seeding programs are already in place and being implemented in various parts of the world today.

The prophecies are unfolding even as you read this.

The relationship between the prophesied apocalyptic events brought on by man and man's ability to control these phenomena today is undeniable. The capacity to harness the weather to produce drought, famine, rain, snow, fog, hail, thunder and lightning, or to deploy chemical or biological substances via the earth's geosphere fits disturbingly well with end-time prophecies.

Seismic Warfare

But Jesus and the prophets also spoke about worldwide geological catastrophes of earthquakes, tsunamis and volcanoes.

Could these also be harnessed and used as weapons of war? Is it possible for man to manipulate the earth's crust in order to induce devastating seismic events?

The most tragic earthquake of all time will occur just after the armies of the earth have gathered at the place called Armageddon. This suggests that this military conflict has something to do with the earthquake which will destroy the cities of the nations that are rising up against one another. As Jesus said, 'nation will rise against nation.' The correlation between war and earthquake is too strong to ignore. It is highly possible that the increase in earthquakes and the cataclysmic worldwide earthquake has something to do with a military strike and counter strike. But could this be?

The answer is yes. Documented evidence clearly shows that nuclear weapons can set off an earthquake.

A devastating earthquake in the Sichuan province of China struck on May 12th 2008. It left 69,195 people dead, 374,176 injured and a further 18,222 missing. A local resident, Mr He, stated that when the earthquake occurred he saw something erupt from the top of a mountain next to the valley. 'It looked like toothpaste being squeezed out. No it wasn't [magma]. It was these concrete pieces. The eruption lasted about three minutes.'

The China News Service reported that paramedics from the People's Liberation Army (PLA) found concrete debris covering the valley around the mountain for almost 1.5 miles. According to reports the thickness of the concrete pieces matched those used in China's underground military bases. An unnamed expert stated he was certain a nuclear explosion had caused the concrete structures to be jettisoned into the air. The report mentioned that at least one of China's nuclear military bases is located in Mianyang City, Sichuan, right near the epicenter.

In fact when television images showed strangely collapsed hills across the province officials were forced to admit there was a network of tunnels underneath which they dubbed their 'Underground Great Wall'. According to researchers China has an arsenal of up to 3,000 nuclear weapons hidden in tunnels.[43]

Moments after the quake Chinese citizens commented on the internet that military special forces had blocked traffic heading towards the epicenter and men in white chemical protective clothing in military vehicles could be seen heading towards the mountain.[44]

In February 2013 it was reported that after North Korea conducted a nuclear test an earthquake was detected in the country and later confirmed by their government. Seismic activity was also detected by the US geological survey and a UN body that monitors nuclear tests, who reported an 'unusual seismic event.' Experts in South Korea, the US and Japan reported the quake 'at magnitudes of between 4.7 and 5.2. Earthquakes of magnitude 3.9 and 4.5 respectively were detected in the North's 2006 and 2009 nuclear tests. The US geological survey said Tuesday's seismic activity had been of magnitude 4.9.'[45]

But what about the possibility of using a tectonic weapon to induce earthquakes?

As far back as 1997 William Cohen, US Secretary of Defense, confirmed the reality of tectonic weapons technology at a conference on Terrorism at the University of Georgia.

Cohen stated, 'others are engaging even in an eco-type of terrorism whereby they can alter the climate, set off earthquakes, volcanoes remotely through the use of electromagnetic waves. So there are plenty of ingenious minds out there that are at work finding ways in which they can wreak terror upon other nations. It's real, and that's the reason why we have to intensify our efforts, and that's why this is so important.'[46]

In 1966, world recognized scientist Professor J F Macdonald, associate director of the Institute of Geophysics and Planetary Physics at the University of California, published papers on the use of environmental control technologies for military applications. Macdonald said, 'the key to geophysical warfare is the identification of environmental instabilities to which the addition of a small amount of energy would release vastly greater amounts of energy.' In the papers Macdonald discusses ocean wave control and earthquake engineering.[47]

Further evidence of the reality of tectonic devices is the existence of a treaty banning such weapons. The 'Convention on the Prohibition of Military or Any Other Hostile Use of Environmental Modification Techniques', signed in Geneva in 1977, states:

'The Convention defines environmental modification techniques as changing -- through the deliberate manipulation of natural processes – the dynamics, composition or structure of the earth, including its biota, lithosphere, hydro-sphere, and atmosphere, or of outer space. Changes in weather or climate patterns, in ocean currents, or in the state of the ozone layer or ionosphere, or an upset in the ecological balance of a region are some of the effects which might result from the use of environmental modification techniques.'[48]

The treaty's reference to the lithosphere means the earth's

crust and upper mantle and refers to the manipulation of this to induce earthquake and volcanic eruptions.

The hydrosphere is the combined mass of both sea and fresh water on, under, and over the earth's surface and refers to the manipulation of this to induce a tsunami. A tsunami is Japanese for 'harbor wave.' A tsunami wave is created by the displacement of large volumes of water, as was the case with the Indian Ocean tsunami that killed over 230,000 people across 14 countries in December 2004. Earthquakes, volcanic eruptions, underwater explosions, landslides and meteor strikes all have the potential to cause a tsunami.

Furthermore the treaty specifically states the prohibition of modification techniques to produce earthquakes and tsunami as a means of destruction:

'It is the understanding of the Committee that the following examples are illustrative of phenomena that could be caused by the use of environmental modification techniques as defined in Article II of the Convention: earthquakes, tsunamis; an upset in the ecological balance of a region; changes in weather patterns (clouds, precipitation, cyclones of various types and tornadic storms); changes in climate patterns; changes in ocean currents; changes in the state of the ozone layer; and changes in the state of the ionosphere.

It is further understood that all the phenomena listed above, when produced by military or any other hostile use of environmental modification techniques, would result, or could reasonably be expected to result, in widespread, long-lasting or severe destruction, damage or injury. Thus, military or any other hostile use of environmental modification techniques as defined in Article II, so as to cause those phenomena as a means of destruction, damage or injury to another State Party, would be prohibited.' [49]

In the 1940's the United States and New Zealand conducted

secret experiments designed to destroy coastal cities with a 'tsunami bomb'. In thousands of underwater tests carried out near Auckland, scientists proved that a series of explosions could have a significant impact and create a tsunami. 'Project Seal' – the name given to the operation – was shelved just months before the atomic bomb was used on Japan.[50] Other projects that looked at ways to cause earthquakes formed part of the project codenamed 'Prime Argus.'

If a 'tsunami bomb' was developed to destroy coastal cities as far back as the 1940's, what on earth do the nations' armies possess in their arsenal today? What about recent tsunamis? Were they naturally occurring as we have been led to believe? Or were they part of a military experiment, or some covert strategy to bring down a nation by stealth?

In 2011 Vladimir Zhirinovsky, a colonel in the Russian Army and high ranking politician, claimed that Russia had the ability to 'destroy any part of the planet' and that '120 million will die' using an arsenal of new technology which involved initiating a tsunami. Zhirinovsky said that the American government had 'no future' and would 'collapse,' whereas Russia had 'lots of money, resources, and new weapons that no one knows about. With them we will destroy any part of the planet within 15 minutes.'

Zhirinovsky also made reference to the tragic 2011 Japanese tsunami and warned, 'And then there will be another tsunami, on the other side of the planet.'[51]

With the knowledge that such weapons exist a gaping question is left hanging in the air concerning a tsunami that occurred in 2004.

On December 26th 2004 the lives of over 230,000 people across 14 countries were ended by the tragic Indian Ocean tsunami. But the terrible loss of life could have been greatly reduced if it were not for a mysterious and monumental failure of the global seismic warning system.

According to reports the advanced global seismic information and positioning systems were fully operational on the day. The quake information was known and available in real time almost immediately to an entire network of seismic organizations, including the Pacific Tsunami Warning Center, a number of US and international government agencies, many officials, scientists, military and intelligence services. All these groups had advanced warning of the impending disaster. A report stated, 'we are not dealing with the failures of a single warning Center in Ewo, Hawaii, but with an entire Worldwide network of seismic information, satellite imagery and other sophisticated data, which was available almost immediately.' The report went on to say that 'while the PTWC [Pacific Tsunami Warning Center] had indeed formally notified Washington and the Military at the Diego Garcia island base, the US government and military already knew, because the seismic data had been processed within minutes by an agency under the jurisdiction of the US Department of the Interior, namely the National Earthquake Information Center (NEIC) based in Golden, Colorado.'

Why then did the entire network not warn of the looming disaster? It was after all one of the largest quakes in history. We will probably never get to know the answer. [52]

In January 2010 a catastrophic magnitude 7 earthquake hit Haiti. Haitian government figures estimated the death toll between 220,000 and 316,000. According to Venezuela's Vive TV unconfirmed reports at the time by a unit of the Russian navy suggested that the devastating earthquake was caused by a United States Navy 'earthquake weapons test', which was intended to be used against Iran but went 'horribly wrong'. Vive TV commented that the purpose of the earthquake weapon was to topple the current Islamic system in the country. Then Venezuelan President Hugo Chavez accused the US of using the tectonic weapon to occupy Haiti.

The report further stated the system used to carry out the test was the sub-arctic facility known as HAARP – 'High Frequency Active Auroral Research Program'.[53]

It might be hard for some to trust the words of Chavez, but more respected voices have questioned the earthquake too.

American Presidential nominee and Baptist minister Chuck Baldwin raised pertinent questions that the mainstream media would never dare ask.

In an article entitled 'What's really going on in Haiti?' Baldwin pointed out that the relief effort by the US military and government, with 20,000 US troops on the ground, was unheard of, and was more akin to a military occupation. Baldwin said, 'simply put, I cannot remember such an all-out "relief effort" by our nation's military and government forces following a natural disaster anywhere – ever!'

Baldwin went on to say, 'for me, there are many things that do not add up regarding what is going on in Haiti. The way the earthquake behaved; the lack of related seismic and tsunamic activity usually associated with earthquakes of this magnitude; the unprecedented involvement of US military forces being used for "relief efforts" even as commanders are desperate to fill combat theaters in Iraq and Afghanistan; the occupation of another independent nation, which occurred at lightning speed; the vast sums of US taxpayer dollars being expended; the devastation done to key Haitian governmental and banking institutions – which were known to be conduits for international financial disbursements – with virtually no devastation experienced anywhere else; and intelligence reports of surreptitious activity circulating all over Europe and Latin America all add up to one big question, What's really going on in Haiti? [54]

Others have also cited the fact that a Haiti disaster relief scenario envisaged just one day prior to the earthquake must have been more than a mere coincidence. The mock drill conducted by the US Southern Command (SOUTHCOM) in Miami was considered to be in 'an advanced stage of readiness.'[55] When the earthquake hit the following day SOUTHCOM took the decision to go live with the system. The report stated, 'on Monday, Jean Demay, DISA's technical manager for the agency's Transnational Information Sharing Cooperation project, happened to be at the headquarters of the U.S. Southern Command in Miami preparing for a test of the system in a scenario that involved providing relief to Haiti in the wake of a hurricane. After the earthquake hit on Tuesday, Demay said SOUTHCOM decided to go live with the system."[56] This begs the question, was it a coincidence or did someone high in the ranks know of the impending disaster? It would not be the first time a mock drill was conducted prior to a disaster event. Both 9/11 and 7/7 were subject to mock drills before the attacks.[57]

Earthquake Lights

Whether the Haiti earthquake was natural or otherwise we cannot of course know with any real certainty. However, claims made by the Venezuelan government that the HAARP research program could have been responsible for inducing an earthquake are not completely without grounds.

HAARP – the High Frequency Active Auroral Research Program is a joint project of the US Airforce and Navy, based in Alaska. HAARP is an ionospheric research instrument designed to focus radio frequency energy for the purpose of manipulating the ionosphere by heating up portions of it. It does this through a ground based 'phased array antenna system', comprising a field of 180 antenna units.

These antennas boil the upper atmosphere with a focused and steerable electromagnetic beam. It is basically a reversal of a radio telescope. Its antennas send out signals instead of receiving them. The heated electromagnetic waves then bounce back onto the earth and literally penetrate everything.[58]

The ionosphere is the region of the upper atmosphere which begins approximately 40 miles above the earth. The ionosphere is composed of electrons and electrically charged atoms and molecules. It plays an important part in atmospheric electricity, and also influences the behavior of radio waves. This portion of the earth's atmosphere is ionized by solar radiation, to which it owes its name the ionosphere.

According to HAARP its purpose is to analyze the ionosphere and investigate potential for developing ionospheric enhancement technology for radio communications and surveillance.[59]

However, HAARP has long been blamed for being more than just a research facility. There are those who say HAARP is being used as some kind of weapon. Often these people are labeled conspiracy theorists by the mainstream media.

But it is not only so called conspiracy theorists that believe HAARP is a weapon. Dr Nick Begich, co-author of *Angels Don't Play this HAARP*, says the fact that HAARP is promoted as an academic research project with the goal of changing the ionosphere for the good of humanity is merely a front for a much more sinister program. US military documents show that HAARP aims to learn how to 'exploit the ionosphere for Department of Defense purposes.'[60]

Furthermore, a European Union Parliament report dated 14th January 1999 confirms HAARP is a weapon. The report referred to HAARP as a 'weapons system which disrupts the climate' and 'a matter of global concern.' The report stated:

'HAARP – a weapons system which disrupts the climate. Regards the US military ionospheric manipulation system, HAARP, based in Alaska, which is only a part of the development and deployment of electromagnetic weaponry for both external and internal security use, as an example of the most serious emerging military threat to the global environment and human health, as it seeks to interfere with the highly sensitive and energetic section of the biosphere for military purposes, while all of its consequences are not clear, and calls on the Commission, Council and the Member States to press the US Government, Russia and any other state involved in such activities to cease them, leading to a global convention against such weaponry.'[61]

The report makes mention of HAARPS ability to aim a high energy beam at a moving target, the potential for an anti-missile system and the ability to penetrate the earth to detect underground military facilities:

'HAARP can be used for many purposes. Enormous quantities of energy can be controlled by manipulating the electrical characteristics of the atmosphere. If used as a military weapon this can have a devastating impact on an enemy. HAARP can deliver millions of times more energy to a given area than any other conventional transmitter. The energy can also be aimed at a moving target which should constitute a potential anti-missile system...Another application is earth-penetrating, tomography, x-raying the earth several kilometers deep, to detect...underground military facilities. HAARP has links with 50 years of intensive space research for military purposes, including the Star Wars project, to control the upper atmosphere and communications. This kind of research has to be regarded as a serious threat to the environment, with an incalculable impact on human life. Even now nobody knows what impact HAARP may have. We have to beat down the wall of secrecy around military research, and set up the right to openness and democratic scrutiny of military research projects, and parliamentary control.'[62]

When asked by the EU to send a US representative to answer questions regarding HAARP the US declined. The report stated, 'on 5 February 1998 Parliament's Subcommittee on Security and Disarmament held a hearing the subject of which included HAARP. NATO and the US had been invited to send representatives, but chose not to do so. The Committee regrets the failure of the USA to send a representative to answer questions...'[63] If it is just a research facility, what do they have to hide?

So it seems then that without doubt we can say that HAARP is indeed a weapon after all. But could it be an earthquake weapon?

In 2008 NASA scientists said they had found a close link between electrical disturbances in the ionosphere and impending earthquakes on the ground below. One study observed over 100 earthquakes with a magnitude 5.0 or larger occurring in Taiwan over several decades. Researchers found that almost all of the earthquakes down to a depth of 35km were preceded by an electrical disturbance in the ionosphere. (64) Excitation of the ionosphere has been observed over many other earthquake locations too. This phenomenon has been described as 'earthquake lights'.[65]

These lights take on a form similar to auroras and can be visibly seen for several seconds and up to ten minutes at a time. Others have described flashes similar to lightning. (66) It is noteworthy that the Apostle John saw a giant electrical storm heralding the devastating earthquake that destroys cities and sinks the island nations. 'And there were noises and thunderings and lightnings; and there was a great earthquake, such a mighty and great earthquake as had not occurred since men were on the earth' (Revelation 16:18, NKJV).

One of the results of the HAARP experiments is that it has created similar lights in the sky. 'Nature' the international weekly journal of science reported, 'one of the most obvious results of the experiments is that they can create lights in the sky that are similar to auroras, the glowing curtains of light that naturally appear in the polar skies when electrons and other charged particles pour down from Earth's protective magnetosphere into the upper atmosphere...HAARP's high-frequency radio waves can accelerate electrons in the atmosphere, increasing the energy of their collisions and creating a glow. The technique has previously triggered speckles of light while running at a power of almost 1 megawatt1. But since the facility ramped up to 3.6 megawatts – roughly three times more than a typical broadcast radio transmitter – it has created full-scale artificial auroras that are visible to the naked eye.' [67]

The fact that HAARP produces the same kind of ionospheric phenomenon should leave us asking a few questions.

American astrophysicist Adam Trombly was asked by journalist Jeane Manning about the possible effects of HAARP-type experiments. Since earthquakes are known to excite the ionosphere Manning asked if the reverse could happen. 'Could pulsed disturbances in the ionosphere set off earthquakes?'

Trombly replied, 'he would not be so naive as just to say, "yes, if they stimulate the ionosphere in this way then they're going to set off earthquakes." However, I would not be so cavalier as to say that if they happen to stimulate the ionosphere at a moment when it is already saturated, or near saturation, that they couldn't set off an event that could induce chaos – where you could end up having a kind of magnetic storming, almost a runaway event up there.' [68]

If HAARP is being used as an earthquake weapon we cannot of course know for sure. However, there is ample evidence that HAARP is indeed a weapon and its connection with earthquakes through the mimicking of 'earthquake lights' is fully documented.

We have also seen that there is more than enough proof that tectonic weapons exist. The ability to set off a tsunami or earthquake is shown by various historical military projects, the claims of politicians, senior army officers, researchers and scientists, and the signing of treaties banning such weapons. Surely this leaves us with only one possible conclusion. Weather and tectonic weapons, such as those described in this chapter, are undoubtedly playing a key role in the formation of the Antichrist world government today. Furthermore the use of such weapons at the battle of Armageddon seems to be a certain reality.

A Nuclear Showdown

Having said that, according to Bible prophecy weapons of far greater destruction than these will also be used. The use of nuclear weapons at the great battle of Armageddon and other end time battles is strongly implied. As the prophet Joel wrote, 'and I will show wonders in the heavens and in the earth: blood and fire and pillars of smoke. The sun shall be turned into darkness, and the moon into blood...' (Joel 2: 30-31, NKJV).

Often throughout the Bible specific details of a verse can be lost in translation. The term "pillars of smoke" (or columns / billows of smoke, depending on Bible version) is the Hebrew word "timeroth" meaning "palm trees", or "palm trees of smoke". Imagine seeing a great plume of smoke rising in the distance that resembled a palm tree. It is of course a perfect description of what we call a mushroom cloud associated with an exploding nuclear bomb.

Furthermore Zechariah prophesied that an unusual plague would all of a sudden befall those during the time of the great battle of Armageddon. 'And this shall be the plague with which the Lord will strike all the people who fought against Jerusalem, their flesh shall dissolve while they stand on their feet, their eyes shall dissolve in their sockets, and their tongues shall dissolve in their mouths' (Zechariah 14: 11-12, NKJV).

What kind of horrifying plague could dissolve eyes and melt human tissue so instantaneously that a person is still standing on their feet as it happens? The Apostle John helps us to understand more. He describes a plague that could be of the kind Zechariah prophesied. It is the plague of 'fire, smoke and brimstone' that has the power to kill a third of humanity (Revelation 9:18).

As the atomic bombs exploded on Hiroshima and Nagasaki, permanent 'shadows' of people were left behind on walls where no person was to be found – instantly vaporized where they stood, just as Zechariah had prophesied. Survivors also described flesh melting and eyes being 'liquefied.'

Murakami Keiko who lived in Hiroshima when the bomb went off said, 'before long wounded people were all around us people badly hurt, people with their flesh melting and drooping because of the burns.' [69]

Setsuko Thurlow who also survived was just 13 at the time. She described the disturbing horrors resulting from the nuclear blast and her words are eerily close to Zechariah's prophetic account. 'They were walking or shuffling with the most terrible injuries. Some people's eyes were liquefied. Some of them, their eyeballs were in their hands. Many more people were just sitting or lying on the ground among the dead bodies and people who were near death.' [70]

John also talks about how the leaders of the nations will eventually come against Babylon. They will be able to consume the city with such intense firepower that it will become totally desolate (Revelation 17 & 18). What kind of weapon other than a nuclear bomb could level a whole city by fire and make it desolate? Certainly no city-destroying weapons of this scale existed at the time these prophecies were made.

Jeremiah tells us more about the coming desolation of Babylon in the end-times (remember that Babylon is also a metaphor to describe the new world order of the Antichrist). Jeremiah declared, 'how Babylon has become a desolation among the nations!' 'For behold, I will raise and cause to come up against

Babylon an assembly of great nations from the north country, and they shall array themselves against her; from there she shall be captured. Their arrows shall be like those of an expert warrior; none shall return in vain' (Jeremiah 50:23 & 50:9, NKJV).

This latter part of the prophecy is intriguing. If we read the verse carefully, the arrow itself shall be like an expert warrior, not the shooter. In Hebrew the word used is sakal which means wise, with insight and comprehension. The word "arrow" in the original is chets, which can also mean a dart, or a javelin, or any weapon that travels through the air. The arrow itself then is intelligent. Two thousand years ago Jeremiah would not have been able to describe the projectiles that exist today in the form of modern missiles, but he seems to imply here the use of some kind of smart (guided) weapon. The final part of the verse also hints at this. 'None shall return in vain.' What kind of arrow, dart, or javelin could hit its target every time with total accuracy? Perhaps only a guided missile! [71]

Based upon this understanding a modern day interpretation of the verse could well read something like this: 'their missiles shall be intelligent and with guided accuracy, so that none of them can miss.'

The early apostles and prophets could not have ever imagined how these prophecies could be fulfilled. However, the horrors of nuclear weapons and their ability to do exactly as the prophecies describe are well known and documented today.

The One-Megaton Bomb

The first effect of a nuclear explosion is a sudden and intense flash of light. This is accompanied by a powerful pulse of heat radiation and a thunderous roar of an enormously powerful blast wave (Revelation 8:5). This intense burst immediately causes everything of combustible material to ignite up to a distance of approximately 8.5 miles (Revelation 8:7). Following this a fireball forms in the air for several seconds, blindingly bright and radiating intense heat. Up to approximately 6.5 miles of the blast every person exposed to the flash would suffer from severe burns and become temporarily or permanently blinded (Zechariah 14:11-12). Still at further distances others would suffer burns as clothing spontaneously combusts.[72]

The first flash would cause thousands of fires to ignite and spread. These combined fires would generate what is called a 'firestorm'. This is when the fires produce an updraft to form their own wind, blowing inwards from every side, increasing the intensity of the fire to above lethal levels (Revelation 8:7 & 9:18). The firestorm winds would be so strong that many survivors attempting to run away from the deadly flames would be sucked in.[73]

Despite knowing of the utter horror and devastation resulting from the nuclear attack against the innocent civilians of Hiroshima and Nagasaki, the proliferation of nuclear weapons continues to this day. Moreover the United States, the only nation on earth to ever drop nuclear weapons of such magnitude over cities, is the very nation that continues to possess some of the highest stockpiles in the world. According to the World Nuclear Stockpile Report the United States currently possess some 7,700 nuclear weapons.

It is estimated that the world's nine nuclear weapons states possess nearly 22,400 working nuclear warheads. Approximately 95% of these are within the United States and Russian arsenals. An important question might be asked here – just who is actually a 'rogue state'? This figure does not include the unsigned countries of the Nuclear Non-Proliferation Treaty. These unsigned countries are Israel, India, Pakistan and North Korea.[74] Since actual numbers are closely held national secrets and other nations unofficially possess nuclear weapons it is therefore impossible to get even close to an exact number.

It is inevitable that there will be a nuclear showdown, and

what is more – in accordance with Biblical prophecy – the confrontation is centering on the Middle East. The dormant seeds or Armageddon have begun to germinate. The escalation of the Syrian crisis in 2013 is one such example. The attempt by the US, UN, NATO and the EU to overthrow President Bashar Hafez al-Assad had the potential to escalate into a much wider conflict. Russia and Iran were involved and China was keeping a watchful eye on events.

The nations of the world are literally setting the stage for the final battle of Armageddon. Armageddon is the ancient fortified city of King Solomon. The name is derived from the Hebrew word har meaning 'mountain' and Megiddo referring to the name of the city. Armageddon overlooks a great valley referred to in the Bible as the 'Valley of Jehoshaphat', which actually means 'the Valley of God's Judgment' (Joel 3:2). It is here that the armies of the world will meet for a monumental military confrontation, outstripping every previous great battle in history.

Israel, the tiny land in which this great battle will be played out, is completely surrounded by twenty-one Arab nations including Iran. Many of these have publicly declared their wish to completely annihilate Israel. According to reports, in 2005 the then president of Iran, Mahmoud Ahmadinejad, quoted from Ayatollah Ruhollah Khomeini that 'Israel must be wiped off the map.' Ahmadinejad was speaking to an audience of 4,000 students at an event called 'The World Without Zionism.'

In words that chillingly echoed the end time battle prophecies of the Bible, Ahmadinejad declared: 'the skirmishes in the occupied land are part of the war of destiny. The outcome of hundreds of years of war will be defined in Palestinian land. Anybody who recognizes Israel will burn in the fire of the Islamic nation's fury.'[75]

As the Bible says, 'and he gathered them together into a place called in the Hebrew tongue Armageddon' (Revelation 16:16).

Chapter 18

Action Stations!

The only thing necessary for the triumph of evil is that good men do nothing
Edmund Burke [1]

When bad men combine, the good must associate; else they will fall, one by one, an unpitied sacrifice in a contemptible struggle
Edmund Burke [2]

Over 4,300 years ago God destroyed the earth in the great flood. But before He did, He mercifully warned the people of the approaching judgment. He set before them a most unusual but unmistakable sign. But the people of the earth, blinded by the pleasures and cares of the world, failed to see the warning. They did not repent of their wicked ways. They carried on as though things would always remain the same.

For over 100 years Noah and his family busied themselves with the greatest nautical construction the world had ever known. This was the unusual and unmistakable sign – the Ark.

With every tree felled, with every sound of saw and hammer, the people of the earth looked on. But although they saw and heard, they didn't understand. They failed to see that disaster was coming but that God was providing a means of salvation.

When the flood waters eventually came only Noah and his family were saved, and the people of the earth were swept away by the torrent of water that burst up from the deep springs and fell down from the skies.

Only eight people out of the entire population of the Earth discerned the signs of the times.

Thousands of years later, just moments after He had uttered the fig tree prophecy, Jesus spoke about this catastrophic event.

'As it was in the days of Noah, so it will be at the coming of the Son of Man. For in the days before the flood, people were eating and drinking, marrying and giving in marriage, up to the day Noah entered the ark; and they knew nothing about what would happen until the flood came and took them all away. That is how it will be at the coming of the Son of Man.' (Matthew 24: 37-39, NIV)

Today as signs of the end-times are being fulfilled with pinpoint accuracy, men and women of faith valiantly preach the gospel message of Jesus Christ in the hope that some will listen and get on board the Ark of God's Salvation.

From what we have seen in this book, there can be no doubt that the world is indeed hurtling towards its prophesied conclusion.

The question is, will the people notice the signs, or will they perish as they did in the days of Noah?

Consider the subjects we have looked at in this book:

- the deception of the masses through propaganda techniques
- the end of national sovereignties
- the destruction of democratic government and the adoption of dictatorial ones
- the resurgence of the Roman Empire

404

- the formation of a one world governmental system taking place through institutions like the European Union and United Nations
- the creation of a world bank through the deepening economic crisis leading to a cashless society
- the burgeoning surveillance grid leading humanity to the mark of the beast
- the increase in persecution of the faithful
- the absence of moral leadership in high places
- the involvement of world leaders in satanic religions
- the creation of a perfect environment in which the Antichrist can rise

These are the signs we are told to look out for.

They show us that 'summer is near'.

Jesus told us to keep watch and to be ready. 'When you see all these things.' Jesus said, 'it is so near, it is at the door!' (Matthew 24:33).

This is a warning for both Christian and non-Christian alike. If we do not act we will be swept away by the torrent of end-time calamities poised to flood the earth in these coming days.

Troubling times are indeed upon us, of this we should not doubt.

Commitment not Compromise

So what then can we do? We cannot sit back in our armchairs and do nothing.
Today a call is going out across the earth to rise up. Action must be taken, both on a spiritual and a practical level.

If you are reading this and you are not a Christian – that is someone who has not yet surrendered their will and life to God through the person of Jesus Christ – now would be the perfect time to humbly submit yourself to God and ask Jesus Christ to enter into your life. Once you have done this, find a Bible-believing church in your area to continue the journey you have begun with God.

If you are already a Christian now would be a good time to check your life before God. The Christian must not be lulled into a false sense of security.

Jesus warned the Christians of the Laodicean church that they were in danger. Jesus used strong words with them. He described them as being 'lukewarm – neither hot nor cold'. Because of this condition Jesus said, 'I am about to spit you out of my mouth' (Revelation 3:16). Jesus went on to warn that because they had become comfortable with earthly things they had believed the lie that they were in need of nothing. But nothing could have been further from the truth. Jesus warned that they were actually 'wretched, pitiful, poor, blind and naked' and in danger of losing their souls.

All too often the security found in wealth and prosperity has slowly drawn the Christian away from the security found only in Christ alone. Without due diligence and care, material gain can so easily lead to a hedonistic lifestyle, a lifestyle diametrically opposed to what is befitting of a true follower of Jesus.

Moreover there are warnings for the Christian who believes that spiritual works of power are a proof of a relationship with him. Jesus said, 'not everyone who says to me, 'Lord, Lord,' will enter the kingdom of heaven, but only the one who does the will of my Father who is in heaven. Many will say to me on that day, 'Lord, Lord, did we not prophesy in your name and in your name drive out demons and in your name perform many miracles?' Then I will tell them plainly, 'I never knew you. Away from me, you evildoers!' (Matthew 7:21-23, NIV)

I do not say these things to instill fear but rather I say them to warn. Let us not casually imagine that all is well with our souls but rather let us daily take action and work out our salvation with awe and trembling. (Philippians 2:12)

Jesus beckons the Christian today. 'Here I am, I stand at the door and knock. If anyone hears my voice and opens the door, I will come in and eat with him, and he with me.'

Only the person who overcomes – that is who continues to realize that without Jesus they are totally destitute and possess nothing of any value to save themselves – will have the right to sit with Jesus upon his throne, just as he himself overcame and sat down with God the Father (Revelation 3:19-22).

As the days draw to a conclusion we must surely desire that God finds us spiritually on fire or hot, not lukewarm or cold – overflowing with the Holy Spirit, attuned to his voice and walking in his ways.

Heaven forbid that on that day we be found lukewarm and full of earthly passions. Let us not be caught out like the unrepentant sinner, bitter towards our brother or sister, engaging in sexually immoral activity, pursuing the latest fashions, wasting time at the movies, watching endless hours of television, dancing and drinking the night away, as though these activities are acceptable in the sight of God.

My dear friend, they are absolutely not. The apostle Paul says, 'what fellowship has righteousness with lawlessness? And what communion has light with darkness?' 'Come out from among them!' entreats the Lord, 'And be separate!' (2 Corinthians 6:14, 17)

Action not Apathy

We must also realize that even though we have signs to show the end is near, we will not know the exact moment. Jesus said, 'but about that day or hour no one knows' (Matthew 24:36, NIV).

In an instant the heavens will disappear with a roar and the elements will be destroyed by fire and everything in the earth will be laid bare. Since everything will end in such a sudden and unexpected manner we are implored in Scripture to be found separated unto God at all times, to be spotless, blameless and at peace with Jesus lest we be taken off guard (2 Peter 3:10-14).

Jesus' return will be sudden, so sudden that it will happen within the blink of an eye (1 Corinthians 15:52).

According to medical science the human eye blinks at a speed of between 300-400 milliseconds. For this reason we are to be like soldiers on guard – alert and awake at all times lest we find ourselves unprepared.

Jesus said that he will come at an hour we do not expect (Matthew 24:44).

Jesus likens his coming to that of a thief, 'Look!' said Jesus, 'I come like a thief' (Revelation 16:15).

The thief analogy is repeated by the Apostle Paul who writes that Jesus will come like a thief in the night. The theme is also picked up by the Apostle Peter and it is carried throughout the gospel warnings. In particular the story of the wise and foolish virgins is told to inspire us to be ready. It is set at night time. The foolish virgins (those who are lukewarm Christians) come unprepared and without power (the Holy Spirit) to light their way to meet the bridegroom (Christ in his second coming). The resulting tragedy is that they are found locked out and unable to enter the wedding feast (the Kingdom of God) (1 Thessalonians 5:2; 5:4; 2 Peter 3:10; Matthew 24:43-44; Luke 12:39; Matthew 25:1-12).

Here we should also take note of Jesus' words to his disciples during that most troublesome night in the Garden of Gethsemane. Jesus told Peter that unless he kept on watching and praying he would fall into temptation. In like manner Jesus is calling upon his disciples in this last hour. Let us not be like the early disciples who failed to keep watch for even one hour. Today let us with persistence watch and pray, lest we become caught up in the cares and pleasures of this world and find ourselves without enough oil to lighten our pathway to the bridegroom.

For the believer then, it is time to attune themselves wholeheartedly to the call of their master Jesus Christ. It is time to stop sitting on the fence of indifference, precariously balanced between two worlds.

For the unbeliever, it is surely time to commit oneself to God, to humbly admit one's sinfulness and surrender one's life to Christ.

Protest not Passivity

As our world becomes darker and darker urgent practical action is required.

There is a duty to be fulfilled in this hour. To sit back and idly watch TV in the imagined safety of our homes while the world outside descends into anarchy around us will soon not be an option.

It is not good enough to believe that since all these things are prophesied all will pan out in the end. Just because we believe these events are happening in fulfillment of end-time prophecy does not give us a license to passivity or idleness. On the contrary it becomes imperative that we confront the darkness. Doing nothing is not an option.

As Edmund Burke famously said, 'the only thing necessary for the triumph of evil is that good men do nothing' (3).

Our inaction is not neutrality. It is complicity in bringing about the Antichrist world order.

In this dark hour God is looking for generals. He is looking for men and women of great faith who will stand up fearlessly in the face of certain persecution, against the death grip of tyrannical government hell-bent on reversing every freedom that so many paid for with their lives.

Where are the William Wilberforces who fought tirelessly for the abolition of the slave trade?

Where are those who will stand up against the global enslavement of humanity today?

Are we to remain asleep, in a drugged up stupor, blinded by propaganda and dumbed down by the mindless nonsense vomited from television screens?

Have we become so conditioned that the subjugation of our nations to foreign unelected bureaucrats has become of no consequence to us?

Are we not angry that they live opulent lifestyles on our money and impose their laws over our laws?

Are we content to be living at a time when Hitler's European dream is being fulfilled?

Are we sitting comfortably watching our ball game as the shadow of United Nation's authoritarianism looms over us?

Are we to continue turning a blind eye to the historical fact that western governments have actively engaged in acts of terror against their own people?

Will we persist in arrogantly labeling anyone a conspiracy lunatic who believes the official version of events is untrue?

Are we content to live in a world of lies when Jesus said, 'I will lead you into all truth?'

Are we disturbed by the encroaching threat of Islamic Sharia law over our lands when at the same time the godless elite stifle free speech, Christian liberty and label Christians 'right wing extremist terrorists'?

How do we feel about being treated like caged animals in a surveillance nightmare rivaling George Orwell's dystopian future?

Are we comfortable having our emails, phone calls, homes and every movement monitored by the state?

Are we going to silently relinquish all our freedoms until we are fooled into accepting the Mark of the Beast?

Do we sit in silence and inaction?

Or do we rise up and fearlessly run to the battle?

There are many practical things we can do in the war against tyranny. We can write letters of warning and protest to our local and national leaders. We can organize or attend peaceful protests around our cities. We can spread the word through social media and produce handout flyers or display bumper stickers. We can stop voting for the mainstream establishment political parties that all work towards the same ends.

The big question is will we refuse to follow government regulations that contravene God's laws?
When government goes against the Word of God we MUST NOT follow them.

There is no Biblical precedent for following dictatorial government when it constrains men and women of faith to sin against God. Time and again we read about the heroes of faith

411

who stood in the face of the elite leaders of their day and refused to bow the knee in surrender to their godless whims.

Romans 13 – the passage written by the Apostle Paul about submission to the authorities – is often regarded as the proof text amongst church pastors and leaders for submitting to government no matter what. It is important to note that Paul does not state that God approves of corrupt government, godless leaders, or unjust legislation, and neither does he mean for Christians to blindly submit to these over the law of God. Indeed Paul often found himself arrested, beaten and imprisoned by the authorities.

Obedience to earthly authority must be the general rule but it is clear from the Bible as a whole that we need not obey government if it involves sinning against God.

Romans chapter 13 has often been taken out of context. Unsurprisingly it has been used to further the aims of tyrannical power and to quell Christian protest. Indeed Adolf Hitler and many German churches used such Scriptures as the Biblical reason not to oppose the Nazi regime.

It should be noted that a church in America employed the same stance on the appointment of president Obama in 2009. The church in Ohio distributed a troubling flyer to its congregation based around the Romans 13 text. The flyer encouraged them to lead the way in supporting Obama because his election was a deterrent against evil. An excerpt from the flyer read:

1. Barack Obama's presidency is appointed by God.
2. Christians should lead the way in supporting Barack Obama's presidency.
3. Barack Obama's presidency can be a force for good and a deterrent against evil.
4. As president, Barack Obama is God's minister to you for good. [4]

Scripture must always be interpreted against the backdrop of all Scripture, and we can see from the Bible that men and women of God fearlessly opposed tyrannical governmental rule and unrighteous political leaders without question and broke the law when necessary.

Courage not Cowardice

It's time to be bold.

Consider the following examples.

The Hebrew midwives Shiphrah and Puah feared God so they refused to obey the command of the king of Egypt to kill the sons born to Hebrew women (Exodus 1:15-7).

Moses was hidden for three months by his parents in defiance of the king's command (Hebrews 11:23).

In protest Moses confronted Pharaoh to his face on numerous occasions (Exodus 5-13).

Esther illegally approached the King (Esther 4:16).

Shadrach, Mischach and Abednego did not heed the decree of King Nebuchadnezzar and refused to worship the graven image (Daniel 3:12-15).

Daniel ignored a thirty day government ban on prayer (Daniel 6:10-17).
God warned the wise men against returning to King Herod despite his clear instructions to do so (Matthew 2:12).

John the Baptist directly challenged King Herod, publicly accusing him of an immoral lifestyle despite knowing that this action would lead to certain imprisonment or death (Matthew 14).

Jesus caused a civil disturbance by overturning the tables of the money-changers. He even fashioned a whip to drive them out and continued to guard the area to prohibit them from returning (Mark 11:1-16).

On being told by the high priestly authorities not to preach about Jesus Christ, Peter and the apostles answered that they should obey God rather than men (Acts 5:29)

Jesus warned us that as the end draws nearer lawlessness will abound (Matthew 24:12). This will amongst other areas manifest itself in anti-Christian legislation. Laws have already been passed that restrict the Christian to act in line with the Bible. This trend will only continue until the Christian is forced to break unrighteous laws.

The day is coming when we will all be faced with this choice.

The question is will we be found obeying the government or will we be found fearlessly obeying God?

Chapter 19

We Will Not Fear!

Hide me under the shadow of your wings

Psalm 17:8

My loving kindness and my fortress, my high tower and my deliverer, My shield and the one in whom I take refuge

Psalm 144:2

If there is one exhortation that I would want to leave with every believer reading this book it would be this: do not be afraid.

What I have written here may be alarming to some. It suggests and indeed confirms that the world is moving at high speed towards the conclusion prophesied in Scripture. But as our global environment becomes more and more turbulent, it is imperative that believers do not give way to anxiety and live out of a centre of fear. As the Bible puts it, we are not to be afraid even though the earth gives way and the mountains fall into the heart of the sea. We are told that nothing can separate us from the love of Christ – that trouble, famine, hardship, government or sword cannot harm and that even death itself has lost its sting.

If we are to accept and alert others to the signs of the times, it is essential that we live in the deep revelation that God is our refuge and fortress – an ever present help in times of trouble – and that we therefore have absolutely nothing to fear. This goes beyond head knowledge and must enter the realm of the heart. It comes only from experiencing the profound, personal relationship we have with the Father through His Son Jesus Christ. As Jesus said, 'peace I leave with you, my peace I give to you; not as the world gives do I give to you. Let not your heart be troubled, neither let it be afraid' (John 14:27).

It is from this experience of God's reassuring and enfolding love that we should look at the events concerning the end times. We must not look on global circumstances from a default setting of fear or foreboding. On the contrary, we should observe them with a certain joy and eager anticipation as we come to realize that these events are the gateway to one of the greatest events prophesied in Scripture – the glorious second coming and return of the Messiah – The King of Kings, Jesus Christ the Son of God. This prospect is one that should bring enormous comfort to every believer's heart for, as the Apostle John wrote, in that day God will wipe away every tear from our eyes. In that day there will be no more death, sorrow or crying and no more pain (Revelation 21:4). In that day we will be invited to live in a city without death.

Let's look again at Psalm 46.

God is our refuge and strength, a very present help in trouble. Therefore we will not fear, even though the earth be removed, and though the mountains be carried into the midst of the sea; though its waters roar and be troubled, though the mountains shake with its swelling. There is a river whose streams shall make glad the city of God, the holy place of the tabernacle of the Most High. God is in the midst of her, she shall not be moved; God shall help her, just at the break of dawn.

The nations raged, the kingdoms were moved; He uttered His voice, the earth melted. The LORD of hosts is with us; the God of Jacob is our refuge. Come, behold the works of the LORD, who has made desolations in the earth. He makes wars cease to the end of the earth; He breaks the bow and cuts the spear in two; He burns the chariot in the fire. Be still, and know that I am God; I will be exalted among the nations, I will be exalted in the earth! The LORD of hosts is with us; The God of Jacob is our refuge."

Here the Psalmist writes, we will not fear. Even though mighty earthquakes strike, resulting in mountains falling into the seas, we will not fear. Even though tsunamis break upon shores and cities, altering the coast line forever, we will not fear. Even though nations may rise up against nations to destroy each other with devastating cruelty, we will not fear. Why will we not fear? We will not be afraid because, as the psalmist says, God is our refuge. He is a very present help. Our God is with us.

Think about it for a moment. Though every edifice on the planet may be shaken and fall, God's fortress will never so much as tremble and certainly will never collapse.

God's fortress is mighty, sturdy, permanent, fixed and safe.

And it is into that high tower, that holy refuge, that believers are called to run.

Oh that we could have a revelation of the wonderful truth that not only God dwells in this refuge and fortress, we are invited to dwell there too!

The heroes of faith knew this.

When Shadrach, Meshach and Abednego stood before King Nebuchadnezzar after they had refused to bow to the king's image, they boldly proclaimed on hearing of their certain death by fire, 'the God we serve is able to deliver us from it, and he will deliver us from Your Majesty's hand. But even if he does not, we want you to know, Your Majesty, that we will not serve your gods or worship the image of gold you have set up.' (Daniel 3: 17b-18 NKJV). These three Hebrew men hid in the fortress of their God and said, 'we will not fear.'

Daniel was thrown into a pit of hungry lions. His faith rested in the full knowledge that God was his refuge. Indeed, such was the peace of God upon Daniel that those ferocious and ravenous lions were not tempted so much as to scratch him, and they became as peaceful as Daniel himself. Daniel had chosen not to fear. His peace extended even to the lions!

Stephen, as he was being stoned to death, was overwhelmed not by the rocks that violently pounded and broke his body but by a vision of Jesus Christ standing in an open heaven beckoning and welcoming him to His side. Such was Stephen's fearless sense of security in God that at the point of death he cried out before his murderers, just like his Master Jesus did, 'Lord do not charge them with this sin.' Stephen found a place of refuge where terror could find no foothold.

The Apostle Paul also hid in this high fortress of God's peace when he was afflicted. He experienced many hardships; he was beaten, stoned, shipwrecked three times and lost at sea, went hungry, thirsty, cold, naked and was imprisoned, yet he wrote that the 'God of all comfort, comforts us in all our tribulation' (2 Corinthians 11:25; 2 Corinthians 1:3-6). Paul knew what it was to run into the high tower of God's mighty presence and peace.

All these men and many more proclaimed at the point of pressure and in the place of persecution, 'WE WILL NOT FEAR!'

And that is what believers today need to learn to do.

How do we do this?

The Psalmist helps us once again when he says – 'God will help her at the break of dawn' and 'the God of Jacob is our refuge'.

Why does the Psalmist here describe God as, 'the God of Jacob'

418

and not 'the God of Abraham?' It is because he wants to draw attention to a powerful lesson about our ability to 'rest,' even when all hell is breaking out around us.

You see, it was Jacob who wrestled with God until the break of day, when he rested. Could it be that through much wrestling (i.e. seeking God with all our heart) we are able to find that place of rest where in God nothing can harm us, regardless of the circumstances raging all around us?

In Proverbs 18:10 we read that 'the name of the Lord is a strong tower and the righteous run into it and are safe.' As soldiers under fire are protected in a strong tower or fortress, so we can take refuge and find protection inside of our 'God-tower', so to speak.

The revelation of this wonderful and blessed truth, that God is our refuge and high tower, and that we can run into our God and become totally hidden and safe in Him, is of paramount importance for living the Christian life in the end of the 'end times.' It empowers us to embrace every hardship with the perfect knowledge that in that difficulty we can dwell safe inside God. We are taken to a place of rest as we experience the true peace of God that the Apostle Paul said surpasses all understanding, and guards our hearts and minds through Christ Jesus (Philippians 4:7 NKJV).

At the end of this book, then, I have to return to the beginning.

Remember what I wrote in chapter 1? All my investigations began with the visitation of an angel who carried a message in just one word, and that word was 'love.'

Love is the key. As I wrote there, if we are to embrace the alarming realities of the earth's final facts (as prophesied in Scripture), then we must live out of a center of love not fear. As the apostle John declared, 'perfect love drives out fear.'

If you have any fear or anxiety in your life about the gathering storms across the globe, then with all sincerity ask your heavenly Father to give you a revelation of his perfect love. By his Holy Spirit, he will surely give it to you (1 John 3.1) and from this you will know that you are a child of God with nothing to fear (Romans 8.15-16).

Without the revelation of God's love, found only in his Son Jesus Christ, there will always be fear in our hearts.

But as soon as we hear Jesus' words, 'the Father himself loves you dearly' (John 16.27, NLT), then all fear is cast out.

Once again it is the psalmist who declares how we should live in these climactic hours of history.

He says, 'be still and know that I am God.'

The safest place in the universe is in the arms of your Father God.

He wants you to know him – not in some intellectual, abstract, or religious way, but in that personal and relational way that Jesus knew the Father.

He wants you to be certain of his love and confident in Him, whatever the circumstances.

To know God in this way, you and I must understand that this kind of relationship is only available through Jesus.

Jesus alone has the keys to the fortress, the high tower, the refuge that is our God.

If you do not yet enjoy this kind of relationship with God, take a moment to be quiet before the Lord and pray a simple prayer in which you say sorry for your sins. Thank God that in Jesus' death you receive perfect forgiveness. Ask Jesus Christ to come into your life as your Saviour and Lord. Finally, ask that the peace of God will come and rest upon your heart and mind and that you will instinctively draw upon the strength of the Lord when trouble and hardship come.

You could end your prayer time by saying something like this:

"Lord Jesus, I come before you now, and acknowledge that you are the God of refuge. Here in this moment I thank you for being my strong tower of protection in every difficult situation that I face. Enable me Lord through the power of your Holy Spirit to live in this reality every day of my life, in Jesus name, Amen."

Now finally remember what the Apostle Paul wrote in Romans 8:35-39:

'Who shall separate us from the love of Christ? Shall tribulation, or distress, or persecution, or famine, or nakedness, or peril, or sword? As it is written: 'For your sake we are killed all day long; we are accounted as sheep for the slaughter.' Yet in all these things we are more than conquerors through Him who loved us. For I am persuaded that neither death nor life, nor angels nor principalities nor powers, nor things present nor things to come, nor height nor depth, nor any other created thing, shall be able to separate us from the love of God which is in Christ Jesus our Lord.'

Let this great truth bring serenity to your soul and with all your brothers and sisters in Christ throughout the earth make this your decree:

'WE WILL NOT FEAR!'

.

Photo Journal –
Europe and the Middle East

Germany – April 2012

RIGHT: A European Union flag adorns the Reichstag parliament. On my visit I was surprised to see EU flags flying all over Berlin. A local commented to me that since the euro crisis they had never seen so many EU flags in the city. This is a perfect illustration of how the economic crisis is being used to further consolidate the elite takeover of Europe.

LEFT: The Seat of Satan. BELOW: the Gates of Hell. Did they influence the past? Are they influencing the EU today?

BELOW: As I walked around Sachsenhausen concentration camp I wept for those who died under such cruel conditions. This camp was used by the Nazis from 1936-1945. The entrance reads 'work makes free'.

But while this camp is a memorial to the past horrors of tyrannical government, will its memory stop the same action from being perpetrated again?

Belgium, Germany & France – October 2012

LEFT: Belgium, Brussels. Within the EU complex of buildings a sculpture of the woman riding the beast as prophesied by the Apostle John. In Greek mythology Zeus the bull rapes Europa the woman. The message is in plain sight – THE RAPE OF EUROPE HAS BEGUN.

RIGHT: I was not surprised to see inside the Brussels visitor center the blatant hatred for nation states. According to the EU, national sovereignty is 'a crying evil.' This, along with many other plaques displayed a clear distain for nationhood.

...national sovereignty is the root cause of the most crying evils of our time and of the steady march of humanity back to tragic disaster and barbarism... The only final remedy for this supreme and catastrophic evil of our time is a federal union of the peoples...

Lord Lothian (Philip Kerr), The ending of Armageddon, 1939

LEFT: Aachen, Germany. A statue of Charlemagne stands on the site of his palace. Crowned in AD 800, Charlemagne is called the 'Father of Europe'. He was responsible for reuniting part of the old Roman Empire – The Holy Roman Empire of the German Nation. Today Germany continues to be a driving force behind the European Union – the prophesied revived Roman Empire. BELOW: Today the Carlemagne Prize is given to champions for the cause of European unification. Notable figures who have been awarded the prize are on display in the town hall.

LEFT: The throne of Charlemagne, Aachen Cathedral.
BELOW: I discovered this Illuminati symbol on a building just outside the cathedral.

BELOW: The Spear of Destiny, Aachen, Germany. In Hitler's satanic quest for world domination he acquired the Spear of Destiny. The spear is said to bestow upon the holder supernatural ability in battle. Both Charlemagne and Barbarossa rulers of Europe possessed the spear while they were in power.

ABOVE: Strasbourg, France. The stained glass window of the Strasbourg Cathedral donated by the Council of Europe in 1956. The 12 halo star above the Virgin Mary is an exact representation of the EU flag.

LEFT: France, Strasbourg. Within the EU complex of buildings. Again the woman rides the beast in fulfilment of the Apostle John's vision. The back end of the beast, in glass, being symbolic of the tower of babel – the EU building. As I looked at the monstrosity I wondered if the message could not get any more graphic. Its clear for all to see – the European Union is raping and plundering Europe.

RIGHT: France, Strasbourg. The EU parliament tower, built to resemble the Tower of Babel and the colosseum of Rome – symbols of rebellion against God and persecution of those who would not bow to Rome.

ABOVE: On entering it was not difficult to imagine the jeering crowds of ancient Rome entertained as political agitators and Christ followers were thrown to the wild animals.

RIGHT: It was chilling to see the EU tower rising above this residential street in Strasbourg. There is no escape for the citizens of Europe as democracy is replaced by tyrannical government.

Switzerland – April 2013

LEFT: Switzerland, Geneva. The Lucis Trust European headquarters is based in this ominous looking building amongst other non government organisations approved by and working with the United Nations. Founded by Alice Bailey the Lucis Trust, formerly the Lucifer Publishing Company distributes occultic books worldwide. According to email correspondence with the Lucis Trust I was told that their bookshop was open to the public. However when I showed up I was hastily told it was not!

England – June 2013

RIGHT: England, Grove Hotel, Watford – Bilderberg 2013. The alternative media's relentless exposé of the yearly secretive meetings of the elite meant it could no longer be hidden. Bilderberg were forced to go public and launch into some kind of PR strategy to deal with it. Here a delegate arrives amid the heckling of waiting protestors.

A global awakening

LEFT: Suddenly Bilderberg was reported by the mainstream media. Predictably the mainstream's take on the group was completely at odds with documented evidence. The reporting served only to stifle the growing awareness to the activities of this shadowy group.

Those suggesting Bilderberg was anything other than the established version were treated in the usual manner and derided as conspiracy theorists. While I was there I overheard a news group talking about how their supervisor had told them they would have access to the delegates at the hotel entrance. If they had known anything about Bilderberg they would have realised that this would not happen. It was interesting to learn first hand how disconnected from true journalism the mainstream press actually are.

Secret plans

RIGHT: Michael Meacher, Labour MP is interviewed at Bilderberg 2013. Meacher commmented, "If you go at the end of the conference...and say to someone, could you just give me a comment about what happened, they will make some polite statement but they are certainly not going to tell you about what was really decided...what is being concerted in terms of their plans is something that is going to be kept entirely secret."

Conspiracy nutcases

LEFT: UK Independence Party and European Parliament member Gerard Batten is interviewed by the Financial Times. Batten commented that anyone who says Bilderberg is more than just a group discussing world problems 'will be branded as some kind of conspiracy nutcase.'

430

Israel – October 2013

Bible confiscation at the Temple Mount, Jerusalem

ABOVE: The Temple Mount in the heart of Jerusalem – the site of the first and second Jewish temples, and the site of the prophesied third Jewish temple. Today the Islamic Dome of the Rock stands here. Although the Temple Mount was reclaimed by the Jews for the first time since the destruction of the second temple in AD 70 after the 1967 six day war, the Israeli government gave jurisdiction of it back to the Arabs.

Here the religious tension is real and felt. While I was on the site Muslim men and women chanted abuse at the few Orthodox Jews on the mount. The Jews were escorted through the crowds by armed police and off the site. Jews and Christians are not allowed to utter a prayer or engage in any act that might be considered a religious one, being kept under the watchful eye of the Muslim police. Upon entry I had my bible confiscated by the Israeli security.

Rock attack on the Hill of Evil Counsel, Jerusalem

RIGHT: This is a view of the Temple Mount from the Hill of Evil Counsel. Historically it is said to be the place where Judas plotted to betray Christ. The hill is where Tony Blair was going to purchase a mansion. It is also where many United Nations staff live. The hill certainly lives up to its name. While I was there a gang of youths chanted at me 'go way', stones were thrown at me and on nearing the bottom of the hill a man hurled a large rock at me.

431

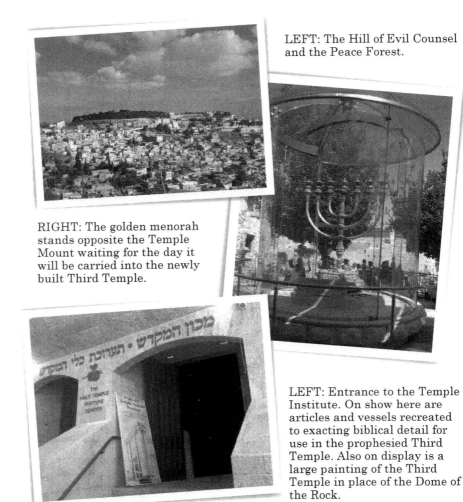

LEFT: The Hill of Evil Counsel and the Peace Forest.

RIGHT: The golden menorah stands opposite the Temple Mount waiting for the day it will be carried into the newly built Third Temple.

LEFT: Entrance to the Temple Institute. On show here are articles and vessels recreated to exacting biblical detail for use in the prophesied Third Temple. Also on display is a large painting of the Third Temple in place of the Dome of the Rock.

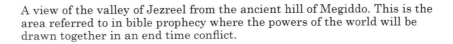

A view of the valley of Jezreel from the ancient hill of Megiddo. This is the area referred to in bible prophecy where the powers of the world will be drawn together in an end time conflict.

The Golden Gate, Jerusalem. According to Jewish belief the Messiah will enter through this gate when he appears. In 1541 it was sealed shut by the Ottoman Sultan Suleiman the Magnificent in order to stop the Jewish Messiah from entering. A Muslim graveyard was also placed in front of it as a further deterrent. This is in the belief that Elijah, the precursor to the arrival of the Jewish Messiah, will not defile himself by entering a cemetery.

View of Jerusalem from the Mount of Olives. From here Jesus prophesied the signs that would lead to the end of the world. (Matthew 24)

In fulfilment of the Apostle John's prophetic end time vision imagery of the woman riding the beast is emblazoned all over Europe.

Mr J Carter,

4th November 2009

The Rt Hon Gordon Brown MP,
10 Downing Street,
London,
SW1A 2AA

Dear Mr Brown,

I am writing today to express my deep concern, sorrow and regret that our free and democratic nation of Great Britain is surrendering itself to the dictatorial ideals of the European Union. The years of subversive and stealth like tactics of the European Union and the way in which the British Government has been beguiled marks a tragic turning in the history of our great nation.

I write to you this day a message from the God of the Bible – please read, take heed and act before it is too late.

The LORD says; "Do not be deceived, I cannot be mocked. They set up kings, but not by Me, They make princes, but I the LORD do not acknowledge them, from their silver and gold they make idols for themselves – that they might be cut off – I the LORD control the course of world events; I remove kings and set up other kings, I the LORD reveal deep mysteries and reveal what lies hidden in darkness."

That which God has not ordained will not succeed. He will depose those who rise against freedom and truth and they will be utterly dismayed, brought low and exposed, He (God) will bring to light everything that is done in secret behind closed doors.

I believe, Mr Brown, that you still hold the power to change the course of our history, to stand in the gap and say no, to make an about-turn, and change the direction of our nation and avert a time of great darkness in our nation.

Thank you for taking the time to read this letter.

Yours sincerely,

Mr Jason Carter

Following my dream encounter of October 2009 I wrote warning letters to Prime Minister Gordon Brown, David Cameron and Her Majesty the Queen.

435

Notes

Chapter 2

1. R W Jepson, *Clear Thinking* (Longmans, 1936)
2. Edward Bernays, *Propaganda* (Ig Publishing, 2004), 71
3. Edward Bernays, *Propaganda* (Ig Publishing, 2004), 10
4. James Sandrolini, *Propaganda: The Art of War*
5. Adolf Hitler, *Mein Kampf*, 180-181
6. Adolf Hitler, *Mein Kampf*, 184
7. David Irving, *Goebbels. Mastermind of the Third Reich* (Focul Point Publications, 1996)
8. Will Stewart, *Hitler planned 'Big Brother' style television to broadcast Nazi propaganda*, (Mail Online, 21 October, 2008)
9. John L. Snell, *The Nazi Revolution: Germany's guilt or Germany's fate?* (Boston Heath, 1959)
10. Barrie Zwicker, *Towers of Deception: The Media Cover-Up of 9/11* (New Society Publisher; Pap/DVD, 2006)
11. Carl Bernstein, *The CIA and the Media* (Carl Bernstein, www.carlbernstein.com)
12. *BBC 'Is £3M Brussels Propaganda Arm'* (Daily Express, 3 February, 2012)
13. Paddy Chayevski's film *Network,* Howard Beale character. (1976)
14. Colin A. Ross, *The CIA Doctors: Human Rights Violations by American Psychiatrists,* (Greenleaf Book Group Press, 2011)
15. Hendricus G Loos describes, *Nervous system manipulation by electromagnetic fields from monitors,* (United States Patent, 6,506,148 January 14, 2003)

Chapter 3

1. Daniel Estulin, *The True Story of The Bilderberg Group* (Trine Day, 2009), 83
2. Daniel Estulin, *The True Story of The Bilderberg Group* (Trine Day, 2009), 84
3. Jim Tucker, *The Bilderberg Diary,* 4
4. Jim Tucker, *The Bilderberg Diary,* 11
5. Daniel Estulin, *The True Story of The Bilderberg Group,* (Trine Day, 2009), 41-43
6. David Rockefeller, *Memoirs* (Random House Value Publications, 2003), 105

7. Daniel Estulin, *The True Story of The Bilderberg Group* (Trine Day, 2009)

8. *Bilderberg Group – Garmisch-Partenkirchen Conference, 23-25 September 1955*, (Wikileaks, 2009), 7

9. Andrew Rettman, *'Jury's out' on future of Europe, EU doyen says* (EU Observer, 16 March 2009)

10. Ambrose Evans Pritchard, *Euro-federalists financed by US spy chiefs*, (The Telegraph, 19 September 2000)

11. Robert A. Pastor, *Toward A North American Community, Lessons from the Old Order for the New* (Peterson Institute, 2001)

12. *North American leaders show unity*, (BBC, 23 March 2005)

13. *US-EU Summit* (White House Archives, George W Bush, www.georgewbush-whitehouse.archives.gov)

14. *EU-US Summit, Washington, 30 April 2007* (Council of the European Union, www.consilium.europa.eu)

15. Luise Hemmer Pihl, *CIA supported British 1975 Yes to EU*, (EU Observer, 18 August 2001)

16. Will Podmore, *British foreign policy since 1870*, (XLibris, 2008)

17. Macer Hall, *EU President van Rompuy to be Highest Paid*, (Express, 20 November 2009)

18. Bruno Waterfield, *Baroness Ashton reaps benefits from EU tax loophole*, (The Telegraph, 23 January 2011)

19. Ambrose Evans-Pritchard, *EU whistleblower in £130m case is fired*, (The Telegraph, 14 October 2004)

20. Ian Traynor, *Who speaks for Europe? Criticism of 'shambolic' process to fill key jobs*, (The Guardian, 17 November 2009)

21. Daniel Hannan, *Herman Van Rompuy: today the EU, tomorrow the world!* (The Telegraph, 21 November 2009)

22. *Lord Christopher Monckton Speaking in St. Paul* (Minnesota Free Market Institute, YouTube Channel, 15 October 2009)

23. Richard Sonnenfeldt, *Witness to Nuremberg: The Chief American Interpreter at the War Crimes Trials*, (Arcade Publishing, 2006), 30

Chapter 4

1. *A 40-Year Wish List*, (The Wall Street Journal, 28 January 2009)

2. Larry Flynt, *Common Sense*, (Huffington Post, 20 August 2009)

3. *Intervention of H.E. Mr. Herman Van Rompuy, New President of EU Council.* (www.eu-un.europa.eu)

4. *Prince Charles Copenhagen speech: 'The eyes of the world are upon you'*, (The Guardian, 15 December 2009)

5.   Alex Jones, *Terrorstorm – A History of Government Sponsored Terrorism* (Disinformation, 2006)

Chapter 5

1.   Alex Jones, *Terrorstorm – A History of Government Sponsored Terrorism* (Disinformation, 2006)
2.   Mae Brussell, Stephanie Caruana *Inside The Hearst Kidnapping, Donald Defreeze Was First Black Patsy In Secret Govt. Plan To Take Over U.S.* (Berkeley Barb, April, 1974, Number 18, www.maebrussell.com)
3.   Trevor Harrison, Slobodan Drakulic, *Against Orthodoxy: Studies in Nationalism,* (UBCPress, 2011)
4.   Kate Connoly, *75 years on, executed Reichstag arsonist finally wins pardon – Dutch activist exonerated under 1998 law – Hitler used fire as pretext to establish dictatorship,* (The Guardian, 12 January 2008)
5.   Daniele Ganser, *NATO's Secret Armies: Operation GLADIO and Terrorism in Western Europe (Contemporary Security Studies),* (Routledge, 2004)
6.   The News Journal, Nov 23rd 1990
7.   Stephen Kinzer, *All the Shah's Men: An American Coup and the Roots of Middle East Terror,* (John Wiley & Sons, 2008)
8.   *Pentagon Proposed Pretexts for Cuba Invasion in 1962,* (The National Security Archives)
9.   David Ruppe, *U.S. Military Wanted to Provoke War With Cuba,* (ABC News, 1 May 2001)

Chapter 6

1.   Mahatma Gandhi, *All Men are Brothers: Autobiographical Reflections,* (Continuum, 2005), 72
2.   Noam Chomsky, *9-11,* (Open Media/Seven Stories Press, 2001)
3.   David Irving, *Goebbels. Mastermind of the Third Reich* (Focul Point Publications, 1996)
4.   *Blair dismisses Iraq weapons doubts,* (BBC, 8 July 2008)
5.   John Glaser, *Antiwar, Iran and the Bomb: A Fabricated Threat,* (20 June 2012)
6.   *Keeping Them Honest with Anderson Cooper,* (CNN, 11 January 2013)
7.   Paul Craig Roberts, *What We Know And Don't Know About 9/11,* (Information Clearing House, 16 August 2006)
8.   *Louis Freeh Charges 9/11 Commission Cover-Up,* (Newsmax.com, 17 November 2005)

9. Dan Eggen, *9/11 Panel Suspected Deception by Pentagon,* (Washington Post, 2 August 2006)

10. *The 9/11 Commission Report,* (W. W. Norton & Co, 2004), 2

11. *The 9/11 Commission Report,* (W. W. Norton & Co, 2004), 5

12. *Hijack 'suspects' alive and well,* (BBC News, 23 September 2001)

13. *Hijack 'suspects' alive and well,* (BBC News, 23 September 2001)

14. David Harrison, *Revealed: the men with the stolen identities,* (The Telegraph, 23 September 2001)

15. *False Identities mislead FBI* (The Guardian, 21 September 2001)

16. David Harrison, *Revealed: the men with the stolen identities,* (The Telegraph, 23 September 2001)

17. *9/11 Conspiracy theory,* (BBC News, 27 October 2006)

18. *Modern Marvels,* (The History Channel, June 2001)

19. *Technical Report Series, High-rise Office Building Fire, One Meridian Plaza, Philadelphia, Pennsylvania,* (FEMA, U.S. Fire Administration, USFA-TR-049/February 1991)

20. *Inferno destroys Madrid skyscraper,* (The Sydney Morning Herald, 14 February 2005)

21. *Fatal Fire destroys Beijing hotel,* (BBC News, 10 February 2009)

22. *Inferno engulfs Shanghai skyscraper,* (The Telegraph, 15 November 2010)

23. *The 9/11 Commission Report,* (W. W. Norton & Co, 2004), 285

24. *Zero: An Investigation Into 9/11,* (Telemaco, 2008)

25. *Zero: An Investigation Into 9/11,* (Telemaco, 2008)

26. Dave Heller, *Taking a Close Look: Hard Science and the Collapse of the World Trade Center* (www.physics911.net)

27. *28-Year Career CIA Official Says 9/11 An Inside Job* (Prison Planet, 7 September 2006)

28. www.implosionworld.com

29. *Zero: An Investigation Into 9/11,* (Telemaco, 2008)

30. *Zero: An Investigation Into 9/11,* (Telemaco, 2008)

31. Jim Yardley, *A Trainee Noted for Incompetence,* (New York Times, 4 May 2004)

32. Thomas Frank, *Tracing Trail of Hijackers,* (New York News Day, Washington Bureau, 23 September 2001)

33. David Ray Griffin, Rob Balsamo, *Could Barbara Olson Have Made Those Calls? An Analysis of New Evidence about Onboard Phones,* (Pilots for 911 Truth)

34. *Blair: No need for July 7 inquiry,* (The Guardian, 14 December 2005)

35. *Blair: No need for July 7 inquiry,* (The Guardian, 14 December 2005)

36. Esther Addley, *7/7 survivors end battle for public inquiry into bombings,* (The Guardian, 1 August 2011)

37. *The Inquiries Act 2005,* (www.publicinquiries.org)

38. *Judge Cory to US Congress: British Inquiries Bill is 'Alice in Wonderland',* (Congressman, Chris Smith, www.chrissmith.gov.uk)

39. *UK: Finucane anniversary – Government must allow public inquiry,* (Amnesty International UK, Press releases, www.amnesty.org.uk)

40. Jason Beer QC, *Public Enquiries,* (OUP Oxford, 2001), 25

41. *Britain is 'surveillance society'* (BBC, 2 November 2006)

42. *Report of the Official Account of the Bombings in London on 7th July 2005,* (National Archives, official-documents.gov.uk, The Stationery Office, 11 May 2006), 4

43. *July 7th 0740 Luton-King's Cross was Cancelled.* (J7: The July 7th Truth Campaign, www.julyseventh.co.uk/july-7-0740-cancellation-confirmation.html)

44. *Report of the Official Account of the Bombings in London on 7th July 2005,* (National Archives, official-documents.gov.uk, The Stationery Office, 11 May 2006), 7

45. *Peter Power's Radio 5 Live Drivetime Interview,* (www.julyseventh.co.uk/media/r5.live.peter.power.exercise.mp3)

46. *Israel was warned ahead of first blast,* (Israel National News, 8 July 2005)

47. *J7: The July 7th Truth Campaign,* (http://www.julyseventh.co.uk/7-7-liverpool-street-aldgate.html)

48. Jeff Edwards, Chris Hughes, *Mirror, Exclusive: The Hunt,* (Mirror, 9 July 2005)

49. *Report of the Official Account of the Bombings in London on 7th July 2005,* (National Archives, official-documents.gov.uk, The Stationery Office, 11 May 2006), 12

50. Sue Reid, *Conspiracy fever: As rumours swell that the government staged 7/7, victims' relatives call for a proper inquiry,* (Mail Online, July 2009)

51. Jane Wardell, *Britain becoming surveillance capital,* (The Associated Press, 29 August 2004)

52. Jeff Edwards, Chris Hughes, *Mirror, Exclusive: The Hunt,* (Mirror, 9 July 2005)

53. *Report of the Official Account of the Bombings in London on 7th July 2005,* (National Archives, official-documents.gov.uk, The Stationery Office, 11 May 2006), 8, 9, 11

54. John Loftus, *Day Side interview with terrorist expert* (Fox News, 29 July 2005)

55. *Report of the Official Account of the Bombings in London on 7th July 2005*, (National Archives, official-documents.gov.uk, The Stationery Office, 11 May 2006), 12

56. *Report of the Official Account of the Bombings in London on 7th July 2005*, (National Archives, official-documents.gov.uk, The Stationery Office, 11 May 2006), 23

57. Jason Bennetto, *Explosives used in bombs 'was of military origin'*, (The Independent, 12 July 2005)

58. Hugh Muir and Rosie Cowan, *Four bombs in 50 minutes – Britain suffers its worst-ever terror attack*, (The Guardian, 8 July 2005)

59. *Advanced bombs were so powerful that none of dead have been identified*, (World Tribune, 11 July 2005)

60. Jeff Edwards, *Mirror News, Exclusive: Was it Suicide?*, (Mirror, 7 July 2005)

61. Kate Connoly, *75 years on, executed Reichstag arsonist finally wins pardon – Dutch activist exonerated under 1998 law – Hitler used fire as pretext to establish dictatorship*, (The Guardian, 12 January 2008)

62. *Strage Di Piazza Fontana Azzerati 17 Anni Di Indagini*, (La Repubblica, 1987)

63. *Guildford Four released after 15 years*, (BBC, 1989)

64. Richard Holt, *Maguire Seven: Fighting for freedom from wrongful conviction*, (The Telegraph, 28 April 2010)

65. *The Birmingham Six: Have we learned from our disgraceful past?* (The Guardian, 12 March 2011)

66. *US sought attack on al-Qaida*, (MSNBC, May 16th, 2002)

67. Michael Meacher, *This war on terrorism is bogus*, (The Guardian, 6 September 2003)

68. Daniel Estulin, *The True Story of The Bilderberg Group* (Trine Day, 2009), 83

Chapter 7

1. *Life in the Spirit Study Bible*, (New International Version, 2003)

2. Mihaljo Mesarovic, Eduard Pestel, *Mankind at the Turning Point*, (Dutton Books, 1976)

3. Gary H. Kah, *En Route to Global Occupation*, (Huntington House, 1996)

4. J. Hampton Keathley, III, *Studies in Revelation, The Message to Pergamum*, 48

5. Neil Hamilton, *Germans Push EU to the Brink*, (Express, November 2011)

6. Rodney Atkinson, *Europe's Full Circle*, (Compuprint Publishing, 1996)
7. Rodney Atkinson, *Europe's Full Circle*, (Compuprint Publishing, 1996)
8. Esteban Buch, *Beethhoven in the Shadows of Berlin: Karajan's European Anthem*, (Dissent, A Quarterly of Politics and Culture, 2009)
9. *Our Hitler, Goebbels' 1942 Speech on Hitler's Birthday*, (Calvin College, German Propaganda Archive)
10. Sidney Kirkpatrick, *Hitler's Holy Relics, A True Story of Nazi Plunder and the Race to Recover the Crown Jewels of the Holy Roman Empire*, (Simon & Schuster, 2011)
11. Jerry E. Smith, George Piccard, *Secrets Of The Holy Lance: The Spear Of Destiny In History & Legend*, (Adventures Unlimited Press, 2006)
12. The Goebbels diaries, 1942-1943, p.359
13. Rick Renner, *A Light in Darkness*, (Harrison House Publishers, 2011)
14. J. Hampton Keathley, III, *Studies in Revelation, The Message to Pergamum*, 48
15. Morris Jastrow, *Descent of the Goddess Ishtar into the Lower World*
16. *Jewish Population of Europe in 1945*, (Holocaust Encyclopedia, United States Holocaust Memorial Museum, www.ushmm.org)
17. *Why the sign of Our Lady reigns over Europe*, (Catholic Herald, 4 December 2004)
18. David Hathaway, *Babylon in Europe: What Bible Prophecy Reveals About the European Union*, (New Wine Press, 2006)
19. David Hathaway, *Babylon in Europe: What Bible Prophecy Reveals About the European Union*, (New Wine Press, 2006)
20. *Euro banknotes: Announcement of the Europa series*, (Official YouTube channel for the European Central Bank, 8 January 2013)
21. *New EU building spares no expense*, (BBC, July 20 1999)
22. *European Parliament*, (Archello, www.archello.com/en/project/european-parliament)
23. Rabbi Daniel Lapin, *Tower of Power, Decoding the Secrets of Babel* (Lifecodex, 2006)
24. Chris Moncrieff, *The EU: 'A German racket designed to take over the whole of Europe'* (Daily Mail, 21 November 2011)
25. Damien McElroy, *Berlin Wall: have Margaret Thatcher's fears about Germany been proved right?*, (The Telegraph, 9 November 1990)
26. Michael Seamark, *Margaret Thatcher feared reunited Germany would 'make more ground than Hitler'*, (Mail Online, 11 September 2009)
27. *Berlin calls for eurozone budget laws* (Financial Times, 16 May 2010)
28. Helen Pidd, *Angela Merkel vows to create 'fiscal union' across eurozone*, (The Guardian, 2 December 2011)

29. Max Keiser, *Germany strangling other EU economies,* (Financial War Reports, 4 September 2012)

30. Tony Paterson, *The Iron Frau: Angela Merkel,* (The Independent, 12 April 2010)

31. *A Curtain went up – Ein Vorhang ging auf, President Herman Van Rompuy pronounces the first Berliner Europa-Rede, Berlin,* (9 November 2010, www.consilium.europa.eu)

Chapter 8

1. James Larratt Battersby, *Holy Book of Adolf Hitler,* (J.L. Battersby, 1952), 8

2. Fritz Springmeier, *Bloodlines of the Illuminati,* (Ambassador House, 2002)

3. Jon E. Lewis, *Voices From the Holocaust,* (Robinson, 2012)

4. Erwin W. Lutzer, *Hitler's Cross: How the Cross of Christ was used to promote the Nazi Agenda,* (Moody Publishers, 2012)

5. Jonas E Alexis, *Christianity's Dangerous Idea,* (AuthorHouse 2010)

6. John Symonds, Kennet Grant, *The Confessions of Aleister Crowley,* (Arkana, 1989)

7. Helena Blavatsky, *The Secret Doctrine Vol II,* 200

8. Helena Blavatsky, *The Secret Doctrine Vol II*

9. Alice A. Bailey, *The Unfinished Autobiography,* (Lucis Trust)

10. Gary H Kah, *New World Religion,* (Hope International Publishing, 1999)

11. *NGO Branch, United Nation Department of Economic and Social Affairs* (www.esango.un.org)

12. *Purposes & Objectives,* (Lucis Trust)

13. Helene Petrovna Blavatsky, (November 1915 to October 1916, Theosophy Magazine), 32

14. *Europe's Track Record,* (West London, UK Independence Party)

15. 'A Room of Quiet' *The Meditation Room, United Nations Headquarters* (www.un.org)

16. *20th Anniversary of the United Nations Meditation Room programme, 15th November 1977,* (World Harmony Run International)

17. Robert Muller, *New Genesis: Shaping a Global Spirituality,* (Doubleday, 1982)

18. *Newsletter of the Aquarian Age Community,* (No. 2, 2012) / Susan MacNeil, Ph.D., *The Spiritual Work Of The United Nations And The Liberation Of Humanity*

19. *20th Anniversary of the United Nations Meditation Room programme, 15th November 1977,* (World Harmony Run International)

20. N H Baynes, *The Speeches of Adolf Hitler, Volume I,* (Oxford University Press, 1942), 743

21. Alice A. Bailey, *The Externalisation Of The Hierarchy,* (Lucis Trust 1957, 1985)

22. Alice Bailey, *Esoteric Healing, A Treatise on the Seven Rays Volume IV,* (Lucis Trust, 1953, 1981)

23. Ronald J. Rychlak, *Hitler, the war, and the pope,* (Bookworld Press, Inc, 2000), 19

24. Joseph Howard Tyson, *Hitler's Mentor: Dietrich Eckart, His Life, Times, and Milieu,* (iUniverse.com, 2008)

25. Susannah Heschel, *The Aryan Jesus: Christian Theologians and the Bible in Nazi Germany,* (Princeton University Press, 2010)

26. Erwin W. Lutzer, *Hitler's Cross: How the Cross of Christ was used to promote the Nazi Agenda,* (Moody Publishers, 2012)

27. Chuck Morse, *The Nazi Connection to Islamic Terrorism: Adolf Hitler and Haj Amin Al-Husseini,* (iUniverse, 2003)

28. Anthony Julius, *Trials of the Diaspora: A History of Anti-Semitism in England,* (OUP Oxford, 2012)

29. *Documents on German Foreign Policy 1918-1945, Series D, Vol XIII, The War Years, June 12–December 11, 1941,* 884

30. Timothy D. Manning, Sr., *The Concordat Between The Vatican And The Nazis, Reichskonkordat (with Hitler, 1933),* (Heritage Foundation Press, 2009)

31. Bob Taylor, *Growing concerns over increased Islamic influence in Europe,* (The Washington Times Communities, 28 December 2012)

32. *Should Turkey join the EU?* (BBC News, 27 July 2010)

33. *Should Turkey join the EU?* (BBC News, 27 July 2010)

34. Soeren Kern, *Belgium Will Become an Islamic State,* (Gatestone Institute)

35. Soeren Kern, *The Islamization of France in 2012,* (Gatestone Institute)

36. Joe Kovacs, *Are You Eating Food Sacrificed To Idols?,* (World Net Daily, 27 January 2011)

37. Soeren Kern, *The Islamization of France in 2012,* (Gatestone Institute)

38. Soeren Kern, *The Islamization of France in 2012,* (Gatestone Institute)

39. *French court approves permit for Marseille Grand Mosque,* (Agence France-Presse, 19 June 2012)

40. Bob Taylor, *Growing concerns over increased Islamic influence in Europe,* (The Washington Times Communities, 28 December 28 2012)

41. Erick Stakelbeck, *UK Islamist Leader: Islam Will Dominate America,* CBN News, 10 August 2012)

42. Andrew Gilligan, *Ken Livingstone: I will make London a beacon of Islam,* (Daily Telegraph, 19 March 2012)

43. Samuel Westrop, *UK Textbook Wipes Israel Off the Map,* (Gatestone Institute, 3 January 2013)

44. Meghan Neal, *Number of Muslims in the U.S. doubles since 9/11,* (New York Daily News, May 2012)

Chapter 9

1. *The White House, Office of the Press Secretary, Joint Press Availability with President Obama and President Gul of Turkey, Cankaya Palace, Ankara, Turkey, April 6, 2009, (www.whitehouse.gov)*

2. Jeff Zeleny, *Obama Says U.S. Could Be Seen as a Muslim Country Too,* (The New York Times, 2 June 2009)

3. Daniel Greenfield, *The Immigration Jihad,* (Canada Free Press, 29 March 2010)

4. Cathy Lynn Grossman, *Number of U.S. mosques up 74% since 2000,* (USA Today, February 2012)

5. Ken Blackwell, Ken Klukowski, *A Religious Test* (The American Spectator, June 2009)

6. *Political correctness gone mad? School in Seattle renames Easter eggs 'spring spheres',* (Mail Online, 14 April 2011)

7. *Ohio Town removes 'Easter' from Egg Hunt,* (The Blaze, March 2011)

8. *Poll: Americans Prefer 'Christmas' Over 'Holiday' Tree,* (Fox Nation, 24 December 2012)

9. Neil Macfarquhar, *At Harvard, Students' Muslim Traditions Are a Topic of Debate,* (New York Times, 21 March 2008)

10. Benjamin Taylor, Aaron D Williams, *The Adhan at Harvard,* (The Harvard Crimson, 13 March 2008)

11. Zia Haq, *Quran quote ripples at Harvard,* (Hindustan Times, 16 January 2013)

12. *Sharia: The Threat to America, An exercise in competitive analysis, report of team 'B' II,* (Center for Security Policy, 2010), 6

13. *Kansas governor signs measure blocking Islamic law,* (USA Today, 26 May 2012)

14. Cheryl K. Chumley, *Cleric in Egypt vows: 'Islamic flag will be raised above the White House',* (The Washington Times, 29 March 2013)

15. Pastor Chuck Baldwin speaks – The 501c3 Government Takeover of the Church, liberty Fellowship of Kalispell, Montana

16. Adolf Hitler, Norman Cameron (translator), R.H. Stevens (translator), *Hitler's Table Talk, 1941-1944: His Private Conversations,* (Enigma Books, 2000)

Chapter 10

1. Anne Broache, *'Obama: No warrantless wiretaps if you elect me'* (CNET, 8 January 2008)

2. Dan Gearino, *Oprah says Obama's tongue 'dipped in the unvarnished truth'* (Quad-City Times, 8 December 2007)

3. *Farrakhan On Obama: 'The Messiah Is Absolutely Speaking'* (World Net Daily, 9 October 2008)

4. Asma Gull Hasan Forbes, *My Muslim President Obama*, (Forbes, 25 February 2009)

5. *Farrakhan On Obama: 'The Messiah Is Absolutely Speaking'* (World Net Daily, 9 October 2008)

6. Scott Helman, *Obama distances himself from Farrakhan*, (Boston.com, Political Intelligence, 15 January 2008)

7. Charles Bierbauer, *Million Man March, Its goal more widely accepted than its leader,* (CNN, 17 October 1995)

8. Jeffrey T. Kuhner, *KUHNER: Jeremiah Wright can sink Obama* (The Washington Times 17 May 2012)

9. Ronald Kessler, *Rev. Wright Was a Second Father to Obama,* (Newsmax, 15 May 2012)

10. Ronald Kessler, *Rev. Wright Was a Second Father to Obama,* (Newsmax, 15 May 2012)

11. Kyle-Anne Shiver, *Obama, Black Liberation Theology and Karl Marx... Revisited,* (American Thinker, 22 August 2010)

12. Madeline Brooks, *Obama's Unique Form of 'Christianity:' No Baptism or Renunciation of Islam Required,* (Canada Free Press, 21 August 2010)

13. Charles C. Johnson, *Was Obama Once An Indonesian Citizen? Here's What We Found When We Went There Looking,* (The Blaze, 5 November 2012)

14. President Barack Obama, *Barack Obama, Dreams from my Father,* (Canongate Books Ltd, 2008)

15. Paul Watson, *As a child, Obama crossed a cultural divide in Indonesia,* (LA Times, 15 March 2007)

16. Nicholas D. Kristof, *Obama: Man of the World,* (New York Times, 6 March 2007)

17. *This Week interview with Barack Obama and George Stephanopoulos,* (ABC News, 15 September 2013)

18. Alex Spillius, *Barack Obama criticised for 'bowing' to King Abdullah of Saudi Arabia,* (The Telegraph, 8 April 2009)

19. Jerome R. Corsi, *Obama's Ring: 'There is no god but Allah',* (World Net Daily, 10 October 2012)

20. Kerry McDermott, *Barack Obama's choice for CIA chief 'converted to Islam' former FBI agent claims,* (The Daily Mail, 12 February 2013)

21. Art Moore, *Egyptian mag affirms Brotherhood infiltration of White House,* (World Net Daily, 3 January 2013)

22. Barbara Bradley Hagerty, *Evangelical Leader Blasts 2006 Obama Speech,* (NPR, 24 June 2008)

23. *A 'New Beginning' in Cairo: The Full Text of Barack Obama's Speech,* (Spiegel Online, 4 June 2009)

24. *Odinga says Obama is his cousin,* (BBC, 8 January 2008)

25. Jerome E Corsi, *Obama Raised $1 Million For Foreign Thug's Election* (World Net Daily, 14 October 2008)

26. Jerome E Corsi, *Obama Raised $1 Million For Foreign Thug's Election* (World Net Daily, 14 October 2008)

27. *Obama's Kenya ghosts,* (Washington Times, 12 October 2008)

28. *About Us, What We Believe,* (Trinity United Church of Christ website, www.trinitychicago.org)

29. Anthony B. Bradley, *The Marxist Roots of Black Liberation Theology,* (Institute for the study of religion and liberty, 2 April 2008)

30. President Barack Obama, *Barack Obama, Dreams from my Father,* (Canongate Books Ltd, 2008)

31. Paul Kengor Ph.D., *The Communist, Frank Marshall Davis: The Untold Story of Barack Obama's Mentor,* (Mercury Ink, 2012)

32. Paul Kengor Ph.D., *Obama's Purge: Why Has Frank Marshall Davis Been Quietly Removed From Dreams From My Father?,* (The Blaze, 3 October 2012)

33. Manning Marable, *The Four Legged Stool that Won the US Presidential Election,* (Socialist Review, December 2008)

34. Victor Morton, *New Obama slogan has long ties to Marxism, socialism* (The Washington Times, 30 April 2012)

35. Antonia Gramsci, *Prison Notebook,* (Lawrence & Wishart Ltd, 1998)

36. Richard Wurmbrand, *Marx & Satan,* (Living Sacrifice Book Co., 1986), 6

37. Richard Wurmbrand, *Marx & Satan,* (Living Sacrifice Book Co., 1986), 6

38. Richard Wurmbrand, *Marx & Satan,* (Living Sacrifice Book Co., 1986), 6

39. Richard Wurmbrand, *Marx & Satan,* (Living Sacrifice Book Co., 1986), 7

40. Gary H. Kah, *En Route to Global Occupation,* (Huntington House, 1996), 116

41. Richard Wurmbrand, *Marx & Satan,* (Living Sacrifice Book Co., 1986), 7

42. Richard Wurmbrand, *Marx & Satan,* (Living Sacrifice Book Co., 1986), 13

43. Richard Wurmbrand, *Marx & Satan,* (Living Sacrifice Book Co., 1986), 7

44. Richard Wurmbrand, *Marx & Satan,* (Living Sacrifice Book Co., 1986), 9

45. *Kissinger on Economy interview with hosts Mark Haines and Erin Burnett,* (First on CNBC, 2009)

46. *From A to Z: What's Wrong With Obama's Birth Certificate?* (World Net Daily, 13 May 2011)

47. Louis Michael Seidman, *Let's Give Up on the Constitution,* (The New York Times, 30 December 2012)

48. Jo Becker, Scott Shane, *Secret 'Kill List' Proves a Test of Obama's Principles and Will,* (The New York Times, 29 May 2012)

49. Andrew Rafferty, *American drone deaths highlight controversy,* (NBC News, 5 February 2013)

50. Ryan J. Reilly, *Eric Holder: Drone Strike To Kill U.S. Citizen On American Soil Legal, Hypothetically,* (Huffington Post, 5 March 2013)

51. Kevin Barrett, *Is Obama killing "kill list" critics?,* (Veterans Today, 13 January 2013)

52. *Stratfor emails reveal secret, widespread TrapWire surveillance system,* (Russia Today, 10 August 2012)

53. *Obama's Plan To Seize Control Of Our Economy And Our Lives,* (Forbes, 29 April 2012)

54. *Newsweek Inauguration Special – The Second Coming Of Obama,* (Lonely Conservative, 19 January 2013)

55. Todd Starnes, *Painting Depicts Obama as Crucified Christ,* (Fox News, 26 November 2012)

56. Joe Newby, *Poster at DNC convention calls Barack Obama 'prophesy fulfilled',* (The Examiner, 4 September 2012)

57. *Newsweek Hails Obama as Messianic 'Second Coming'?* (Christian News, 21 January 2013)

58. Jonathon M. Seidl, *As Seen At The Dem Convention: The Calendar That Uses John 3:16 In Reference To Obama,* (The Blaze, 3 September 2012)

59. Yasmine Hafiz, *Boy Prays To And For Obama,* (Huffington Post, 14 August 2013)

60. Yasmine Hafiz, *Boy Prays To And For Obama,* (Huffington Post, 14 August 2013)

61. James Nye, *'You are good, Barack Obama. You are great': Fury as mother uploads video of little boy appearing to pray to the President,* (Mail Online, 13 August 2013)

62. Yasmine Hafiz, *Boy Prays To And For Obama,* (Huffington Post, 14 August 2013)

63. *Jamie Foxx Calls Obama 'Our Lord And Savior' At Soul Train Awards, Causes Furor Among Christians,* (The Huffington Post, 27 November 2012)

64. *Florida professor: Obama an 'apostle' sent to create 'heaven here on earth'* (The Examiner, 12 November 2012)

Chapter 11

1. 'The President and the Press' speech by John F Kennedy at the Waldorf-Astoria Hotel, April 27th 1961, (www.jfklibrary.org)
2. Mike Hanson, *Bohemian Grove: Cult of Conspiracy*, (Rivercrest Publishing, 2012)
3. Jonathon Oliver, Caroline Graham, *Tony Blair's gissa-job trip, partying with the super rich in America*, (Mail on Sunday 29 July 2006)
4. David Garrett Jr, *Hacked photos show Colin Powell, actor at Bohemian Grove*, (The Examiner, 13 April 2013)
5. *Gay Porn Star Services Bohemian Grove Members*, (New York Post, reposted by InfoWars, 22 July 2004)
6. James Warren, *All The Philosopher King's Men. President Richard Nixon, John D. Ehrlichman, and H. R. Haldeman*, (Harper's Magazine, February 2000)
7. *Animal House*, (Russia Today, 15 July 2011)
8. Cathy O'Brien, Mark Phillips, *Trance-Formation of America*, (Reality Marketing Inc, 2005)
9. *Occult Activities at the Elite Bohemian Grove in Northern California Exposed! Alex Jones Tells His Story*, (Info Wars)
10. *Occult Activities at the Elite Bohemian Grove in Northern California Exposed! Alex Jones Tells His Story*, (Info Wars)
11. Philip Weiss, *Masters of the Universe Go to Camp: Inside the Bohemian Grove*, (Spy Magazine, November 1989), 59-76
12. Mark Dice, *The Illuminati: Facts & Fiction*, (Resistance Manifesto, 2009)
13. *A Guide to the Bohemian Grove*, (Vanity Fair, April 2009)
14. *Guccifer emails link Tony Blair to top-secret Bohemian Grove gathering*, (Russia Today, 25 March 2013)
15. Cathy O'Brien, Mark Phillips, *Trance-Formation of America*, (Reality Marketing Inc, 2005)
16. Mike Hanson, *Bohemian Grove: Cult of Conspiracy*, (Rivercrest Publishing, 2012)
17. *19 Facts About Abortion In America That Should Make You Very Sick*, (The American Dream, 19 February 2012)
18. *Society for the Protection of Unborn Children, Student info on abortion*, (www.spuc.org.uk)

19. *Killing babies no different from abortion, experts say,* (The Telegraph, 29 February 2012)

20. Jerome R. Corsi, *Science Czar's Guru Backed Eugenics,* (World Net Daily, 9 December 2009)

21. Jerome R. Corsi, *Holdren's Guru: Dispose Of 'Excess Children' Like Puppies,* (World Net Daily, 9 December 2009)

22. Elizabeth Flock, *Bohemian Grove: Where the rich and powerful go to misbehave,* (Washington Post, 15 June 2011)

23. Benjamin Franklin L. Camins, *Hillary Is the Best Choice: Ten Top Historical Voting Patterns that Show Americans Are Ready to Pick a Woman President,* (iUniverse, 2007)

24. Antony C Sutton, *America's Secret Establishment, An Introduction to the Order of Skull & Bones,* (Trine Day, 2004)

25. Antony C Sutton, *America's Secret Establishment, An Introduction to the Order of Skull & Bones,* (Trine Day, 2004)

26. Ron Rosenbaum, *The Secret Parts of Fortune,* (Harper Perennial, 2001)

27. Sarah Lawless, *The Witch Of Forest Grove, Dem Bones: Skulls And Bones In Magic & Ritual,* (28 September 2010, www.sarahannelawless.com)

28. Maria Glod, *Odd Fellows Have Skeletons in Their Closets – and Their Walls and Attics,* (LA Times, April 2001)

29. Stephanie Reitz, *Geronimo's Descendants Sue Yale's Skull And Bones Over Remains,* (Huffington Post, 18 February 2009)

30. Stephanie Reitz, *Geronimo's Descendants Sue Yale's Skull And Bones Over Remains,* (Huffington Post, 18 February 2009)

31. Rebecca Leung, *Skull and Bones,* (CBS News, 11 February 2009)

32. Rebecca Leung, *Skull and Bones,* (CBS News, 11 February 2009)

33. Malcolm C. Duncan, *Duncan's Masonic Ritual and Monitor,* (Crown)

34. Albert G Mackey, *The Symbolism of Freemasonry,* (Published 1882)

35. Ron Rosenbaum, *The Secret Parts of Fortune,* (Harper Perennial, 2001)

36. Jim Kouri, *Satanic or ritualistic crime and murder,* (The Examiner, 14 April 2009)

37. Ronald B. Flowers, *Sex Crimes: Perpetrators, Predators, Prostitutes and Victims,* (Charles C. Thomas Publisher, 2006)

38. *Today, Meet the Press, Guest: George W. Bush,* (NBC News, 13 February 2004)

39. *Today, Meet the Press, Guest: John Kerry,* (NBC News, 2004)

40. McKay Coppins, *Obama Advisor Brought Secret Society To White House,* (Buzzfeed, 9 February 2012)

41. Antony C Sutton, *America's Secret Establishment, An Introduction to*

the Order of Skull & Bones, (Trine Day, 2004)

42. Antony C Sutton, *America's Secret Establishment, An Introduction to the Order of Skull & Bones,* (Trine Day, 2004)

43. Alex Jones, *Dark Secrets Inside Bohemian Grove – The Order of Death,* Documentary film, 2001)

Chapter 12

1. Charles G. Finney, *The Character, Claims And Practical Workings of Freemasonry 1869*

2. *Writing on 'Zionism versus Bolshevism',* (Illustrated Sunday Herald, February 1920)

3. Albert G Mackey, *The Symbolism of Freemasonry,* (Published 1882)

4. *UK Politics, Tally of Freemason Judges Revealed,* (BBC News, 10 November 1998)

5. *Brother Winston,* (MQ Magazine, Issue 3, October 2002)

6. *Who's Who,* (United Grand Lodge of England, www.ugle.org.uk)

7. *Handshakes and Trouser Legs – Secrets of the Freemasons,* (The Telegraph, 9 March 2012)

8. Sarah Oliver, *Freemasons open a lodge at Buckingham Palace...but the Queen isn't amused,* (Mail Online, 8 March 2008)

9. *Handshakes and Trouser Legs – Secrets of the Freemasons,* (The Telegraph, 9 March 2012)

10. *Freemasons in the police leading the attack on David Cameron's riot response,* (The Telegraph, 20 August 2011)

11. *Masonic Influence in the EU,* (The Brussels Journal, 17 April 2011)

12. *Masonic Influence in the EU,* (The Brussels Journal, 17 April 2011)

13. *Receiving GODF by the President of the European Commission, The Grand Orient de France,* (9 April 2008)

14. *Demoley – Building Tomorrow's Leaders Today since 1919, Bill Clinton Inducted May 1, 1988*

15. John Robison, *Proofs of a Conspiracy,* (Published 1798), 84

16. Library of Congress: George Washington Warns of Illuminati

17. Mackey's Encyclopedia of Freemasonry

18. John Robison, *Proofs of a Conspiracy,* (Published 1798), 11

19. John Robison, *Proofs of a Conspiracy,* (Published 1798), 11,12

20. John Robison, *Proofs of a Conspiracy,* (Published 1798), 12

21. Albert Pike, *Morals and Dogma of the Ancient and Accepted Scottish Rite of Freemasonry,* 189

22. Gary H. Kah, *En Route to Global Occupation,* (Huntington House,

1996), 115

23. Masonic Service Masonic Service Association Publisher, *The Pocket Encylopedia of Masonic Symbols,* (Literary Licensing)

24. Albert Mackey, *Mackey's Encyclopedia of Freemasonry,* (Kessinger Pub Co)

25. Christopher Haffner, *Workman Unashamed: The Testimony of a Christian Freemason,* (Lewis Masonic, 1989), 39

26. Albert Mackey, *Encyclopedia of Freemasonry and Its Kindred Sciences,* (The Masonic History Company, 1920)

27. Encyclopedia of Judaism by Sara E. Karesh, Mitchell M. Hurvitz

28. Albert Mackey, *Encyclopedia of Freemasonry and Its Kindred Sciences,* (The Masonic History Company, 1920)

29. Albert Pike, *Morals and Dogma of the Ancient and Accepted Scottish Rite of Freemasonry,* 321

30. Charles G Finney, *The Character, Claims and Practical Workings of Freemasonry,* (1869), 47

31. Charles G Finney, *The Character, Claims and Practical Workings of Freemasonry,* (1869), 55

32. Gary H. Kah, *En Route to Global Occupation,* (Huntington House, 1996), 140

33. Andrew Glass, *President Bush responds to Iraqi invasion of Kuwait, Sept. 11, 1990,* (Politico, 11 September, 2009)

34. *Public Papers of the Presidents of the United States: George H. W. Bush, 1991, Book I,* (6 March 1991, www.gpo.gov)

35. Andrew Hammond, *Pyramids pulsate as Egypt greets new millennium,* (Reuters, 31 December 1999)

36. Lytle W. Robinson, *Edgar Cayce's Story of the Origin and Destiny of Man,* (Berkley, 1985)

37. Henry Wallace, *Statesmanship and Religion,* (Round Table Press, 1934)

Chapter 13

1. The World Council of Religious Leaders, The Millennium World Peace Summit of Religious and Spiritual Leaders (www.millenniumpeacesummit.org)

2. *A common word between us and you? A global agenda for change,* (Tony Blair Faith Foundation, 7 October 2009)

3. Hugh O'Shaughnessy, *Tony Blair's Faith Foundation inspires ridicule,* (The Guardian, 13 May 2009) / Michel Schooyans, *Obama and Blair. Messianism reinterpreted,* (Chiesa Espresso Rebubblica)

4. Laura Donnelly, *Homeopathy Is Witchcraft, Say Doctors,* (The Telegraph, 15 May 2010)

5. *Alternative Medicine or Witchcraft? Europeans Cast Critical Eye on Homeopathy,* (Spiegel, 16 July 2010)

6. *Homeopathic Remedies,* (News Medical)

7. *Use of ADHD drugs 'increases by 50% in six years',* (BBC News, 13 August 2013)

8. *Use of ADHD drugs 'increases by 50% in six years',* (BBC News, 13 August 2013)

9. Mike Adams, *Americans Drowning in Prescription Drugs,* (Natural News, 4 September 2010)

10. Bill Berkrot, *Global drug sales to top $1 trillion in 2014,* (Reuters, 20 April 2010)

11. Mike Adams, *Americans Drowning in Prescription Drugs,* (Natural News, 4 September 2010)

12. Mike Adams, *Americans Drowning in Prescription Drugs,* (Natural News, 4 September 2010)

13. Dr. Larry Dossey, *Creating Disease: Big Pharma and Disease Mongering,* (Huffington Post, 18 June 2010)

14. Dr. Larry Dossey, *Creating Disease: Big Pharma and Disease Mongering,* (Huffington Post, 18 June 2010)

15. Carl Elliott, *White Coat, Black Hat, Adventures on the Dark Side of Medicine,* (Beacon Press, 2011)

16. Daniela Perdomo, *100,000 Americans Die Each Year from Prescription Drugs, While Pharma Companies Get Rich,* (AlterNet)

17. Gary G. Kohls, *How Psychiatric Drugs Made America Mad,* (AlterNet)

18. Christopher Bryson, *The Fluoride Deception,* (Seven Stories Press, 2006), 355

19. *Fluoride Alert, Fluoride & Intelligence: The 37 Studies,* (Flouride Alert, www.fluoridealert.org/studies/brain01/, 16 May 2013)

20. *Is Fluoride Safe?,* (The Independent, February 2008)

21. *Ancient meteorite causing modern problems,* (Canwest News Service, 29 January 2008)

22. Christopher Bryson, *The Fluoride Deception,* (Seven Stories Press, 2006), 355

23. *Is Fluoride Safe?,* (The Independent, February 2008)

24. Barry Groves, *Fluoride: Drinking Ourselves to Death?,* (Newleaf, 2001)

25. *Psychiatric Drugs Cause Violence,* (Citizens Commission on Human Rights, www.cchrint.org)

26. Jenny Deam, *James Holmes' psychiatrist warned he may pose threat,* (LA Times, 4 April 2013)

27. James Barron, *Children Were All Shot Multiple Times With a Semiautomatic, Officials Say,* (New York Times, 15 December, 2012)

28. *Friends: Newtown Gunman's Mother Home-Schooled Son, Kept Arsenal Of Guns,* (CBS News, 16 December 2012)

29. Adolf Hitler, Norman Cameron (translator), R.H. Stevens (translator), *Hitler's Table Talk, 1941-1944: His Private Conversations,* (Enigma Books, 2000)

30. *Amsterdam to get statue to honor prostitutes,* (Reuters, 19 January 2007)

31. *Katy Perry's Dad Refers To Her As A 'Devil Child' In Sermons?* (Huffington Post, 6 May 2013)

32. *Madonna Battles Rabbi Over 'Slut' Comment,* (World Net Daily, 3 June 2004)

33. Sut Jhally, *The Spectacle of Accumulation: Essays in Culture, Media, And Politics,* (Peter Lang Publishing Inc, 2006), 194

34. Millennium Peace Summit, The World Council of Religious Leaders, About the World Council, (www.millenniumpeacesummit.org)

35. Millennium Peace Summit, The World Council of Religious Leaders, About the World Council, (www.millenniumpeacesummit.org)

36. David Limbaugh, *Persecution: How Liberals are Waging War Against Christianity by* (Harper Perennial, 2004), 269

37. David Limbaugh, *Persecution: How Liberals are Waging War Against Christianity by* (Harper Perennial, 2004), 269

38. Larry Witham, *U.N. plans to bring together 1,000 world religious leaders,* (The Washington Times, 14 July 2000)

39. *If you build it, he will come,* (Temple Institute, June 2012)

40. Rowena Mason, *Tony Blair: the EU needs a president,* (The Telegraph, 29 October 2012)

41. BBC News, Bringing God into politics by Nick Assinder, 4 March 2006

42. Michel Schooyans, *Obama and Blair. Messianism reinterpreted,* (Chiesa Espresso Repubblica)

43. *Blair under fire over plans to move into historic Jerusalem palace,* (Daily Mail, 22 January 2008)

44. Tim Butcher, *No room at the inn for Tony Blair,* (The Telegraph, 20 July 2007)

45. Simon Walters, *An identity crisis for Blair: Former PM describes Jerusalem as 'home',* (Daily Mail, 12 April 2009)

46. Matthew Kalman, *Cost-cutting exercise sees Blair on move – into millionaires' row,* (The Independent, 27 June 2011)

47. *Blair: Obama win opens way to revive peace talks,* (Reuters, November 7 2012)

48. Nicholas Watt, *Barack Obama makes Tony Blair his unofficial 'first friend'* (The Guardian, 5 February 2009)

49. Daniel Martin, *Love letter to America: Gushing tributes to Obama and Bush in U.S. version of Blair memoirs,* (Daily Mail, 3 September 2010)

50. *Tony Blair take two: Ex PM 'poised for political comeback with Labour after advising Obama on election battle'* (Daily Mail, 20 May 2012)

51. *Tony Blair reads the Koran daily to stay 'faith literate'* (The Indian Express, 13 June 2011)

52. *Tony Blair reads the Koran daily to stay 'faith literate'* (The Indian Express, 13 June 2011)

53. *I read the Holy Quran everday: Tony Blair,* (The Express Tribune, 13 June 2011)

54. Ian Drury, *I read the Koran every day, says former prime minister Tony Blair who claims it keeps him 'faith-literate',* Daily Mail, 13 June 2011)

55. Nahla Mahmoud, *Here is why Sharia Law has no place in Britain or elsewhere,* (National Secular Society, 6 February 2013)

56. *Shariah For Dummies,* (World Net Daily, 27 August 2010)

57. Ibn Warraq, *Virgins? What virgins?,* (The Guardian, 12 January 2002)

58. Nahla Mahmoud, *Here is why Sharia Law has no place in Britain or elsewhere,* (National Secular Society, 6 February 2013)

59. *Tony Blair's sister-in-law converts to Islam,* (The Guardian, 24 October 2010)

60. Daniel Shane, *Saudi to keep ban on churches – minister,* (Arabian Business, 26 April 2013)

61. *Woolwich attack: the terrorist's rant,* (The Telegraph, 23 May 2013)

62. Ned Simons, *UK, Woolwich Attack: David Cameron Targets 'Conveyor Belt To Radicalisation',* (The Huffington Post 3 June 2013)

63. Matthew Champion, Richard James, *Boris Johnson: Neither Islam nor UK foreign policy to blame for Woolwich attack,* (Metro News, 23 May 2013)

64. Ezra Levant, *Multiculturalism doesn't work,* (Toronto Sun, May 25 2013)

65. Mark A. Gabriel, *Islam and Terrorism,* (Charisma House, 2002), 81, 82

66. *Tirmidhi Sahih, Vol. 9,* 74; *Abu Dawud, Sahih, Vol. 5,* 207; Ali b. Abi Talib, Abu Sa'id, Umm Salma, Abu Hurayra

67. Abu Abdullah Ahmad bin Muhammad bin Hanbal Ash-Shaibani, *Musnad Ahmad Ibn Hanbal, Vol. 1,* (Darussalam), 99

68. Mohammed All Ibn Moulana Zubair Ali, *Signs of Qiyamah,* 39

69. Umm Salamah, Ummul Mu'minin, *Sunan Abu Dawud, Book 36, No. 4273,*

70. Mark A. Gabriel, *Islam and Terrorism,* (Charisma House, 2002), 91

71. Mark A. Gabriel, *Islam and Terrorism,* (Charisma House, 2002), 92, 93

72. *Sahih Muslim, Book 1, No. 0293*

73. *Sahih Ashrat as-Sa'at*, as quoted in Kabbani, 236

74. *Al-Sadr and Mutahhari*, prologue, 3

75. Sunan Abu Dawud, Book 37, Number 4310, Narrated by Abu Hurayrah: see also Sahih Bukhari Volume 3, Book 43, Number 656

76. Muhammad Ali Ibn Zubair, *Who is the Evil Dajjal (the "anti-Christ")?*

77. Muhammad Ali Ibn Zubair, *The Signs of Qiyama*

78. Samir Khalil Samir, *Fr. Samir: This too is Islam. The video of the beheading of a young Tunisian convert by Samir Khalil Samir*, (Asia News, 6 August 2012) / *Islam Threat, Beheading of Christian in Tunisia*, (17 August 2012)

79. Samuel Shahid, *The Last Trumpet: A Comparative Study of Christian-Islamic Eschatology* (US, Xulon, 2005), 254

Chapter 14

1. *Reflections and Warnings – An Interview with Aaron Russo*, (Info Wars)

2. Edwin Black, *IBM and the Holocaust*, (Dialog Press, 2012)

3. *Dogs in England must be microchipped from 2016*, (BBC, 6 February 2013)

4. Stephanie Condon, *Va. Lawmakers Oppose Forced Microchip Implantation, and the Antichrist*, (CBS News, 10 February 2010)

5. *Human Microchips Seen As 'Device Of Antichrist' By Some In Virginia House*, (Huffington Post, 12 April 2010)

6. *Apocalyptic Talk Stokes Microchip Implant Debate*, (AOL News, 2 November 2010)

7. Todd Lewan, *Chip Implants Linked to Animal Tumors*, (The Associated Press, 8 September 2007)

8. CBS News July 15, 2010

9. *VeriTeQ Acquisition Corporation Acquires Implantable, FDA-Cleared VeriChip Technology and Health Link Personal Health Record from PositiveID Corporation*, (Business Wire, 17 January 2012)

10. *www.veriteqcorp.com*

11. *Reflections and Warnings – An Interview with Aaron Russo*, (Info Wars)

12. *Shadow Government*, (Cloud Ten Pictures)

13. Declan McCullagh, *Chip implant gets cash under your skin*, (CNET, 25 November 2003)

14. *Barcelona clubers get chipped*, (BBC News, 29 September 2004)

15. *Chip implant makes its debut at VIP British club*, (The Observer, 17 January 2005)

16. *VeriChip Health Link* (television commercial, 24 April 2008) / *VeriChip TV Ad Confirms Critics' Fears: They Want Everyone Implanted,* (CBS News, 9 November 2010)

17. *Parents look to microchip children,* (CNN, 3 September 2002)

18. *U.S. Military Seeking Implantable Microchips in Soldiers,* (The New American, 8 May 2012)

19. *Post-9/11 Security Fears Usher in Subdermal Chips,* (World Net Daily, 2 April 2002)

20. Andrew Donoghue, *CeBIT: Quarter Of Germans Happy To Have Chip Implants,* (TechWeek Europe, 2 March 2010)

21. *PayPal goes after Oz and Amsterdam high streets,* (Finextra, 15 November 2012)

22. *Cash not always welcome at Apple stores,* (ABC Local News, 17 May 2010)

23. Anna Tims, *Why cash is no longer king,* (The Guardian, 5 July 2012)

24. Anna Tims, *Why cash is no longer king,* (The Guardian, 5 July 2012)

25. *McDonald's upgrades – cashiers out, computers in,* (NBC News, 16 May 2011)

26. Amal Graafstra, *Hands On, How radio-frequency identification and I got personal,* (IEEE Spectrum, 28 February 2007)

27. *www.sparkfun.com*

28. *Chipless RFID Ink: Somark Innovations Announces Successful Animal Tests Of Biocompatible Chipless RFID Ink In Cattle And Laboratory Rats,* (RFID Solutions Online, 11 January 2007)

29. Bill Christensen, *Invisible RFID Ink Tattoos For Cattle, People,* (Technovelgy, 2007)

30. *Wearable Electronics Demonstrate Promise of Brain-Machine Interfaces,* (News Wise, 12 August 2011)

31. John Horgan, *The Work of Jose Delgado, a pioneering star, The Forgotten Era of BRAIN,* (Scientific American, Inc, 2005)

32. John Horgan, *The Work of Jose Delgado, a pioneering star, The Forgotten Era of BRAIN,* (Scientific American, Inc, 2005)

33. Jose M. Delgado, *Physical Control of the Mind: Toward a Psychocivilized Society,* (Harper Collins, 1969)

34. Jose M. Delgado, *Physical Control of the Mind: Toward a Psychocivilized Society,* (Harper Collins, 1969)

35. Jose M. Delgado, *Physical Control of the Mind: Toward a Psychocivilized Society,* (Harper Collins, 1969)

36. Jose M. Delgado, *Physical Control of the Mind: Toward a Psychocivilized Society,* (Harper Collins, 1969)

37. Mitch Waldrop, *DARPA and the Internet Revoluiton,* (www.darpa.mil)

38. *DARPA funding computer-mediated telepathy*, (Frontline 15 May 2009)

39. *Pentagon plans for telepathic troops who can read each others' minds... and they could be in the field within five years*, (Mail Online, 9 April 2012)

40. *Emerging Cognitive Neuroscience and Related Technologies. Committee on Military and Intelligence Methodology for Emergent Neruophysiological and Cognitive / Neural Research in the Next Two Decades*, (National Research Council, National Academy Press, 2008)

41. *Saudi 'Killer Chip' Implant Would Track, Eliminate Undesirables*, (Fox News, 18 May 2009)

Chapter 15

1. *Yahoo to Users: Let Us Read Your Emails or – Goodbye!*, (StartPage, 30 May 2013)

2. *Waking up to a surveillance society*, (Information Commissioners Office, Press Release, 2 November 2006)

3. *Top 5 cities with the largest surveillance camera networks*, (Vintechnology, 4 May 2011)

4. Ginger Gibson, *Ron Paul: 'Glee' in administration after 9/11*, (Politico, 8 December 2011)

5. *Surveillance Under the USA Patriot Act*, (American Civil Liberties Union, 10 December 2010)

6. Glenn Greenwald and Ewen MacAskill, *NSA Prism program taps in to user data of Apple, Google and others*, (The Guardian, 7 June 2013)

7. Glenn Greenwald and Ewen MacAskill, *NSA Prism program taps in to user data of Apple, Google and others*, (The Guardian, 7 June 2013)

8. Vanessa Allen, *Google finally admits that its Street View cars DID take emails and passwords from computers*, (Mail Online, 28 October 2010)

9. Charlotte Meredith, *Now Google is threatened with criminal action over Street View data theft*, (Express, 21 June 2013)

10. Verne Kopytoff, *Google has lots to do with intelligence*, (SFGate, 30 March 2008)

11. Kimberly Dozier, *AP Exclusive: CIA following Twitter, Facebook*, (The Seattle Times, 4 November 2011)

12. Thomas Houston, *Julian Assange: Facebook Is 'Appalling Spy Machine'*, (Huffington Post, 2 May 2011)

13. Andrew Bomford, *Echelon spy network revealed*, (BBC News, 3 November 1999)

14. *European Parliament 1999-2004 Session Document*

15. Ryan Gallagher, *Governments turn to hacking techniques for surveillance of citizens*, (The Guardian, 1 November 2011)

16. Jesse Emspak, *Chips for dinner: Edible RFID tags describe your food,* (New Scientist, 10 June 2011)

17. Duncan Campbell, *How NSA access was built into Windows,* (Telepolis, 1999)

18. Anna Leach, *Woz: Cloud computing trend is 'horrendous',* (The Register, 6 August 2012)

19. *Smart TVs can spy on their owners,* (Russia Today, 14 December 2012)

20. Tech Device Reviews, *New Apple iOS 6 Gives Government Back Door Access To Control Your iPhone,* (June 19, 2012)

21. Mark Milian, *Security-Enhanced Android: NSA Edition,* (Bloomberg Business Week 3 July 2013)

22. *Michael Hastings sent chilling e-mail hours before crash,* (Fox News, 25 June 2013)

23. *US Department of Homeland Security, Analyst's Desktop Binder, / National Operations Center, Media Monitoring Capability, Desktop Reference Binder,* (Department of Homeland Security, 2011)

24. Philip Bump, *Google 'Pressure Cookers' And 'Backpacks,' Get A Visit From The Cops,* (Nextgov, 1 August 2013)

Chapter 16

1. H.G. Wells, *The New World Order,* (1940)

2. *Matthew 24:9, New Living Translation*

3. *Matthew 24:21, Amplified Bible*

4. John Foxe, *Fox's Book of Martyrs,* (Zondervan, 1978)

5. John Foxe, *Fox's Book of Martyrs,* (Zondervan, 1978)

6. John Foxe, *Fox's Book of Martyrs,* (Zondervan, 1978)

7. John Foxe, *Fox's Book of Martyrs,* (Zondervan, 1978)

8. John Foxe, *Fox's Book of Martyrs,* (Zondervan, 1978)

9. Tim Stanley, *Pro-abortion activists chant 'Hail Satan!' at a Texas rally. Satan doesn't need this kind of bad publicity,* (The Telegraph, 4 July 2013)

10. *Street Preacher Brutally Beat Down During Seattle 'Gay Pride' Event,* (Christian News, 5 July 2013)

11. *Family Research Council Shooter Gets 25 Years,* (CBS News, 19 September 2013)

12. Todd Starnes, *Christian Preachers Brutally Beaten at Gay Pride Festival,* (Fox News, 5 July 2013)

13. *Violent Pro-Abortion Mob Attacks Pro-Life People Praying at Catholic Church,* (Life News, 3 December 2013)

14. *FEMEN crashes Christmas service, nude woman plays Christ in Church,* (Euronews, 26 December 2013)

15. *EU: Free Speech on the line,* (Evangelical Now, November 2009)

16. *EU: Free Speech on the line,* (Evangelical Now, November 2009)

17. *EU: Free Speech on the line,* (Evangelical Now, November 2009)

18. Baroness Miller of Chilthorne Domer, *They Work For You, Keeping tabs on the UK's parliament & assemblies, Public Demonstrations (Repeals) Bill*

19. Heather Clark, *Federal Appeals Court Upholds Government Established Free Speech Free Zones,* (Christian News, 3 August 2012)

20. Fox News, Army Labeled Evangelicals as Religious Extremists

21. *Military Warned 'Evangelicals' No. 1 Threat,* (World Net Daily, 5 April 2013)

22. *MIAC Strategic Report, The Modern Militia Movement,* (Constitution Society, 20 February 2009)

23. *Truman Library, Semi-Annual Report, January 1 – June 30, 1946*

24. Roy L. Brooks, *When Sorry Isn't Enough: The Controversy Over Apologies and Reparations for Human Injustice,* (New York University Press, 1999), 212

25. *Guantanamo detainees were tortured, medical exams show,* (The Associated Press, 18 June 2008)

26. *'Everybody in Guantanamo has been tortured or abused' – former detainee,* (Russia Today, 6 July 2013)

27. William Bigelow, *Feds Buy Two Billion Rounds of Ammunition,* (Breitbart, 18 February 2013)

28. *1.6 Billion Rounds Of Ammo For Homeland Security? It's Time For A National Conversation,* (Forbes, 11 March 2013)

29. *Homeland Security under investigation for massive ammo buys,* (Russia Today, 30 April 2013)

30. *Silence of the Homelands: Why is DHS stockpiling guns and ammunition?,* (Russia Today, 23 March 2013)

31. *Silence of the Homelands: Why is DHS stockpiling guns and ammunition?,* (Russia Today, 23 March 2013)

32. *Why Are Tens of Thousands of Plastic "Burial Vaults" Stacked in a Field Near Madison, Georgia?* (Cryptogon, 20 July 2008)

33. Bob Unruh, *Why is the National Guard Recruiting for 'Internment Cops',* (World Net Daily, 7 August 2009)

34. *FM 3-39.40, Internment and Resettlement Operations,* (February 2010), 2-8

35. *FM 3-39.40, Internment and Resettlement Operations,* (February 2010), 1-12

461

36. Caroline Brothers, *Obscurity and confinement for migrants in Europe*, (The New York Times, 30 December 2007)

37. Helena Smith, *Greece to open new detention centres for illegal migrants*, (The Guardian, 29 March 2012)

38. Richard Cottrell, *End The Lie, First new concentration camps in Europe set to sprout on Greek soil*, (End The Lie)

Chapter 17

1. *Fear can Kill*, (BBC News, 3 March 1999)

2. *Fear can Kill*, (BBC News, 3 March 1999)

3. *Fear can Kill*, (BBC News, 3 March 1999)

4. Fraser Cain, *Red Moon*, (Universe Today, October 2008)

5. *Seeing red: How a lunar eclipse and volcanic ash create colourful phenomenon for moon-gazers*, (Daily Mail, 16 June 2011)

6. *Volcanic ash: effects and mitigation strategies*, (US government documentation, www.volcanoes.usgs.gov/ash/health)

7. Clifford Krauss, *The Scramble for Access to Libya's Oil Wealth Begins*, (New York Times, 22 August 2011)

8. John Vidal and Helen Weinstein, *RAF rainmakers 'caused 1952 flood'*, (The Guardian, 30 August 2001)

9. Spencer C. Tucker, *The Encyclopedia of the Vietnam War*, (Oxford University Press, USA, 2001)

10. Chen May Yee, *Malaysia to Battle Smog with Cyclones*, (Wall Street Journal, 13 November 1997)

11. *Iran VP claims country's drought is part of West's weather war on Islamic republic*, (Daily Mail, 18 July 2012)

12. Alok Jha, *Obama climate adviser open to geo-engineering to tackle global warming*, (The Guardian, 8 April 2009)

13. David Gardner, *Obama may fire pollution particles into stratosphere to deflect sun's heat in desperate bid to tackle global warming*, (Daily Mail, 9 April 2009)

14. Liz Bestic, *Is aluminium really a silent killer?*, (Telegraph, 5 March 2012)

15. Liz Bestic, *Is aluminium really a silent killer?*, (Telegraph, 5 March 2012)

16. Francis Mangels, *Scientific Obervations*, (Global Skywatch)

17. *What in the world are they spraying?*, (Truth Media Productions, 2010)

18. *What in the world are they spraying?*, (Truth Media Productions, 2010)

19. *Why in the world are they spraying?*, (2012)

20. USPTO Patent Full-Text and Image Database, (www.uspto.gov/patents)

21. USPTO Patent Full-Text and Image Database, (www.uspto.gov/patents)

22. Liz Bestic, *Is aluminium really a silent killer?*, (Telegraph, 5 March 2012)

23. Col Tamzy J. House, Lt Col James B. Near, Jr. LTC William B. Shields (USA) Maj Ronald, J. Celentano Maj David M. Husband Maj Ann E. Mercer Maj James E. Pugh, *Weather as a Force Multiplier: Owning the Weather in 2025, (*A Research Paper Presented To Air Force 2025, August 1996)

24. Col Tamzy J. House, Lt Col James B. Near, Jr. LTC William B. Shields (USA) Maj Ronald, J. Celentano Maj David M. Husband Maj Ann E. Mercer Maj James E. Pugh, *Weather as a Force Multiplier: Owning the Weather in 2025, (*A Research Paper Presented To Air Force 2025, August 1996), 19

25. *Monsanto To Introduce Genuity DroughtGard Hybrids In Western Great Plains,* (CropLife, 11 September 2012)

26. *Delivering Genetically Engineered Crops to Poor Farmers,* (The International Food Policy Research Institute, December 2009)

27. Col Tamzy J. House, Lt Col James B. Near, Jr. LTC William B. Shields (USA) Maj Ronald, J. Celentano Maj David M. Husband Maj Ann E. Mercer Maj James E. Pugh, *Weather as a Force Multiplier: Owning the Weather in 2025, (*A Research Paper Presented To Air Force 2025, August 1996)

28. Col Tamzy J. House, Lt Col James B. Near, Jr. LTC William B. Shields (USA) Maj Ronald, J. Celentano Maj David M. Husband Maj Ann E. Mercer Maj James E. Pugh, *Weather as a Force Multiplier: Owning the Weather in 2025, (*A Research Paper Presented To Air Force 2025, August 1996), 19

29. Jerry E. Smith, *Weather Warfare,* (Adventures Unlimited, 2006)

30. Robin McKie, *Genetically modified crops are the key to human survival, says UK's chief scientist,* (The Guardian, 23 January 2011)

31. *Monsanto Says GM Wheat 'Isolated Incident,' But Lawyers Bet There Will Be More,* (Forbes, 5 June 2013)

32. *Genetically Modified Soy Linked to Sterility, Infant Mortality,* (Institute for Responsible Technology)

33. John Vidal, *Study linking GM maize to cancer must be taken seriously by regulators,* (The Guardian, September 28 2012)

34. Alice Wessendorf, *Frankencrops Coming to a Roadside Near You,* (Healthier News, 30 August 2010)

35. Matt McGrath, *Agent Orange chemical in GM war on resistant weeds* (BBC News, 19 September 2012)

36. Jonathan Benson, *'Agent Orange' crop chemicals challenged by coalition of US farmers and food companies,* (Natural News, 22 April 2012)

37. Marie-Monique Robin, *The World According to Monsanto: Pollution, Corruption, and the Control of the World's Food Supply,* (The New Press, 2012)

38. *Agent Orange In Vietnam Program, History: Agent Orange/Dioxin in Vietnam,* (Aspen Institute)

39. *'Last ghost' of the Vietnam War,* (The Globe and Mail, July 12 2008)

40. *'Last ghost' of the Vietnam War,* (The Globe and Mail, July 12 2008)

41. *Hungary destroys more than 1,200 acres of GMO corn by fire,* (The Examiner, 29 May 2013)

42. David Adams, *Could you make a genetically targeted weapon?,* (The Guardian, 28 October 2004)

43. *China 'has up to 3,000 nuclear weapons hidden in tunnels', three-year study of secret documents reveals,* (The Daily Mail, 1 December 2011)

44. Wu Weilin, *Nuclear Explosion Occurred Near Epicenter of the Sichuan Earthquake, Expert Says,* (The Epoch Times, 3 June 2008)

45. Justin McCurry, Tania Branigan, *North Korea stages nuclear test in defiance of bans,* (The Guardian, 12 February 2013)

46. *DoD News Briefing: Secretary of Defense William S. Cohen.* (US Department of Defense, April 28 1997)

47. Gordon J F MacDonald, *Unless Peace Comes,* (1968)

48. *US Department of State, Convention on the Prohibition of Military or Any Other Hostile Use of Environmental Modification Techniques,* (www.state.gov/t/isn/4783)

49. *US Department of State, Convention on the Prohibition of Military or Any Other Hostile Use of Environmental Modification Techniques,* (www.state.gov/t/isn/4783)

50. Eugene Bingham, *Devastating tsunami bomb viable, say experts,* (The New Zealand Herald, 28 September, 1999) / Emily Bourke, *Military archives show NZ and US conducted secret tsunami bomb tests,* (ABC Australia, 3 January 2013)

51. *Secret Weather Weapons Can Kill Millions, Warns Top Russian Politician,* (The European Union Times, 17 May 2011)

52. Prof Michel Chossudovsky, *Indian Ocean Tsunami: Why did the Information Not Get Out?,* (Global Research, 17 June 2005)

53. Andrew Moran, *Russian Report: U.S. weapon against Iran caused Haiti earthquake,* (Digital Journal, 23 January 2010)

54. Chuck Baldwin, *What's Really Going On In Haiti?,* (News With Views, 26 January 2010)

55. *A Haiti Disaster Relief Scenario Was Envisaged by the US Military One Day Before the Earthquake,* (Global Research, 21 January 2010)

56. Bob Brewin, *Defense Launches Online System To Coordinate Haiti Relief Efforts,* (Nextgov, 15 January 2010)

57. Prof Michel Chossudovsky, *7/7 Mock Terror Drill: What Relationship to the Real Time Terror Attacks?,* (Global Research, 7 July 2013)

58. Jeane Manning, Dr. Nick Begich, *Angels Don't Play This HAARP, Advances in Tesla Technology,* (Earthpulse Press, 1997)

59. *www.haarp.alaska.edu*

60. Jeane Manning, Dr. Nick Begich, *Angels Don't Play This HAARP, Advances in Tesla Technology,* (Earthpulse Press, 1997)

61. Maj Britt Theorin, *European Parliament report on the environment, security and foreign policy, Committee on Foreign Affairs, Security and Defence Policy,* (14 January 1999)

62. Maj Britt Theorin, *European Parliament report on the environment, security and foreign policy, Committee on Foreign Affairs, Security and Defence Policy,* (14 January 1999)

63. Maj Britt Theorin, *European Parliament report on the environment, security and foreign policy, Committee on Foreign Affairs, Security and Defence Policy,* (14 January 1999)

64. Paul Rincon, *Plan for quake 'warning system',* (BBC News, 5 June 2008)

65. *November 29, 1975 Kalapana Earthquake,* USGS, Hawaiian Volcano Observatory, www. hvo.wr.usgs.gov/earthquakes)

66. David Finkelstein, James Powell, *Earthquake Lightning,* (Nature Journal)

67. Naomi Lubick, *Artificial ionosphere creates bullseye in the sky, Auroral experiments make glowing plasma patch,* ('Nature' International Weekly Journal of Science, 2 October 2009)

68. Jeane Manning, Dr. Nick Begich, *Angels Don't Play This HAARP, Advances in Tesla Technology,* (Earthpulse Press, 1997)

69. A-Bomb Survivor's Story, My Hiroshima by Murakami, Keiko

70. Tom Robbins, *A-Bomb Survivors Tell Their Stories in Brooklyn,* (The Village Voice, 15 December 2010)

71. Koinonia House, Technology and the Bible by Chuck Missler

72. Alan F. Phillips, M.D., D.M.R.T., *The Effects on The Inhabitants of a City of The Explosion of a Nuclear Bomb,* (3:AM Magazine)

73. Alan F. Phillips, M.D., D.M.R.T., *The Effects on The Inhabitants of a City of The Explosion of a Nuclear Bomb,* (3:AM Magazine)

74. Robert S. Norris, Hans M. Kristensen, *Global nuclear weapons inventories, 1945-2010,* (Bulletin of the Atomic Scientists)

75.   Nazila Fathi, *Wipe Israel 'off the map' Iranian says,* (The New York Times, 27 October 2005)

Chapter 18

1.   David E. Leininger, *Lectionary Tales for the Pulpit,* (CSS Publishing Company, 2007)

2.   Elizabeth M. Knowles, *The Oxford Dictionary of Quotations,* (OUP Oxford, 2009)

3.   David E. Leininger, *Lectionary Tales for the Pulpit,* (CSS Publishing Company, 2007)

4.   Paul Joseph Watson, *Church Document Encourages Congregation To Obey Government,* (Info Wars, 4 March 2009)

Help get the message out –
'LIKE', 'SHARE' & 'FOLLOW'
Trumpet Blast Warning
on Facebook or Twitter

www.facebook.com/trumpetblastwarning

www.twitter.com/NewProphecyBook

www.trumpetblasttv.co.uk

To order more copies
of this book visit:

www.trumpetblastwarning.co.uk